FRIEDRICH HEER

THE
HOLY ROMAN
EMPIRE

TRANSLATED BY JANET SONDHEIMER

FREDERICK A. PRAEGER, Publishers

NEW YORK · WASHINGTON

BOOKS THAT MATTER

Published in the United States of America in 1968
by Frederick A. Praeger, Inc., Publishers
111 Fourth Avenue, New York, N.Y. 10003

German text © 1967, by Friedrich Heer
English translation © 1968 by George Weidenfeld and Nicolson Ltd.
London, England
Library of Congress Catalog Card Number: 68-30935

Printed in Great Britain

CONTENTS

ILLUSTRATIONS

ILLUSTRATIONS

38 Christ in Majesty; on the tympanum in the narthex at Vézelay, *c.* 1120 (*Janine Niepce*)
39 Signature of Pope Calixtus II on the last page of the Concordat of Worms, 1122. Rome, Archivio Segreto Vaticano
40 Bishop Adalbert receives his crook from Otto II; detail from the bronze doors of Gniezno (Gnesen) Cathedral, first half 12th century (*Bildarchiv Foto Marburg*)

HOHENSTAUFEN (*between pages 82 and 83*)
41 Arcade in the Hohenstaufen castle of Wimpfen, *c.* 1200 (*Lala Aufsberg*)
42, 43 Frederick Barbarossa with his chancellor Otto of Freising, and Empress Beatrice; figures on the porch of Freising Cathedral, 12th century (*Lala Aufsberg*)
44 Tomb of Henry the Lion and his wife Matilda in Brunswick Cathedral, mid-13th century (*Bildarchiv Foto Marburg*)
45 Dreams of Charles the Great before the Battle of Pamplona; from the Shrine of Charlemagne in Aachen Cathedral, 1200–15 (*Ann Münchow*)
46 Charles the Great receives two bishops who bring him a letter from Constantine; 13th-century window in Chartres Cathedral (*André Held*)
47 Head of '*Justitia Imperialis*' from the Bridge Gate at Capua, *c.* 1234 (*Albert Renger-Patzsch*)
48 Henry VI at the Siege of Naples; miniature from the *Liber ad Honorem Augusti* by Pietro da Eboli, *c.* 12... Berne, Bürgerbibliothek, Cod.120 f.109
49 Frederick Barbarossa as a crusader; dedicatory miniature from a manuscript of the *Historiae Hierosolymitanae* of Robertus Remensis, second half 12th century. Rome, Biblioteca Apostolica Vaticana, Cod.Vat.Lat.2001 f.1
50 Detail of an episode from the fourth crusade; from the detached pavement, 1213, of the Basilica of S. Giovanni Evangelista, Ravenna (*Josephine Powell*)
51 Imperial eagle of the Hohenstaufen on a baroque altar frontal from the Hohenstaufen tombs. Palermo, Cathedral Treasury (*Lala Aufsberg*)
52 Frederick II; miniature from his *De Arte Venadi cum Avibus*, 1258–66. Rome, Biblioteca Apostolica Vaticana, Cod.Pal.Lat.1071 f... (*Scala*)
53 Frederick II with his wife and two sons; relief on the pulpit in Bitonto Cathedral, Apulia, by Magister Nicolaus, 1229 (*Lala Aufsberg*)
54 Tomb of Archbishop Siegfried III of Eppstein (d. 1249), who crowns two kings, in Mainz Cathedral (*Dom- und Diözesanmuseum, Mainz*)
55 Seal of Bishop Conrad von Scharfenberg, 1200–24. Speyer, Historisches Museum der Pfalz (*Lala Aufsberg*)
56 Seal of Richard of Cornwall as Roman Emperor, 1257 (from a cast). London, British Museum
57 Capture of the anti-imperial prelates by the Pisans, 1241; illustration from Matthew Paris' *Chronica Maiora*, mid-13th century. Cambridge, Corpus Christi College (by courtesy of the Master and Fellows), Ms.16 f.146

HABSBURGS, LUXEMBURGS, WITTELSBACHS (*between pages 106 and 107*)
58 Rudolph von Habsburg; detail of the Habsburg window from St Stephen's Cathedral, Vienna, Vienna court school, *c.* 1390. Vienna, Historisches Museum der Stadt Wien (*Bildarchiv der öNB*)
59 Pope Boniface VIII; copper statue by Manno di Bandino, 1301. Bologna, Museo Civico (*Alinari*)

viii

COLOUR ILLUSTRATIONS

I

SACRUM ROMANUM IMPERIUM

HOLY Roman Empire: to some of its subjects in the seventeenth and eighteenth centuries, this most remarkable of all the structures thrown up by the Old Europe was already a 'monstrosity', a 'skeleton', a 'ghost', even before its final demolition by the French Revolution and Napoleon. In France, as in England, medieval chroniclers and political thinkers fell early into the habit of ignoring the Empire as a non-entity, though this did not preclude intense political interest in its territories. By the end of the Hohenstaufen era (1250), if not before, it was already tantalizingly clear to popes, kings, princes and political thinkers that there in the heart of Europe was an institution whose power had all but drained away but which nevertheless eluded all external and internal attempts to grasp at it – just as it eludes the categories of political theorizers who think in terms of the nation state.

Kings and emperors, predominantly of German descent, strove as vainly for mastery over the Empire as did popes who were by birth Italians or Frenchmen. There were moments when imperial bishops and ecclesiastical electors presumed to act as regents of the Empire, for example Peter Aspelt, whose tombstone shows him as a great bishop crowning two kinglets (*reguli*) Kings of the Romans. The ecclesiastical imperial aristocracy had its lay counterpart, closely linked to it by blood, which occupied a thousand years – if we include the Carolingian prelude – with its contentions for power in the Empire. Kings of England, France and Spain competed for the imperial crown, either for themselves or for collateral branches of their dynasties.

Large and important rival empires were set up, right on the Empire's doorstep, or at least in open confrontation with it: witness the states founded by the Normans in Sicily and southern Italy, as also in England. The French monarchy conquered France with its 'king's churches', the Gothic cathedrals, and through this same agency (Gothic was known as the 'French style') went on to make its first cultural conquest of Europe. The university of Paris founded an empire ruled by reason, an intellectual empire of the intelligentsia, one of whose functions was to provide the kings and princes of Europe with trained officials and collaborators. Francis I, Louis XIV, Napoleon, saw themselves as the Holy Roman Empire's legitimate heirs.

Popes waged a thousand-year-long battle with emperors for the right to Rome, the Papal State and Italy and for supremacy in the church. Echoes of this conflict reverberated as late as 1904, when Cardinal Puzyna of Cracow, as spokesman for the

I

emperor of Austria (at best, emperor of 'the secret Holy Roman Empire') vetoed the election of Rampolla in the papal conclave.

Men revered the Holy Roman Empire as the bastion built against the coming of antichrist. The Holy Roman Emperor saw himself as the chief defender of the church, indeed of all Christendom. For all that, Empire and Emperor had no more formidable rival, or indeed enemy, than the Roman Pope. What was more, this papal hostility weighed most heavily in the balance at precisely those moments when the Empire was in greatest danger, whether from the Turks, the French or the Protestants.

If the Pope and the French king were rivals to the Empire, so also, and at times to an even greater degree, was Spain. Medieval kings were addressed as emperors in their own right, the reason being that they were rulers of several states. This honour they took as a matter of course. Spanish acceptance of empire as a mission, and of the claims this mission entailed, was delayed until the time of Charles v. It was only then, and with initial reluctance, that Spain embarked on building up the world empire which carried the double eagle to America and across the Pacific to the Philippines. This was an empire in which Madrid always kept one anxious and mistrustful eye on Vienna, for Spanish 'imperialism' was the heir and rival, friend and foe of the Holy Roman Empire. Both empires, the Spanish and the Holy Roman, are commemorated in the dollar and 'dollar imperialism' of our own day. The dollar is the nominal descendant of the *Joachimstaler* (for centuries the currency of the Empire). The two vertical strokes and wavy band of the dollar sign – to many a sacred symbol indeed – first adorned, as the emblem of the Spanish monarchy, *taler* made from South American silver. The strokes stand for the Pillars of Hercules, which together with a legend-bearing scroll (the wavy band) made up the sacral-political device of Charles v and his empire [plates 106, 109].[1]

Behind the Spanish and Holy Roman empires lies yet 'another' *imperium*, whose device is the celebrated line from Virgil's *Fourth Eclogue* foretelling the rebirth of the Golden Age, a prophecy which medieval men took to refer to Christ. It is Virgil, as the first poet-prophet of the Roman Empire who conducts Dante, poet-prophet of the medieval Holy Roman Empire through Hell and Purgatory to the threshold of Paradise. Dante's paradise has its roots in the palace garden of the Persian king, in the primal age of world monarchy, and the same can in a sense be said of the gardens of Versailles and Schönbrunn. 'Emperor's yellow', in Peking and Vienna alike the imperial colour and reserved strictly for use on imperial buildings, is yet another reminder that the Holy Roman Empire and its successor, the Austrian imperial monarchy, belonged to an order which had endured for five thousand years.

In 1958 Prince Karl Schwarzenberg, whose forebears were numbered among the princes of the Empire, published a study (*Adler und Drache*) in which he traces out the symbols of this five-thousand-year order. The concluding sentence runs: 'Five thousand years measure the flight path of the imperial eagle as he makes his way from the temple towers of Eridu towards the setting sun and the evening mists veiling the

[1] See below p. 160.

I The imperial crown of the Holy Roman Empire; its octagonal form relates to the Heavenly Jerusalem, the bow to world dominion, the cross to Christ, Emperor of Heaven – the emperor is his representative on earth. Whoever possessed this embodiment of 'the Empire' was lawful emperor.

future of the atomic age.' The post-Copernican era was launched with the first space rockets. In the not so distant future the new Columbus, *homo cosmonautus*, may be planting pockets of himself and his life-style in some galaxy, just as his forebears once planted colonies first round the Mediterranean and later in the two Americas. This open cosmos presents man with a challenge he finds hard to bear.

The terrors of the irrational, of the empty and unknown, are so immense that they can be mastered only through action, knowledge and experience. In the past, man's existential affirmation of himself was clothed most readily in military-political forms, forms which with the overthrow of the five-thousand-year order have become all the more perilous. Within the old order man inhabited what the Romans described as an *urbs deis hominibusque communis*, a household common to gods, men, beasts, all living things. There might be times when this household was in open disorder: it appeared in this light to the Hebrew prophet in Nineveh, to Roman poets and politicians who lived through the unending civil wars which preceded the triumph of Augustus, to Dante and the medieval German mystics, to a Nicholas of Cusa, a Leibniz or a Goethe. As a great sacral-political order the household was continually threatened from within or without, by foreign conquerors, by regicides and renegades, by pretenders to the throne, by rulers who were either too strong or too weak. Yet all these enemies, and especially those who were the order's bitterest foes, were seeking in their own fashion to renew it; if they seized power it was to re-establish continuity. This could even be said of Napoleon and those who followed him. The conception of the Holy Roman Empire as a unique barrier against the coming of antichrist still had a place in the thought of Bellarmine, one of the most important papal theorizers of the early modern period; more significant still, it is also implicit in the thought of constitutional philosophers and theorists of the eighteenth and nineteenth centuries.

The idea that while the Holy Roman Empire still existed – in one of its metamorphoses if not in its own person – the end of the world and the Last Judgment would be postponed was the great theme of the medieval theologians of the Holy Roman Empire and of its poets and literary champions at critical moments in its history. This conviction concealed within itself the realization that the Holy Roman Empire was the last manifestation of an age-old sacral-political order in which 'gods', men, beasts, all living things, dwelt together under the protection of one or more great houses. The houses were those of the world emperors, rulers whose insignia, down to the end of the Holy Roman Empire, continued to be those proper to the Emperor of the Heavens. The imperial eagle was a battle standard in the time of the earliest Mesopotamian kings and afterwards among the Sumerians; it went into battle with the Roman legions and the troops of Frederick II of Hohenstaufen, just as in the battles of the First World War it accompanied the armies both of His Apostolic Majesty the Emperor of Austria and of the Tsar of All the Russias. The double eagle, officially incorporated into the arms of the Empire in the fifteenth century in the reign of Sigismund, is first found in Mesopotamia. Our seven-day week is a sacred division of time presided over by the seven Chaldean planetary deities, and we inhabit the holy places made safe by the tutelary powers of the old gods and their earthly representatives.

The Holy Empire, under constant threat of corruption and collapse (the *desidia* of the Hohenstaufen documents), again and again found itself in need of protection and rebirth, *renovatio*. Hence the programmatic names assumed by so many emperor-kings, names which invoke saviour forebears whom their descendants hope to reincarnate. Assyrian, Babylonian and Egyptian rulers had all used programme names, some of them quite revolutionary in character, like that of Pharaoh Amenophis IV (1383–1365 BC). He called himself Echn Aton, 'ray of the sun', and composed a hymn to the sun which is taken up word for word in Psalm 104. Without knowing it, many christian households still recite the prayer of this sun ruler – 'all eyes wait upon Thee, O Lord . . .' as a grace before meals.

Recent excavations under St Peter's have unearthed a third-century mosaic of a sun god mounted on his chariot; on one side of the figure is the word *helios* (sun), on the other *Christus*. If Christ was the 'true sun', the Emperor of the Heavens – who in Europe was entitled, as his true successor, to wear his mantle and bear his emblems of authority? Was it the Emperor or the Pope? Between the eleventh and the thirteenth centuries the contest between these two powers took on an increasingly terrifying aspect. The contest ended in 1250 with the collapse of the old Empire. This was followed, half a century later, by the 'Babylonian captivity of the church', that is to say, the removal of the papacy to Avignon, where it was under the thumb of the French king.

Ostentation, extravagance and pomp are inseparable from imperial celebration and ceremony, whether in Augustan Rome, Byzantium or Vienna. We shall understand more clearly why this should be so when we appreciate that their underlying purpose was to replenish the sun-given splendour and power of the Holy Empire, which seemed perpetually threatened by decay and its hosts of enemies. The nimbus which encircles the emperor in Byzantine and early medieval portraits is the aura, *Hvarna*, the heavenly blaze of triumph emanating from the light and might of the sun which plays about the head of the Persian king. The sign of the cross, which carried Constantine, founder of both Empire and Papacy as christian world powers, to victory at the Milvian bridge, already hangs from the neck of the Assyrian king: to him it symbolized the sun and the four corners of the world, and he wore it as a sign of strength and salvation. Lordship of the world meant lordship extending over the four quarters of the heavens.

The time is December 1916, the scene Budapest, whither Charles I of Austria has come for his coronation as king of Hungary. (On the same day a negative answer was received from the allies to the peace feelers put out by Austria-Hungary and Germany). Charles is crowned with the sacred crown of St Stephen (part Byzantine, part papal in origin and on a par with the imperial crown) and invested with St Stephen's sword. He swears the oath for his kingdom of Hungary. The paladins proffer him the ancient sword of the Holy Roman Empire, the imperial sword of

4

St Maurice, which was probably made for Emperor Henry III. Inscribed on one face of the hilt is the ancient victory song to Christ once chanted in the *Laudes* which followed imperial coronations: *Christus vincit – Christus regnat – Christus imperat*. The next ceremony is at the Sankt-Georgs Platz, where a mound has been made of earth sent in chestfuls from every county in Hungary (the orb of the Holy Roman Empire is said to contain earth from the four quarters of the globe). As befits the king of a nation of horsemen – once Asiatic, now steeped in European tradition – Charles rides up the mound and from the summit brandishes the sword to all four points of the compass in symbolic reference to the Magyar claim to world dominion.

Charles I, Emperor of Austria and King of Hungary, was the last to bear the saving name of Charles the Great which had been invoked by so many 'renovators' of the Holy Roman Empire, from the Ottonian emperors to the Hohenstaufen, from Maximilian I to Napoleon. Charles is a name as programmatic as Belshazzar, the name of the last king of Babylon, which means 'may God protect the king'. In the nineteenth and twentieth centuries God was no longer protecting the emperors and kings of the old empires. The last couplet of Heine's famous poem *Belsazar* was found scratched on the wall of the cellar in which the Tsar's family was shot.[1] As recently as 1881, the Egyptian populace had broken spontaneously into the age-old lament for the dead when the royal mummies were brought to Cairo after their three thousand years of seclusion in the Valley of the Kings. Earlier in the century Heine noted in his *Reisebilder* a little incident which had occurred in Mexico. Bullock had dug up an ancient stone image dating from heathen times; next morning he found it wreathed in flowers. 'And this,' says Heine, 'after the Spanish had destroyed the old religion of the Mexicans with fire and sword and spent three centuries going over their souls, ploughing them up and sowing the seeds of Christianity.' Today it is the images of the emperors that lie in ruins. Historians tend to be prophets after the event (and nowadays sometimes even before it) but they have no means of knowing what power order will assume in the psyche of the nations the role occupied for the past five thousand years by the great households of the sacred empires. Will there be an 'Emperor of America' (apart from the one envisaged by George Bernard Shaw)? Or perhaps an Emperor Atom? International conferences of the United Nations Commission on Atomic Energy take place at the Hofburg in Vienna, only a few paces from the resting place of the imperial crown. In 1938 Hitler had the crown taken from Vienna to Nuremberg, where it was no stranger, having been kept there from 1424 until 1796. Kennedy, Khrushchev, the Shah of Persia, many potentates, leading statesmen, presidents, pretenders to thrones and dictators have stood in our day in the presence of the imperial crown of the Holy Roman Empire.

Primitive forms of the imperial insignia are to be found in the Sumerian, Babylonian and Assyrian empires. The crown represents the heaven hat of the King

---

[1] *'Belsazer ward aber in selbigen Nacht*
  Von seinen Knechten umgebracht'.
'And on that same night, Belshazzar was slain by his servants.'

of the Heavens. Sceptre, orb, sword and star-strewn mantle represent the claim to rule the cosmos. The vestments are the vestments of a high priest, the thrones triumphal chariots. The designs for *trionfi* made by Dürer and other German masters of the Renaissance for Maximilian I, the *grandes entrées* in honour of Charles v, hark back to the ceremonious parading of divine effigies of the god-king in the holy and universal empires which preceded the Holy Roman Empire. In solemn processions the Emperor rides beneath a canopy representing the sky, in other words Heaven [plate 104]. Whether in Babylon or in the Vienna of Francis Joseph, the ruler has a sacred ritual of prayer and liturgical observance to perform. (How greatly things changed with the triumph of the papacy is shown by the fact that the place under the canopy in the Corpus Christi procession was thenceforth reserved for the 'All Holiest', borne by priests, the Emperor being left to walk behind.) The Emperor ploughs, hunts, makes war, honours his sacred forebears. The Holy Empire is a feasting, celebrating community, in which banquets, festivals, war, 'war dramas', mock battles and the chase are bound inextricably together. We shall find this significant constellation recurring throughout the thousand years of the Holy Roman Empire's history. Francis Joseph, the last emperor of ancient lineage, was as much of a Nimrod as Nimrod himself.

The birthday of Emperor Francis Joseph fell on 18 August, a day of 'sky-blue imperial weather'. The popular belief that prosperous harvests, good weather, cosmic harmony on earth, are dependent on the ruler came as naturally to the Irish and Anglo-Saxon monks and other intellectuals who frequented the Carolingian court as it did to the ancient empires of the Euphrates and the Nile and to the 'Blacks and Yellows' (imperial loyalists) of the Danube monarchy. The ruler was the guarantee that these benefits would continue, the guarantee of the great peace.

The peace had to be cosmic, embracing both the heavens and the earth. On earth the peace-giving function of the Emperor of the Heavens was exercised by the emperor ordained by God. The Empire was a federation of peoples led by the Emperor, a federation in which *concordia provinciarum*, harmony between the members, prevails. The charters of the emperors of the Holy Roman Empire invoke the One and Undivided Trinity and promise peace 'to the faithful of God and of the Empire', employing a sacral formula which goes back to ancient Roman and pre-Roman times. At the Versailles Peace Conference the Portuguese delegate (a professor of the ancient university of Coimbra) proposed without success that the treaties which were supposed to end the First World War (but failed to do so) should open with an invocation to the Trinity.

For its *fideles*, the Holy Roman Empire was a zone in which peace prevailed. To have peace within the Empire it was necessary to fight the 'infidel', the 'heathen' (the *gentes* of the Bible), the 'heretic'. In his own interpretations of his office, the Emperor was the supreme defender and protector of the church. Here was intractable material for conflict. Exactly how was the Emperor to exercise this protectorate over the church? Did it also give him rights, albeit regarded initially as purely 'temporal' rights, over the Pope and his possessions? What should be the Pope's reaction to this exalted and high dangerous patronage? What gave the Holy Roman Empire its title? Did it derive from Aeneas, from that *pius Aeneas* in whose honour Aeneas Silvius Piccolomini, who had been secretary to Emperor Frederick III, called himself Pius on becoming pope? Did it derive from Caesar? From Augustus, creator of peace and order in the Augustan age, whom the Middle Ages honoured because he prepared the way for the *Pax Christi*? Did it derive from Christ himself, who had conferred the temporal sword on the Emperor and the spiritual sword on the Pope, for the governance of Christendom? From St Peter? From the papacy?

Charles the Great, regarded by all emperors of the Holy Roman Empire as their illustrious forebear, took the title not of 'Roman Emperor' but of 'Emperor ruling the Roman Empire'. We have Einhard's word for it that the 'Roman emperors' would have been greatly displeased by the establishment of a second imperial office through Charles' coronation on Christmas day 800. The Roman emperors in question were purple-born emperors, enthroned in the 'second Rome', the Golden City on the Golden Horn, in other words Constantinople. The problem whether there could be two emperors would vex the minds of many future statesmen of the west.

The issue of the official Vienna gazette for 15 August 1804 contains a patent published in the name of the fifty-fifth christian Roman emperor, Francis II. Already 'Perpetual Enlarger of the Empire, King in Germany, Hungary, Bohemia, Galicia and Lodomeria, Archduke of Austria, Duke of Burgundy and Lorraine, Grand Duke of Tuscany, etc.', this Roman emperor was now assuming for himself and his successors in the Habsburg hereditary dominions the additional title of Emperor of Austria. Earlier in the year, in May, Napoleon had been proclaimed 'Emperor of the French'. On 2 December, in the presence of the Pope, he crowned himself in Notre-Dame. On 7 December the Austrian imperial patent was solemnly proclaimed from the loggia of the church Am Hof in Vienna. A year later, on 2 December 1805, Napoleon inflicted a terrible defeat on the Austrian and Russian forces at Austerlitz. He could now proceed with the 'final' demolition of the old Empire. He prevailed on a number of German princes to come together in a Rhenish League, which then declared its secession from the Empire. Next Francis II was called on to divest himself of the imperial crown, in terms so threatening that he had no choice but to comply. He did so on 6 August 1806, and at the same time dissolved the 'Roman Empire', an act for which he had no legal justification.

In February 1806 Napoleon urged his uncle, Cardinal Flesch, to impress upon the church that 'I am indeed Charlemagne, the sword of the church and its emperor'.

Paris has not forgotten the victories won by Napoleon; they are commemorated in monuments, in the names of streets and squares, even of underground stations. Paris, on a par with Rome, Madrid, Vienna and London, asserts the old claim of the French kings to be the true successors of Charles the Great. The 'true Franks' are not the 'German Franks' but the French. German princes became Franks in virtue of their coronation in Aachen (Aix-la-Chapelle), Charles' seat, or in Frankfurt, Charles' city.

The King of the Romans was 'Frankish' to the end (witness Goethe's account of the coronation of Joseph II in Frankfurt in 1764); the groundwork of the Holy Roman Empire was Carolingian. 'Frankish' and 'Roman' and 'Christian' came to mean 'Roman Catholic'. Historically speaking, how did all this come about?

2

THE EMPIRE OF CHARLES THE GREAT

WE do not know where Charles the Great was born, nor with complete certainty when, though it was probably 2 April 742. He died on 28 January 814 at Aachen. Aachen has been a place of pilgrimage for christian emperors, kings, princes and potentates for over a thousand years. The kings in Paris (and even the kings of England) have honoured it with gifts; Louis XIV had his eye upon it. It was at Aachen that Churchill received the Charlemagne prize. Charles the Great, Charlemagne, made his appearance as recently as 1945 as patron of a West European federation based on a Franco-German condominium and on the potential of the industrial states of the European Economic Community.

Charles the Great built up a European empire which fell apart soon after his death. Yet structures from Carolingian Europe determined the basic features of European political and social life and the institutions of the church, culture and education in Europe until 1806, and were still an influence down to 1914. Standing outside this Europe were the Scandinavian states, the British Isles, the Islamic Mediterranean region and that part of Eastern Europe from which the great antagonist, the imperial monarchy of the Rhomaioi in Constantinople, parried and deflected thrusts from Carolingian Europe and later went over to the counter-attack. This 'other' Europe came up against Carolingian, papal, 'Frankish' Europe in Italy and the Balkans (until well on into the Middle Ages almost to the gates of Vienna, since the Eastern Church had monasteries in Pannonia), in Moravia and in parts of Russia. It is surely significant that to the Byzantines and the Muslims of the Near East, as much later to Indians and Asiatics, all West Europeans were 'Franks'. Charles the Great, assisted by his Frankish warriors, bishops and monks (the latter fought a miniature war of their own against the Irish and Anglo-Saxon missionary monks and bishops), and his imperial officials, built up his *imperium* through a series of hard-fought campaigns. Creating the peace of the Empire (in Charles' day known in the west as the '*imperium Romanorum atque Francorum*'), is seen to depend on fighting wars, though until we reach the Thirty Years War, the first full-scale European war, the wars are admittedly confined to relatively small areas and engage what are by modern standards only very small forces.

Charles' most significant achievements, which led to the formation of a German core to Europe, were the subjection of the Saxons and the destruction of the 'tribal duchy' of Bavaria,[1] which had in Tassilo its last great leader. The old Saxons (not to

9

be confused with the inhabitants of the later electorate or of the Saxonies of modern times) occupied regions lying between Westphalia and Holstein which in future would be part of Germany; they possessed an indigenous 'pagan' culture and were led by a strong and self-confident aristocracy.

Their forcible conversion to Christianity at the hands of Charles the Great made the Saxons members, and before long upholders, of the Empire, and turned them into Germans and Europeans. Starting with some of Charles' own contemporaries, chroniclers and critics down the centuries have not failed to stress the violence of this conversion. Even today, the double aspect of this religious-political incorporation of the Saxons into the Europe of Charles the Great still merits close attention. It was Saxons, Saxon imperial bishops, abbots and abbesses, nobly born men and women, ecclesiastical and lay, who built up the Holy Roman Empire afresh in the tenth century, after its collapse under Charles' successors. Without its Saxon foundations, the thousand-year Empire is inconceivable. In the tenth and eleventh centuries, Ottonian-Christian culture, literature, architecture and spirituality were unique and led Europe. Without this christian Saxony there would be no Empire, no Holy Roman Empire. But the wounds went deep and did not completely heal. Resistance to the Empire and to Rome, to Rome's catholicity and to Latin culture, was deep-rooted in these one-time Saxon regions right down to the time of Hitler; it was here that he was able to build up his first and most stable support in northern Germany. A hundred years before Hitler, Heinrich Heine had already noted this mental undercurrent:

It is said that there are still old men in Westphalia who know where the ancient images of the gods lie buried; they tell their youngest grandchild on their death bed, and he then guards the precious secret in his taciturn Saxon breast. In Westphalia, which was once Saxony, not everything buried is dead. A man who wanders its ancient oak woods may still hear the sound of antique voices, may still catch the echo of those deep-sounding incantations which well up with greater fullness of life than all the literature of the Mark of Brandenburg. Once as I wandered through these forests I passed close to the Siegburg, ages old, and a mysterious awe shuddered through my soul. 'Here,' said my guide, 'once dwelt King Wittekind,' and he gave a deep sigh. He was a simple wood-cutter and carried an enormous axe. If it came to the point I have no doubt that even today he would strike a blow for King Wittekind; and woe to the skull on which his axe falls! (*Elementargeister*, 1836)

In 785 the Saxon leader Widukind (Wittekind) was baptized 'of his own free will'. The Saxon territories were forced to accept a christian religious structure and a harsh Frankish administration. Centuries later, Charles IV, the Luxemburger who was the first and only emperor between Otto IV and the fall of the old Empire to set foot in northern Germany, endeavoured as part of his general policy of reconciliation (between Germans and Czechs, Rome and East Rome) to bring about a second peace between Widukind and his own illustrious 'ancestor', Charles the Great. Having found the grave of the Saxon duke in a state of decay, Charles IV had the monument restored and placed on the tombstone the armorial bearings of Charles the Great and of Bohemia. This policy of reconciliation diffused its influence as much over the past (still, for all that, the 'unsubdued' past) as over the future. Many are inclined to dismiss the Luxemburg emperor as a mere philistine, but he had a better insight into historical depth-psychology and its metapolitical and political chain reactions than many more recent politicians and historians.

Another Widukind worshipper was Heinrich Himmler, whose father was tutor to a Bavarian prince and who in his own youth was a server at Mass. Himmler venerated the 'pagan' Widukind, and regarded himself as the reincarnation of the Saxon Henry I, whose tomb he opened and whose cathedral he turned into a cult centre for his SS.

The foundation legend of Kremsmünster, the Bavarian monastery founded by Tassilo in 777, relates that a son of this last independent Duke of Bavaria met his death near the spot from a wild boar (probably a totem animal of the Tassilo clan); to this very day the monks consume a wild boar once a year in memory of Tassilo's son. Ten years after Kremsmünster was founded Charles liquidated Tassilo's 'empire'. Bavaria, like Saxony, was divided into counties under the control of royal counts and joined Saxony as a vital component and opponent of the Empire. First the Welfs and then the Wittelsbachs would be contenders for the imperial crown, and Wittelsbach Bavaria, not infrequently in alliance with the French, would at times stand in open opposition to the Empire.

As a result of Charles the Great's eastern campaigns against the Slavs and the Avars whole regions from the mouth of the Oder to Croatia and the Adriatic became exposed to imperial influence. South of the Pyrenees, a Spanish mark was established against the Arabs and Barcelona captured; the Balearic Islands were another recent conquest. In 778 a small rearguard of Charles' northward returning army, led by Ruodland ('Roland'), was annihilated by the Basques at Roncesvalles. In the twelfth century France would make the *Song of Roland* its 'first Marseillaise'; the crusading spirit of the epic woke to life a fiery French 'nationalism' which readily equated the 'heathen dogs' (the Saracens) of the eighth century with the Germans of the twelfth.

There is no Empire without Rome. The debate among historians over the meaning and function of Charles the Great's imperial coronation and over the intentions of the two protagonists, Charles and Pope Leo III, bristles with as many problems as the coronation and its resultant chain reaction presented at the time.

On Christmas Day in the year 800 Charles heard Mass in St Peter's. Whilst his head was bent in prayer, Leo III placed on his forehead a gold circlet in token of an imperial crown, and the Romans acclaimed him Emperor: 'To Charles Augustus, crowned by God, the great and peace-giving Emperor of the Romans, life and victory!' Einhard in his life of Charles the Great asserts that Charles was taken by surprise and feared the jealous indignation of the Greeks.

Modern research has shown that it is no longer possible to speak of the coronation as in any sense a surprise gesture. But we are still entitled to assume that the more immediate and remoter participants in the event attached to it differing conceptions, hopes and fears. To the Franks in general the coronation must have seemed a thorough-going and visible vindication of their faith in Christ (and in St Peter): it demonstrated that Christ, King of the Franks and war leader of the God-chosen Frankish people, had elected Charles to lead them on earth. The clerical intelligentsia of non-Frankish scholars who had flocked from the British Isles, Spain and Italy to Charles' court, and through their letters and other writings openly canvassed Charles' future assumption of the imperial office, had the satisfaction of seeing Charles established as the protector of all Roman Catholic Christians: Charles therefore had the obligation to bring the many tribes, peoples, princes and rulers constantly feuding with one another beneath the umbrella of his empire, to realize the peace of Augustus and the peace of Christ as the peace of Charles. To the Romans on that day Charles had appeared in the Roman garments (tunic and chlamys) he so greatly disliked: he appeared, that is to say, as a Roman emperor and his coronation as a completely 'standard' Roman imperial coronation [plate 1]. More concretely, he appeared to the Romans as the master of their long-standing Lombard enemies, as their champion against the much detested Byzantines (who nevertheless had their partisans, in Rome as well as in southern Italy), and not least as master of the Pope.

The Romans' resentment of the papacy persisted throughout the Middle Ages and almost into our own day. Their search for protectors against the 'oppressive' rule of their bishop was of long duration (the fourteenth-century coronation of Emperor Ludwig the Bavarian by a layman was but one episode), but in the year 800 one thing at least seemed plain: Leo III, the pope who fell on his knees in the Romano-Byzantine fashion to pay homage to the newly crowned emperor, recognized in Charles his protector and master. As a personality Leo is something of an enigma. In the previous year he had fled from his Roman enemies to take refuge with Charles at Paderborn in Saxony; the charges the Romans brought against him were to some extent disposed of by an oath of purgation he took (with an eye to making himself fit to carry out the coronation?) at a hearing in Rome presided over by Charles himself.

Charles conceived himself as the protector of western Christendom and took energetic steps to organize, guide and control it. He divided the imperial church into twenty-one archbishoprics, Rome being in his eyes the first. He summoned church councils, saw to it that controverted doctrinal questions were settled according to his own views (as against those of Byzantium) and devised a Romano-Frankish liturgical order so enduring that the liturgy of the Roman Catholic Church retains a Frankish imprint down to this day. Charles was convinced he had received a mission from God (throughout the Middle Ages God and Christ were closely assimilated), from Christ, the illustrious leader of the Franks, to convert the infidels, in other words the Saxon and other tribes living on the borders of his empire. He himself was not unduly astonished that the interests of Christ and of Emperor Charles should so closely coincide, but over the centuries the identification struck men as increasingly debatable; it ultimately became so insupportable that it sparked off the great conflicts of the Holy Roman Empire.

Charles' coronation at Rome would have been impossible without the massive superiority of Frankish fighting forces in western Europe and the manifest weakness of a papacy which from the time of Pope Stephen II (752–9) had been in the habit of taking refuge with the Franks from the constant harassments of the Lombards. Nor should the fact that the third force, Byzantium, was currently hampered by disputes over the succession be overlooked. A bold plan for dealing with Byzantium by a marriage between Charles and the Empress Irene was wrecked by Irene's dethronement, but it is interesting to see the 'great dream' of the spectacular political marriage brought into play at this juncture, since this was a solution the dynasties of old Europe, and not least the Habsburgs, would so often strive and struggle for. It was the Ottonians who first brought a purple-born princess into the Empire, and then only after protracted and difficult negotiations.

Charles had altogether five wives – in order, a Frank, a Lombard princess, a Swabian, an East Frank and another Swabian, not to mention numerous mistresses and concubines (in this he resembled David and Solomon, whom he honoured as his exemplars and forebears because they were the ancestors of Christ). He intended his marriages as a means of reconciling the peoples within his empire. At the back of the 'great dream' of the great political marriage lies the ancient and noble idea that mankind forms one family. *êwa*, the word from which the German word for marriage (*Ehe*) is derived, signifies the great order in heaven and the lawful order upon earth. Marriage thus establishes on earth the basis for the one and indivisible order of law and peace.

It was this order Charles and his associates hoped to achieve by their strenuous efforts to unify the vast empire. Royal counts administered the counties (*gaue*), and the counts in turn were controlled by itinerant royal commissioners. Annual empire-wide assemblies of bishops and counts meeting at court concurred in Charles' legislative and administrative decrees. The imperial church was made responsible for education, for the culture and moulding of the people.

One Emperor, one Church, one Christianity, one Empire (Aquitaine and the Lombard kingdom had their own organs of government, instituted by Charles): to a large extent this work of unification was never realized. The legislation tended to remain so much parchment, the ordinances of synods so many pious hopes, to which neither opulent bishops and abbots nor the great army of 'uncultured' popular clergy would or indeed could subscribe. Nevertheless, as a programme, as a grandiose design, Charles' empire exercised a potent fascination down the centuries, on the Ottonian and Hohenstaufen emperors, on Maximilian I and Charles V, on Louis XIV and Napoleon. Napoleon sought to impose on his own Europe, that is on Spain and Italy and the kingdoms he set up on the soil of the old Empire, a reformed legal code supported by the unifying influence of the French language and literary culture. This ambition must surely be seen as successor to the great enterprise attempted by the men round Charles the Great: just as Charles (who, however painstakingly he crooked his fingers, still could not write) sought by imposing one script (the Carolingian minuscule), one Franco-Roman clerical culture, one liturgy and one legal code to make the one empire a unity, so too did Napoleon seek to regiment Europe, using as his 'metre-stick' (the metric system was invented in the French Revolution) the laws, judicial system, traffic regulations, and on occasion the economic controls, which he himself ordained.

Down the centuries voices have been raised in protest against this 'monstrosity' of a 'universal monarchy'. In the seventeenth century, French propaganda directed by Richelieu and Mazarin dangled before the German princes and public the horrifying spectre of the Empire as just such a rigidly centralized monarchy; and this vision, be it noted, was conjured up by a French monarchy in process of building up its own state through the suppression of all dissenting political and religious groups and movements, even those whose dissent was purely intellectual. Here, if anywhere, was the true descendant of Charles' empire.

The Holy Roman Empire developed into something very different from the centralized Carolingian state. The Empire did not turn into a 'universal monarchy' nor into a dictatorship. It most certainly did not become a 'state' of the national variety, the kind which owed its beginnings to the patience and resource shown by men in twelfth-century England, France and Sicily.

In the Middle Ages the Empire was not a territorial expression but first and foremost a union of persons on the basis of fellowship. It nevertheless rested on Carolingian foundations, and would continue to do so down to 1806. However unstable and problematic Charles' empire itself might appear, with its bureaucracy and legislation designed to promote an imperial culture [plate 2] and its 'Carolingian' renaissance brought about by the intelligentsia streaming from many lands to Charles' court, the political, ecclesiastical and intellectual structures whose lineaments first emerged to view in Charles' Europe showed astonishing powers of endurance. These structures were truly fundamental to the creation of a central European 'old Europe', which on the intellectual plane stretches from Rhabanus Maurus to Goethe (who composed a German version of Rhabanus' *Veni creator spiritus*) – from one Rhineland Frank to another. It is no accident that in the Middle Ages the Carolingian inheritance can be summed up as consisting of two things, the imperial domain and 'the Empire'. All the monasteries of the Holy Roman Empire whose abbots ranked as princes of the Empire were founded during the Merovingian or Carolingian period. The imperial church, first and last the mainstay of the Holy Roman Empire, retained Carolingian characteristics until its dissolution by Napoleon in 1803.

In the Carolingian Empire forty-two noble families (at least nineteen of them related to the royal house) occupied the most important positions in the imperial administration. It is common form for anyone who wants to count for anything in Europe to trace his ancestry back to Charles the Great. John Foster Dulles, credited by his friends and detractors with sharing 'Carolingian' Adenauer's ambition to revive Carolingian Europe, set about it with the help of professional genealogists. Against these efforts to provide Charles with eminent political descendants must be set the researches of serious Swiss historians (perhaps not without ulterior motive) which have proved a Carolingian descent for many Swiss citizens, not all of them by any means people of the first importance.

Implicit (and magically implicit) in the achievement and person of Charles the Great was an elemental force. Something of this force emanates from his throne of stone in the cathedral at Aachen. Charles took up residence in his new palace at Aachen, the 'Charlestown' above all others, about the year 786. He was attracted to the place by its thermal waters; Einhard, who superintended the building work, speaks of the king's pleasure in 'exercising his body by frequent swimming, in which he was so adept that none can rightly be said to have surpassed him. Indeed, it was on this account that he built a royal citadel at Aachen and lived there without interruption during the last years of his life, until his death.'

A royal citadel: Charles' nimbus, his saving strength, his 'prestige', rested from start to finish on the fact that he was king of the Franks, the people beloved and chosen by Christ. In Europe, as in all ages whenever sacral royal power has developed (the last kings of the old type are at present dying out in Africa), monarchy has its roots in archaic, magical depths. At bottom, the king is a magus (the kings of ancient Egypt wear an imitation lion's tail, like the master magicians in prehistoric cliff and cave drawings). He is 'god' on earth, high priest (like Melchizedek). He bears the power and attributes of divinity, of priests, of magicians. The Carolingians, with the help of the Pope, had deposed, desacralized, the Merovingians, who, vested with the magic of their flowing sacred locks, had once progressed on their sacred ox-wagon through the lands of saints related to their dynasty. The inheritor of their saving strength was Charles, and after him the French kings (in the nineteenth century restoration period, royalist supporters still expected the kings to touch for 'king's evil' – scrofula).

Charles' throne at Aachen [plate 6] stands at the top of a flight of steps, like the throne of Solomon, the 'true king of peace'. Theodor Haecker has described Charles' throne as 'the most awe-inspiring, the most meaningful, of all German national monuments'. Charles was no '*Deutscher*', but in his time the early form of the word '*deutsch*' (meaning the same as 'vulgar', in contrast with Latin) makes its appearance. Charles ordered a collection to be made of the old songs and lays of the Germans, most of which were magical incantations. In its original meaning the Latin *carmen* (hence 'charm') stands not for the incantation as such but for the magic it produced. Charles was folkish in his way of life. His dress was 'Frankish' – linen shirt, short linen drawers, knee-length surcoat, stockings, stout foot-gear made from goat leather and a long-haired travelling cloak. The dreaded Saxons went into battle in their cherished straw hats, from which they refused to be parted. Charles and his men fought accoutred in iron helmets, iron armlets and iron plates to protect breast and shoulders. They had chain shirts reaching to knees and elbows; their weapons were the sword, lance, round shield, spear, javelin and battle-axe.

The real foundation of Charles' power was the unbroken strength of his Franks and of the tribes they subdued. Equally real – as an expression of unbroken belief in their saving strength – was the Franks' conviction that they were in no way inferior to the tribes who had sustained the old empires of the past, the Medes, the Persians, the Greeks and the Romans. The sentiment is made explicit in the preface that Otfried of Weissenburg wrote for his *Harmony of the Gospels*.

Why should the Franks alone fail in not starting to praise God in the Frankish tongue? True, it is not yet so polished and hedged about with rules, yet it has its own ordered usage which is beautifully simple. Why should the Franks be unfit to come together in unity, the Franks who assuredly do not lag behind the Greeks and the Romans, the Medes and the Persians? They are as valiant as the Romans, and no one can say the Greeks offer them any challenge.

In the decades following 800 an idea, or rather an ideology, started to develop in Frankish circles to the effect that the Greeks had handed over the *imperium* to the Franks as the 'people of the Empire'. The first mention of a *translatio imperii* having occurred in 800 dates from about 850 and comes from a Frankish-Lotharingian source, the *Life* of Willehad, first archbishop of Hamburg, which is known to have been written in the monastery of Echternach. This was not the interpretation placed on the imperial coronation by Charles and his followers in 800; nor can the idea of such a transference be traced to Charles at any time before his death. Papal politicians and curial ideologists – with help from the *Donation of Constantine* (a document confected at Rome about this period which purported to be Constantine's grant of Rome and the Papal State to the Pope) – would later develop the translation theory into an ideology of papal world dominion and a formidable weapon against the Emperor: the Pope, having once conveyed the *imperium* away from the Greeks, could withdraw it again, perhaps to hand it over to the 'true Frank' in Paris.

However far removed Charles and his circle may have been from the translation theory (for them grace flowed directly from God onto the King and Emperor; the Emperor was crowned by God; Charles himself crowned his son Louis; Louis – Ludwig – bore the ancient and sacral name of the first converted Merovingian, Chlodwig), in certain significant matters Charles did effect a translation. The stones for building his Aachen he translated literally from ruined Roman buildings in Trier, Cologne and Aachen, columns and marble work he brought from Ravenna [plate 4]. Moreover, through the medium of his court scholars, he carried over into his Empire the ancient and venerable wisdom handed down from a single and sacred antiquity, *antiquitas*.

The 'authoritative humanism' (Walter Rüegg) of the Carolingian era pressed ancient words and names into service as redemptive slogans and claims to power: the Charles who is 'David' [plate 13], 'Solomon', and 'Augustus' is strengthened and fortified against Byzantium. It was thought that words found in sacred books, in the Bible – the book of salvation – or in the works of doughty Roman and Greek sages (though the latter were increasingly suspect) should suffice to break the power of 'pagans' and 'heretics' – people who refused to trust in the great oneness of Charles' empire (one God, one Emperor, one Faith, one Empire, one Culture).

'Plurality ceases as a dimension with the number two.' As a sweeping statement it could be said that ever since Carolingian times the 'Franks' (that is the West Europeans, the Latins) have been men incapable of counting up to three. For three read plurality: plurality and polychromy in the Godhead and in mankind, plurality in society. The voice of Greek christian spirituality speaks with Clement of Alexandria of the hundred flowers encouraged to blossom under the benign influence of the Trinity. The Carolingian west interpreted Three-in-Oneness with all the emphasis on the 'One' God, and was very soon in difficulties over the very idea of a Three-in-One. 'Greek' minds interpret the threefold Godhead as a 'process' unfolding itself in world history (becoming, growth, and change are all bound up with it). 'Roman' and 'Frankish' minds interpret the 'Three-in-Oneness' as a single, indivisible, inseparable mighty Oneness, in which God the Father and God the Son flow into one another, and the Holy Spirit plays a remarkably subdued and subterranean supporting role.

The after-effects of the Trinitarian disputes which convulsed Charles' empire were felt long beyond his time. In 792 he had Felix of Urgel condemned as a heretic at the Council of Regensburg. This Spanish bishop (Spain retained its reputation with the papal curia as the motherland of heresies into the sixteenth century) insisted on emphasizing the humanity of Jesus Christ. The victorious theologians of the Carolingian court thought otherwise: for them Christ was all God, the *One* God.

The Carolingian gospel was a lordly doctrine and a doctrine of lordship; this was how Charles ordered his clergy to preach and proclaim it to the people. It speaks not of the suffering Christ, the 'poor Christ', the Christ of the 'destitute', but of the God-Christ, the King of noble lineage [plate 5]. It is fitting here to recall that in Charles' empire large numbers of smaller folk were being successfully reduced from freedom to unfreedom. 'Of their own free will' (in fact, with little choice if they were to avoid the burden of military service or oppression by the powerful), peasants and smaller land-owners were commending themselves and their property to the military and legal protection of greater lords, and in particular of monastic and other ecclesiastical landlords. The land registers of monastic and other foundations chart this process clearly enough. Thereafter, the Middle Ages in the main would know only various forms of dependent peasantry.

Great gulfs separated the Anglo-Saxon, Hiberno-Scottish, Spanish and Lombard-Italian clerics who frequented Charles' court from the broad mass of 'uncultured' clerics who still took part in the pagan sacrifices, or at least in the richly magical rituals customary among their tribes and people. The extent to which Carolingian Europe, superficially unified, was itself aware of these contrasts is shown by the political and ecclesiastical measures resorted to by Charles and his collaborators in the battle against the Spanish 'heretics'.

Felix of Urgel was condemned as a 'heretic' at Regensburg in 792. *Roma locuta, causa finita*: 'when Rome has spoken, a matter is no longer open to dispute'. The tag (in this particular formulation belonging to a much later period) lays bare an illusion which has had tragic, if not lethal, consequences for Europe: for as its later history shows, not one of the 'heresies', not one of the 'non-conforming' religious, theological or politically 'deviant' ideas which first emerged to view in the Empire of Charles the Great has ever been 'rooted out'. They are alive and at work today. Here we shall only point out how they are interwoven into this particular 'Spanish' affair.

Soon after Felix had been condemned at Regensburg the controversy flared up again. A Spaniard, Migetius, came forward with an interpretation of the Trinity which in many respects anticipated the view of world history first conceived *in nuce* by Joachim of Flora in Greek southern Italy at the end of the twelfth century, and later given a more radical and political slant by his disciples. This view postulated three dispensations, the kingdom of the Father (coinciding with the Old Covenant), the kingdom of the Son (coinciding with the historic life of the Empire and the Papal Church), and the kingdom of the Holy Spirit, of the 'Everlasting Gospel', which was yet to come. Through acting upon history, the Trinity was bursting the 'middle age' wide open. Hence the old *imperium* and the old *ecclesia* – Empire and Papal Church – are seen as ephemeral epochs, justified merely by their chronological place in the history of a mankind on its way to a greater future. In the Trinitarian doctrine of Migetius, God the Father was incarnate in David, God the Son in Jesus, God the Holy Spirit in St Paul. Bishop Elipandus of Toledo retorted by asserting that the human nature of Christ had no part in the Godhead, and Felix came to his support, interpreting Elipandus' 'adoptionist theory' (i.e. that God had 'adopted' the human Jesus) as a contractual master-servant relationship (a similar interpretation would be advanced by Bishop Eberhard of Bamberg in the twelfth century). Felix introduced a missionizing note into his adoptionist doctrine: 'We are all, like Jesus, adopted by God as his sons, and like him have received the same grace'.

The controversy spread all over Charles' empire, drawing in Rome and Aachen. After his condemnation at Regensburg Felix had taken refuge in Arabo-Spanish territory, probably with Elipandus in Moorish-Christian-Jewish Toledo. On the intervention of a number of bishops, the matter was raised again in 793–4 at the Council of Frankfurt, in the presence of Charles the Great acting in his capacity as 'external bishop' of his 'orthodox' imperial church. (East Roman emperors had regarded themselves as 'external bishops', and made sure their court theologians respected them as such, ever since the days of Constantine). Felix was again condemned, and once again found bishops willing to intercede on his behalf.

In the spring of 800 Felix finally recanted, having allowed himself to be 'convinced' by Alcuin, but he left behind him when he died a tract which revived the old 'heresy'.

The Europe which had been unified with such daring, energy and violence was an unquiet continent. After Charles' death the imperial structure fell apart. It will be more meaningful in this context – for the historian as for the alert individual anxious to gain in appreciation and knowledge of his past – to speak not of blame but of causes.

One overwhelming personality had forced the most heterogeneous components into the mould of one great empire. Under Charles' sons these components asserted

The Empire of
Charles the Great

1 Charles the Great, the father and
protector of the Holy Roman
Empire. Ottonians, Salians and
Hohenstaufens try to 'renew' his
Empire, and all imperial
coronations hark back to his.

2 Charles the Great, one of his sons and a scribe. The Carolingian 'renaissance' marked the beginning of a European culture and society based on the written word.

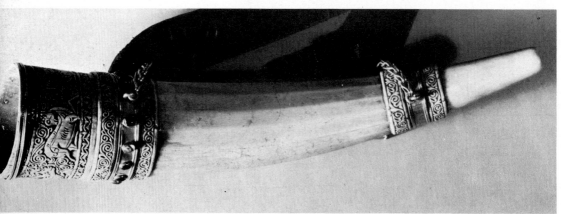

3 'Charles the Great's hunting-horn'. The hunt played a part in imperial ceremonial in the five-thousand-year-long tradition of Empire.

4 The Octagon in Aachen Cathedral, with the twelve-turreted chandelier (symbolizing
the heavenly Jerusalem; this dates from the twelfth century), preserves the ancient holy
number eight (Persia), a sacred symbol of the City of God.

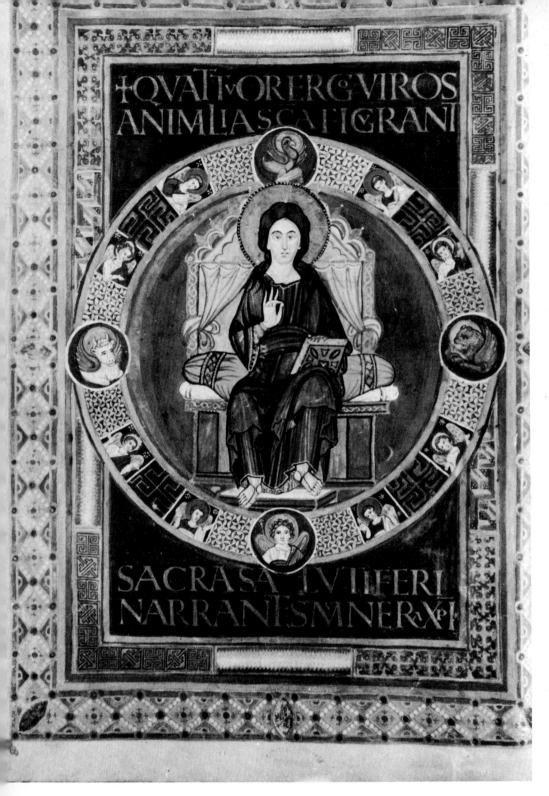

5 Christ in Majesty. The Carolingian world was subject to the one God-King, Christ, and his representative on earth, Charles the Great.

6 The throne of Charles the Great. This sacred stone seat (like the Stone of Scone) harks back to the throne of Solomon.

7 A Byzantine empress (*c.* 500). The continuing Roman Empire in the east viewed with disfavour the upstart Frankish Empire.

8 The Tassilo Cup in Kremsmünster, a memorial of Duke Tassilo, the last ruler of an independent Bavaria. This work of art combines elements from almost all the cultures that came together in the Carolingian Empire.

9 Louis the Pious (814–40). While the Empire was declining, Carolingian culture was bearing its first fruits.

10 Lothar I (840–55). The division of Charles' Empire among his sons and grandsons gave rise to France, Burgundy, Germany and Italy.

11 Charles the Bald (875–7). His court saw the first flowering of the intellectual culture of the new Europe, e.g. Scotus Erigena.

12 Charles the Fat (881–7) with his wife. All the Virtues, the benign powers of Heaven on earth, are gathered round the emperor whose imperial power is failing.

13 King David, venerated as Charles's ancestor, playing the lyre. Carolingian illuminated manuscripts are religious-political manifestations of Carolingian culture.

14 'In the beginning was the Word': the initial words of St John's Gospel, from a bible of Charles the Bald. Carolingian culture was literally based on the word of the Bible, on classical education, on the written word which the Carolingian reform of handwriting itself made possible.

their own rights. The single empire had its episcopal and monastic champions (Louis the Pious hoped to restore the unity of the Empire through a reforming clergy), and was at times supported by members of the higher nobility. But the institutions and communications which could have brought about a real and enduring unification of Carolingian Europe were lacking. There was no imperial bureaucracy with a vested interest in holding the Empire together. Such officials as did exist were becoming feudal lords, each intent on creating a great or small 'empire' for himself. There was no economy geared to the Empire. Attempts to construct an economy based on money were soon frustrated. Carolingian Europe, at any rate in the central regions, reverted to an economy based purely on the land, and it was this return to an agrarian culture which largely contributed, on the political plane, to the triumph of feudalism. The great landed proprietor catered for his own needs; the most immediate requirements were met by exchanges on a small scale in local markets.

There was a return to the epic barbarism of the Merovingian period, a time renowned for the cruel, murderous, treacherous and self-destructive actions of its great families. Termagant women, faithless bishops, treacherous, self-seeking magnates once again took the stage and played their fatal roles. It is not difficult to see why Judith, the second wife of Louis the Pious, whose life was lived 'between times', has the reputation of a 'she-devil'. As a young woman she gathered 'humanists' at her court; in her later years she surrounded herself to the public indignation with sorceresses and soothsayers and was in the habit of invoking demonic powers – a witches' kitchen out of Macbeth. In the violence of their passions and their obsession with intrigue, some of the women of this age seem indeed the very incarnation of Lady Macbeth and her sinister powers.

Louis the Pious [plate 9], created co-emperor by his father in 813, came to grief because of the quarrels between the sons of his first and second marriages. His own vassals nearly all betrayed him, and when his army deserted to his sons at the 'Field of Lies' (Rotfeld, near Colmar), Louis himself confessed, from his retreat at Soissons, that his culpable errors made him unfit to rule. True, he regained his crown because of the continuing bad blood between his sons and kinsmen, but Louis remained throughout the Middle Ages the classic example of the disempowered ruler, the ruler who had lost his royal saving power, his sacral dignity and invulnerability, his territories, his property, his vassals, his wife and his sons.

A new beginning was made with the treaties of Verdun and Coulaines. Verdun, in later days under the Empire known as Virten, has been much fought over. The area surrounding the fortress of Verdun claimed the lives of one and a half million German and French soldiers in the First World War; in front of Verdun, almost unremarked, the old 'theatrical' style of warfare, in which man and man fought face to face as a work of artistry and skill, met its death. This same Verdun, where for the first time in a thousand years of war the battle became one between materials rather than men, was the place where France and Germany were born.

The Empire was divided between three brothers. Ludwig the German was assigned the major part of the German territories (East Francia), Charles the Bald the major part of the French, together with Brittany and the Basque lands (West Francia). Lothar [plate 10], who was emperor, received the two imperial cities, Aachen and Rome, the Frankish heartland round the Meuse and the Moselle, Burgundy and Italy; and as emperor he was nominally supreme in the Empire. But in 855 Lothar died, his three sons failed to produce any legitimate heirs, and for practical purposes the leading historical roles fell to the other two kingdoms, East and West Francia. Nevertheless, Lothar's middle kingdom remained of unique importance for Europe: as a 'middle Europe' it was the first to foster the development of a European character and consciousness. The area it covered now embraces the Benelux countries and parts of France and Switzerland. In the later Middle Ages, as Burgundy, it was ruled by princes audacious enough to make it a prosperous and brilliant state wedged between France and the Empire so that Burgundy's fate came to be at the mercy of the Habsburgs and the kings in Paris. Charles v, 'the Burgundian', embroiled his beloved native land in the 'world politics' of his day; the country was overrun by Spaniards and Frenchmen, by troops and governors sent by the Habsburgs and from the Empire, all contending for the prize. Burgundy still exerted a fascination over that terrifying simplifier of our own century who was so anxious to build his own Europe: Hitler, and still more, Himmler, envisaged the creation of a new-old Burgundy as a middle zone between Greater Germany and a France reduced to a smaller compass (similar to that which it occupied between the ninth and mid-twelfth centuries).

For French historians the history of France begins in 843, the year of the treaties of Verdun and Coulaines. Charles the Bald (823–77) is listed as the *premier roi de France* [plate 11]. At that date 'Germania' is a wholly vague concept, whereas 'Gallia' already appears firmly present in outline. The treaty concluded between Charles the Bald and his vassals at Coulaines a few months after Verdun has been called 'the foundation charter of the West Frankish kingdom'.

While the great Empire was wasting away, in West and East Francia substantial nuclei were in painful process of formation. Robber bands preyed on the countryside. Arab pillagers set fire to Marseilles. There was an Arab bridgehead at Pontresina in the Engadin – *pons Sarracenorum*. Each year Danish fleets swooped down from the north manned by 'Normans' who sacked the coasts and voyaged up the Seine as far as Paris. In the time of Charles III [plate 12] they penetrated to Aachen, Metz, Rheims. The Saracens captured Palermo and Bari. In 846 they pillaged St Peter's, the 'golden Rome' of the Franks, whose attachment to Rome arose from their peculiar Petrine belief. In 884 the Saracens destroyed the monastic citadel of Monte Cassino (destroyed again, after much bitter fighting, in the Second World War). The Slavs, under Swatopluk, a christian Moravian prince, were founding a Greater Moravian Empire stretching from the Fichtelgebirge up to the gates of Vienna (perhaps already the capital of a vast Slav Empire in the seventh century, under Samo the Frank) and thrusting deep into Russia.

As we take stock of this troubled Europe, which was apparently relapsing into – or indeed perpetuating – the long centuries of the folk migrations, we find Germany, France and Burgundy emerging as the successor states of Charles' empire. Italy, meanwhile, was reverting to indigenous rulers, who were perpetually feuding with one another.

At one moment it seemed that leadership of the dying Empire might be destined to pass to the vigorous Arnulf of Carinthia, bastard grandson of Ludwig the German. He deposed Charles III at the Diet of Tribur (on the Rhine), defeated the Normans at Louvain (891), gave battle to the Moravians, and in answer to an appeal for help from Pope Formosus swept through northern Italy and was crowned emperor at Rome. A fatal heart attack shortly after the coronation removed Arnulf from the scene Under his son, Ludwig the Child, conduct of affairs passed to prelates like Archbishop Hatto of Mainz and to a Franconian family, the Conradins. In 910 little Ludwig was defeated near Augsburg by the Magyars, who since 900 had been making annual raids, first on Bavaria and later also on Saxony and Thuringia.

Europe, in the form of Charles' empire, had only recently been taken from the cradle by its two fathers, Charles the Great and the Pope. Now it was apparently left fatherless. The prevailing mood of the monastic chronicles, written in islands of uncertain peace which were constantly visited by floods from storms far and near, is one of profound pessimism. In the tenth century, 'the dark century' of later historians, the lights of hope were going out, especially in western and southern Europe Yet it was precisely in this Europe, whose face was darkened by perpetual feuding and warfare, that the Holy Roman Empire came into being – as the Ottonian Empire.

3

THE OTTONIAN EMPIRE

THE imperial crown of the Holy Roman Empire has remained since 1800 in Vienna, a dazzling memorial and witness to the Empire's majesty. It was probably made for the coronation of Otto the Great in 962. From that day forward, although the Empire was at no time a German national state, Germany was to be its chief prop and stay.

The popes, who would be the emperors' great rivals in the Holy Roman Empire and in Christendom at large, had profited from the quarrels between Charles the Great's heirs and successors during the ninth century. The claims to authority some of them then advanced anticipate the mounting claims of the popes between Gregory VII and Innocent IV. In 833 we find Gregory IV asserting that the Pope is not a brother to the bishops but their 'father'. Pope Nicholas I (858–67), known as 'the Great', held that the church was co-extensive with the earth and that his office made him the rightful judge of terrestrial emperors and kings. He distinguishes between a 'legitimate, lawful ruler' (*verus rex*) and the unlawful 'tyrant'. Later popes would develop this duty of adjudicating on the merits of candidates for the Empire into a high political art and a means of exercising power. In the era of the Ottonian and early Salian emperors, however, the boot was on the other foot and it was the Emperor who determined who was the lawful Pope.

The self-assertiveness of the ninth-century popes was greeted by other ecclesiastics with a mixture of amazement, apprehension and resentment. Archbishop Gunther of Cologne expostulates over the effrontery of Nicholas I in counting himself an apostle among the apostles and behaving as though he were emperor of the entire world, and the chronicler Regino of Prüm also comments disparagingly on the pope's habit of giving orders to kings and tyrants, 'as though he were lord of the world'.

The popes, in short, possessed a religious-political doctrine whose essential features were clear-cut well before the rise of the emperors. Whatever the vicissitudes and catastrophes experienced by individual popes, this doctrine provided a firm inner core for the building up of papal power in centuries to come. The Holy Roman Emperor of the period covered by the Ottonian, Salian and Hohenstaufen dynasties (962–1250) had at his disposal an ideology and continuity on a par with the papal doctrine, but in practice individual rulers again and again found themselves left to stand on the own feet, relying on their own potency and vitality.

This was an adolescent Europe in more senses than one. The heroines of courtly epic are girls of twelve or thirteen; men married early, came early to high ecclesiastical and secular office and died an early death.

Most of the emperors were under twenty-five when they came to the throne; only Lothar was in his fifties, only Henry I and Conrad III in their forties. The emperor's colleagues were just as youthful. Men quickly adapted themselves to the hardships and dangers of itinerant government which entailed a ceaseless round of journeys on horseback between the North Sea and the Mediterranean, undertaken without benefit of maps or proper roads. Of the sixteen regularly constituted rulers between Otto the Great and the Interregnum, Frederick I lived to be about sixty-five, Otto I and Lothar III reached sixty, but no others lived as long. Seven emperors contracted fatal illnesses (malaria, dysentery, and so on) in Italy. Frederick I met his death by accident whilst on crusade, Conrad III returned from crusade fatally ill. Philip of Hohenstaufen was murdered, Otto IV deposed. Only five died a more or less natural death.

The late medieval dances of death show Death, the Emperor's greatest enemy, snatching him away. Respect for death, preparation for death, contemplation of death, celebration of death in the solemnities of funeral procession, burial and funerary monument, informed the lives, work, thoughts and feelings of Habsburg rulers from Maximilian I to Maria Theresa. Some might say that the Habsburg burial place, the vault of the Capuchins in Vienna is one of the places where the memory of the old Empire is kept most green.

There was nothing romantic and little that was numinous about the political climate in which the Frankish Conrad I (911–18) and his Saxon rival Henry I (919–936) – to whom Conrad on his deathbed despatched the royal insignia in designation of his successor – laid the foundations of the Ottonian Empire. The collapse of the Carolingian state and its system of county organization had left the 'tribes' to fend for themselves against threats from Danes, Slavs and Magyars. In this emergency they rallied round their dukes.

There were four main tribes, the Saxons, Bavarians, Franks and Swabians, and one smaller group, the Thuringians; the Lotharingians, in their two dukedoms of Upper and Lower Lotharingia (Lorraine), also come into the picture. On the death of the last German Carolingian (Ludwig the Child) in 911 the tribes in a free election chose Conrad, Duke of the Franks, as king of the *regnum Theotonicum* (a name given by one annalist to the new kingdom in 920).

The 'Germans', then, are the four great tribes who in military emergency choose for themselves leaders, dukes. The dukes in turn elect a 'super-duke' as king and fight under his leadership. The essential feature is that the king should occupy the role of leader only to ward off external attack; at other times he is to receive only the occasional marks of respect due to his rank. This has a close bearing on the peculiar weaknesses inherent in the imperial office right down to the end of the Holy Roman Empire in 1806. No matter what his title, whether that of 'German King', 'King of the Romans', 'Emperor' or 'Roman Emperor Elect', the supreme head of the Empire which was created in the tenth century was never acknowledged by its members as their monarch.

The tribes elected the king, the tribes comprised the kingdom and its army; and even when the 'tribal duchies' started to crumble away, diets whose competence extended over the whole tribal territory continued to meet, magnates from all over the region were still required to attend sessions of the ducal court. A general assembly of magnates, which met only under threat of extreme emergency (independence reasserted itself the moment each magnate set out on his homeward way) had sufficient faith in Henry, Duke of the Saxons, to elect him king: even as king, they felt, Henry would still be true to his ducal origins. King Henry refused the anointing and coronation which Heriger of Mainz, following Carolingian precedent, offered him immediately after his election. In the historical claptrap of 'German Nationalist' and Nazi publicists this significant gesture is made to appear a rejection of 'Rome' and 'clerical' status in favour of a 'national' kingship protesting its Germanness. Henry's refusal has to be seen in the light of his situation in 919: it was not for him, so recently a duke himself, to raise himself above the other dukes. Rather, he had to rely on them for support, more than ever necessary at this time of dire emergency. When the Saxon duke rejected this coronation, Rome and an imperial coronation were not uppermost in his mind. But he had not turned his back on them. In 919 he was weighed down by the cares of the moment; things were different in 936 when he designated his son Otto as his successor. In the first years of his reign Henry had neither an arch-chaplain nor a chapel of royal clerks, that is to say, no developed chancery. The charters of the first five years of his reign were drafted and written by a single scribe, a notary named Simon.

Henry I married as his second wife Mathilde, a direct descendant of the great Saxon leader Widukind. This forceful woman, who bore Henry five children, brought him a rich patrimony in Westphalia as well as the inestimable benefit of union with her sacred stock. It was in this Saxon environment that the idea that it meant something to be 'a German' was born, an idea which as the tenth century brought further wars and woes also took root in the other tribes. It was 'German' to strive for security by entering into a bond of loyalty towards God and God's friends, the influential saints, just as it was 'German' to enter for the same reason into a bond of friendship with fellow-travellers on this harsh earth, the princes and dukes of one's tribal kindred – or, if those proved faithless, with friends in the church.

Henry I acquired from Rudolf of Burgundy an object which became the victory-bringing sacred symbol of the Saxon Ottonian Empire and was revered for the next thousand years as one of the holiest of the imperial insignia. This was the Holy Lance [plate 15] whose trail leads back from Burgundy into the Lombard kingdom and from Italy back again to Jerusalem (later it was identified as the spear Longinus thrust into the side of the crucified Jesus [plate 25]). His possession of the lance places Henry, the Saxon duke who strove to prove his sacral kingship in the only admissible manner, by victory on the field of battle, directly in line with his son Otto the Great, who as emperor would wear the star-strewn mantle and the tunic fringed with tintinnabula. Tunic and mantle formed part of the vestments of the biblical high priest. And it was the high priest who wore the *ḥoshen*, the breastplate set with twelve precious stones whose names were the names of the twelve tribes of Israel. The crown of the Empire [colour plate 1] incorporates two such groups of twelve stones, on the front and on the neck-plate; one or other must surely have been intended to perpetuate the symbolism of the *ḥoshen*. The Ottonian Emperor is representative of the high priest, of Christ the Priest King, who succeeded the kings of God's ancient people. Four potent saviour figures – Solomon, David, Isaiah confronting King Hezekiah in his sickness, and Christ the ruler of all – occupy the four intermediate plates of the crown, summoning the Emperor to his bounden duty. Keeping faith with Christ the King and his own sacred ancestors, supported on earth by his true 'friends' – in other words by princes, dukes, kings, popes and bishops – the Emperor is to lead God's people to war and victory. The splendour and frailty of the Ottonian conception of empire already stand revealed. What could be finer, what more right and proper, than a Holy Empire conceived as a great federative league, based on trust rather than subjection, composed of friends from within and without (at their head the Pope, both as bishop of Rome and king's friend), the whole under the leadership of the Emperor-king? But what would happen, and here is the crux, should these friends lay and ecclesiastical prove unfaithful?

King Henry used the security of the nine years' truce he purchased for his Saxons from the Magyars to build up a fighting force in which mounted men predominated. He fortified monasteries and market centres against attack. He battled successfully with the Slavs, capturing Brennabor (Brandenburg) in 929, and in 933 gave the Magyars their first defeat, at the river Unstrut. His relations with the powerful tribal dukes were governed by foresight and good sense, and he consolidated his prestige by establishing friendly connections with Burgundy and Anglo-Saxon England. At Epiphany in 935 King Henry mediated between the kings of France and Burgundy at Ivois on the Chiers; he also concluded a treaty of friendship with France and Burgundy on his own account. It was on this occasion that King Rudolf of Burgundy gave him the miracle-working Holy Lance, whose iron point, studded with gold crosses, contained nails from Christ's passion. Possession of this sacred relic, said to have been given by St Helena to Constantine the Great, was 'symbol and proof of his claim to Italy and to the imperial office'. The German king had thus acquired two more friends, the kings of France and Burgundy.

By way of concluding his account of Henry and his deeds, the Saxon chronicler Widukind of Corvey[1] remarks that when all the neighbouring peoples had been subdued 'he finally resolved to set out for Rome; but being attacked by illness, he

---

[1] The body of St Vitus, patron saint of the Saxon kingdom, had been translated to Corvey in 837. St Vitus, to whom Charles IV dedicated his cathedral in Prague, also became the patron saint of the Bohemian kingdom.

renounced the journey'. It appears, then, that Henry himself intended to go to Rome to receive the imperial crown.

Otto I, Henry's eldest son to be born in wedlock, was brought up as a child of the people and without benefit of a literary, clerkly education. His early liaison with a Slav woman of noble birth (captured in the wars of 928–9) issued in an illegitimate son, William, who as archbishop of Mainz at one of the great turning points of history stood up for the rights of the Slavs against his father. Otto married as his first wife Edgitha, sister of the English king Athelstan. Otto presented his father-in-law (whose fame was celebrated by a German poet) with a magnificent gospel book; his wife received as her wedding gift the town of Magdeburg, since Carolingian times a place of first importance in the commercial traffic with the Slavs. Edgitha rebuilt it after its destruction by the Magyars and in 946 was buried in the cathedral.

Otto was chosen king by the Franks and Saxons; the formal ceremony of election by all five tribal duchies and the consecration and enthronement took place at Aachen on 7 August 936. Aachen was the imperial city of Charles the Great, 'Otto's exemplar from the day he began to rule'.

The election was in two parts, the ecclesiastical and lay princes acting separately by their own wish. The lay princes set Otto (who had donned Frankish clothing – in becoming king the Saxon became a Frank) on a throne in the cathedral forecourt and pledged him loyalty and support against his enemies. The people raised their right hands to show their assent in the election and shouted 'victory and salvation' (*Sieg und Heil*), a salutation of substance in that it gave the election legal force. The rite of consecration (which had been administered only seven weeks previously to the Carolingian king in France) was presided over by Heriger of Mainz who had emerged the victor from a dispute with the other archbishops, Cologne and Trier, over which of the three should take precedence. Standing before the altar he handed the king the sword with which to fight the enemies of Christ, the mantle in token of a faith kept burning until death, the sceptre and staff with which to chastise his subjects and protect the weak. Then the archbishops of Mainz and Cologne anointed and crowned the king. The sacred rite was brought to its culmination and conclusion by two deeply archaic ruler-cult rituals: enthronement on Charles' seat, 'from which he could see all and by all be seen', and a royal banquet in the palace, at which the four dukes did the honours, Gilbert of Lotharingia as chamberlain, Eberhard of Franconia as steward. Hermann of Swabia as butler and Arnulf of Bavaria as marshal. An impressive picture of 'German' unity: people and princes shoulder to shoulder beside their king.

Otto's efforts to give substance to this new kingdom led, soon after the coronation, to a series of conflicts within his own family and with the dukes, conflicts which dragged on until 955, the year of the battle at the Lech. Otto's elder half-brother Thankmar died a rebel. His younger brother Henry allied himself with Dukes Eberhard of Franconia and Gilbert of Lotharingia, with Louis IV of France and Archbishop Frederick of Mainz. Conspiracies, reconciliations, and new defections

The Ottonian Empire

15 The Holy Lance, the most sacred
object of the Ottonian Empire. More
even than the imperial crown it
embodied this Empire's claims to
authority, in political, military and
religious spheres, particularly towards
the east.

16 Christ in Majesty with Otto I, who carries a model of Magdeburg Cathedral. Emperor Christ is invoked to bless the eastern mission of Emperor Otto I, who intended Magdeburg as a German Rome to unite Eastern Europe to his Empire.

18 St Udalrich blesses two abbots. From Ottonian times the hierarchy of the Church was as powerful an element in the Empire as the secular hierarchy.

17 Otto II. Germania, Francia, Italia and Alemannia, as embodying the four continents of the Christian world of Europe, pay homage to the emperor.

19 Chalice of St Udalrich. The name of Udalrich, bishop of Augsburg and comrade-in-arms of Otto I, is inseparably linked with the victory over the Hungarians at the Lech and the foundation of the Ottonian Empire.

20 Christ in Majesty, with the Virgin and St Maurice (patron of the Ottonian eastern mission), is adored by Otto II, Empress Theophano and the future Emperor Otto III in the traditional Byzantine proskynesis.

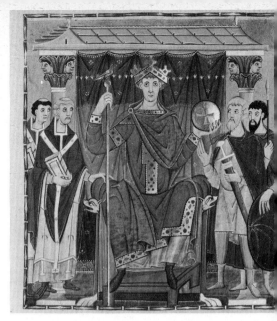

21 The four provinces of the Empire, Sclavinia, Germania, Gallia and Roma, pay homage to Otto III. The unhappy identification made by St Boniface of Slav and slave (Sclavinia = slave/Slav land) has blighted German policy towards the east down to the twentieth century.

22 Lead bull of Otto III. The inscriptions contain his whole programme *in nuce*: he intends, as the reborn Augustus, to renew the (ancient) Roman Empire (OTTO IMPERATOR AUGUSTUS: RENOVATIO IMPERII ROMANORUM).

23 (*opposite*) A crown, attributed to Otto III. The Emperor's crown was placed on a crucifix: Emperor Christ.

24 St Michael, protect
of the Empire and
leader of the Heavenly
Emperor's host, and
Christ are adored by th
tiny figures of Empero
Henry II and Empress
Kunigunde. Henry II
donated this altar-
frontal to the cathedral
he founded in Basel.

26 (*opposite*) From
Henry II's Gospel
Lectionary: Emperor
Christ himself crowns
the emperor and
empress; the apostles
are only bystanders at
this sacral act. Roma
(with the walled crown
and allegories of the
Provinces and the Virtu
pay homage to the
king-emperor in Heave
and to his representativ
on earth.

25 Bronze door of
St Bernward at Hildes-
heim, 1015: Cruci-
fixion. Here for the firs
time Christianity has
penetrated to the com-
mon people; we see
not Emperor Christ
reigning from the
Cross, but an ordinary
man of the people who
is crucified by his
fellow-men, and
mourned by them.

TRACTANDO IUSTUM · DISCERNITE SEMPER HONESTU
STILE CONUENIAT · CONSULTUM LEGIS UT OPTAT ·

SOLUIMUS ECCE TIBI · REX CENSUM IURE PERENNI ·
CLEMENS ESTO TUIS · NOS REDDIMUS ISTA QUOTANNIS ·

followed one upon another, seemingly without end. In between there were successful expeditions into Bohemia and northern Italy, where in 951 Otto secured for himself the title of 'King of the Lombard kingdom' and married Adelheid of Burgundy. A particularly grave threat to Otto was the rebellion of his sons in 953–4, which led to a grand coalition of all his enemies, the Magyars included.

This brings us to the eve of the battle at the Lech, whose thousandth anniversary in 1955 was commemorated with such pride in the Federal Republic. At Augsburg, the city closest to the site of the battle, the ecclesiastical and secular rejoicings took place in different settings and at different times; in the days of Otto I lay and ecclesiastical magnates were equally divided. Some of the motives inspiring the celebrations of 1955 are obvious enough. At that time Adenauer was pressing at Bonn and in Rome the claims of the Federal Republic to be regarded once more as the shield and protector of the christian west against the anti-christian east; the Magyars of 955 (like the Turks of 1683) stood in for the enemies of the *Reich* of 1955. The underlying perspectives are more arresting still. 'In the sight of God a thousand years are but a day' may be a pious platitude, but there is no denying that it was in the age of Otto the Great that structures basic to the religious, political, social and intellectual development of Germany first came into being or at least received their definitive form.

Many consequences followed from the victory of Otto I at the Lech: his own future assumption of the imperial office, the final establishment of the German imperial church as a political force of the first order, the refoundation of the Bavarian Ostmark of Austria, the establishment of the Hungarian (Magyar) kingdom under the crown of St Stephen, and the initiation of the eastern policy followed by Germany from 955 down to 1945. Nothing of this was known to Bishop Udalrich of Augsburg when on 8 August 955, clad in his vestments and without benefit of shield, cuirass, helmet or sword, he stood at the Osttor (later the Barfüssertor), where the assault was fiercest, and gave his people courage to stand firm. The attack repulsed, Udalrich spent the night in prayer. Having sent nuns to process praying and chanting through the streets, he himself repaired to the cathedral where he stretched himself full length on the ground and implored the Mother of God to protect the people and deliver the city. When morning came Udalrich administered the viaticum to his people. The Magyars broke off their attack, having learned from Berchtold, son of Arnold the Count Palatine, the news of Otto's approach.

Mention of Berchtold reminds us that the Magyars, those deadly foes of Christendom, were already deeply embroiled in the internal politics of the German world. Contemporary writers describe the Magyars as monsters, devilish malformations of the human species. In the words Widukind of Corvey puts into Otto's mouth before the battle, they were 'enemies of God and man', 'enemies of Christ'. During the Investiture Contest and its aftermath we shall find popes and emperors denouncing one another as enemies of God, precursers of antichrist, everything monstrous. There would even be sharp criticism of the victor of the Lechfeld for his marches on Rome.

27

27 Imperial Crucifixion. Christ on the Cross reigns as Emperor in liturgical vestments with the imperial crown (not the crown of thorns) on his head as triumphant victor over death and the devil.

Otto I's Roman expeditions, undertaken to re-establish the Empire and the imperial office, are described by Benedict, a monk of Monte Soracte, as 'pillage' of the once highly-famed city of Rome by the barbarian 'king of the Saxons'.

It remains true, however, that the appearance of the outwardly strange and savage Magyars in German lands was a great shock, even though there was little to choose between their plundering raids into German and Bohemian territories and the type of feuding then endemic in Christendom. In the course of a feud between Otto I and the French king Louis IV, fought out on French soil in 946, both armies plundered and devastated the regions they passed through. Some of Otto's closest kin took part in the rebellion of his son Liudolf, and showed themselves just as merciless as the Magyars in their depradations on German soil. Augsburg itself was seized by Liudolf from its loyal bishop and plundered.

The jubilators of 1955 might rejoin that these Magyars were pagans, and as such 'quite different' from other human beings. But it is important to remember that the western Christians of the ninth, tenth and even later centuries had their roots in 'pagan' archaic and barbarian soil – which in part accounts for their vitality. 'Barbaric' is the only word for the situation Otto I had to deal with at Rome. A century of carnage had been ushered in by the murder in 882 of Pope John VIII, who had fought with great energy against the Saracens. One of his kinsmen gave him poison to drink and then finished him off with a hammer. The atmosphere is thick with the primitive ferocity of murderous clan warfare, as celebrated – and exorcized – in the Norse sagas and in the *Nibelungenlied* (in its earliest form itself a product of the battle at the Lech and its aftermath), and for that matter in the plays of Shakespeare, the great memorialist and vanquisher of our European Middle Ages.

Udalrich of Augsburg, so his friend and biographer tells us, came to a diocese in which the clergy had run to seed: they permitted pagan practices to flourish in the countryside unchecked and took part in them themselves. But there is another way of looking at this: the magic and lustre shed by Otto the Great and his loyal servant Udalrich were due to the fusion in their own persons of the archaic with the new, the pre-christian with the christian. In this lies the true magic, the compelling power, the monumental appeal of Ottonian culture. Bishop Udalrich [plates 18, 19], military leader and priest, ruled his people soberly and with a harsh sense of justice; he showed himself friendly towards God and his family, towards the clansmen of his house and bishopric; he took pleasure in feasting and festivals and was ever mindful of the honour due to his noble birth. It was concern for this honour and for the rank attaching to his house that prompted the octogenarian Udalrich, with Otto's approval, to institute his nephew Adalbert as his successor in the see during his own lifetime, thus incurring the serious displeasure of the other German bishops. In Otto, Udalrich had at his side a king in whom magical 'pagan' and christian elements intertwined, as in Romanesque sculptural ornament or in the initials worked by the great book-illuminators of the Ottonian century.

Widukind's account of Otto's demeanour at the battle at the Lech is wholly consonant with this fusion within his person of the pagan and the christian. Otto knew that his saving potency as king was at stake in the battle. Its outcome would prove whether he was indeed the mighty one strong to save who could secure peace for his people, fruitful harvests for the land and fame and immortality for his warriors. Right up to the eve of the battle this royal potency was still in doubt, endangered by serious conflicts with his closest clansmen and with rebellious tribal dukes. To make sure of it, Otto invoked all the saving powers and forces that he knew: St Laurence, to whom on the morning of the battle he vowed a bishopric at Merseburg in the event of victory; the Archangel Michael, standard bearer of the Empire and of the hosts of heaven, whose battle ensigns pulsed with divine energy; St Maurice, whose lance the king carried into battle, so linking himself directly with the saving energy which flowed from Christ the conqueror. Maurice, as patron saint of Magdeburg, which Otto was later to develop as 'a capital of the German east' in exploitation of the opportunities opened up at the Lech, became the patron saint of Otto's eastern policy.

Once Otto had armed himself for the decisive battle with all the resources which the 'high and holy friends of God' placed at his disposal, the mighty ones of Heaven brought up reinforcements in the shape of the happy co-operation of the elements: rain which fell in the night frustrated the enemy in his wicked designs, the cloudless sunshine of the dawning day gave 'God's people' hope and confidence. The connection between fine weather and the life-giving potency of the Lord's anointed continued to be made in the popular mind down to the time of Emperor Francis Joseph and his 'emperor's birthday weather'. Francis Joseph inherited his title 'Apostolic Majesty' from the kings of Hungary, whose power dated from the time when the hold of the roving razzia commanders over the Magyars was finally broken: the most potent of these leaders was Bulcsu, hanged by Otto I on the Lechfeld as an act of desacralization.

Otto's own sacral power, to which Widukind affixes names handed down from antiquity – *divinus animus, caelestis virtus, fortuna, constantia, virtus* – was vindicated by his victory on the field of battle. At the finish, Widukind relates, his men proclaimed him *imperator*, emperor. 'It was victory in battle which gave the *imperator* his title, since in the realm of ethnology it is always battle and not descent which determines the divine verdict ... the sacral significance of victory in battle stamped on the hegemonial imperial office its military origin and charismatic character' (H. Beumann). Immediately after the battle came the victory celebration, a sacral feast uniting the living and the dead in a common commemoration: the proceedings, as Widukind monkishly remarks, were conducted *secundum errorem paternum*, in accordance with the 'erroneous' usage of the pagan forefathers.

The 'pagan' Hungarians, or rather their forebears, are known to have been in contact with Christianity from the sixth century at the latest. At the time of the battle at the Lech the two most powerful Magyar chieftains, Gyula and Bulcsu, were already christians. Gyula, who operated in the Theiss region, imported Greek priests and monks to convert his people. Bulcsu, like Gyula, had been baptized in Constantinople and awarded the exalted and honorific title of a patricius of the Byzantine Empire. It is also a fact that for some decades past the Hungarians had been in the habit of allying with German magnates, Bavarians in particular. As late as July 955 a Magyar embassy reminded Otto of the 'old friendship' between the Hungarians and the Germans.

The juxtaposition in modern Hungarian of words of Bulgar, Slav and Greek origin with those borrowed from church Latin is evidence of the tensions of this early period of Hungarian history, when Byzantium and Rome contended in the background for dominance over this east European no-man's-land, determining its fate for the next thousand years. An essential part of the process was the grinding down of the national Slav churches between the pressure applied on the one hand by the Germans and on the other by the Byzantines.

It was the tragedy of the Balkans that the consolidation of Germany under Otto I took place at a time when Byzantine military activity was also at its height. In 960–61 (when Otto I was making his plans to develop Magdeburg), Romanus II recaptured Crete from the Arabs, who had held it since 823; his successors occupied Cilicia and Cyprus, and by the time this Macedonian dynasty became extinct (1028) its aggressive policies had extended the Byzantine sphere of influence as far as Armenia. In Europe the Byzantine imperialists had three goals of conquest: the Balkans, the Hungarians and Moravians, and ultimately Russia. The superior might of Byzantium, which crushed the Bulgarian Balkan empire, in the tenth century brought even western Europe within the range of its imposing influence. A tenth-century English king will describe himself as *imperator* in his charters, and from about 930 Greek styles such as *basileus* and *monarcha* are adopted (presumably to indicate superiority over the *reguli* and *subreguli*, the various petty kings ruling in Britain). These Greek-sounding titles may also have owed something to the Anglo-Byzantine trading connections which existed at this period.

Rome was too weak to be of any assistance to Bulgar rulers in their quest for protection against Byzantine and German overlordship, just as Rome had failed the Bavarian dukes a couple of centuries earlier. They, too, had looked to Rome to uphold the independence of their church – and with it their political independence – against the aggressive Franks and the equally aggressive Frankish church. At the Lech, it was a Bavarian magnate (Berchtold) who brought the Magyars news of Otto's approach. Bavarian magnates had used Hungarians as their allies and feuding partners for over half a century. The battle at the Lech in fact grew out of the war inside Germany, to which it forms the climax.

One year before the battle the rebellious dukes and magnates of Bavaria and Lotharingia, acting through Arnulf of Bavaria (Berchtold's father), had reached an understanding with the Hungarians. Among the rebels was Otto's son Liudolf, who provided Bulcsu with guides to conduct him into Franconia, the region where his father's power was chiefly concentrated. In Bavaria the situation was more than usually confused, because of strife which had broken out between its duke, Otto's brother (already exhausted by his long years of conflict with the king) and his nephew Liudolf. Widukind notes that even the bishops were irresolute, inclining to both parties. In spring 955 Herold of Salzburg was blinded on Duke Henry's orders and placed under captivity at Säben in South Tyrol. There followed mutual recriminations between Henry and Liudolf over which of them had called in the Hungarians.

Otto's greatest victory was won before the battle was even fought: the shock produced by the Hungarian inroads into Bohemia and vast stretches of German territory during 954 was great enough to enable Otto to form a combined host of Franks, Swabians, Bavarians and Bohemians. Absentees from the battle included the Saxons, who were tied down by the Slavs of the Elbe, the Lotharingians, Henry of Bavaria (dying from a wound sustained in his war with Otto) and Liudolf. Without this unexpected victory in 'internal politics', the battle at the Lech could never have been fought. Its most lasting effect was on the same plane: the battle identified the Germanic element as the most significant in the Empire and in the imperial, Ottonian church.

Carolingian culture, from which German, Ottonian culture ultimately emerged as a creative distillation, had been the combined achievement of Spanish, Irish, Anglo-Saxon and Italian intellectuals and French humanists (Lupus of Ferrières surely merits the description). It was the work, that is, of a 'floating intelligentsia' living under court protection and permitted to indulge in the written and spoken expression of high-flying speculations (Scotus Eriugena), an intelligentsia in a state of awareness removed by centuries from that of the people. The position of these people was not dissimilar to that of the Erasmian humanists at the court of Charles V or of the French intellectuals at the courts of Frederick the Great and Catherine of Russia.

The crystallization of what was Ottonian, German, eliminated many floating and fluctuating elements. In place of the Carolingian culture, with its court academy of letters and cathedral schools, with its Irish and Anglo-Saxon intellectuals asking awkward questions (Virgil of Salzburg, for example, who wondered about the existence of men in the Antipodes), there now emerged a monastic and episcopal culture firmly planted upon the ground. From now on, and until the days of Charles V, German culture would take no further interest in a *plus ultra* in this world (though it would show plenty of interest in the world beyond).

It was in the decades following the battle at the Lech that the great German cathedrals, which were such characteristic witnesses to the German Middle Ages – until reduced to rubble at the end of the last war – first started to take shape. These churches were God's strongholds. They proclaimed that the faithful God assured his faithful servants power, peace and security. Their two poles, the eastwork and the westwork,[1] declared that there was a partnership on earth and in heaven between imperial bishop and king-emperor, as the servants of Christ, King and Emperor of

[1] See p.73.

31

Heaven. The Ottonian system, which remained the basis of the imperial church until 1803, left behind in these churches a record whose imprint was clear and strong.

The well-being of the Empire was indivisible. It declared itself through successes and victories, internal and external. Bishops and imperial abbots therefore had a duty to support the Empire with their own weapons – prayer, the sacrifice of the Mass and the divine liturgy – and with their 'aids' (economic contributions from their great resources and the no less important military support furnished by their vassals). This was the age when 'German-ness' was born, brought most significantly to birth in the battle at the Lech. In this battle Otto demonstrated his royal saving power by creating peace on German soil: he had forced mutually warring lords to act in unison and had banished forever an invading power whose outward aspect was terrifying. In so doing, Otto had provided an area of peace for an incipient Germany, a Germany which on the surface continued to be a very loose federation of tribes and peoples, even of *regna* (kingdoms). For the incipient Germans, still unsettled by the anxiety and unrest of the migration period (whose shock effects have still not completely died away – in 1945 they even received some reinforcement), he procured through his victory a significant measure of confidence and security.

This is the place to speak of the peculiarly German faith in power. Fundamentally, it is a faith rooted in mistrust of the 'wicked world', a world full of devilish enemies (the Devil himself is the *alt boese viant*, the old arch enemy), a world of discord and unrest, in which feud, war, perjury and murder are masters. Lamentations over the perfidy of this world assail our ears from the tenth century down to our own day. This feeling that the world is past hope has tended to drive the Germans to succumb to one of two temptations. The first is a despairing Manichaeism: the world is split to the core between the friends of God, who are few, and the minions of the Devil, who are many; the only way to break out of the 'situation' (*laga*, in Old German an ambush from which all exits lead to death) is through a prayer born of sheer desperation – with or without action. Hence people are 'pessimists' or 'optimists', those who pray or those who act. The other temptation is to succumb to what is at bottom a no less despairing Pelagianism: man is free, completely exposed to all winds and weathers; he can assert himself only through mastering the material world, including – terrifying thought – its human material.

As was clearly recognized by great German theorists of the Empire, for example Nicholas of Cusa and Leibniz, the Ottonian order represents an attempt, with important historical consequences, at connecting up these two poles. The righteous man serves God and the world, and wins fame and honour in heaven and on earth through faithful service, in a religious-political sense, in the Ecclesia, 'Christendom', whose lawful representatives on earth are the Lord Emperor and his bishops. For Widukind of Corvey, the highest bishop is not the silent pope but a German imperial bishop, the pontiff of Cologne or of Mainz.

The so-called Ottonian system of Empire, which transferred to the bishops a preponderant weight and major responsibility, thus making the imperial church the corner-stone of the Empire, was not, therefore, as has often been said, merely a 'solution of expediency' forced on Otto because the lay magnates had shown themselves 'faithless'. The system rested on deep psychological foundations. It was a German attempt at a *concordantia catholica*, an attempt at paving over the peculiarly German temptation (engendered by the troubled centuries of the folk migrations and their aftermath) to flee the world in despair and to despair of the world's sickness. '*Sieg Heil*': all raise their right hands and so confirm the choice of Otto as king. For us the salutation has a sinister ring from its associations with the terrifying man from Braunau-am-Inn. In its full meaning the salutation – *salus et victoria* – implies that all 'salvation', the salvation of body and soul, is committed to the *dux* (duke, *Herzog*), the leader (*Führer*) of the host, in the expectation that he will render it back as a benefit.

Otto made his clerical brother Brun a duke. Ruotger, Brun's pupil and biographer, in fact calls him 'archduke', to stress the exceptionally full powers he wielded. Brun was brought up in Utrecht by Israel, its Irish bishop, from whom he received a sound education (the learning of Irish clerics was still far superior to that of the continentals). In 940 Brun became his brother's chancellor and afterwards archchaplain; in 953 he was made archbishop of Cologne and in the same year – at the age of twenty-eight – duke and vice-regent in Lotharingia. He proceeded to fill the most important westerly sees with his own trusted men, men he knew would serve the interests of his brother and the Empire.

Brun had to wait until 1870 for his canonization: threatened with the loss of the Papal State, the hard-pressed pope of the day turned for help to Bismarck, in an appeal different yet not wholly dissimilar from that of his predecessors to the German rulers a thousand years earlier. Canonizations are very frequently, if not always, politically inspired. Kings and princes like to have as many of their relatives as possible accorded the dignity of their own altar. Joan of Arc was canonized after the First World War, an olive branch offered by the Holy See to the 'atheistical Republic' and an honourable recognition of France's enormous human losses in the war; in Rome the victory was construed as victory over 'Protestantism'. The canonization of Charles the Great, promoted by Frederick Barbarossa and his bishops and promulgated by an anti-pope, was recognized only in dioceses which had a history going back to Carolingian times. Udalrich of Augsburg, Otto's great friend and political supporter, the episcopal hero of the battle at the Lech, is the first saint known to have been formally canonized by Rome, by the Roman Catholic, Latin, Church. Previously 'saints' were by and large those whom the people venerated as such. Pope Alexander III, in the twelfth century, still found it necessary to warn the Swedes not to make saints of high-placed individuals who died in their cups.

Udalrich of Augsburg stood out as a man of friendship, as the friend and fellow-clansman of his king and emperor, the friend of the saints in heaven and of his clerical and secular family on earth. But this Udalrich, the Udalrich we read of rejoicing in God and the world in the *Life* written by Gebhard, his friend and colleague, was not acceptable to Rome as a saint. For the purpose of canonization it was necessary to submit to Rome a biography larded with the expected hagiographical clichés.

Victory in battle had made Otto sure of God and the world. He could now go on to make sure of the regions bordering the 'German' space so recently secured, regions from which 'insecurity' might still break in. These included the Slavonic north-east and the Italian south, the operational field of the great Byzantine foe, whose unseen presence had stood behind Bulcsu, Patricius of the Empire of the Rhomaioi, at the Lech. Moreover, Byzantium might still hope by missionary endeavours to increase her ecclesiastical and political influence in other regions: in Hungary,[1] Bohemia, Moravia and Poland.

The Russian princess Olga, widow of Rurik's son Igor, was converted to Christianity in Constantinople in 953. Two years later, in the same year as the battle at the Lech, Otto won a victory at the Recknitz in Mecklenburg which subdued all the Slavs as far as the Oder. Olga established contact with Otto and in 961, shortly before his imperial coronation, the German king dispatched Adalbert, a monk of St Maximin's, Trier, to Kiev as a missionary bishop. But Adalbert failed and the Byzantines awoke to what was happening. Evangelized from Byzantium, Russia was cast into the intellectual and spiritual mould which was to last for centuries – even into our own day. Had Rome and the imperial church succeeded in their missionary effort to Russia during the Ottonian century, the structure of Europe would be very different.

In the event Adalbert became the first pontiff of the archiepiscopal see of Magdeburg, founded ten days after Otto's imperial coronation [plate 16]. Otto intended that Magdeburg, as the 'capital of the German east', should have no limit set to its missionary territory to the east, as is clear from the harsh and laconic language of the foundation charter: its mandate was to subdue to the yoke of Christ the peoples beyond the Elbe and the Saale. The unlimited scope of this commitment, which brought immediate protests from the bishops of Mainz and Halberstadt, from Saxon magnates, and ultimately from the pope (in 968 John XIII fixed Magdeburg's boundary at the Oder), lays bare the *hohe Mut* (high daring) of the Ottonian claim. There can be no doubt that Otto I regarded the assimilation of the Slavs on the Oder, the Elbe and the Saale as his chief mission. The battle at the Lech cleared the air, militarily speaking, in the south-east and made it possible to concentrate on the north and east. It remained for Rome to provide him with the appropriate personal quali-fications: investiture with the imperial office which made him *ipso facto* lord protector of Christendom, and papal support in sustaining the heavy labour of performing his duties in that office, which in Otto's case meant the pursuit of warfare and missionary endeavour.

The missionary bishopric of Merseburg was founded in fulfilment of a vow Otto

---

[1] The Eastern Church had monasteries near Vienna until the twelfth century, when the Cistercians, 'the Jesuits of the twelfth century', captured Pannonia for the west and the Latin Church by establishing their own houses in the region.

II Christ crowns Henry II emperor (all papal pretensions are thereby dismissed – the imperial office derives directly from God-Christ). He is supported by saints of the Holy Roman Empire: on his right hand, which holds the Holy Lance, by St Udalrich; on his left, which holds the sword, by St Emmeran.

made to St Laurence on the eve of the battle at the Lech. Slavs had played a prominent part in some of the most important experiences of his formative years. As a young man he had fought in the Slav wars of 928–9, he spoke a Slavonic tongue, a high-born Slav was the mother of his son William. From all this it seems quite likely that Otto felt a genuine personal involvement in the terrestrial and celestial welfare of the Slavs on the borders of his empire. This would also be in keeping with Saxon tradition: Saxon magnates, including some of Otto's contemporaries, formed alliances with pagan Slav princes (as did Henry II, the only emperor to be canonized). Other Saxon magnates flatly refused to fight Slavs who were related to them by kinship or marriage. When he was six years old, Otto III was taken on a campaign against the Slavs to fire the determination of Germans reluctant to fight.

Having decided on the subjection of the Elbe Slavs as far as the Oder, Otto appointed Hermann and Gero margraves of the border marches and in 948 founded the missionary bishoprics of Oldenburg, Havelburg and Brandenburg, subordinating them to the see of Mainz. Conversion was by the sword. The 'German' God demonstrated his power to save through victory in battle. Between 938 and 950 the war against the Slavs was conducted with the utmost brutality. Widukind of Corvey marvels at the resilience of the Slavs, who suffered terrible losses, defeats often being followed by multiple hangings. 'But even so, they choose war rather than peace and count all misery cheap in comparison with precious liberty; for this is a dour race, capable of bearing pain, accustomed to the barest sustenance, and what our own people take to be the heaviest of burdens, to the Slavs is a form of pleasure.' German soldiers who fought in Russia during the Second World War described the Russian people's capacity for suffering in almost identical terms.

In the Middle Ages relations between the German peoples (in particular the Saxons) and the Slavs were complex, many-layered: if there was hatred and suspicion, there was also respect and even profound understanding. The clash between the different peoples in the east was harsher and more brutal than that between Germans and French in the west. What in the west amounted to rivalry and disputes over orders of precedence, in the east took the form of bitter hostility. After 925 the western boundaries of the German peoples and of the Empire remained unchanged until the later Middle Ages, and even then underwent no fundamental alteration; as regards the French, German culture was on the defensive. It was otherwise in the east. Here, following the defensive stance of the ninth century, partially maintained into the tenth, German conquest and settlement advanced with a powerful thrust. The advance was at the expense of a people already characterized by St Boniface in the eighth century as born slaves; he called the Slavs a 'stinking and despicable race'. Writing a century later, Abbot Eigil of Fulda relates how another eighth-century abbot, Sturmi, met Slavs bathing in the Fulda and recoiled in disgust at the stench of their bodies. Germans and Slavs could not bear one another's 'smell'; American negroes and southerners have the same difficulty. In 981 a baptized Slav chieftain wanted his son, who had been with the German host in Italy, to marry the niece of the

Saxon duke Bernhard II. Margrave Dietrich disapproved: 'one does not give one's kinswoman to a dog'.

Medieval German writers (Arnold of Lübeck, Helmold of Bosau, author of the *Slav Chronicle*) describe the Slavs as 'corrupt by nature, born criminals', singling out the Poles especially as brutal robbers and murderers. 'Treachery', *incerta fides*, is an inborn characteristic of all Slavs: one can place no faith or trust in them.

That the mistrust between Germans and Slavs was mutual is illustrated by an anecdote from the *Miracles of St Henry the Emperor* compiled by a member of the Hildesheim cathedral school. An aged Wend was advised to touch the relics of Henry II as a cure for blindness but resignedly refused on the grounds that no Wend could expect help from a German.

The situation in the north-east in the spring of 955, the year of the Lechfeld, duplicated that in the south. Two Saxon magnates, Wichmann II and Ekbert the One-Eyed, allied themselves with Nako and Stoinef, Abodrite Slav chieftains, and encouraged them to make raids on Saxony. At the Recknitz on 16 October 955 Otto won a second major victory, which directly paved the way for the tragedy of Germany's eastern policy. German historians working on this period in the years preceding the Second World War came to the conclusion that Germany's political, military, economic and human resources were in no way commensurate with the demands made by Otto's aggressive eastern policy. Moreover, as Theodor Mayer pointed out as early as 1931, the Saxon nobility of the day were resistant to any idea of German colonization east of the Elbe: they could not expect to exact from German christian peasants the heavy dues and services they could from pagan Slavs.

The techniques of land improvement needed for effective settlement (draining marshes, for example) were only mastered centuries later. The siege methods of the German armies were inadequate to deal with the fortified constructions they found in the east. Some three centuries would pass before it was possible for German peasants to go east to claim the soil so long and so vainly contested by the German sword. In 1938 – when Hitler's storm clouds were already threatening the sky above Vienna and Prague – Konrad Schünemann drew up a balance sheet of Germany's eastern campaigns: out of the one hundred and seventy-five undertaken between 789 and Frederick I's first Polish campaign, a third could just about be said to have achieved their immediate military objective, a quarter were semi-successful and the rest were a failure. Twenty expeditions ended in total disaster for a German army.

It was not only military but also intellectual and spiritual resources that were lacking. Otto's empire had no 'surplus' of clerics and no reforming orders who might have dedicated themselves to the mission of evangelizing the east. Otto already had great difficulty in finding a priest and a bishop in response to the appeal made by Olga in 959. His first choice, Libutius, a monk of St Alban's, Mainz, died in 961. Adalbert, who was eventually sent, was consecrated bishop of the Russians against his will and returned after six months having accomplished nothing.

Nevertheless, Otto's designs were grandiose. The newly founded archbishopric of

Magdeburg was to rank second to Constantinople; in the words of a recent German historian (R. Holtzmann), it was to be a 'German Rome'. The new metropolis was assigned its suffragan sees at the synod of Ravenna in October 968: Havelberg, Brandenburg, the new bishoprics of Merseburg, Zeitz and Meissen and the newly created Polish see of Posen (Poznan). Otto's thoughts were even turning toward Prague. Magdeburg was given primacy over all the churches on the right bank of the Rhine; following the Roman pattern, it was to receive an endowment of twelve cardinal priests, twelve cardinal deacons and twenty-four cardinal subdeacons.

Polish, Bohemian and Hungarian princes were quick to perceive the danger of having a German pope, or at least a German patriarch, as ecclesiastical patron of the German eastern mission. But the first protest came from within Otto's immediate family circle. Otto's plans for Magdeburg, which left the creation of new sees entirely at his own discretion, was first laid before the Pope in 955, probably immediately after the victory at the Lech. William of Mainz, a German prelate of the first rank and the son of King Otto and his Slav concubine, at once wrote Pope Agapetus II a letter in which he exposes the ideological base of his father's intended subjugation and christianization of the Slavs: the king's sole concern, he alleges, is not conversion but power, political subjugation. Eventually, as has been mentioned, Pope John XIII fixed the eastern boundary of Magdeburg at the Oder (968), thereby assuming, as the Protestant historian Hashagen has pointed out, a papal responsibility for the protection of hitherto independent nations who now felt themselves menaced by the superior might of the Empire.

We have seen that Otto I had to contend for his imperial office in a world in which Byzantium was riding high, and that he had proved himself and his saving powers in two great victories; he was now seeking to legitimize his eastern policy through coronation as emperor. The pope who crowned him on 2 February 962 – the date generally taken as marking the foundation of the 'Holy Roman Empire' – represented an enfeebled papacy which might be expected to support Otto's imperial policy for Italy as well. Through Otto and the Ottonian dynasty 'orphaned' Europe might once again acquire trustworthy fathers strong in saving power, that is to say, king-emperors, popes, imperial bishops and abbots worthy of their office.

The degeneracy into which the papacy had fallen is blatantly obvious. The murder of John VIII in 882 had set off a kind of chain reaction. The darkest period is ushered in by the macabre proceedings of Pope Stephen VI, who in 896–7 had the corpse of his predecessor, Pope Formosus, disinterred, robed in the papal vestments and placed on the throne to be judged. (Hochhuth's criticism of Pius XII in his play *The Representative* seems quite innocuous by comparison.) Stephen ordered the blessing fingers to be hacked from the dead pope's right hand and the corpse thrown into the river. A few months later Stephen himself was strangled; the archaic hatreds stored up in Rome had made it a den of assassins. Soon, in the words of Cardinal Baronius, the great historian of the Counter-Reformation, it had also become a 'pornocracy'.

The pope who invited King Otto and his wife Adelheid to Italy and who crowned

Otto emperor on 2 February 962 was an illiterate tyrant who had turned the Lateran into a brothel. In the following year he was deposed at a synod presided over by the emperor, but after Otto's departure reinstated himself, took a terrible revenge on his enemies and died on 14 May 964, a week after being surprised in adultery by the deceived husband and so severely beaten that he never regained consciousness. John XIII, the pope who crowned Otto II emperor at Christmas 967 (the twelve-year-old boy was crowned during his father's lifetime), kept his place only because he was backed by the emperor. His successor, Benedict VI, was strangled by adherents of the anti-imperial party. The imperial will to reform showed itself with the eleva-tion to the papacy of Peter of Pavia (Otto II's arch-chancellor in Italy) as John XIV; after Otto's death he fell into the hands of an exiled anti-pope (Boniface) who threw him into prison and starved him to death.

A year later this anti-pope was himself murdered and his mutilated corpse dragged through the streets. His successor was John XV, detested for his avarice and nepotism; he was the pope who invited Otto III to be crowned emperor and it was he who pronounced the first papal canonization, that of Udalrich of Augsburg in 993. The emperor's efforts to rid Rome of abuses led next to the appointment of the first German pope, who was immediately followed by the first French pope. The German was Otto I's grandson Brun, who reigned as Gregory V. When he died aged thirty in February 999 he had reigned for just under three years. For the next three years the pope was Otto III's friend and tutor, the highly cultured Gerbert of Aurillac, a native of Aquitaine, who reigned as Sylvester II. The entry into the new millennium thus coincided with the first laborious stages of the ascent of the papacy to the position of Europe's leading religious and political power.

The most stinging of all medieval attacks on the corrupt papacy was perhaps that delivered by Bishop Arnulf of Orleans at a great French synod held in June 991 at Verzy (south-east of Rheims). The papacy, he said, was once an ornament of the church; now it had collapsed into ignorance, crime and ignominy. Why should any bishop worthy of the name bow before it? Arnulf of Orleans was on friendly terms with Gerbert of Aurillac, whose influence can be detected behind this speech. The synod proceeded to the deposition of another Arnulf, archbishop of Rheims. The next incumbent of this much-coveted see was Gerbert of Aurillac.

In this synod and the circles it influenced a 'Gallic' note is already audible: the French clergy and their kings display a robust self-confidence in their dealings with Rome and the papacy. Only French clerics felt, as they feel to this day, that they were intellectually and spiritually superior to the 'uncultured' prelates of Rome. Rome was afraid of these Frenchmen, as it would later fear the Spanish; and Rome feared the Emperor. Out of the twenty-five popes who reigned during the Ottonian era, the emperors appointed twelve and deposed five.

Reform in the church between the tenth and twelfth centuries stemmed from the activities of monastic reforming movements originating in the region occupied by the old Lotharingia, that is, in that middle Europe which looked intellectually towards

France but which had such close ties with the Empire. Gorze, Cluny, Cîteaux and Prémontré (the mother houses of the Cistercians and the Premonstratensians) generated movements which were still vigorous in this region during the twelfth century, and from them a fresh wind blew towards Rome. Without this encouragement, the papacy as it became under Gregory VII and Urban II is inconceivable. The Ottonian emperors, above all Otto III, most European of emperors, looked to these Lotharingian reforming movements for help in carrying out their own intended reform of the church.

German historians seized the opportunity offered by 1962, the thousandth anniversary of the Holy Roman Empire (designated 'Roman' under Otto II, 'Holy' under Frederick I in the twelfth century, 'of the German Nation' in the early fifteenth century), to ventilate the problems attaching to its foundation. Did it imply a claim to world dominion? Or was '*dominium mundi*' merely a 'literary flourish' (Tellenbach)?

From the time of Otto I the German kings were also rulers of the kingdom of Italy; in 1033, under Conrad II, they acquired a third kingdom, that of Burgundy. Rule over three realms (Germany, the major part of Italy and Burgundy) was, it seemed, enough to make their ruler into an emperor; in its turn, the imperial dignity seems to have become the clasp and crown which held this trinity together. Starting in the time of Conrad II, the imperial chancery by slow degrees came to use the term '*Imperium Romanum*' as the normal description of this complex. The same idea, that rule over several 'kingdoms' makes an 'emperor' is also found during the tenth century in England and in Spain: an imperial monarchy denotes supremacy over other kings and a kingship augmented by victories over heathens.

Outside the Empire men of the tenth and eleventh centuries used the term '*Imperium Romanum*' in a threefold sense: first, it could describe a state with local territorial limits (Rome, the Papal State, on occasion Italy); second, it could describe the trio of Germany, Italy and Burgundy; third, it could have a universal meaning, though this was largely devoid of any content of lordship (*Imperium Romanum* = *Imperium Christianum*, that is to say European Christendom).

The imperial coronation of Otto I in 962 laid on him one particularly significant obligation, the defence of the Roman Church (*defensio ecclesiae Romanae*); although quite what was meant by the 'Roman Church' was not entirely clear. Principally it meant that the Emperor had a duty to protect the Pope in Rome and in his Papal State. It was this kind of protection the popes of the nineteenth and early twentieth century (down to the First World War) had in mind when they looked to the emperor in Vienna or to other protectors (Bismarck, Napoleon III, even the Tsar on occasion) for the defence of their Papal State.

From Otto I onwards the imperial office appears permanently bound up with papal coronation and the German kingship. The validity of both ties would later be vehemently contested. Nor did contemporaries of Otto the Great and his successors allow their possession of the imperial office to go completely unchallenged. Objections were voiced not only by the holder of the senior imperial office in Byzantium but also in Lotharingia, France, England and Italy. It was being said in Utrecht soon after Otto's imperial coronation that Bishop Radbod, who died in 917, had prophesied the coming humiliation of the Franks (that is the French) and the elevation of Germania through the imperial office, but had declared that neither state of affairs would last for long. At some time before 954 a monk named Adso (who afterwards became abbot of a West Frankish monastery), writing in Toul – and thus inside Otto's empire – dedicated a treatise *De ortu et tempore Antichristi* to Gerberga, queen of the West Franks. Adso maintains it is the duty of the West Frankish kings, as the true kings of the Franks, to shore up the already crumbling *Imperium Romanum* and so postpone the coming of antichrist; the last emperor of all would finally lay down his crown and sceptre on the Mount of Olives. The German counterpart of this apocalyptical French emperor does not appear until the twelfth century, when he is introduced by a Bavarian monk into the Tegernsee play of Antichrist.

West Frankish chroniclers allude only briefly to Otto's imperial coronation (Flodoard of Rheims) or ignore it altogether (Richer). Yet Richer was Gerbert's pupil. Gerbert himself would plead passionately at the Ottonian court for the universal and christian idea of empire; yet while still living in France he took an eschatological view of the Roman Empire, whose ruined state was then so evident, and had written on behalf of the Capetian king to the Byzantine emperor proposing a political alliance with Byzantium and recognizing Byzantine pretensions to the Roman Empire. The pattern of an anti-imperial alliance in which Paris and Byzantium (or Paris and the Sultan) were partners was thus early established.

Abbo of Fleury's thoughts on the imperial question are helpful to the claims of his French kings. Every king, he says, sets up the *Imperium Romanum* within his own borders; all christian kings and emperors have the same task, to defend the church and the faith and to carry out ecclesiastical reform. Helgald of Fleury (writing after 1042) extols Robert, the second Capetian king (996–1031) as the 'great Emperor of the Franks': of all the kings the earth has seen, not one since David has been his equal. The Capetians were installed in France in the mainstream of the Carolingian imperial tradition. For Ralph Glaber, a Cluniac monk, the French king and the Emperor stood on an equal footing; *terror Caesarum*, the 'Caesars' rule of terror', was a thing of the past, vanquished by Christ. The peoples who had once lived in subjection to Rome were starting to take their revenge.

English chroniclers make no mention of the imperial office held by Charles the Great in the ninth century and allude to later emperors only in the briefest terms; in the twelfth century they begin to be highly critical of the Germans as emperors, and indeed as Germans. King Knut, who was present at the imperial coronation of Conrad II in Rome in 1027, allowed himself to be called *Imperator*.

In the tenth and eleventh centuries educated clergy and monks in Italy were in close contact with West Frankish reformers, monks and men of letters. These connections contributed to the formation of a body of French-Italian feeling critical of the German emperors. At this point it is important to make one thing plain: the outsiders we find describing the Empire or the imperial office as 'German', by way of derogation, are the Empire's enemies. The educated Italian clergy by and large accepted the imperial office and the ideology of world dominion, but were at the same time deeply resentful of alien, 'German', rule. Regrets over the decline of Italy and of the Romans, coupled with complaints concerning German overlordship, were being voiced in the eleventh century at Monte Cassino. The discontent many Italians felt with the Ottonian and Salian emperors was assuaged by contemplation of prophetic sayings, for example the utterance of the 'Tiburtine sibyl' which predicted that the Emperor of the Apocalypse would come in the eleventh century, from Byzantium. The chronicler of Salerno regards Byzantium as the true seat of the Roman Empire. Romans and popes questioned the validity of the Germans' tenure of the imperial office. Otto I's intervention in Rome is criticized as totally unjustified in view of Constantine's transference of lordship over Rome to St Peter and the Pope. This version of the translation theory had been current since the ninth century and was based on the Donation of Constantine. Otto III rejected the Donation as an out-and-out forgery (which indeed it was), because he wanted Rome to be his capital city. 'There is no clearer indication of the position of the imperial office at this date than the fact that Eternal Rome could not become the Emperor's residence' (Heinz Löwe). In Rome Otto the Great and his successors were confronted with two great opponents playing the same game, Byzantium and the Papacy.

All the threads of European history, the threads of English, French, Burgundian and above all Italian history, come together at the Ottonian court. As ruler over the nations, captain of conquering armies, propagator of the faith, director-in-chief of western policy, Otto impressed himself on the consciousness of the great men of the Empire, on the army and on the people, as in truth a new Charles.

The words are those of an Italian of our own time, Giorgio Palco. Otto I occupied northern Italy for the first time in 951, having responded to appeals for help from Adelheid of Burgundy, backed up by Pope John XII, against Berengar of Ivrea, an aspirant to the Lombard crown. In 961 Otto assumed ruling powers in Italy, and in 962 was crowned emperor at Rome. When John XII then allied himself with the Hungarians and with Adalbert, Berengar's son, he was deposed by an imperial council held at Rome with Otto presiding. This pope's crimes were more than a merely parochial concern.

The assumption of the imperial title, which involved claims in Italy, led inevitably to a clash with Byzantium. The whole of southern Italy, the old Magna Graecia, was intellectually a Greek province and long continued to be so. As a 'rebellious', anti-Roman city, Naples retained 'liberal', 'Greek' characteristics almost into our own day (for example, Benedetto Croce and his circle). Byzantium still had a substantial following among the cultivated Italian clergy and the Roman aristocracy, who resented the 'uncultured German barbarians'. After a war of fluctuating fortunes Otto the Great managed to assert his authority in the south. The marriage of Otto II with

Theophano, the talented, beautiful and strong-willed niece of the Emperor John Tzimisces, brought a partial reconciliation with Byzantium. On 14 April 972 Pope John XIII officiated in St Peter's at their marriage and at Theophano's coronation as empress [plate 20]. One year later, on 7 April 973, Otto the Great died in Thuringia and was buried in his beloved Magdeburg, close to his English wife.

Otto the Great left behind him a very loose-knit empire, a structure based on the good faith of its members. It leaned heavily on the imperial bishops and abbots and on a band of eminent women. Two of Otto I's closest female relatives, Mathilde his mother and Adelheid his second wife, became saints of the Roman Church; in their cloisters Ottonian abbesses fostered a cultural world which produced an outstanding figure in the poetess Hrotsvith of Gandersheim; notable empresses such as Theophano, Kunigunde and Gisela came to play a leading role in the fortunes of their dynasties. Unsupported by law books or officials, for a long time with only a very modest chancery at its disposal, the Empire of Otto the Great maintained friendly relations with France, Burgundy and Denmark, with the new duchy of Poland and before long even with the Hungarians. It was dependent on the loyalty of the men who wielded the real power, the dukes in the duchies and the bishops in the bishoprics.

The youthful Otto II (973–83) [plate 17] suffered heavy defeats at the two points where this Empire was most vulnerable. A revolt of the oppressed Elbe Slavs wiped out all that had been achieved through missions and colonization, and in 982 a combined Arab and Byzantine force defeated him off Capo Colonne in the gulf of Taranto. The casualties included Henry, Bishop of Augsburg, and some of the great lay magnates of the Empire. The fleeing emperor was rescued by Kalonymus ben Meschullam, a Jew of Lucca, who gave him a horse on which he swam out to a Greek vessel which refused to take him on board. The emperor had to return to the shore, where the Jew was still standing, 'anxious over the fate of his beloved lord'. Still on the Jew's horse, the emperor managed to outdistance the pursuing Saracens and reached a second ship, whose complement included a Slav warrior from his own following, Henry Zolunta, who helped him to safety. Otto II, the Roman emperor, owed his preservation from his Saracen and Byzantine enemies to the good offices of a Jew and a Slav. He later invited Kalonymus to Mainz, where he won for himself a name as a learned rabbi.

In the Holy Roman Empire Jews were protected by letters of privilege and the laws of the Empire, by emperors, imperial bishops and individual princes; during the nineteenth and early twentieth centuries Jews fled from the pogroms of Russian Poland and Tsarist Russia to the protective regime of the Emperor in Vienna. The Babenbergs, like the Habsburgs after them, early attracted notoriety and suspicion on account of their 'friendship towards the Jews'. The Rhenish towns (for example, Trier, where Karl Marx grew up) had probably been centres of Jewish settlement from late Roman times; here in particular lived a German Jewry whose outlook was conservative in the extreme and remained so to the bitter end. Conservative in their theology, these Jews were also conservative in their faith in the Empire, a faith which they transferred in due course from the old Holy Roman Empire to Bismarck's Germany and to the Emperor in Vienna; in fact they evolved Empire-loyalties of their own, which in the Kaiser's Germany made victims in their own fashion of men like Ballin and Rathenau. Jews 'atoned' in Hitler's extermination camps for their unshakeable trust in the *Reich* (which was *Reich* [empire] no longer) and in German justness. In former centuries they had died in front of those imperial cathedrals which continued until 1944–5 to stand on their Ottonian foundations, having withstood the conflagrations of a millennium. When 'holy Cologne' and its triconch churches went up in flames, when ancient Hildesheim, the creation of two Ottonian bishops, Bernward and Godehard, was collapsing under a hail of bombs in February and March 1945, German Jewry, whose financial power for centuries was a mainstay of emperors, kings and German princes (Jews were the 'managers' of their courts), whose contribution in the nineteenth and early twentieth century enriched German science, culture and art, itself already was annihilated, reduced to ashes.

Bishop Godehard of Hildesheim bequeathed his name to the St Gotthard pass. Bernward of Hildesheim became tutor and counsellor to Otto III. Otto II died at Rome on 7 December 983 at the age of twenty-eight, in the presence of Theophano and Pope John, who administered the last sacraments. He was buried in 'Paradise', the vestibule of St Peter's; his tomb was an antique Roman sarcophagus, closed with a porphyry lid. Porphyry was the stone sacred to emperors, to the Roman Emperor: Frederick II lies encased in porphyry at Salerno. In due course the triumphant popes would also take to porphyry. In 1618 – another critical moment for the Empire, when it was just plunging into the Thirty Years' War – the rebuilding of St Peter's led to the removal of Otto II to a new tomb in the vaults of the Vatican. The only German emperor to die in Rome, he rests there alongside a number of popes, among them his kinsman, the German Gregory V.

In the Middle Ages Otto III was called the 'wonder of the world'. He was anointed and crowned king by Archbishops John of Ravenna and Willigis of Mainz at Aachen on Christmas day 983 when he was only three years old, before it was known for certain that his imperial father was dead. He died at Paterno on Mount Soracte at the age of twenty-one (on 24 January 1002) and was buried in the cathedral at Aachen; in his life he had paid Charles the Great the homage due to an illustrious ancestor and exemplar.

The child was king, since regency was unknown to German law. In practice government was carried on by two women, who held their own against strong male opposition. The first was Otto's mother Theophano, styled in contemporary documents 'Theophano, Empress by the Grace of God' (*imperatrix augusta*) or even 'Theophanius, Emperor by the Grace of God'. When she died in 991 conduct of affairs passed to Otto's grandmother, Adelheid, who as 'mother of the kingdoms' – an admiring contemporary description – remained in control until her death in 999. Adelheid and Theophano between them succeeded in holding the Empire together at its centre.

Otto III, in the words of a contemporary 'the handsomest offspring of the handsome emperor', was taught first by John Philagathos, a Greek from southern Italy, and afterwards by Bernward, the Saxon he so rewardingly made bishop of Hildesheim. There is a much-quoted letter from the youthful Otto to Gerbert in which he implores him not to be discouraged by his Saxon greenness but to kindle in him the Greek subtlety buried like a spark beneath the ashes. Otto III did not forget the debt he owed to his 'Greek', 'Roman', Saxon and Frankish predecessors. This young man, who might through his marriage have united the two imperial offices of East and West Rome, was certainly not the unstable dreamer, the irresponsible intellectual, the visionary with no sense of *Realpolitik*, so often depicted by the German nationalist school of historians.

The Saxon *rusticitas* which Otto wished to exchange for Greek *subtilitas* rooted him in the most archaic tradition. The contemporary anecdote which relates how he opened up Charles the Great's tomb at Aachen, took parings from his holy forebear's fingernails, drew one of his teeth (a 'lucky tooth') and dressed in some of his clothing, is not incredible; these were objects which could confer on him their saving powers. This precociously adult young man (early maturity was common in the Middle Ages, when expectation of life was short and men and women plunged into it with heightened sensibilities and vigour) wanted to absorb into himself all that was sound in the Roman and Neo-Roman (Byzantine) tradition, as also in Christian tradition going right back to the time of the Apostles, whose representative he took himself to be. He envisaged the Europe of the future as a 'league of nations' in which the new kings of the peoples then growing to adulthood as part of the western family, the Poles and the Hungarians, were linked to the Emperor and the Empire by ties of friendship, not as subjects but as partners. In promoting his policies, Otto chose to work through 'old' imperial bishops, whose indigenous roots predisposed them to a folk form of Christianity; but he did not ignore the wakening intelligentsia of southwestern Europe, who drew their intellectual sustenance from an Arabic-Greek-Mediterranean culture (Gerbert of Aurillac). Otto also relied on men thrown up by the monastic reform movements whose leavening influence was now permeating the whole of Europe, reaching out from Lotharingia into France, Spain, northern and southern Italy and Slavonic eastern Europe. Young though he was, Otto was very realistic in his appreciation of movements which had a great future in Europe.

Otto III realized that a Europe conceived as a religious-political union of peoples and as a zone wide open to movements of intellectual and spiritual reform needed a staunch and trustworthy head. This could be none other than the Roman pontiff. As we have seen, however, Arnulf of Orleans, Gerbert's friend, had only recently declared that Rome lacked any vestige of culture, spirituality and integrity. The Ottonian conception of the imperial office entailed raising the papacy from its provincial narrowness and corruption to a position of European esteem.

In 996 Otto celebrated Easter (12 April) at Pavia, where the Italian lords once again confirmed his election as king. While he was there envoys came from the Romans requesting him to designate a new pope in place of John xv, who had died. 'This marked a return to the order of Charles the Great and Otto the Great: the king nominated the new pope, election and consecration followed' (Robert Holtzmann). Otto's nominee was his chaplain Brun, a grandson of Otto I, who reigned as Gregory v; when he died, Otto nominated Gerbert, the first French pope, who reigned as Sylvester II. Both popes took programmatic names with a sacral-political significance. As Gregory, Brun should reincarnate Gregory I, that greatest of popes who had presided in Rome at a turning point in history; as the second Sylvester, Gerbert should with Otto III, his new Constantine, restore the sacred unity of Empire by reconciling Rome (both Romes), Church and Christendom. Otto regarded Justinian as his first predecessor as emperor of the west; on the seals he used as emperor Otto is represented as a Greek basileus with full beard [Plate 23]. At high festivals Otto appeared as 'monocrator', vested in a rose-coloured dalmatic embroidered with golden eagles; his shoes were studded with eagles, dragons and lions, the imperial and royal beasts of antiquity. His official robe – a cosmic world mantle – was sewn with 365 little bells, one for each day of the annual cycle of the heavens. In illuminations to his ornate manuscripts we see the emperor receiving homage from the four powers of his empire – Rome, Germania, Gallia and Sclavinia; he sits enthroned on the curule chair, surrounded by ecclesiastical and lay magnates [plate 21].

Otto had a markedly developed feeling for propaganda: everything he did, said, ordered, should have some programmatic significance. The intentions and claims of the Empire were to be proclaimed not only in his charters, which one might expect, but also through material objects and emblems. Byzantine diplomacy already owed much to the careful attention the Greek emperors and their lay and ecclesiastical officials paid to such procedures: sacral-political gifts, marks of honour, crowns, the hands of purple-born princesses and remoter female connections, all were bestowed according to the rank considered suitable for the recipient, who might be a 'friend', a patricius, or a threatening barbarian prince it was desirable to woo. The example was not lost on Rome, where the popes adopted power emblems, vestments, thrones, and the style of imperial charters for their own solemn transactions.

Otto III clearly recognized that a papacy prepared to be seen, lauded and acknow-ledged as ruler of the world was a danger to himself. In January 1001 he changed his sacral title 'Servant of Jesus Christ', assumed only a year before, into that of 'Servant of the Apostles'. In this capacity the Emperor himself became the representative of St Peter, who was regarded as the ruler of the *Patrimonium Petri*, the Papal State. The Pope's claim to rule the Papal State (and much more besides) rested on the forged Donation of Constantine and on grants and confirmations of grants made by a series of rulers, starting with Pepin and ending with Otto I in 962. Otto III was asked by his German pope, Gregory v, to restore to the papacy the eight counties of the Pentapolis. This request, made in 996, was refused; nor was there any renewal of Otto's grant, known as the Ottonianum. Otto III eventually restored the eight coun-ties to 'his' second pope, his mentor Sylvester. The action was performed 'out of love for the Lord Sylvester', but the grant is addressed to St Peter and the charter convey-ing it is an imperial manifesto. The power struggle between pope and emperor which men of succeeding centuries would watch with bated breath, the 'struggle for Rome', for the leadership of Christendom, had already begun. Otto III defines his position: 'we affirm that Rome is the capital of the world, we testify that the Roman Church is the mother of all churches.'

In his imperial city of Rome the emperor had granted to St Peter, of his own free will, counties belonging to the Empire. The emperor retained his superior pro-prietary right over these counties, as he did over the territories of the German churches. The young emperor alludes explicitly to the past incompetence of popes in administering their property, much of it fraudulently acquired by means of forged deeds. Unflattering imperial comment on the handling of affairs in papal Rome runs like a red thread through all the centuries down to the nineteenth, when we find even the conservative powers of the 'Holy Alliance' criticizing Pope Gregory XVI in 1832 for the corruption of his Papal State. Otto III, the 'servant of the Apostles', was the first to expose the Donation of Constantine before the eyes of Christendom as a forgery (even so, popes of succeeding centuries continued to rely on the Donation in their struggles with the Emperor, as long as it suited their case). Otto III saw Rome as the *urbs regia*, the city of the emperors, and not as the city of the popes [plate 22]. The popes, he declared, had first squandered the property of the Roman Church and then tried to replenish it by robbing the Emperor. The Donation of Constantine was a botched-up fraud; the grant made by Charles the Bald, to which the papal side attached equal importance, had been invalid from the outset, since it gave to the Roman Church lands Charles did not himself possess.

Otto III had no faith in curial Rome, and had good reason to distrust the Romans. During his last stay in Rome he was besieged by rebels on the Aventine but made a successful break-out to reach Castel Sant'Angelo, Bishop Bernward leading the way with the Holy Lance. Otto appointed a Saxon magnate, Ziazo, his deputy in Rome with the title *patricius Romanorum*. It was at such times of dire emergency that the imperial office became concrete, with the emperor in arms, around him the small band of men faithful through thick and thin, a few bishops and troops, and a handful of aristocratic 'deputies', who held onto the fortresses and towns in Italy so long as was feasible.

We do not know how the young emperor, had he been allotted a longer span, would have organized the empire at its German core. Probably he would have created a type of dual monarchy not unlike – despite dissimilar circumstances – the dualism of the Danube monarchy (in which the kingdom of Hungary had its centre in Budapest and the 'Imperial Council of the United Kingdom and Provinces' repre-sented the remaining peoples in Vienna). His two capitals would have been Aachen and Rome. Aachen as a capital implies entry into the Carolingian inheritance, lordship over the heartland of the German tribes. It also implies renunciation of the 'digressive' eastern policy of Otto the Great, a retreat from Magdeburg. The emperor who established a capital at Rome staked out a claim to wealthy southern Italy and its superior financial resources, to lordship of Italy – in which control of the papacy was not of least importance – and declared his connection with the religious movements of southern, central and northern Italy.

Otto III, who journeyed as penitent, petitioner and pilgrim to the graves of his saintly friends Adalbert and Romuald, was a frequenter of monasteries, caves and sanctuaries; he went to Monte Cassino, to Monte Gargano – where there was an important shrine to the Archangel Michael, standard-bearer of the Empire – and to Serperi near Gaeta. In April 999 he spent fourteen days in penitential exercises in a cave at the church of San Clemente not far from the Lateran in Rome. It must not be supposed on this account that Otto III was haunted by 'apocalyptic' fears of antichrist of the kind unjustly associated with the year 1000. He was far from being obsessed by German apocalyptical pessimism, and much nearer to a Greek pneumatic optimism. Otto was preparing himself for a difficult undertaking. He realized his plans would arouse opposition among many of his Germans and in the imperial church (where his most important collaborators and power centres were located). What he did was to deliver the Poles and Hungarians from the rule of the German imperial church and the threatening weight of oppression implicit in the claims of its leaders. Given the continuing weakness of the papacy, it is possible that this 'intermediate' Europe – Poland, Bohemia and Moravia, Hungary – would otherwise have turned instead to Byzantium, thereby committing itself to that East European hemisphere which in Russian-Communist eastern Europe still bears visible traces of Byzantine influence.

Otto III, friend and venerator of Adalbert of Prague – a Czech on whom Italy left its mark – was very close to the various Italian spiritual revivalist movements of his day. He himself early attained to a profound spirituality which made him capable of a higher form of *Realpolitik*, one which looked to the future. Rightly understood, Otto's ideas should be a source not merely of interest but even of excitement to Germans and other Europeans who today are still hidebound by a narrow-minded *Realpolitik* tied to the pursuit of day to day interests, and to the fetishist belief in power which goes with it. At that date the German masters of the imperial church thought a 'realistic' eastern policy meant establishing bishoprics or perhaps arch-bishoprics in Poland, Bohemia, Moravia or Hungary. They were careful to keep these foundations subordinate to their own power centres, Mainz, Salzburg, Magdeburg or Passau. Once these bishoprics had been set up in the name of the German church, it was 'realistic' to follow up with evangelization and political penetration. Faced with the prospect of being taken over by force, princes of Poland, Moravia, Bohemia and Hungary who were on the verge of becoming christians recoiled in alarm and looked for allies in Rome and Byzantium.

Otto III recognized this danger and offered himself to these princes as an ally, a 'brother'. This young man had a clearer and more sober vision than the *Realpolitiker*, the ecclesiastical and secular magnates, who now turned against him. An eastern expansion on the scale they envisaged was beyond the mental resources and energies of the narrowly German part of the Empire. Otto III accordingly took the bold step

47

of creatively reducing his grandfather's creative achievement. The great work of construction achieved by Bernward (Otto's faithful comrade in arms and collaborator) in Hildesheim [plate 25], the magnificent Saxon-Ottonian art and culture for ever linked with the names of Bernward and his successor Godehard, was begun by renouncing the mission to the Slavs. There was enough to set in order at home.

In December 999, the last month of the last year of the first christian millennium, Otto left Rome. In March he came to Gnesen, to the tomb of his martyred friend Adalbert. His guide was Boleslav Chabry, a friend with whom he had fought three Slav campaigns. 'As soon as he sighted the longed-for city,' says Thietmar of Merseburg, 'he proceeded barefoot with humble prayer.' What follows, however, stirred Thietmar to an instantaneous protest which was echoed by Bishop Unger of Posen and Archbishop Gisiler of Magdeburg, as by German historians of later generations. Otto III set up a Polish archbishopric of Gnesen with three suffragan sees, Kolberg, Cracow and Breslau. Boleslav was honoured with the titles 'friend and confederate of the Roman people', 'co-worker of the Empire' (*cooperator imperii*) and patricius. He received a golden circlet and a replica of the Holy Lance which is still preserved in the treasury of the cathedral at Cracow, the ancient royal city of the Polish kingdom. The emperor furthermore remitted the tribute the Polish leader had been forced to pay in respect of land on the left bank of the Warthe. It was Otto's intention that Poland and the rest should become confederate states of varying status, like those which had surrounded the old Roman Empire. *Romanum Imperium* admittedly signified the hegemony of the Emperor; but the hegemon refrained from interfering in the internal affairs of his 'friends'. Within their own boundaries, the friendly and confederate states of the Empire enjoyed a freedom not always found today within the confederacies of either east or west (where interference in the internal affairs of member states is not confined to vital economic matters). Otto III intended to develop this system of alliance and friendship still further, but was prevented by death. His tenure of the imperial office is the first occasion on which we find the Empire being projected as a model, primarily as a model for a federation of European peoples. The Emperor was hegemon, enjoyed rights of leadership, but chiefly was pre-eminent in honour. This Empire was what we should call an umbrella organization; it united in the loosest possible form ethnic groups of greatly varying size and held them together by the most diverse of ties. In Otto's design the Empire comes astonishingly close to some of our contemporary projects for federations of states designed to encompass in one grand union peoples and societies of widely different social composition and mental outlook.

This is especially clear when one looks at Otto's second model, Hungary, which he also envisaged as a prototype for further alliances. Heartened by the generosity shown by Otto at Gnesen, Waic (Stephen I) decided to opt once and for all for the west, for the Latin church and Latin civilization. He married Gisela, sister of the Duke of Bavaria, and with Otto's help converted his country to christianity. He too received a replica of the Holy Lance, and a king's crown in place of the patrician's diadem.

With the agreement of the emperor (who was acting in conjunction with the pope), the Hungarian king founded an archbishopric in his capital city of Gran and provided it with a number of suffragan sees. The first metropolitan was Ascherich (Anastasius), a German cleric sent by Otto; he crowned Waic, either in 1000 or 1001, with the crown sent by the pope for King Stephen I. Through his restraint, Otto III had demonstrated to the Poles and Hungarians that it was possible to attach oneself to western civilization, Latin culture and the Latin church, to become the friend and ally of the Emperor, without having to become a German.

Up until this decisive moment, the Byzantine church and its civilization could hope to press on through Hungary with that reconquest of Europe which Justinian and his ambitious lieutenants had intended to launch from their bridgehead of Ravenna, the 'sacred citadel'. Otto III's intended bridgehead was Rome, where he meant to reign as 'servant of the Apostles' – thereby placing himself on an equal footing with the eastern *'isapostolos'*, the 'equal of the Apostles', the 'new Constantine', the 'new Justinian'. In the thirteenth century, at the height of the papal counter-challenge to the Emperor, Pope Innocent IV would be addressed by the Sultan of Egypt as 'the thirteenth apostle'. If Otto III had allowed and even encouraged the Poles and Hungarians to submit to St Peter, it was because he saw himself as St Peter's deputy. Later popes would try to rally the peoples and states of Europe to a crusade against the 'German' emperor, a crusade preached not just once but time and time again.

Otto III died unmarried, having failed to win his Byzantine princess. He was succeeded by his uncle, Duke Henry of Bavaria (who was born the day before Otto the Great died), the last in the male line of descent from Henry I [colour plate II]. This future saint (he was canonized in the twelfth century) fought a long war with the Poles (1003–18), in which he did not scruple to make use of the pagan Liutizi. As a result of this war Bohemia was annexed to the Empire. Henry persuaded the childless Rudolf of Burgundy to name him as heir to his crown and received Basel as a surety. The Heinrichsmünster in Basel and the magnificent gold altar frontal which Henry commissioned for the cathedral survive to this day as a reminder of this pious king and emperor [plate 24].

Pope Benedict VIII, the emperor's ally, the pope who crowned him emperor in 1014 and in 1020 fought at his side against the Byzantines in southern Italy, presented Henry II with an orb. Henry handed it over to Cluny, whose reforming abbot was also his ally, there to be dedicated to Christ, Emperor of the World [plates 26, 27]. To Henry II – as to all pious emperors and kings – piety did not, however, consist in being otherworldly, 'unrealistic'. Henry II is famed for his adroitness in making his imperial bishops and reforming abbots useful servants of the Empire. They were in fact to carry the Empire, financially, administratively, politically. In 1007 Henry made Bamberg into a bishopric. It is there that he lies buried, together with his wife Kunigunde, who was also later canonized. Bamberg was to be a base for the consolidation of imperial rule and for the conversion of the Slavs in the Thuringian region, which was now slowly gaining headway. The Elbe was becoming a frontier of the Empire.

In 1009 Brun of Querfurt, who had collaborated with Otto III in his eastern plans, won the coveted martyr's crown whilst working among the Prussians. Shortly before this last missionary journey he wrote Henry a letter 'conceived in the deepest distress' imploring the emperor to resume good relations with the Poles and to give up his alliance with the Liutizi.

Henry died childless on 13 July 1024, leaving no dispositions for the succession. Henry had no great love for the man the majority of the princes would elect, but neither did he wish to decide against him in advance. On her husband's death his wife took charge of the imperial insignia – these were themselves 'the Empire' – and eight weeks later handed them over to Conrad II, the new, unanimously elected king.

REXROGATABBATEM. MATHILDIMSUPPLICATATQ.

4

THE EMPIRE OF THE SALIANS

THE Salian emperors (1024–1125), who came of the old Frankish national stock, were descended in the female line from the Ottonian dynasty and became the forebears of the Hohenstaufen. Their century saw the medieval Empire first at its peak and then almost immediately thereafter on the brink of disaster.

Conrad II (1024–39) was educated as a layman and a knight and was well-disposed towards the aspiring petty aristocracy. Acting with speed and severity, he disposed of German, Burgundian and Italian opposition and soon won general acceptance. In 1026 he had himself crowned at Milan with the iron crown. His imperial coronation at Rome was in the presence of the Anglo-Danish king, Knut the Great, and of Rudolf III of Burgundy. The device *Roma caput mundi tenet orbis frena rotundi*, which appears as the legend on his seal, he took seriously and in a self-asserting sense: Rome was the imperial city, the city of the 'King of the Romans' (Conrad was the first to use this title as a preliminary to the full imperial dignity), and as such it should live under Roman rules. Rome was imperial, not papal.

Conrad was a Frank and relied on his bishops, who were happy enough to support him. In 1033 the bishop of Constance burned a bull of Pope John XIX: centuries later Constance would be the scene of a council held under imperial auspices at which popes and anti-popes were judged. The archbishop of Mainz addressed Conrad as *vicarius Christi*, thus using a sacral-political title the popes would later claim for themselves. Conrad was ruthless in dealing with bishops who opposed him on political grounds. He arrested and deposed Aribert of Milan, who had crowned him with the iron crown but afterwards became his enemy, and banished three more bishops, Piacenza, Cremona and Vercelli. Burchard of Lyons languished in chains for years.

On the death of Rudolf III, the last king of Burgundy, the successful emperor entered Nordburg and was crowned king of Burgundy at Payerne (Peterlingen, in French Switzerland). Germany, Burgundy and Italy henceforward make up the Empire – geographically speaking, and looked at from the outside, an extremely powerful complex. Internally, however, this association gave rise to continual political, diplomatic and military friction. There were difficulties enough with the lay princes in the German sector (and soon with the ecclesiastical princes as well). To these were added struggles with the aspiring Italian towns; it was against Conrad II that they first tried out their military strength. Apart from the towns, there were the

E

III Canossa. Henry IV, through the mediation of Matilda of Tuscany and the abbot of Cluny, comes as a penitent to Pope Gregory VII. Germany never forgot this moment of political ignominy. Bismarck made 'We will never alliances formed by the nobility with the bishops for mutual protection against the man from Germany at a time when no support was forthcoming from debilitated papal Rome. In Burgundy, the rule of the Empire never extended over the whole of the old kingdom but was at most confined to western Switzerland, the Free County of Burgundy (Franche Comté), Savoy and Mount Cenis.

Conrad, a martial emperor, made the Polish duke Mesko his vassal and forced the Liutizi of Brandenburg, Henry II's former allies, to pay him tribute. He died in 1039 at Utrecht and was buried in the cathedral he founded at Speyer [plate 28]. This massive stone edifice is the last resting-place of all the Salian emperors. With its walls metres thick, it is the embodiment of security and self-evident dignity – far removed from Romanesque self-torment over Hell or the paradisal art of Gothic. Even the wish of the hapless Henry IV to be buried in Speyer was at length granted.

Henry III (1039–56) represents imperial power at its zenith [plate 29]. He was Conrad's son, but he had received a thorough schooling and tried to compensate for the harsh and violent deeds of his father. He restored Aribert of Milan to his see, made the duke of Bohemia, and for part of his reign the king of Hungary, a vassal of the Empire, and as king-priest, *rex sacerdos*, conceived it his mission to reform the church. With the support of the monastic reform movement – or at least one of its significant branches – Henry presided in 1046 over the Synod of Sutri at which two popes were deposed. He then had Bishop Suidger of Bamberg elected pope (Clement II) and was crowned by him as emperor. Henry was responsible for the election of three more German popes:[1] Damasus II, Leo IX and Victor II. Leo IX was the emperor's cousin; Victor II (formerly Bishop Gebhard of Eichstätt) was also related, though at a greater distance, to the ruling house.

It should not, however, be assumed from these papal elections that the emperor intended them as a means of providing for his 'cousinage'. Henry set great store on seeing men of less than noble birth, as well as educated noblemen, raised to the throne of St Peter. His cousin Leo IX (1046–54), for all that he had been bishop of Toul and count of Eggisheim, was determined to uphold what he conceived to be papal rights, even against the emperor. It was this pope, indeed, who set the papacy on its upward path. He gathered round him at Rome a considerable band of collaborators from Lotharingia and the monastic reform movement. Leo's Lotharingian and other sympathizers included Frederick, brother of Duke Godfrey of Upper Lotharingia, Hubert of Moyenmoutier and Hugh Candidus, and thus represented circles influential both in monastic reform and in the political opposition to the emperor, a convergence which would be momentous for the future of the imperial office. The group also included the monk Hildebrand, afterwards Pope Gregory VII, who had recently returned to Rome from Cologne, whither he had accompanied the deposed and exiled Pope Gregory VI – and Cluny had figured in his itinerary. The immediate aim

---

[1] Non-Italian popes have never lasted long in the Roman climate: its fatal effects in curtailing the reign of Hadrian VI – Charles V's ex-tutor – was a severe blow to hopes for a reformed Catholicism in the sixteenth century.

of the papal reformers was to free the clergy from the 'world', in other words from the superior power and authority of secular lords who appointed them to serve their own churches. This could only be done by tearing the priest away from his wife and family circle. Eliminate simony (the sale of spiritual office) along with clerical marriage, and the clergy could be turned into monks. All great purifiers and radical revolutionaries want to make men into monks: one thinks of Robespierre, but it also applies to Lenin, since he trained his professional revolutionaries to renounce love and the world of women, all binding attachments to other individuals.

Henry III in his time experienced only the rumblings of the approaching world storm. He had his warnings. Bishop Wazo of Liège once told Henry: 'our priestly consecration dispenses life, your royal consecration leads to death'. Then there was Archbishop Halinard of Lyons, who as a monk refused to render Henry the oath of fealty. On the political plane, there was the marriage of Godfrey the Bearded of Upper Lotharingia (who was also in touch with the opposition in southern Germany) to Beatrice of Tuscany, widow of Margrave Boniface of Canossa, which produced a Lotharingian-Tuscan alignment soon to be complemented by an alliance between the papacy and the Normans; the two together formed the basis of an *entente cordiale* which – with changing partners and buttressed by the monastic reform movement – would sustain the papacy in a struggle destined to last from 1076 to 1250. This struggle, from which the popes would eventually emerge victorious, was now in its preliminary stages.

We in our day can look back over a millennium filled with clashes between popes and emperors, kings and other lay rulers, between popes and cardinals, bishops, theologians and monks. In none of these collisions was the clash so momentous, so impassioned or so lethal as in the two great crises, the Investiture Contest of the eleventh century and the German Reformation of the sixteenth. Luther was a monk in whom erupted, from an archaic underground, the faith, hope and despair of a people never fully convinced that God was faithful and perpetually afraid that the Devil was mightier. In the eleventh century this revolutionary role was assumed by the monk Hildebrand, in the description of Peter Damian a 'holy Satan'.

The power structure of the Roman Church, now the conservative principle in Europe, takes its groundwork from the revolution effected from Rome under Gregory VII. In the nineteenth century, forward-looking Catholics, liberals and progressives, were always hoping to see the Pope at the head of popular movements for national and social freedom. They hoped in vain. Many were totally unaware of the lengthy and indirect paths which linked their own call for 'freedom' and 'liberties' with Gregory VII's call for 'freedom of the church': *libertas ecclesiae* was the rallying cry with which the monk-pope mobilized the men of the streets, first in the Italian towns and later in Germany, against a feudalized, anti-reforming aristocracy of bishops and abbots, and against king and emperor.

No pope since has ventured thus to mobilize 'the streets'. The popular fury which broke out at Milan in the form of hatred for a wealthy higher clergy and an outcry against 'simonaical, whoring and adulterous priests' marks the eruption of an anti-clericalism present in latent form throughout the Middle Ages. This type of anti-clericalism (strikes – with papal sanction – against 'simonaical priests', abuse and manhandling of priests, mocking at the sacraments) would erupt again with the Cathars and the Albigensians, with Wyclif, Hus, Calvin and Zwingli; it paved the way for the various anti-ecclesiastical manifestations, vandalisms and iconoclasms which characterized the sixteenth to nineteenth centuries. In the eleventh century anticlericalism was made to further the cause of a pope and a papacy convinced that all measures were appropriate if they promised liberation from an overlordship exercised by 'worldly' rulers and the clergy they controlled.

The old 'Lord Bishops' who had grown up in the imperial service grew mortally afraid. 'This dangerous man,' says Archbishop Liemar of Bremen of Gregory VII, 'thinks fit to order bishops as though they were stewards on his estates; if they do not do everything he wants, they must either come to Rome or be suspended without judgment.' This 'old' imperial clergy, together with the monarchy, stood for the conservative principle (the Constantinian-Carolingian and Ottonian tradition). They rested their case upon history. As one scholar has observed, 'by his conduct through-out, Henry IV presents his case as none other than an appeal to history and customary law'. Gregory VII had his reply: 'The Lord says, "I am the truth and the life"; he has not said, "I am custom, the old law".'

The outcome of the great conflict was decided in advance, against the Empire and its 'worldly' king-emperor, by one fateful short-circuiting action. After some skir-mishes and a few more serious clashes between prelates of the German-Italian imperial church and Gregorian reformers, on 24 January 1076, at a synod held at Worms and attended by twenty-six out of about forty German bishops, Henry IV declared the pope deposed. The north Italian bishops, meeting at Piacenza, concurred in the decree.

It was these bishops who brought disaster on the young king, who already had behind him a youth filled with painful and humiliating experiences. The tragedy of the conservatives, brought as they were for the first time face to face with a revolution (after this revolution true conservatives would virtually cease to exist, though there would be reactionaries in plenty), was that they had no conception of what was in store. They did not even know their enemies, so that their own momentary victories contributed to their adversary's great triumph, a triumph decisive in world history.

Emperors had been deposing unsuitable and insubordinate popes ever since the days of Charles the Great; Henry's father had deposed no less than four. There seemed no reason why the self-confident rulers of the German and Italian imperial church should not also depose the 'monk Hildebrand', a plebeian of dubious antecedents, an 'impudent' and 'false' monk. Three years after he had been installed in office, it was now declared that Gregory had never lawfully been pope.

'You are condemned by the sentence of all our bishops and our own; therefore depart, vacate the usurped apostolic see. Let another ascend the throne of St Peter, one who will not disguise violence under the cloak of holy writ but will teach the unfalsified doctrine of the blessed Peter. We, Henry, king by grace of God, with all our bishops, charge you: descend from thence, descend from thence.'

Gregory's response was immediate. On 22 February he declared the king deposed for rebelling against the church, excommunicate for spiritual disobedience. The pope released Henry's subjects from their oaths of fealty. The son of the king-priest Henry III, who had worn all the attributes of cosmocracy, was declared an outlaw. Gregory published his anathema in the form of a prayer addressed to Peter, prince of the apostles, from the Lenten Synod at Rome. 'And so I *bind* him, in trust in thee, that the peoples may know and be convinced that thou art Peter and on thy rock the Son of the living God has built his Church and the gates of Hell shall not prevail against it.'

'We waited, with a crowd of strangers, for half an hour in St Peter's, and then the pope came down. He went and kissed the foot of St Peter and prayed with his head against it and then he went to the priedieu prepared for him in front of the Confession of St Peter, as it is called. The relics had been placed on the High Altar.' This description comes from a letter written on 20 March 1870 by Bishop Ullathorne, who was present at the First Vatican Council. The pope in question, Pius IX, was preparing himself for the difficult final stage in carrying the dogma of papal infallibility. His Petrine belief had roots as archaic and magical as that of the Franks of the early Middle Ages and of Gregory VII, the monk from the people.

'And so I *bind* him, trusting in thee . . .': Gregory was as much convinced as any wizard, magician, shaman, high priest or priest-king from the depths of the preceding millennia (nothing pejorative is intended by the comparison), that through his sentence of excommunication he could move heaven and earth. To bind, to anathematize, to chain: magical incantations and the Romanesque sculptural ornament in cathedral and village churches made manifest the magically strong binding power of excommunication (as later of witches). This pope from the people, native of a country famed in the Middle Ages for its magic arts, convinced that as St Peter's successor he was called upon to bind and loose in heaven and on earth, began to assume on earth the cosmic attributes of the Emperor. *Quibus imperavit Augustus, imperavit Christus*: Christ was the only legitimate successor to Augustus-Caesar and Christ's successor was the Pope. The Pope was the common father and lord of all Christians (*communis Pater et dominus*). On him, as St Peter's successor, was laid the charge *universo orbi imperare*, to rule the entire world. Anyone who placed himself beyond and above papal commands was exposing himself to the sin of idolatry, since the commands of the Pope were issued *ex parte omnipotentia Dei*, by God's authority.

Gregory stood for the Petrine belief in its fullest sense and pressed it to its ultimate conclusion. In a letter to Terdelvach, King of Ireland, we find him declaring that Christ has placed St Peter above all the kingdoms of the world; the successor of St Peter has the right to depose kings. 'Cursed be he that keepeth his sword from blood' (Jer. 48.10) was a text Gregory was fond of invoking against kings, the 'worldly' rulers. Again, the apostolic and royal power are to one another as the sun is to the moon. The dignity of the priest is to the power of the king as gold is to lead. The king owes his office to the Devil: the Devil causes men to leave the path of righteousness and the king is placed there merely as the servant of the church, to punish the wicked. Good kings at all times offer obedience to the church. Kings disobedient to her are wicked kings, minions of the Devil. The king is 'useful' when he carries out with the sword what the Roman Church determines. His consecration makes the humblest cleric the superior of any 'worldly' ruler. An exorcist is more than the Emperor, he is a spiritual emperor, *spiritualis imperator*. In taking his stand against the 'worldly' and reprehensible, Gregory tapped archaic beliefs, steeped in magic. Worldly rulers, and this includes Henry IV (in Gregory's eyes merely the 'German king') sponsor wicked material things, all the evil world of womankind. The equation 'worldly' = 'German' = 'wicked' probably formed in Hildebrand's mind during his exile in Cologne, where he was confronted by the brilliance and pomp of the German imperial church, the brilliance which would later repel Bernard of Clairvaux. As for the 'worldly' king, he seemed matter personified.

The struggle against 'godless materialism' (which still has marked political overtones) was directed in Gregory's day first and foremost against the worldly king, the worldly clergy and the laity. Gregory's own solution was to turn both secular clergy and laity into monks.

Modern Catholic morality is still essentially monastic in emphasis; the sins the layman confesses are primarily those 'of the flesh', the sins of a celibate clergy. In his effort to impose clerical celibacy and to deliver the clergy from their attachment to 'blood and soil', Gregory laid the foundations of structures which still remain part of European man and of Roman Catholicism. It goes without saying that for centuries after Gregory, and until well into the Counter-Reformation, priests (and bishops) continued to live with their concubines, popes and prelates continued to sire noble bastards, some of whom made history. Celibacy nevertheless remained the goal, a prodigious goal, and the attempt to impose it set off a chain reaction: whether the charge was negative or positive depends on the standpoint of the observer.

Celibacy created an activist clergy. A cleric who was detached from the world was ready to go to the ends of the earth to preach the gospel on orders from the Pope or his religious superior, and to burn himself up in the task. This peculiarly western dynamicism – it is alien to the ethos of the eastern church – is closely linked with celibacy.

Where the sexual drive is successfully sublimated, celibacy makes a man willing for sacrifices and capable of an all-embracing charity. Through celibacy, it is possible for priestly father-natures to develop, which in times of stress have brought confidence, help and 'edification' to many.

Celibacy also activates drives which impel men to overweening ambition, greed, vanity, envy and contentiousness. The unbridled clerical passion for contention – the quarrel of one order with another, of bishop with cathedral chapter, of country priest with his neighbouring priest, of theologian with theologian, party with party – has from the eleventh century kept the christian world in a state of constant turmoil; as an emotion it is bound up with the sexual envy and hatred felt by the celibate cleric for the layman living in the world.

Whatever else it may be, a theology which peoples the 'wicked world' with demons, preaches hell-fire, and systematically induces fear into christian souls through threats of Hell and the Devil, is a theology of war and civil war, of death and destruction. Today every depth psychologist is aware of the close connection between such elements, where they are present in a life lived under the enormous strain of celibacy, and an unsuccessfully sublimated sexual drive.

Gregory VII unleashed tremendous energies which in turn set up tremendous disorders. He kindled more hatred in Europe than any other ruling figure since the days of the Neronian emperors. It was a case of one hatred against another. Gregory's partisans imputed to Henry IV as much turpitude as any man can well impute to another; Gregory, conversely, was charged not only with being of non-noble and disreputable ancestry, but also of having cleared his path by poisoning his four predecessors. During the Investiture Contest political propaganda swiftly reached great heights of calumny and mutual denunciation – assertions that the enemy was possessed by the Devil, that he was beyond redemption, and so forth – just as it did in the last struggle between Frederick II and the pope, and again in the Reformation.

As lawful possessor of the keys of Heaven, the pope-monarch stood outside and above the law. According to Gregory, privileges conferred by the Roman Church could be altered or revoked at any time, 'should necessity or greater utility demand it'. The law allowed the Pope to disregard conciliar decisions. The excommunicated king was rightless. Heresy was high treason against the Pope.

In the *Dictatus Papae*, Gregory's private statement of intent, we read *Solus uti possit imperialibus insigniis* ('only the Pope has the right to the imperial insignia, vestments and emblems of power'), a phrase inserted as a perpetual reminder and example to Gregory's successors.

Gregory VII, the ill-educated monk of inferior descent (he was also small, pallid and ill-favoured) planned to build up a European league of peoples in the form of one great European system of vassalage, in which individual states would be bound to St Peter by legal-political ties. He made a good start: submissions came from the principality of Capua in 1077, Dalmatia in 1073 and 1077, Hungary in 1074, Russia in 1075, Corsica in 1077, Saxony in 1081, Provence in 1081. The last pope to entertain this vision of the nations combining under papal leadership was Pius XII. He expressed it most clearly in 1938, when as Cardinal Secretary he attended the World Eucharistic Congress in Budapest. The crusade on this occasion was directed primarily against Russia. In the letter he addressed to the Russian people dated 7 July 1952, Pope Pius XII, consistently enough, supported his case with a reference to Gregory VII, the pope who was ready to admit the Russian king Isyaslav and his son into the protective relationship offered by the papacy.

Gregory's crusading plans pointed in two directions: outwards, toward the unifica-tion of all christian peoples, inwards toward the suppression of heretics. He was the first to give concrete form to the crusading idea: like Pius XII, he was convinced it was his urgent duty to snatch Christendom from the claws of antichrist. Urban II, who subsequently summoned Europe ('Europe' was itself a concept formulated by papal Christendom) to the First Crusade, made his appeal with direct reference to Gregory VII. The first summons to crusade against a heretic was issued by Pope Paschal II, who in 1102 called on Count Robert of Flanders and his men to fight the 'arch heretic' Henry IV.

The tremendous claim of the Pope to lead the whole of Christendom – in the struggle with East Rome as in everything else – entailed the desacralization of Empire and Emperor: the latter's status had to be reduced to that of a 'German king', a king like all other kings who was only legitimate if he fulfilled his obligation to obey the successor of St Peter.

Henry IV, who had grown into a tall, well-favoured young man, in the early and crucial stages of his contest with Pope Gregory VII had no inkling of the daemonic personality and genius confronting him in the 'false monk' Hildebrand; nor were his bishops able to enlighten him. In the course of the wars which filled the next thirty years this unhappy king was abandoned and betrayed by his ecclesiastical and secular magnates and eventually even by his sons. He grew nevertheless to a greatness of his own: despite his many defeats, this 'King Mark' (Mark is the ill-fated king in Gottfried of Strassburg's *Tristan*) preserved the dignity befitting a ruler of the Salian house, the dignity which has left its record in the stones of Speyer cathedral. His was a 'natural' dignity, anachronistic in view of the new spirituality and secularity then emerging in Europe to reveal themselves, at the height of the Investiture Contest, as a fatal and impious duality. To men within the Empire, clerics and laymen alike, the new prospect was terrifying. 'How pitiable a face the Empire presents! It reminds us of what we read in one of the comedians (Plautus), to wit, "We are all doubled", and so it is: the popes are doubled, the bishops doubled, the kings doubled, the dukes doubled.'

The remark is made by the contemporary annalist of Augsburg. In 1555 Augsburg would witness the first attempt, in the religious Peace of Augsburg, at giving legal recognition to the *de facto* split within the Empire into a Catholic and a Lutheran body. Monk Luther's revolt is inconceivable without monk Hildebrand's: the German answer to the desacralization of the Empire and the Emperor was to desacralize the Papal Church and the Pope.

The excommunication of Henry IV in February 1076 was followed by an avalanche of defections. The diet of princes which met at Tribur in October demanded that the king absolve himself from the decree of excommunication within a year and a day, and invited the pope to come to Germany. Gregory VII, no stranger to Germany, set out on his journey. Henry now resorted to a cunning counter-ploy, which took both his German enemies and the pope by surprise. In midwinter, with his wife Bertha of Savoy, he crossed the Mont Cenis pass and came to Canossa, a castle belonging to Countess Matilda of Tuscany. There, in the garb of a penitent, barefoot and hair-

28 Speyer Cathedral. This citadel of God still embodies the self-confident purpose of the Salian kings and emperors.

29 The Virgin Mary as Queen of Heaven receives a book from the hands of Emperor Henry III, whose reign formed the climax of the Salian Empire. With her other hand Mary blesses Empress Agnes.

30 Tomb of Rudolf of Swabia, the anti-king, in Merseburg Cathedral.

31, 32 A crown and a crucifix from the grave of Henry IV at Speyer.

33 Henry IV with his sons Henry and Conrad and three princes of the Church. The
unhappy Henry IV fought his family, and ecclesiastical and lay princes, to the bitter end.

34, 35 Henry IV (*left*) surrenders the Empire to his son Henry V at Aachen in 1099, handing him the royal insignia, crown, orb and sword; and (*right*) Henry V receives the imperial insignia from Pope Paschal in Rome in 1111. Now at last the surrender of the empire to the papacy seems complete, and the dream of the Gregorian popes appears to be fulfilled.

36 Panels from the imperial throne in the palace at Goslar, founded by the Ottonians and rebuilt by Emperor Henry III.

37 Emperor Augustus as emperor of the world, *c.* 1120. Augustus was venerated as having prepared the way for Christ's world empire of peace, and was seen as the patriarch of the Holy Roman Empire.

38 (*opposite*) Christ the King, at Vézelay. It was here that Bernard of Clairvaux, in the sight of this terrifying King of Heaven, coerced Emperor Conrad III and the French king Louis VII into the Second Crusade.

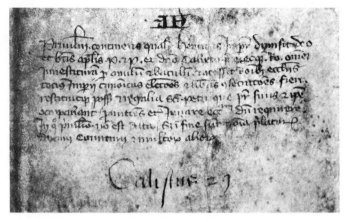

39 Signature of Pope Calixtus II on the last page of the
Concordat of Worms, the agreement which ended the
investiture struggle that had shaken the papal Church to its
foundations.

40 Panel of the cathedral door at Gnesen: Adalbert of Prague receives the crozier from
the hand of Emperor Otto II. This relief showing a bishop receiving his crozier from
the emperor was made in the first half of the twelfth century and is a programmatic
rendering of the emperor's powers confirmed by the Concordat of Worms.

shirted, he implored the pope to lift the ban of excommunication [colour plate III]. 'Canossa' – the spectacle of the penitent-king (as his enemies described him) standing for three days in snow and ice before the castle gates – inflamed German passions even in the nineteenth and twentieth centuries.

Gregory was very quick to recognize that his enemy had gained a political advantage by standing outside the castle gates at Canossa. With reluctance, the pope yielded to the persuasions of Countess Matilda (who had Salian connections) and Abbot Hugh of Cluny and lifted the ban of excommunication. Henry promised to accept the pope as arbiter. The German opposition was disillusioned by this retreat on the part of 'their' pope, but nevertheless fought on. Rudolf of Swabia was elected as anti-king [plate 30] and the Empire declared to be not hereditary but elective.[1]

In the civil war which followed, the anti-king lost his advantage; this was taken as a divine judgment and he soon met his death. A second anti-king, Hermann of Salm, found no solid support. Henry was again excommunicated. But repeating the decree diminished its force, just as the wholesale decrees of excommunication and interdict issued by popes of succeeding centuries against towns, bishops and monarchs (even Elizabeth I of England was excommunicated), also devalued themselves.

Gregory would hear of no compromise and was insistent both on a radical prohibition of lay investiture[2] and on close scrutiny of episcopal elections. His intransigence gave the king, supported by German and Italian bishops, a chance to recover the political and military initiative. In 1084 Henry marched on Rome, deposed Gregory in St Peter's, had Archbishop Wibert of Ravenna enthroned as Pope Clement III, and was himself crowned emperor by this anti-pope. As a demonstration it was spectacular; but the days of Henry III were not to be recalled. What had passed at Sutri in 1046 for an imperial reform of the church carried out by its supreme protector in 1084 appeared in its true light, as one of the many acts of violence committed at Rome by which a political pretender tried to impose his own candidate as pope. Gregory turned for help to the Normans, but under Robert Guiscard they pillaged Rome so thoroughly that Roman resentment forced Gregory to withdraw from the engagement.

Gregory died at Salerno, exhausted and in exile. Embittered, he amended the text from Psalm 45 which runs, 'Thou hast loved righteousness and hated iniquity, wherefore God, even thy God, hath anointed thee with the oil of gladness above thy fellows' so that it read 'I have loved righteousness and hated iniquity, *wherefore* I die in exile'. Men of the early Middle Ages (and of much later periods) were fond of citing and reciting biblical texts of this kind as high authority for the bond between

---

[1] Opposition forces within the Empire constantly revert to this concept of the Empire as a freely elective office, particularly in later centuries when with the backing of French propaganda and French money efforts are made to protect the Empire against the hereditary claim of the Habsburgs.

[2] What Gregory objected to here was the investiture of bishops with episcopal ring and staff by the lay ruler prior to consecration by the archbishop and bishops of the province, since this implied that the bishop's appointment was determined by his acceptability to the ruler [T].

God and the world: God in His majesty will reward His heroes with terrestrial great-ness and glory. Gregory had found it otherwise. The chasm between God and the world had cracked irremediably open. The desacralization of the Empire and of every 'worldly' power not only exposed them to secularization but at the same time smoothed the path towards an autonomous 'statist' evolution.

Hildebrand came to Germany as an exile and died an exile in Salerno, as his enemies may have thought a heavily defeated man. In 1606, in the period of the Counter-Reformation, when the Thirty Years' War was not far over the horizon and the pope's feud with the England of Elizabeth I, fought with the weapons of excommunication and all possible military and political resources, was still a matter of recent history, Gregory VII was canonized. This plebeian, this 'little man', had been the greatest pope of the Middle Ages. Innocent III and Innocent IV, able men but totally uncreative, supported by an army of curial canon lawyers and other clerical advisers, expanded the imperial authority of the Roman Church and brought it to the peak from which it shortly thereafter fell. Gregory VII had no such resources; scholastic theologians and canon lawyers only started to emerge from the universities in any numbers in the late twelfth century. He thus lacked the enormous bureaucratic and political apparatus within the curia which was at the disposal of an Innocent III. His way was prepared for him by a mere handful of highly-gifted and like-minded colleagues and pioneers, pre-eminent among them Humbert of Silva Candida ('our Emperor is Christ'). The revolution from Rome – the only European revolution ever initiated by a pope – was Gregory's work. His successors, carefully and tirelessly, continued to build on the foundations he had laid.

A conspicuous example of a pope who followed up Gregory's work was his next successor but one, Urban II (1088–99). A Frenchman and a Cluniac, Urban led Europe, 'Christendom' (so described in his proclamations), minus the excommuni-cated 'German king' and the Holy Roman Empire, into the First Crusade, which he proclaimed at the Council of Clermont in 1095. The emperors in Constantinople looked on this 'Frankish' enterprise as a wilful misunderstanding of their need; they had asked for auxiliary troops, not for an army of invasion. Eastern churchmen were alarmed and repelled by the spectacle of western bishops at the head of an army. To the 'west', for which it acted as a precipitant, the crusade was a welcome means of curbing an aristocracy which was exhausting itself in permanent feuds, of providing land for younger, landless sons, and of vindicating the pope's claim to lead the Europe he himself 'created'.

In the German territories of the Empire the crusade sparked off the first persecutions of the Jews, brought in like a contagion by crusading bands from further west. In Mainz alone – the city where the Jew who had saved the life of Otto II had become a rabbi – these crusaders killed over a thousand Jews. Archbishop Ruthard could do nothing to prevent it, though the Jews were under his protection and he had even taken money for his good offices. When Henry IV instituted a vigorous inquiry on behalf of the Jews thus exploited, Archbishop Ruthard took refuge in rebellious

Flanders and became Henry's bitter opponent. Henry took the Jews under his own royal protection, thus inaugurating the Jewish *Kammerknechtschaft*, the special relationship linking the Jews of the Empire directly with the Emperor or King. This system was expanded under Frederick I and Frederick II and continued into the later Middle Ages.

Henry IV fought on both in Germany and in Italy. His ill-luck continued to dog him, as members of his family circle one by one deserted to the political opposition [plate 33]. His adulterous second wife Praxedis, daughter of the Grand Prince Vsevolod of Kiev, escaped from custody with the help of his enemies and appeared as 'crown witness' against her husband at a synod in Constance. His son Conrad deserted him and allowed himself to be crowned King of Lombardy. Yet before the century in which the imperial office had reached both its zenith and its nadir was out, there seemed a good chance that the king would re-establish himself at least in the German part of the Empire, where a general peace (*Landfriede*) would crown and sanction the reconciliation.

The new century, the twelfth, during which the structures of the new Europe would develop – in the church, in the western, secular, state, in town life, in art, with the emergence of Gothic as the first European style – brought catastrophe to the emperor-king, who was once again excommunicate. Where he was concerned, it seemed, anything was permissible. Abetted by ecclesiastical and lay magnates and by the pope, yet another son, the future Henry V, rose against his father, took him prisoner and extorted from him the renunciation of his rights as ruler [plate 34] and a revolting confession of his sins. Dishonoured and disgraced, Henry IV managed to escape to the loyalist cities of the lower Rhineland and died at Liège on 7 August 1106. Peasants came to touch the king's corpse with their seed-corn, hoping from the contact to obtain a rich harvest. In their eyes, the saving-power of the king-emperor had not been broken by the ban imposed by an alien church. 'Every inch a king' – the Shakespearean tag may justly be applied to Henry IV: mellowed by his errors and the blows of fate, he never sacrificed the dignity and obligations of his office. The conflict between Henry and Gregory has brought much grist to the mill of German poets.

Would Henry V (1106–25) revenge on the pope the father he had betrayed and in whose footsteps he would himself soon tread? He did indeed march on Rome, with the entire German host, and there wrested from Pope Paschal II (imprisoned for a time in St Peter's, together with all the cardinals present in Rome) a pact which incensed the reformers. Under this pact the pope was forced to crown him emperor [plate 35] and to promise that Henry would not be excommunicated once he left Rome. On his return from Italy, Henry had his father's body ceremoniously interred in Speyer cathedral [plates 31, 32].

In the pact (made at Sutri in February 1111) Henry had tried to turn to the emperor's advantage the distinction between *temporalia* and *spiritualia* which Gregory VII had used to support and justify his offensive against kings and emperors.

Henry turned the screw with a vengeance: if the church was really so eager to be purely spiritual, freed from all 'worldly' baseness and material burdens, he for his part was only too willing to oblige. He, as king and emperor, renounced the investiture of bishops, but in return the church should renounce the imperial lands it had held as fiefs ever since the days of Charles the Great. Render to Caesar that which was Caesar's! Under this scheme the German imperial church would give back the *regalia* (fiefs and secular jurisdictions) and in future live on tithes and private benefactions.

Paschal II had accepted this proposal – hence the outcry from reformers and others in ecclesiastical circles – and confirmed it in two documents. He was the only pope (just as Francis was the only saint) who was courageous enough to detach himself from the 'medievalism' of the Roman Church. This medieval period of the church outlived the Papal State and lasted until the death of Pope Pius XII. Its essential characteristic was the church's view of itself as a legal corporation, neither willing nor able to surrender a single right, or indeed a single possession (even one which had passed centuries earlier into other hands) – not even for the sake of something greater and more 'spiritual'.

Furthermore, Paschal II was not prepared to excommunicate the emperor and persisted in this resolve, despite intense subsequent pressure from reformers and supporters of the papacy; in fact he kept in contact with the emperor until his own death in 1117.

In April 1111, while he was the emperor's prisoner, Paschal had even conceded to Henry that investiture with ring and staff should precede consecration. The reformers attacked this privilege (known as the agreement of Ponte Mammolo) as a *pravilegium*, a depravity.

It is not known whether Henry, like Ludwig of Bavaria after him, descended on Rome accompanied by a band of anticurial clerics (he had one such in his chancellor, David), men of the temper of Marsilius of Padua and the Spiritual Franciscans, who in Ludwig's time wanted to force Rome to return to the 'church of poverty'. However that may be, the turbulent events in and around Rome in 1111 resulted in a further decade of discord. On the death of Paschal the emperor's nominee, Burdinus, was installed as anti-pope. Pope Gelasius II, finding a pro-imperial party had the upper hand at Rome, took refuge in France. The next pope, Calixtus II, was elected at Cluny. He excommunicated Henry and a new and bitter conflict seemed in prospect. Calixtus, however, who belonged to the higher Burgundian nobility and was related to many of the great houses of Europe (including the Salians), was a personality of considerable stature. He recognized that the ecclesiastical, religious and social disorders troubling the Empire were themselves a consequence of the conflict which had now lasted nearly half a century.

On 23 September 1122, in an open meadow outside Worms, it was announced that a concordat had been concluded [plate 39]. This Concordat of Worms, as is the case with all constructive peace treaties, had been preceded by protracted negotiations.

For the emperor the most important result was that he remained master of the imperial church in the German territories of the Empire. Admittedly, episcopal and abbatial elections were to be conducted 'canonically', 'freely', but in Germany (as in England), the king had the right to invest with the sceptre *before* consecration took place [plate 40]. The bishop- or abbot-elect swore an oath of fealty, was enfeoffed with the *regalia*, and only then proceeded to ecclesiastical investiture with ring and staff. In case of disputed elections the king, after consultation with the bishops, could decide on his own nominee. In Italy and Burgundy, however, a bishop-elect was merely required to petition the king for investiture with the *regalia* within six months of his election and consecration. In these regions, therefore, the influence of king and emperor was greatly diminished.

The Concordat of Worms emphasizes the contraction of the Holy Roman Empire to its narrowly German territories. During the long years of conflict under Henry IV and Henry V, we see new structures and power centres emerging within this part of the Empire. The imperial church seems split into two parties, one siding with the king, the other, a 'Gregorian' party, with the pope. The towns, especially the Rhineland towns, force their episcopal governors to grant them a degree of self-government (sometimes, though not always, with royal support). Ecclesiastical and secular lords build up territorial lordships. The higher nobility, which naturally includes the dukes, win a voice for themselves in important royal and imperial decisions. New dynasties come to the fore. The old Welfs separate from the younger; this younger branch becomes increasingly embroiled in imperial politics and in the person of Otto IV will eventually contest the imperial crown. Another Otto, the nephew of Otto IV, is the common ancestor of the Welfs of Brunswick (who lasted until 1918), the Welfs of Hanover (extinct in 1866), and the Welfs of England (1714 to the present day). The Welf dynasty has the singular distinction of having worn three different imperial crowns: Otto IV became Emperor of the Romans, Ivan III (VI) Emperor of All the Russias, Victoria of England, Empress of India. The ancient Welf pride survived many injuries and humiliations: King George V of England, 'as a Christian, a monarch and a Welf', refused to take second place to the King of Prussia.

Another dynasty, the Zähringer, rose to importance under Henry IV, who in 1098 created for Bertold II of Zähringen a Swabian dukedom of Zurich. The dynasty had great opportunities for development in the German-Swiss-Burgundian region (the Zähringer are still remembered as the founders of Berne and Fribourg), but in 1218 became extinct. The Zähringer patrimony passed to the counts of Kyburg and eventually to the Habsburgs.

And there were the Hohenstaufen. Emperor Henry V died of a cancerous ailment in 1125, at the age of forty-four and in the midst of a fresh conflict with lay and ecclesiastical opponents. Cancer is not only a modern disease; but it seems – as is only to be expected – to become especially prevalent at critical and revolutionary periods of human history, periods in which men are obliged to 'transpose' themselves, physically and psychically. Monica, St Augustine's mother and an extraordinary woman in her own right, died of cancer, at the turning-point between Antiquity and the Middle Ages. Henry v, a man faced with an extraordinary challenge, also died in one of Europe's periods of revolution. Childless, he appointed as his successor his nephew Frederick of Swabia, of the house of Hohenstaufen.

5

SACRUM IMPERIUM:
THE EMPIRE AND IMPERIAL IDEOLOGY
UNDER THE HOHENSTAUFEN

THE heir designated by Henry v was not elected. The ecclesiastical and lay princes who had emerged inside Germany as victors in the Investiture Contest met in the presence of the papal legate and elected Lothar of Supplinburg. On Lothar's death the designated heir (Henry the Proud) was again passed over, in favour of Conrad III of Hohenstaufen. The princes, with papal backing, thus did their best to prevent the imperial office from becoming hereditary. They realized that any weakening of the office and every break in continuity gave them fresh opportunities for enlarging their own possessions, rights and influence. This was what they understood by the 'freedom' of the Empire.

Lothar III (1125–37) might have gone down to history as the founder of a powerful line of Welf emperors had not the curia and the princes decreed otherwise by thus passing over his son-in-law Henry the Proud. Lothar had given Henry both Saxony and the margravate of Tuscany and on his deathbed delivered to him the imperial insignia. Since Henry also possessed Bavaria, he was well on the way to having an 'empire' of his own; had he become emperor it would have formed a powerful core to the Holy Roman Empire, since it stretched from the North Sea deep into Italy and incorporated many estates belonging to the Welf dynasty; these served as a bridge between the two duchies of Saxony and Bavaria, now united in one hand.

In 1125 Lothar was fifty, in the eyes of his contemporaries almost an old man. He was cautious enough to pay due heed to the movement for church reform which had in Bernard of Clairvaux its most outspoken leader. During a period of schism Lothar conducted Bernard's pope, Innocent II, to Rome and was crowned emperor; the pope also invested him with the Tuscan lands of the Countess Matilda.

The policy the Saxon Lothar pursued in the north-east of the Empire linked up with the earlier efforts of Otto the Great in which mission, conversion, colonization and the acquisition of territory went hand in hand. Bishop Otto of Bamberg preached the 'German God' to the Pomeranians. Holstein was given to Adolf of Schauenburg, who razed the Wendish settlement at Lübeck and founded a German one in its place.

Lübeck became the chief city of the Hanse, in which the 'Wendish' towns were to play an important role. Albert the Bear, founder of the Mark of Brandenburg, received the Nordmark. Meissen and Lusatia went to Conrad of Wettin, ancestor of the Saxon princely houses. Lothar III thus laid the foundations for Brandenburg–Prussia and the new Saxony, powers destined to play a leading part in the Empire from the time of the Reformation.

The Diet of Merseburg in 1135 shows Lothar at the height of his power in the Empire. The rulers of Poland and Denmark were present as his vassals, Duke Boleslav III of Poland carrying the emperor's sword when the imperial train entered the church. Bohemia, too, was subject to him. The next year Lothar was persuaded by Pope Innocent II and a number of Italian, Byzantine and Bernardine princes, enemies of Roger of Sicily, to enter the Norman kingdom of southern Italy. In later days the papacy would do everything in its power to keep the 'Germans', that is the Hohenstaufen, out of southern Italy and Sicily. But it was the papacy which had first invited, indeed enticed, the Germans into these southern parts, just as the curia, on the death of Lothar, worked for the election of the Hohenstaufen Conrad III as ruler of the Empire.

The position was that Pope Innocent II had been ousted from Rome by Pope Anacletus II, Innocent having been elected first but in a very hasty election and by a minority of cardinals, while Anacletus had secured the votes of the majority. Innocent fled to France and there won the support of Bernard of Clairvaux. Bernard once described himself as the 'chimera of the century'. For all his smallness of stature, he radiated a fascinating, daemonic 'charm'. He was also a man of great loves and hates. Among Bernard's hatreds was the 'Jewish' Pierloni clan, to which Anacletus belonged. The Pierloni were descended from a Jew named Benedict who had been baptized at some time before 1050. The family had subsequently done useful service to the curia. Anacletus, an educated and cultivated man, had to bear the full brunt of the hatred of the Bernardine monastic following and of other 'anti-semitic' kindred spirits. His support was Roger of Sicily.

Innocent II induced Lothar to take part in a joint expedition against Anacletus and Roger. Roger soon declared his willingness to detach Apulia as an imperial fief for one of his sons and to surrender another son as a hostage. But Innocent was for pressing on until the entire Norman kingdom had been destroyed. The Germans, whose men refused to go on fighting in that hot and unwholesome climate, were against the plan. Moreover, there were growing symptoms of disagreement between the pope and Henry the Proud, in which the emperor also became involved. The upshot was a decision to retreat. On the way back Lothar died, utterly worn out. He is buried in Königslutter cathedral.

The period that follows bears the stamp less of Conrad III, the first of the Hohenstaufen (1138–52), than of Bernard of Clairvaux. Conrad was the first ruler since Henry I not to seek imperial coronation. Bernard, who died in 1153, scored some great personal triumphs, which from another point of view might be regarded as spectacular failures: he secured the Church's condemnation of Abelard, the father of scholasticism and the first to attempt the moulding of a young European intelligentsia, and hounded to his death Arnold of Brescia, Abelard's pupil, a reformer whose memory is still cherished by opponents of papalism. Bernard persuaded the young French king, Louis VII, and Conrad III to embark on a crusade (1147-9) which ended in catastrophe. Bernard's activities stirred up fresh persecutions of the Jews in the Rhineland towns, while at the same time Saxon noblemen, with the approbation of Bernard and his pope, Eugenius III, embarked on a Wendish crusade which jeopardized everything past missionary work had so laboriously achieved. Bernard's solution, however, was to 'convert the heathens or destroy them'.

Bernard summoned men to crusades: in the Holy Land, against the Wends. He also summoned men to do battle with 'heretics' and 'rebels' – the 'rebels' were the Romans, who refused to allow Pope Eugenius to rule in Rome and chose Arnold of Brescia as the leader of their republican uprising. From this it was a short step to a fateful question which Roman canon lawyers serving the greatly strengthened papacy of the early thirteenth century would not fail to pose: should not the crusade in Europe for the overthrow of the church's enemies – heretics, infidels, dynasties such as the Hohenstaufen who were enemies of God – take precedence over the crusade beyond the seas to the Holy Land?

The accursed – by the popes – house of Hohenstaufen owed its accession to the throne to an adroit manoeuvre on the part of the curia reminiscent of the manoeuvre which had secured the election of Innocent II. Archbishop Adalbero of Trier, supported by a minority of the princes and with the connivance of a cardinal legate, arranged for Conrad to be elected before the time appointed. As a rival king Conrad III had made a poor showing even against Lothar III; on his own merits he could never have carried the day against the Welfs. Knowing the weakness of his position, he designated as his heir not his eight-year-old son, Frederick of Rotenburg, but his nephew, Frederick of Swabia. The Hohenstaufen era had begun, and with it the Holy Roman Empire of the German Nation.

The vision of this empire – *the* Empire – harboured by a German nationalist-liberal and conservative bourgeoisie and lovingly encouraged by historians and poets, sees it set in a Middle Ages transfigured by romanticism. This is the empire of Kaiser Rotbart, Frederick Barbarossa, the one empire which was a fusion of power and spirit, a combination of political importance on a world scale with an independent German knightly civilization whose influence radiated out from the heart of Europe. This empire was what men would later term a 'power order' and its emperor was the ruler of all christian peoples. Barbarossa died on crusade. But the old Emperor of the old and glorious Empire did not die: he sleeps in Kyffhäuser, the holy mountain, and when Germany reawakens will return. The collapse of Kaiser Wilhelm's 'empire' was followed in conservative German Protestant and Catholic circles by a revival of a religious-political form of empire romanticism (the Kyffhäuser Bund). The period after the Second World War saw performances in south Germany of the *Ludus de*

Antichristo, a mid-twelfth-century play which exalts the Emperor as the sole shield against antichrist, the sole protection against an envious, wicked East and a jealous West.

Frederick I, 'Barbarossa': his very appearance had a tincture of splendour, a radiance which fascinated contemporaries as it has fascinated posterity. Never gross, delicate of limb, with a clear skin soft as a boy's and red-blond hair and beard, wherever he went – to the tourney, into battle, to the chase, to his solemn crown-wearings – he appeared the very paragon and patron of a European chivalry.

The poorly endowed Count Frederick of Büren (Barbarossa's grandfather) had been singled out as a likely ally by Henry IV, who gave him Swabia and the hand of his daughter Agnes in marriage. Frederick removed his family seat from the small moated castle of Büren to the peak of Hohenstaufen. Karl Hampe, an outstanding historian of the German Empire, is surely justified in regarding Barbarossa's struggle with the Lombard towns as a kind of resumption of the Investiture Contest.

Frederick I, son of a Welf mother and related to the Carolingian, Ottonian and Salian dynasties, wanted to revive the Holy Roman Empire of Charles the Great and the Ottonians. At all events this was what some of those responsible for his religious-political propaganda claimed on his behalf and certain public gestures in the grand style, for example the canonization of Charles the Great, point the same way [plate 45]. Being also of a practical turn of mind, he wanted to revive as far as possible those imperial rights in Italy, Burgundy and Germany which his predecessors' *desidia* – their culpable negligence – had allowed to lapse. In addition he needed allies in and outside the Empire, and some form of private domain. Frederick's efforts to add to Hohenstaufen possessions soon earned him the hostility of greater, middling and lesser lords. Historians and political writers with nationalist-liberal, 'Little Germany' tendencies award the Habsburgs a black mark because of their ambitions to carve out a 'private domain' for themselves. But it was what all princes and lords ambitious to achieve or defend a commanding position had to do, in the Empire as in England and France: the French monarchy carried the day in France because it possessed the strongest private domain. Frederick II of Hohenstaufen[1] had plans for creating a broad band of Hohenstaufen possessions stretching from his estates in the west and south-west by way of Cham to Eger, and for making a kingdom based on Austria the centre of Hohenstaufen power in the Empire; he thus provided the Habsburgs with a direct precedent.

To do full justice to Frederick I we must look first at his deeds, or, to borrow Otto of Freising's term, at his *Gesta*. After considering his political and military exploits, his defeats and his victories, we can then turn to a separate consideration of the other aspect: the self-stylization of his imperial intentions contained in the imperial liturgy, in Frederick's festivals and ceremonials, and in the religious-political propaganda put out by his collaborators and partisans.

The first stages of his reign were laborious. In the German part of the Empire he

---

[1] The original emperor of the Kyffhäuser legend, which was transferred to Frederick I at a later date.

gained ground only slowly, appointing his supporters to bishoprics and abbacies and granting them territory and estates. Having divorced his first wife on grounds of her adultery, he married Beatrice of Upper Burgundy who brought him a rich marriage portion [plates 42, 43]. His six Roman expeditions brought him into conflict with the Italian towns and with the papacy. In Germany he scored a success through his alliance with the Welfs in the person of his cousin Henry the Lion, to whom he granted not only privileges east of the Elbe but also the duchy of Saxony and the duchy of Bavaria, the latter shorn of the newly created duchy of Austria. This Austrian duchy, endowed with special privileges which were later a great bone of contention, he granted to a Babenberger, Henry Jasomirgott. It was when this dynasty became extinct in 1246 that Frederick tried to acquire Austria for the Hohenstaufen.

The well-endowed Henry the Lion and his cousin Frederick I worked together in harmony for twenty years.

Under a treaty made at Constance in 1153 Frederick allied himself with Pope Eugenius III: they had two enemies in common, the Romans (still in revolt under Arnold of Brescia, to whom they had offered the imperial crown) and the Normans. But friction between Frederick and Pope Hadrian IV (1154-9) – Nicholas Breakspear, the first and only English pope – threatened to bring a clash with the papacy closer. These difficulties were composed and Frederick crowned emperor; but as soon as his army had withdrawn Hadrian made an alliance with the Normans. At the Diet of Besançon the chancellor of the Empire, Rainald of Dassel, professed himself eager to relax the accumulated tensions: there was the matter of Hadrian's letter in which he described the imperial crown as a *beneficium* granted by the Pope. Now *beneficium* meant both 'fief' and 'benefit'. Rainald, who interpreted the vital word as fief, was perhaps out to pick a quarrel. The pope's representative at Besançon was Roland Bandinelli, now presumed by modern scholars (probably correctly) to have been the author of the theory current in the curia that the papacy had transferred the imperial office from the Greeks to the Romans and could equally well transfer it again elsewhere. Bandinelli would subsequently become Pope Alexander III and Frederick's great adversary. Rainald's fears were not groundless, and as imperial chancellor he succeeded in rallying the imperial bishops to a unanimous protest, whereupon Hadrian explained that by *beneficium* he had meant 'benefit'.

Spurred on by this success, Rainald pushed the emperor further than he was prepared to go. To understand the fourteen years of warfare in Italy which followed, it is necessary to realize that by and large the Italian lands – still in no way homogeneous in the sense of being an Italian nation – were economically far more advanced than their hinterland. Italy, the 'garden of the empire' as Dante called it, yielded products, treasures and riches, which Frederick was anxious to enjoy. In 1156 at the Diet of Roncaglia the emperor saw to it that the sovereign rights, the *regalia*, which had been lost to the Empire during the Investiture Contest received legal confirmation. By instituting imperial officials in the towns, the emperor hoped to tap their economic power for the benefit of the Empire. Later emperors succeeded in doing this in Germany through the compacts they made with wealthy patricians, for example the Fuggers. Frederick I had no success with the Italian towns, the Lombard towns proving especially recalcitrant. They revolted and sought an alliance with the new pope, Alexander III. A minority of the cardinals elected the pro-imperial Octavian as Victor IV, and it was Victor who was recognized as pope by the imperial church. The result was a schism which lasted for seventeen years (1159–77).

Alexander took refuge from the emperor in France. He secured recognition for himself first in France and then in England, that is, from princes who were not part of the Empire, and as time went on increasingly within the Empire itself.

Rainald of Dassel, the emperor's chancellor, overreached himself. On the death of Victor IV he was still not prepared to bow to reality and we find him presiding over the election of three more anti-popes. Defeat at Milan in 1162 only spurred him on to a still more radical anti-Alexander and pro-imperial line of policy. The Lombard League, which was formed from towns united in their opposition to the emperor, named their stronghold Alessandria, in honour of Alexander III. This defensive and offensive league at one time included as many as twenty-two towns and had Milan at its head. Despite isolated successes, Frederick could not hold his own against it, especially when at a crucial moment Henry the Lion withheld his troops (Chiavenna). In 1176, after his defeat by the Lombards in the battle of Legnano, the emperor at last began to realize that the long evolution by which the Italian communes had risen to a high degree of political and economic independence could not be reversed. In 1177 he reached an agreement with the pope at Venice. The church had suffered greatly through the schism and the Peace of Venice (we shall come across it again as a celebration of the imperial liturgy) was a genuine compromise. The emperor recognized the pope and acknowledged his sovereignty in the Papal State, while Alexander III recognized the emperor's overlordship of the imperial church.

The Lombard towns felt the pope had betrayed them and fought on until 1183. Under the Peace of Constance made in that year the emperor recognized their League (Alessandria had its name changed to Caesarea) and agreed to the free election of town magistrates; he would invest them and they in return would swear him fealty. Supreme jurisdiction remained with the Emperor.

Under Frederick I one can already see imperial Italy taking its future shape. The towns were in practice already a long way towards being independent, yet even at times when they were in conflict with the emperor they still protested their respect for the dignity of his office and their wish to remain subject to it. Imperial Italy, especially after Barbarossa's last Italian campaign (1184–6), was treated as an organized possession of the Empire in northern and central Italy. It was governed through German overlords, who when left to their own devices (as was often the case) tried to maintain themselves through a series of shifting alliances.

At Milan, now friendly again, Frederick I married his son Henry to Constance, who became heiress to the Two Sicilies. This marriage the pope viewed with alarm, since it held out a threat of encirclement which must endanger his independence. Urban III, formerly archbishop of Milan, took steps to bring Frederick's enemies inside Germany, in particular the Welfs with their English connections, into a grand coalition. The Hohenstaufen replied by forming an alliance with Philip Augustus of France against the Welfs and the Angevins. This Hohenstaufen-Capetian friendship lasted until the death of Frederick II: St Louis of France refused to support the popes in their war on the 'infamous clan'. The death of Urban III (1187) restored peace between Frederick and the papacy.

While the emperor was occupied in Italy, his wealthy cousin, Henry the Lion, had been at work building up and fortifying a realm of his own in Saxony, along the Baltic and in Mecklenburg. He captured Lübeck, made the dukes of Pomerania his vassals, and clothed Brunswick in ostentatious magnificence. The Welf treasure, the lion of Brunswick, and Brunswick's lofty cathedral still testify to the days of Welf splendour under Henry the Lion. In 1158 he founded Munich, which became a rival capital in opposition to the Empire and the Emperor – a role it retained into the twentieth century.

Frederick I in fact had no capital city. He was almost continually on the move, an *imperator viator* who found his lodging in episcopal palaces, in Carolingian and Ottonian palaces which he restored, and in castles. His rich cousin went in 1172 on pilgrimage to Jerusalem, to the '*alt erbelant*' of Christ, the true King and Emperor. This pilgrimage, and Henry's munificent gifts to churches, were intended in part as acts of expiation, for in his rise to power he had injured not only many secular lords but also pillaged or destroyed many churches.

After concluding the Peace of Venice with the pope, Frederick set about 'settling his account' with Henry the Lion. The complaints of the successful Welf's numerous enemies gave him grounds for summoning Henry to appear before his high court, a summons which he issued three times in vain; after the third non-appearance Frederick outlawed Henry and broke up his Welf empire, an act whose consequences were greater than any other in the Empire's internal history. The duchy of Saxony was split up and the duchy of Bavaria further truncated through the loss of the Tyrol and the establishment of a duchy in the Steiermark (Styria). Frederick gave the new Bavaria to Otto of Wittelsbach, whose dynasty continued to reign in Bavaria until 1918. Henry the Lion took flight, surrendered, attempted to foment insurrections, eventually submitted for good. He kept Brunswick and Lüneburg. The truly royal funerary monument erected to Henry and his wife Matilda in Brunswick cathedral is testimony to his high importance and his greatness [plate 44]. The burial place of Frederick Barbarossa (probably near Tyrus) has passed into oblivion.

The victors in the struggle with Henry the Lion were the middling territorial princes and a number of ecclesiastics. The archbishop of Cologne acquired a duchy of Westphalia, created from the Cologne and Paderborn dioceses of the old duchy of Saxony. The key political position in north-west Germany which this rich endowment created for the archbishopric of Cologne would in future be coveted by the

Wittelsbachs, the Habsburgs and by Brandenburg-Prussia. The bishop of Würzburg also acquired a duchy, in eastern Franconia.

The last years of Frederick's reign were shot with splendour: at Whitsun in 1184 the knighting of his sons Henry and Frederick was celebrated with a feast which united all the chivalry and minstrelsy of Europe. In 1187, at a diet in Mainz, the emperor took the cross [plate 49]. On 10 June 1190 Frederick drowned while bathing in the river Saleph and the crusade collapsed.

The propaganda and acts of the Hohenstaufen emperors surrounded their Empire – *Sacrum Romanum Imperium* – with a halo. The Empire thus aureoled is presented to Christendom as the highest ranking and indeed unique representative of political power. This self-stylization and deliberate self-exaltation continues without interruption until the death of Frederick II (1250). The liturgies of the Empire only make sense when it is realized that these emperors (Frederick I, Henry VI and Frederick II) and their collaborators were perpetually conscious that the Empire was in a permanent state of siege.

For German monks of the eleventh and twelfth centuries (as later for Luther and his spiritual sons) the besieger was the '*alt boese viant*' (the collective name given in the Hohenstaufen era to the Devil and all his earthly confederates). In the time of Frederick I and his successors the Holy Roman Empire was threatened by a powerful opposition inside Germany, but above all by a hostile pope and by the emperor in Byzantium. French, Anglo-Norman, Norman and Spanish kings resented the preeminence of the Empire and deliberately sought – so Hohenstaufen statesmen were convinced – to undermine it. Confronting this multifarious attack stood the equally deliberate political and religious-political activity of the self-styled Holy Roman Empire.

During the decisive decade 1157–67, the Empire had Rainald of Dassel as its protagonist and leading propagandist. Born into the famous Saxon family of the counts of Northeim, Rainald went to school in Hildesheim and rose to be canon and provost of its cathedral. Hildesheim was a place of ancient stone churches and strong-walled monasteries, a place where God and the world met. Its great period had been in the tenth century, under the guidance and artistic patronage of Bernward and Godehard. In the twelfth century the cathedral chapter, which had a high reputation throughout Germany, still delighted in the old pomp and ceremonies. Rainald never forgot his connection with Hildesheim and when he was chancellor of the Empire made the chapter a gift of twelve *mansi*[1] with the stipulation that as a reminder of his benefaction the canons were to enjoy a feast each year from its revenues.

Rainald created something of a stir at the start of his career by opposing (successfully) a decree being debated at the Council of Rheims in 1148 which forbade the clergy to wear brightly-coloured furs. 'The clothes make the man'. Classes and individuals (always of the noble class) have long fought over questions of 'honour' and precedence, striving for recognition of their special position through observance

[1] A *mansus* represented a landholding large enough to maintain a single family by its produce.

of protocol in sitting and standing and the right to wear sumptuous clothing and display special emblems. In the same way, Rainald fought for the '*honor imperii*', for the legal standing and dignity of the Empire, which its many enemies belittled.

He was trenchant when he faced the French King Louis VI on the bridge over the Rhône near St Jean de Losne on 18 September 1168, declaring that the Emperor alone had the right to choose the Pope. His master Frederick I had admittedly invited the provincial kings (the '*armen kunege*', '*kunegelin*' of contemporary German poetry) to discuss the ending of the schism. But they had no right to appoint the Pope, and would be the first to object if the Emperor intervened in an appointment to one of their own sees. Archbishop Rainald of Cologne was wholly in his element when in 1167 he led his knights in a successful engagement against the Romans near Tusculum.

Rainald had a fresco painted in the church of St Patroclus at Soest showing the kings of Judah wearing their sacred crowns, sacral power-emblems of the sacral rule of his own king and emperor, Frederick I. Rainald carried off as his most precious booty from defeated Milan the relics of the Three Kings and brought them to Cologne; and it was Rainald who set in train the canonization of Charles the Great. The holy kings of Judah and Charles the Great were brought in to reinforce the *honor* of the Empire and the potency of its emperor – their successor, their son, their 'heir'.

But the Empire was under attack. This was brought home to the Germans living in the early fifties of the twelfth century by the *Ludus de Antichristo*, a play composed, and probably also performed, at the monastery of Tegernsee (an imperial foundation).[1]

This 'Play of Antichrist' has features which are characteristically German and very much of the Hohenstaufen imperial period. It is a unique dramatic illustration of the programmatic phrases which occur in imperial manifestoes addressed to 'all the faithful of God and of the Empire', and which harp on the theme that Christendom depends for its well-being on the one true and lawful terrestrial representative of the King of Kings and Emperor of Heaven. It depends, in fact, on the benevolence and grace of the Emperor Frederick, whose *clementia*, *honor* and *imperium* are a reflection of the divine majesty. The *Ludus* is a celebration of the imperial liturgy.

The stage consists of two elevated rostra facing one another (in this it resembles the old Romanesque German cathedrals with their two poles, eastwork and westwork, allowing space for double choirs). On the west (the good west, strong in saving power) we have the Papacy, Christendom and the Emperor, flanked by the Greek and French kings. On the east (the apocalyptic east) stands the temple of the Lord, one of whose side turrets is the King of Jerusalem, the other being Jewry, the old chosen people. In this tense setting the French and Greek kings assert their claim and the king of Babylon wrestles with Emperor and Christendom, thus revealing themselves as precursors of Antichrist.

---

[1] During the baroque era, and even earlier, important monastic foundations which boasted an imperial salon or imperial apartments would arrange theatrical and musical performances for visiting imperial highnesses, in honour of the harmony prevailing between God in heaven and his representative on earth.

THE HOLY ROMAN EMPIRE

The first message of this liturgical drama is that the Empire has decayed because of the *desidia* or failings of its earlier rulers. Through his chastisement of the impious petty kings the Emperor restores the Empire to its former position. The Emperor is the leader of the Church, of Christendom. The Pope sits as a silent dummy on the thronework of the Emperor: he must yield to him just as 'Brother Leo' once yielded to Charles the Great.

Paganism, resting its case on *ratio* (a first and pointed attack on the rationalistic scholasticism of the French) pleads for a plurality of gods. But there is but one *Fides*, one unique religious-political faith: one God, one Church-and-Christendom, one Pope, one Emperor. At this point in the *Ludus* Church sings the hymn to the Trinity.[1] There is a poem by Walther von der Vogelweide in which the Hohenstaufen family as it walks in liturgical procession to a solemn coronation is made into a symbol of the Trinity.

After the last strains of Christendom have died away, Antichrist begins his work of destruction. This can only happen when the Emperor, having first chastized the French and defeated the King of Babylon and the Infidel, lays down his crown and sceptre on the altar in Jerusalem. Only when the Empire abdicates can Antichrist begin to triumph.

'Hypocrites' (heretics like Arnold of Brescia) prepare his way. They assert that God has no love for a wealthy imperial clergy. Antichrist, the new King of kings, demands and receives divine reverence from the kings of the world.

The author now makes a harsh attack on the French. They, so he alleges, have discovered in advance the *ritus*, the religious-political style proper to Antichrist. By their theological subtlety, their diabolical dialectical pseudo-cleverness, they have helped him to his throne. With no show of resistance the French King submits to Antichrist and accepts his gifts. The only resistance comes from the German people, the *populus furibundus*,[2] which raises its horns against his *religio*. The petty kings who marshal their armies against the German King (so-called because he has now abdicated as Emperor) are repulsed. The German King sings the hymn of the 'Fatherland', which treats of blood and honour and of the cunning and deceit of the enemy. Here the vocabulary strikes a chord remarkably familiar from our recent past.

Eventually, and this is of the utmost interest in the field of popular psychology and metapolitics, Antichrist works miracles (he heals a leper and revives a warrior apparently dead), which win over even the pious and warlike Germans. The German faith in political miracles, a faith in which power and magic, irrational trust in the saving power and charisma of the leader, are closely intermingled, was invoked by Hitler with his talk of 'Providence'.

---

[1] Imperial charters were regularly issued in the name of the Trinity as patron and protector of the Empire. Compare the 'Trinity' columns found in imperial baroque and the anti-cosmos use of 'Trinity' as the code name for the atomic bomb.

[2] '*Teutonicus furor*', the Latin west's expression for the warlike propensities of the Germans, is here made to recoil against the emissaries of Antichrist.

Antichrist kills the resurrected prophets Enoch and Elijah, who have unmasked him, beats down Synagogue and invites the kings to pay him homage and adoration and attend at his solemn coronation. And only now is he annihilated by a thunderbolt from the true Emperor of Heaven. The *Ludus de Antichristo* has two peaks, both of them scenes of coronations: one is the surrender of the imperial crown to Christ the King by the Emperor, the other the attempted self-coronation of Antichrist.

Frederick I attached the highest importance to celebrating the liturgy of the church as the liturgy of the Holy Roman Empire. Imperial diets were made to coincide with festal crownings (which in this form went back to the Ottonians) and with the high festivals of the church. Laetare Sunday, which falls in the middle of Lent and whose office contains a reference to the city of peace (*Jerusalem, id est visio pacis Jeruscholajim*) and the advent of the heavenly kingdom, was a favourite season for these high ceremonies. The coronation of Frederick as German king took place on Laetare Sunday 1152. According to Otto of Freising, Christ was present at this coronation as both king and priest, since another Frederick was consecrated bishop on the same occasion.

For the Hohenstaufen all imperial diets had the character of divine services; they were public acts of the celestial kingdom. It was as representative of the '*cheisir aller kunige*', the Emperor of all kings, that Frederick as king of kings wore the imperial crown. The imperial diet which met at Fulda on Palm Sunday 1157 (the day when the church's liturgy celebrates the entry of the Christ the King into Jerusalem), summoned the faithful of the Empire to do battle against diabolical *superbia*, in other words the rebellious pride of the Milanese. The Diet of Würzburg held at Whitsun 1165 was made the occasion when the German episcopate was required to take the fateful oath binding them to Frederick's anti-pope, Paschal III. At Christmas 1165 the imperial diet was summoned to meet at Aachen and Charles the Great was canonized. The knighting of the emperor's sons took place at Whitsuntide 1184. The *curia Christi*, the 'Diet of Christ' was summoned for 27 March 1188 at Mainz. At this diet the emperor yielded the presidency to Christ and prepared for the 'journey', the campaign which should take him to Christ's '*erbelant*'. From Laetare Sunday 1152 to Laetare Sunday 1188 the circle of an impressive world of ceremony runs full circle, a world in which propaganda, acts ecclesiastical and imperial, proclamation of imperial claims, warfare, judgment and stylized self-presentation are designedly and inseparably linked.

It was the concern of Gregory VII and his reformers, as equally of the scholasticism developing in Paris during the twelfth century, to separate God from the world (first from the 'wicked' world, then from the rational, immanent world, within itself obeying only the laws of nature): the Gregorians were vehement in their approach, radical and aggressive (in the monkish and ascetic fashion); the schoolmen sober, scientific and rational. Sustained by the old confidence (with its roots in primitive magic) that a single great harmony united God, the world, the cosmos, man, animal

75

and object, a confidence which at popular level was still unbroken, Hohenstaufen propaganda set out to demonstrate that God and the world belonged together, as did emperor, imperial clergy and pope. Emperor and Pope reign side by side as equals. That was how it appeared to German ecclesiastics and Italian jurists and even to a non-German contemporary, Vincenz Kadlubek, who was a Pole. The compiler of the *Schwabenspiegel*, the great thirteenth-century law book, still takes the same view. *Regnum* and *sacerdotium* belong inseparably together. Anyone who seeks to separate them or to play one off against the other is an enemy to God and the Empire.

Ecclesia, 'church', is a single Christendom, in which the Emperor bears the secular and the Pope the spiritual sword, and it is always understood that as supreme advocate and protector of the church the Emperor has the right and obligation to see that everything within it is ordered with justice: his writ runs in Rome as in every town and village of the Holy Roman Empire. It must be emphasized that the emperor does not claim 'world dominion' in a modern totalitarian sense. He concedes to the kings and kinglets who were vassals of the Empire (Bohemia, for example) the full exercise of this tutelage over the churches in their own lands.

There was one God, one Church, one Emperor. Frederick accordingly addressed his charters and edicts to 'the faithful of Christ and of the Empire'. By the same title, as representative of the divine majesty, he had the right to reward the 'good', those whose belief in the Empire was orthodox, and to punish the 'wicked'. A rebel against the Empire was equally a rebel against Emperor Christ.

Rainald of Dassel evolved an imperial liturgy of vengeance – vengeance which was not the arbitrary action of an individual but a just judgment reached according to a strictly prescribed ritual. Probably the most impressive and terrifying celebration of this liturgy took place at Milan in March 1162, on the name-day of the emperor, when the surrender of the starving Milanese was turned into a ritual pageant. One has the impression its stagers intended to reproduce in sacral *imitatio* a Last Judgment of the kind seen on the portals of Romanesque cathedrals, where Christ appears as the terrible judge [plate 38]; Pope Alexander III had already fled before this vengeance into France. The liturgy opens with Frederick enthroned as it were at Lodi, the town loyal to the emperor. At a blast from the trumpet (the Last Judgment again) the advancing trains of Milanese citizens, their wives and children, prostrate themselves. On the following day the emperor pronounces sentence. As rebels against God, Emperor and Christendom, all have been disobedient and are deserving of death. The emperor then pronounces the complete destruction of the proud and handsome city of Milan and the deportation of its inhabitants. He appears as *judex rex tremendus*, the awe-inspiring judge-king, celebrating an awesome ritual in which terror and 'joy' are closely intermingled: the 'joy' lies in the emperor's grace, the prospect of his mercy. Imperial *clementia* has taken over the office of the divine. His sentence is the sentence of God: *ex sententia divina . . . ponimus*.

We have seen that the Empire's judgments, charters, punishments, rewards and pardons are acts ascribed to God. This identification, to which at the height of the twelfth century there seemed no limit, stirred men to outspoken protest and opposition. John of Salisbury, the great English humanist who ended his days as bishop of Chartres, asks: 'Who has appointed the Germans judges over the christian peoples?' The Lombard towns, while respecting the Empire, will fight to force the emperor to treat with them in the legal forms of secular practice – a code far removed from that of sacral justice, in which the legal pronouncements of God, the Emperor and the Empire merge into one another.

Heinrich der Glichezare, perhaps one of the Alsatian noblemen who opposed the emperor, characterizes Frederick Barbarossa in his satirical epic *Reynard the Fox* (*c.* 1182) as 'King Wickedness', the deceived deceiver, the passer of false judgments. Berthold of Zähringen, writing significantly enough to Louis VII of France, describes the emperor as 'destroyer of the laws'. Men do not trust the emperor and have no faith in the Holy Roman Empire; the future looks black, and so in retrospect does the past. As the price of peace with the Lombard towns Frederick demanded from them recognition of the Laws of Roncaglia as codified by the jurists of Bologna. Christian of Mainz, the emperor's negotiator, in putting this demand invoked the memory of Henry IV, asserting that the honour of the Empire required a return to the legal position in Italy as it had been in his day. In answer the Lombards' jurists pointed out that no man still living could remember the institutions of 'Emperor Henry' and furthermore that the 'emperor' in question had been no orthodox christian ruler but a tyrant. They went on to say that the honour of the Empire made it imperative to stick to this opinion, since that 'emperor' had laid hands on Pope Paschal, destroyed many churches and blinded bishops. It would be better for men of the present not to recall such atrocities.

The portrait which emerges is of a 'barbarian emperor' in which Neronian features are blended with recollection of 'crimes' committed by various rulers from the more immediate past. It is clear that this image of the alien tyrant was widely current in Italian circles, and also influenced certain anti-German intellectuals further afield.

Frederick Barbarossa knew how heavily his Empire was under attack. In the course of his long conflict with Pope Alexander III he came to see that agreement with this pope was essential if his rule was to be recognized as legitimate. The stage management of the peace celebrations at the impressive ceremonies which took place in Venice on 24 and 25 July 1177 is thus of exceptional significance. This was another great moment in the liturgy of the 'Holy Empire', as becomes clear from accounts written by two eyewitnesses who were in fact adherents of Alexander, Bodo and Romuald.

The first meeting between the emperor and the pope took place on 24 July. Having ritually divested himself of his imperial mantle the emperor prostrated himself as a sinner before the pope and kissed his foot. This ritual 'abasement' was at once followed by a ritual 'elevation' as the pope, with tears in his eyes, raised to his feet again as emperor a Frederick converted from a 'lion' into a 'lamb' and gave him the kiss of peace. This was the signal for the assembled Germans to proclaim to the world

77

with powerful voice (*excelsa voce*, says Romuald, with a *Te Deum* which reached to the stars, says Bodo), that *regnum* and *sacerdotium* were again at one. Then the emperor conducted the pope, Alexander walking at his right hand, into the choir of St Mark's and received his blessing. The supreme advocate of Christendom had resumed in due form his protectorate over the church.

The unity between emperor and pope was demonstrated the following day (the feast of St James)[1] at a festal high mass in St Mark's. The emperor, in his clerical role of *ostiarius*, with rod in hand first expelled the laity from the choir (the place reserved for the priesthood, the consecrated) and then cleared the pope's way to the altar. During the mass, which was sung by the German clergy alone and in its most elaborate form, the emperor remained in the choir with his German ecclesiastics. Most of the leading bishops of the imperial church had been branded as 'schismatics' for fighting on Frederick's side and preaching his cause; some had even been appointed to their office by Frederick and one of his (anti-)popes. Alexander now received them back into the bosom of the Roman Church. After the gospel the pope preached a sermon on peace; after the creed the emperor and princes presented the pope with gifts, recalling the gold and other offerings the Three Kings presented to King Christ. Finally, the pope administered the sacraments to the emperor. Frederick, the erstwhile 'schismatic' 'ex-Augustus' and 'tyrant', had once again become a sacral emperor.

On 1 August, at the Venetian palace of the Patriarch of Aquileia (Aquileia usually took an intermediate position between the Empire and Rome) there was a festal banquet, a 'peace celebration'. On his right hand, the pope had the emperor, on his left Archbishop Romuald of Salerno, who had just concluded a treaty with the emperor on behalf of the king of Sicily – that same Romuald who was such a scrupulous reporter. In his oration Pope Alexander gives full rein to his rhetoric: this is the day the Lord has made, for the emperor, who as a schismatic and an excommunicate was dead, is alive again. Let the whole world rejoice in this joyful peace. *Una fides, unus Dominus, una sit et ecclesia.*

One Faith, One Lord, One Church – the pope interprets it in his own way. He, the pope, has led the emperor back into the fold of unity, the Church of Christ. In his reply (delivered in German with Christian of Mainz interpreting), Frederick confesses that as a sinful man and prone to error, he had allowed himself to be led astray into his seventeen-year-long campaign against Alexander through listening to the promptings of evil men. But the emperor, as a skilled diplomat, could not allow this admission to loom too large. To him it signified no surrender of his claims, nor of his position in law as he understood it. The record of the peace treaty issued for Alexander III on 17 September 1177 reiterates in the *arenga* the old religious-political formula which Frederick had used at the start of his campaign for the renewal of the *Sacrum Imperium* a quarter of a century before: the imperial majesty is directly

---

[1] Santiago de Compostela was one of the great pilgrim centres of western Christendom and had associations with the cult of Charles the Great as a crusading emperor.

charged by the King of Kings to preserve a peaceful order throughout the world. God himself has appointed him, Frederick, to be emperor of the Roman empire and its lord.

German, Provençal, Lombard and Italian poets sang Barbarossa's praises at the height of his power. His uncle, Bishop Otto of Freising, the great historical thinker of the German Middle Ages, saw in Frederick the prince of peace, the saviour of the decaying Empire, the bringer to Christendom of health, security and cosmic peace, *pax et securitas*. Frederick's proud son, Henry VI (1190–97), brought the Empire to a pinnacle of power and exposed it to the conflicts which would lead the Empire to disaster [plate 48]. Henry may possibly have been a *minnesänger*, if he was indeed the author of the songs ascribed to 'emperor Henry'. He had been very well educated and fought hard in pressing the Empire's most far-reaching claims. Through his wife Constance he considered himself the heir to all the Norman possessions and pretensions: he wanted to annex Tunis, Tripoli and the Balkan peninsula to the *imperium*. Since the Normans plied with their swift ships to Constantinople, Henry's political imagination was caught by the idea of capturing this further prize of such beauty and fairy-tale richness. He planned to conquer the Byzantine empire, or at least to bring it into close alliance through a marriage or a treaty. Henry VI looked on this 'eastern land' with the eye of the falcon greedy for its prey. He betrothed his brother Philip, Duke of Tuscany, to Irene, daughter of Emperor Isaac Angelus II, and secured from Isaac's successor Alexius payment of an annual tribute. The Kings of Armenia and Cyprus (Leo and Amalric) became Henry's vassals. German *ministeriales* (ennobled vassals of servile birth) were made princes in Italy and imperial officials introduced into the Papal State. He envisaged making Germany, imperial Italy and Sicily the broad base of a hereditary Hohenstaufen empire, for which he tried to win the support of the German princes. Henry had his son Frederick, born barely three years before his own death, elected his successor.

Throughout his reign Henry VI was surrounded and threatened by conspiracies and revolts, first by Henry the Lion, then by a Norman opposition party in which his own wife Constance was involved and finally by a great north German conspiracy supported by England. That the emperor succeeded in breaking out of this menacing circle was due to an extraordinary stroke of luck. King Richard Coeur de Lion had made an enemy of Duke Leopold of Austria while both princes were with the crusading force before Acre. Richard set out for home by the land route, travelling in disguise for fear of his many enemies. But he was recognized in an inn at Erdberg just outside Vienna. Leopold held him prisoner in the castle of Dürnstein and eventually delivered him over to the emperor, who knew how to make good use of his illustrious prize. He extorted from Richard a promise to pacify his German allies, a huge ransom, and an oath of homage. Richard was in an acutely embarrassing situation. He must have been afraid the emperor would hand him over to his English enemies and may perhaps have heard that the latter were offering the emperor substantial sums to prolong his captivity.

It was Henry VI, backed by Richard and the towns of Pisa and Genoa, who fitted out the Empire's first fleet. Henry's fleet carried his crusading army to Palestine. The emperor took the cross at the Diet of Bari in 1195, and appointed his wife Constance as regent of the Two Sicilies. Disturbances and conspiracies in Sicily prevented him from taking ship himself and he died at Messina on 28 September 1197. In Italy revolts immediately broke out and the Germans were expelled by Constance from Sicily. In Germany there was open war. Henry's brother, Philip of Swabia, assumed the crown, but only after hesitation. The opposition had meanwhile elected as king Otto IV, the favourite nephew of Richard Coeur de Lion and the son of Henry the Lion. The papacy, having already excommunicated the dead Henry VI, now excommunicated Philip of Swabia and in the person of Innocent III intervened in Germany's internal quarrels on the side of the Welfs. Between 1198 and 1208 Germany was ravaged by civil wars and disputes over the succession.

The contenders for the crown were two young men who differed fundamentally from one another in nature and disposition. Philip was refined, delicately bred, courtly, a 'sweet young man' in the description of Walther von der Wogelweide, courtly and noble in the best sense of the word. The sixteen-year-old Otto had grown up during the Welf exile at the Anglo-Norman court; he was greedy, brutal and inwardly insecure. Some people credited him with a plan for turning the brothels into a public institution. Such was the candidate Innocent promoted by all possible means, until to his horror he realized that the Welf meant to extend his power into Italy and as far as Sicily, so that from him the pope must fear only the worst. Meanwhile, starting in about 1204, Philip was gaining ground. But just as the pope was slowly coming round to him as the likely victor, the Hohenstaufen was assassinated in the bishop's palace at Bamberg, by the Bavarian Count Palatine, Otto of Wittelsbach.

Philip was murdered on 21 June 1208. On 4 October 1209 Innocent crowned Otto IV emperor in Rome. At the end of November, having resumed his plan for the conquest of Italy, Otto was summarily excommunicated by Innocent, who then agreed to the election of his ward, Frederick of Sicily [plates 52, 53], as anti-king.

Frederick started his rise to power by going to Rome to become Innocent III's vassal, by renouncing Sicily in favour of his son Henry, and by forming an alliance with Philip Augustus of France. German support for the Hohenstaufen quickly gathered strength.

The fate of the Empire was decided by a single battle, in which the contestants were on one side the French monarchy and on the other the Anglo-Norman monarchy and its Welf allies. At Bouvines (south-east of Lille), on 27 July 1214, Philip Augustus defeated the numerically superior fighting strength of Emperor Otto IV and dispatched to his Hohenstaufen ally the gilded imperial eagle from the captured imperial standard. A German chronicler pinpoints the battle as the moment when the reputation of the Germans among foreigners started to decline.

Otto's luck had deserted him and he died in 1218. Veit Valentin (a German historian of Huguenot descent) has described Frederick II as the 'first European man'; to his contemporaries he was the 'terror of the world', the 'marvellous transformer', and as such feared, respected, much hated and probably totally unloved. Before all this, however, he was an *enfant humilié*, a humiliated child. Georges Bernanos, painfully aware that Christendom was disgracing itself and that Europe was sliding into the Second World War, said the same of the 'terrifying simplifier' who was Adolf Hitler.

Originally Frederick was to have been called Constantine, a programmatic name which would have proclaimed to all the world both his father's Norman aspirations and his imperial Roman belief and general intentions. Frederick Roger, as he actually became, was the son of a mother who hated all Germans (including her husband). Soon orphaned, the alert, highly gifted child was bandied hither and thither, belonging nowhere and surrounded all the time by courtiers and intriguers. He grew up in comfort but in a state of inward isolation and spiritual neglect, in a land where poverty, luxury, slavery and harsh government were openly on view and where Norman, Sicilian, Arab, Greek, Jewish, Latin and Italian elements intermingled.

'The God of the Jews would not have been so loud in his praises of the land he gave his people had he known of my Sicilian kingdom,' Frederick is said to have remarked in Palestine. Mendicant friars whose master was the Pope preached against the Emperor in the squares and streets of Italy; propaganda against this free spirit, this 'antichrist', spread by word of mouth throughout Europe.

The culture of Frederick II's court in Sicily and Apulia belongs to that culture of the 'Three Rings' which has become familiar to the public of more recent centuries through the parable of the rings in Lessing's *Nathan the Wise*. Frederick's remark about the three great impostors, Moses, Christ and Mohammed, was familiar currency in this Mediterranean culture which stretched from Bagdad to Toledo. It expressed in negative form the fact of a fruitful coexistence between Jewish, Islamic and Christian culture. Frederick had his kindred spirits, among his own contemporaries Alfonso the Learned (Alfonso the Wise is a mistranslation), who was descended on his mother's side from the Hohenstaufen and in 1253 was a candidate for the Empire, and in the next generation Dinis of Portugal (1279–1325). Alfonso was a great patron of learning, commissioning translations from Hebrew and Arabic and founding at Seville a Latin-Arabic college for physicians and teachers of both religions; as governor of Murcia he had already established a school for Christian, Jewish and Islamic children. Alfonso is reported to have said that had he been consulted about the creation of the world he would have arranged things very much better, and the saying could equally well have come from Frederick II. Dinis, who founded the university of Lisbon (later transferred to Coimbra), was like Frederick a poet. He carried through an 'improvement programme' reminiscent of Frederick's activities in his centralized Sicilian state: he built canals, encouraged agriculture and foreign trade, set up a controlled economy and instituted a very 'modern' tax system which seems to have borne heavily upon his subjects.

Frederick II had great technical gifts. He experimented with nature, and his enemies alleged that he even conducted fatal experiments on human subjects. His university of Naples, which he founded as a rival to papal Bologna, might be described as the first modern 'state' university. Its aim was to train officials, jurists and physicians for service to the state. The foundation charter makes provision for high financial rewards and dignities for the professors and for grants and cheap lodgings for the students.

Frederick II meant to turn the practice of politics into a high art, on a par with warfare and the chase, an art demanding seriousness of purpose, skill and a respect for one's partners' interests. This highly rational approach is especially evident in his German policy. Frederick was quite ready to recognize that the secular and ecclesiastical princes had risen to a position of territorial sovereignty and confirmed the *Constitutio in favorem principum* which the princes wrested from his son Henry at Worms in 1231. In this document the princes are for the first time described as 'territorial rulers', *domini terrae*. The *Landfrieden* of Mainz, 1235, the first law of the Empire to be published in German, by implication defines the Empire as a league of princes within the framework of a monarchy. Alongside the territories of the princes, which are largely independent as regards internal policies, there exists a species of imperial government, embodied in the judge of the imperial supreme court (*Reichshofrichter*). The emperor's aim was to strengthen the courts, safeguard communications and preserve the Empire's remaining *regalia*. Here we already find present *in nuce* the very things which a handful of imperial officials went on defending right down to the end of the Empire in 1806: an imperial jurisdiction, secure communications and a small number of imperial rights.

The excommunicated Frederick II was rational – to his enemies shockingly so – in the way he fulfilled his crusading vows. He negotiated with the Muslims to obtain a kingdom comprising Jerusalem, Bethlehem, Nazareth and the adjoining littoral. He guaranteed the Muslims freedom of worship in the mosque of Omar at Jerusalem, concluded a ten-year truce with them and crowned himself king in Jerusalem with the Davidic crown. When Napoleon crowned himself in Notre Dame it was with the pope standing by; the patriarch of Jerusalem replied to Frederick's self-coronation with an interdict.

The emperor brought reason to bear in building up his state in Sicily and imperial Italy. He appointed imperial officials, set up a bureaucratic system of taxes and courts, and got together a mercenary army and a fleet. He erected fortifications at strategic points and used the lesser knights to break the opposition of the higher nobility.

This supremely rational reinforcement of his power in Sicily and Italy brought Frederick into collision with the equally rational power drive of the popes, who to secure their rights and claims made use of all the irrational religious and religious-political movements they found at their disposal. The popes saw Frederick as a lethal threat; he ignored or made light of their rights and demands, while his possessions, on the one hand in Sicily and southern Italy and on the other in northern Italy and Tuscany, held the Papal State in a pincer-grip. Hence the crusade against the

41 Arcade of the Hohenstaufen palace at Wimpfen. The imperial palaces or castles were strong-points of the Empire and provided lodging for the emperor on his perpetual travels.

Hohenstaufen

42, 43 Frederick
Barbarossa with his
uncle and chancellor,
Otto of Freising, the
greatest historian of
the German Middle
Ages; on the right
Frederick's empress
Beatrice, who intro-
duced western,
specifically French,
elements into
Hohenstaufen
courtly life and
literature.

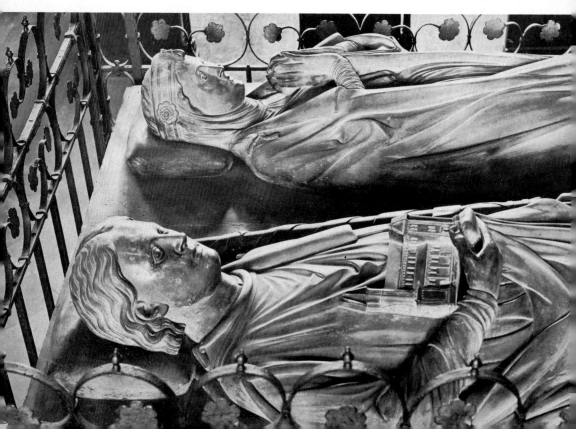

45 (*above*) Charles the Great on the silver reliquary at Aachen. Frederick Barbarossa had him canonized by his antipope as patron of the Hohenstaufen empire.

46 (*right*) Charles the Great receives from two bishops a letter of Constantine's. 'Charlemagne', seen here in a window at Chartres, was regarded in France down to Napoleon as the pattern and patron of all French claims to European hegemony.

44 (*left*) Henry the Lion and his wife Matilda. Henry's powerful Welf 'empire' presented Frederick Barbarossa with a dangerous rival he was forced to destroy.

47 This head of *Justitia Imperialis* from Capua with its antique beauty symbolizes the ideal of imperial justice proclaimed by Frederick II, 'the sun of righteousness'.
48 (*opposite*) Henry VI at the siege of Naples. From the *Emperor's Book* of Pietro da Eboli: the southern kingdom of the Hohenstaufen, based on Sicily and Naples, fought for its life with words and weapons against powerful native opposition and the papacy.

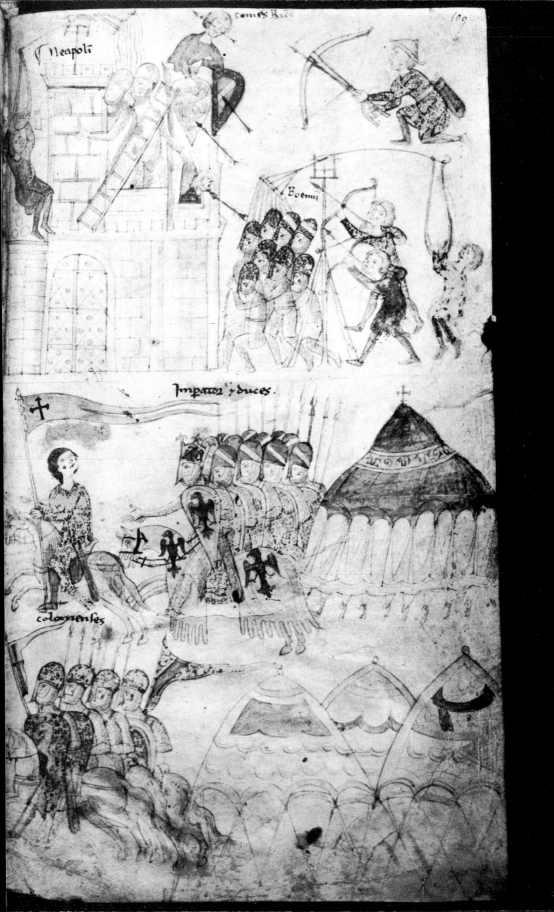

49 Frederick Barbarossa as crusader. Taking part in the crusade was the supreme justification of any Christian prince's title to rule.

50 An episode from the Fourth Crusade, which led to the capture of Constantinople by the Latins, a peak moment in the thousand-year-long conflict between East and West Rome.

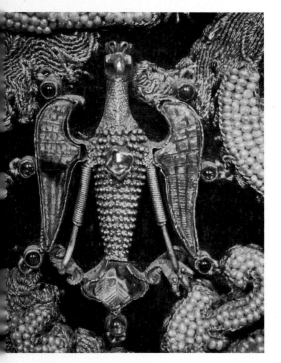

51 The imperial eagle of the Hohenstaufen set on a baroque vestment from the dynasty's burial vault at Palermo. The eagle was an important symbol in the ideology of the Empire down to the nineteenth century.

52 Frederick II as seen in his book on the art of falconry. This emperor is at once feudal lord and the forerunner of 'Enlightened' despots, down to the eighteenth century.

53 Frederick II with his wife and two sons: the sculptor, Magister Nicolaus, has shown great artistry in composing the emperor's tragic domestic relations.

54 (*left*) Archbishop of Mainz (Siegfried III von Eppstein) crowning two kings during the period when the Holy Roman Empire was disintegrating.

55 (*top right*) Seal of Bishop Conrad von Scharfenberg. As chancellor in turn to Otto and Frederick II, he contributed substantially to later Hohenstaufen government.

56 (*bottom right*) Seal of Richard of Cornwall as Roman Emperor. Anglo-French rivalroften took the form of rivalry for influence in the Holy Roman Empire.

57 Anti-imperial ecclesiastical princes making their way to the Council of Lyons aboard aGenoese ship are captured by pro-imperial Pisans, 1241. The struggle for the Holy RomanEmpire is still a struggle for the Church.

'antichrist' Frederick preached with such fervour by preachers and publicists, by mendicant friars and by the Italian and non-German partisans of the curia.

Bernard of Clairvaux had exalted the Pope as the representative of Christ, the Lord's anointed, the God of Pharaoh (*vicarius Christi, christus Domini, Deus Pharaonis*). Innocent III adopted the same ominously exalted position, which Alvarus Pelagius would later state explicitly: as the 'God of Pharaoh' the Pope was the God of the Emperor, *Papa est Deus imperatoris*. Frederick II's answer to the pope's claim to be God's unique representative was an imperial messianism. He proclaimed his message from the chancel of the cathedral at Pisa (a city loyal to the emperor and afterwards an asylum for the anti-papal and radical disciples of Joachim of Flora): God has appointed the imperial office for the maintenance of peace, security and justice upon earth; the Empire is a divine institution; its rights, its courts, its edicts are all sacred; the Emperor is appointed directly by God.

Imperial officials and propagandists preached an ideology of the Empire which threw into even sharper prominence themes and formulations already advanced by the imperial chancery under Rainald of Dassel. Many of their pronouncements and proclamations strike a sinisterly hybrid note, they are in fact 'Byzantine', but in the adverse sense. One has the impression of a religious-political ideology being hammered out with cold deliberation. Briefly, everything to do with the Emperor – his court, his tribunals, his legislation, his ceremonial occasions – is to be held sacred and inviolable.

A deliberate attempt is made to fuse the sacral character of the ancient Roman *imperium*, the numinous aspect of ancient Roman politics and statecraft, with a christian Caesarism. The emperor is Christ's heir and successor. Jesi, Frederick's birthplace, is aligned with Nazareth, analogies are drawn between the emperor's lifelong endeavours as prince of peace and the life of Jesus. We are invited to compare the 'sufferings' of the emperor (in a Herculean task) with the passion of Jesus Christ.

This monstrous presumption becomes more comprehensible when some of the reasons for it are borne in mind. There was first the immoderacy of papal claims, to which (as it appeared to Frederick and his collaborators) 'justice' could only be done by a corresponding immoderacy on the imperial side. Men well beyond the emperor's Italian circle of supporters felt the urgency of finding some counterweight to a papalism of this stamp. Dante may have condemned Frederick II to Hell, but he adopted large chunks of his imperial ideology. If the emperor was now 'invested' with the old and more recent sacral names, dignities and emblems of power (as in Visigothic Spain at the time when kings first received ecclesiastical unction and coronation), it was to protect him against the never-ending plotting and attacks on his life. Anathematized and excommunicated several times over, Frederick was never out of danger.

Frederick was surrounded by disloyalty, treachery, plots and conspiracies. His son, Henry, joined the Lombards in their revolt of 1234 and died his father's prisoner in 1242. Frederick's chancellor, Peter of Vinea, committed suicide. In 1245, at the

Council of Lyons, the emperor was once again solemnly condemned, expelled from the church as a heretic and deposed as emperor. In Germany, Frederick and his son Conrad were faced with two successive anti-kings – Henry Raspe and William of Holland. In Italy there were constant revolts against the harsh rule of Frederick's *podestàs* to be suppressed. In 1249 the Bolognese finally succeeded in capturing Frederick's illegitimate son Enzio, the King of Sardinia, who as General Legate was head of the Italian government, and he remained their prisoner until his death in 1271. The restless, peripatetic, vulnerable emperor died on 13 December 1250 at Fiorentino in Apulia.

As emperor, Frederick II had chosen Justinian for his sacral prototype. Frederick meant men to revere his state as an 'imperial church' (*imperialis ecclesia*), in which he himself was the high priest of justice and his functionaries and officials its lesser clergy. The Hohenstaufen line was the *stirps caesarea*, the imperial line, in which the divine emperors from '*pius Aeneas*' downward lived again.

Innocent III and his successors wanted the dominion they exercised over the church and the world in their capacity as Christ's Vicars (the programme-title coined by Bernard of Clairvaux) to be understood and acknowledged in a double sense as a vicariate of Christ as High Priest and of Christ as King.

During the Carolingian period men thought of the king predominantly as the representative of God (*vicarius Dei*), in the Ottonian and early Salian period as the *vicarius Christi*; in the twelfth and thirteenth centuries the title *vicarius Dei* received a fresh lease of life and a new basis. The popes destroyed the old unity of the church as the Christendom in which pope and emperor ruled jointly and side by side. 'The *sacerdotium* had destroyed the old form of the *ecclesia universalis* as its province; it now began to erect on the basis of the purely functional existence still ascribed to it an ecclesiastical monarchy, a *regnum ecclesiasticum*' (Friedrich Kempf, s.j.).

The dynasty of the counts of Segni was known in later days simply as the 'counts', the Conti. Count Lothar Segni (his forename takes us back to the old Carolingian kingdom of Lotharingia) studied in Paris and Bologna, developed into a canon lawyer and a theologian and in 1190 was made a cardinal. As Pope Innocent III (1198–1216) at the peak of his career he could fancy himself the master of two empires: a western Latin empire and the eastern empire set up by the crusaders after their atrocious sack of Constantinople during the Fourth Crusade (1202–4). This, though eastern, was also a Latin empire and the pope was its sponsor.

As a pope Innocent III is a significant figure, but unlike Gregory VII he was not truly creative as an individual. This conclusion is confirmed by Friedrich Kempf, the historian of the Pontificia Universitas Gregoriana who has dedicated a lifetime's devoted research to Innocent's achievement.

At his accession Innocent III found the curia already in possession of well-defined political objectives: to maintain papal suzerainty over southern Italy; to extend the Papal State and papal possessions in central Italy in conformity with the privileges granted by past emperors and the Matildine donation; and to consolidate and develop the authority of the pope as sovereign within the Papal State. Innocent's own pro-gramme during the early years of his pontificate was to restore papal government in Rome and the Papal State, to recover his suzerainty over the kingdom of Sicily and to win back the territories in central Italy: he aimed, that is, at a partial concentration of Italian powers under the leadership of the pope.

The Hohenstaufen defined their attempt to restore imperial authority in central Italy as '*recuperatio*'. Innocent III, as leader in Italy of the struggle against the German 'barbarians', now proceeded to 'recover' the lands that they had occupied. He also aspired to become suzerain of the kings of Europe. Fealty was forthcoming from Portugal, King Peter II of Aragon in 1204 entrusted the pope with the wardship of his successor, who was a minor, and Poland, Hungary, Galicia and Lodomeria, Serbia, Croatia and Bulgaria all submitted themselves in varying forms to the authority of the pope. Otto IV and Frederick II started by calling themselves 'Emperor by grace of God and the Pope'. Innocent saw himself as the new priest-king Melchizedek and the leader of Christendom at large. To John of England he may even have sent a ring as symbol of investiture (Adrian IV had sent an emerald ring to Henry II when he was planning the conquest of Ireland in 1155). While Philip of Swabia and Otto IV contended for the German crown, the pope was developing the ideology which claimed the kings of the nations as vassals of the pope and the Empire as his to dispose of.

One important strand in Innocent's thinking was the idea that collective guilt was incurred by a clan or group, an idea with which we of the twentieth century are dismally familiar. Philip was unacceptable to him because of his descent from the Hohenstaufen, a clan demonstrably hostile to the church. To prove it Innocent adduced a long series of outrages perpetrated by Henry V, Frederick I and Henry VI.

The medieval popes' deployment of history for political ends was among their strongest weapons. Popes indeed made history by manufacturing it and any precedent needed as a legal title was invented. This is paralleled at a lower level by the numerous forgeries emanating in the twelfth century from religious houses. When it came to inventing a past consistent with present and future claims, the popes needed to look no further back than Gregory VII. Gregory had deduced the Pope's right to levy the tax of Peter's Pence in France from a charter attributed to Charles the Great which relates to the foundation of a hospice for Frankish pilgrims in Rome. Gregory could maintain that Saxony belonged to the Holy See because two Saxon churches were dedicated to the Prince of the Apostles in Charlemagne's day. Through supporting his opponent, Innocent III was determined to deliver Philip's Hohenstaufen kingdom a devastating blow. And as Kempf points out, 'the pope mentions among the positive qualities recommending Otto IV his descent from the Welf and royal English lines'.

More significant still is Innocent's reference, seven times in three years (1199, 1200, 1202–3), to the *translatio* doctrine propounded in the sixties of the twelfth century by partisans of Alexander III (who may have invented it himself while he was still

Roland Bandinelli). Alexander used the threat of 'translating' the Empire back to the Greeks to bring pressure to bear on Frederick I. Innocent III asserted that the Empire and the disputed succession were matters for the Pope, since in the time of Leo III the papacy had transferred the imperial office from the east to the west. In his famous letter to Duke Berthold of Zähringen dated March 1202 (which the pope himself had included in the first collection of his decretals under the heading *Venerabilem*), he declares that the church transferred the imperial office from the Greeks to the Germans in the person of Charles the Great. The Holy See was the less disposed to encroach upon the electoral right of the princes because in the last resort it derived from the Holy See itself.

Two French canonist sources refer to the pope as *verus imperator* and in one place to the emperor as *vicarius papae*. The Pope is the true Emperor, the Emperor the Pope's vicar. How dizzying and lonely was the eminence on which Innocent saw himself enthroned we can gather from a sermon he preached to the Romans on one anniversary of his consecration: 'Indeed, as you see for yourselves, this menial set over the family is in truth the vicar of Jesus Christ, the successor of Peter, the anointed of the Lord, the God of Pharaoh: he stands between God and man, below God and above man, smaller than God, greater than man, judge over all and judged of none, for as the Apostle says, "He who judges me, the same is the Lord"' (I Cor. 4. 4). The human world was committed to St Peter in its entirety and the power to rule it devolves on the Pope.

In the *Decretale per Venerabilem* Innocent III defends his action in legitimizing children born to Philip Augustus of France out of wedlock by pointing out that the French king recognized no secular superior; he could therefore submit to the jurisdiction of the Holy See without infringing the rights of a third party. Canon lawyers who rejected an imperial world dominion seized on this passage as evidence for their case. It also became the prop and stay of French kings and other monarchs outside the Empire who were eager to assert their independence: 'within his own realm the king is emperor (and pope!).'

Innocent III claimed the right to make kings. Derived from the Roman imperial constitution, this right was at first exercised by emperor and pope jointly; after the Investiture Contest we find emperor and pope acting separately. To Innocent III it no longer signified establishing a title to rule but was merely a matter of conferring a higher rank – and in this honorific sense he conceded the right to the emperor he had himself raised, confirmed and consecrated.

The Pope's much debated and much quoted *plenitudo potestatis*, his 'claim to world dominion', is explicable only when it is realized that as bishop of Rome the Pope was never sure of 'his' own city. Always at the back of his mind was the fear of becoming an imperial bishop, the subordinate of an emperor who kept his court in Aachen, Rome or Palermo. The popes and their curial politicians were panic-struck at the prospect of a hereditary Hohenstaufen empire with bases in Sicily and Tuscany which might ally with the republican-minded antipapal Romans and make the pope a prisoner. It was this panic which drove them to plot the extermination of the entire Hohenstaufen clan.

The papal design to exterminate – the only possible word – the sons and heirs of the excommunicated heretic Frederick II was to be accomplished through the French. The French pope Urban IV (1261–4) brought in Charles of Anjou, brother of King Louis IX of France, to campaign against King Manfred of Sicily, half-brother of King Conrad IV who had died in 1254. Manfred fell in the battle of Benevento and his three sons languished for thirty to forty years in strict Angevin confinement. King Conrad's son, the young Conradin, marched from Swabia on Rome, was elected Senator by the Romans, fell captive to Charles of Anjou and on 29 October 1268, together with his friend Frederick of Austria, was beheaded at Naples.

The square in Naples, before whose gloomy and oppressive buildings the last of the Hohenstaufen met his death by execution, stands today as it did then. On this spot the revolutionary papacy, whose crusades to desacralize the Empire had started under Gregory VII, set a precedent which prepared the way for the desacralization of all Europe's sacral monarchies. The executions of the English and French kings (in the English and French revolutions) stand in its vicariate, for execution is in a class on its own, quite different from murder or even regicide. Thus while the Pope as *vicarius Christi* had 'annilated' the Emperor as *vicarius Dei* and *vicarius Christi*, from this vicariate there sprang yet another.

The papacy had triumphed over the Empire of the Hohenstaufen and played its part in rooting out the 'infamous clan'. It reigned in a 'christian Europe' riddled from Italy to Provence, from France to the Rhine, and soon also in Bohemia, by sectarian and other enemies of the Roman Church. Even Rome was rarely safe for the Pope to live in for any length of time. The spiritual resources of the papacy had been over-strained, exhausted, and diverted into propaganda and crusades against the Pope's political enemies.

Between 1250 and 1273 the Holy Roman Empire was engulfed in the Interregnum, 'the terrible time without an emperor'. Candidates were proposed but failed to win acceptance: William of Holland (elected at one time as anti-king to Conrad IV), Richard of Cornwall [plate 56], brother of Henry III of England, King Alfonso the Learned. Italy too was plunged into feuds, with Ghibellines and Guelfs at loggerheads in town and country, killing and outlawing one another and labelling themselves as imperial or papal supporters as occasion demanded [plate 57].

The crisis of the Empire and the crisis of the Church were terrifying to live through. In twelfth-century Germany and Italy the painful experience stimulated thinking men to attempt a philosophy and theology of world history. These writers, as they reflect on progress and decay, consciously or unconsciously hold up for us a mirror to the history of their epoch, the epoch which saw the rise and decline of the Empire and the decline and rise of the Church.

Underground eddies of this historical thinking reached Friedrich Hegel as he in turn reflected on world history in the last days of the Holy Roman Empire, and they re-emerge (some of them clearly identifiable) in his philosophy. In the Middle Ages the movement comes to a peak in the thought of two contemporaries, Meister Eckhart (*c.* 1260–1327) and Dante (1265–1321). At the end of the twelfth century it is concentrated in Joachim of Flora, who postulated the coming 'reign' of the third Empire of the Holy Spirit, in which the old Holy Roman Empire and the old Papal Church would be overcome.

The emergence of figures such as Rupert of Deutz, Hugh of St Victor, Anselm of Havelberg, Otto of Freising, Hildegard of Bingen, Ekbert of Schönau, Gerhoh of Reichersberg and finally of Joachim of Flora is a phenomenon unparalleled until we reach the pullulating abundance of the last days of the Empire, the epoch of Goethe, Schelling, Hegel and Hölderlin.

Twelfth-century German scholars and theologians who reflected on the meaning of world history dwelt on a number of themes. They expounded world history as the unfolding of the Trinity (Rupert of Deutz is an early example). They wrestled with the concept of progress: was progress a perpetual renaissance, a *renovatio imperii*, a perpetual harking back to the same origins and heroic beginnings, or is there a development from these origins, a development which surpasses what is past and makes innovation something greater than the merely evil, sinful and heretical practice which papal encyclicals (down to the nineteenth century and after) condemn it as being? Was there an authentic *novus ordo*, or were there only to be new orders, of the kind currently proliferating in a church being rejuvenated by monks?

A deep pessimism, such as still retains a hold over German piety and spirituality, filled twelfth-century German theologians as they contemplated the destinies of Empire and Church. In the eighth, 'apocalyptical', book of his *Historia de duabus civitatibus* (the two cities are those of Christ and Antichrist), Otto of Freising observes that the texts he has applied to the 'falling away' of the *regnum* are interpreted by others as applicable, and with the same force, to the Roman see. Otto, a bishop of the Empire, poses himself the *gravis questio de regni ac sacerdotii justitia dissensio*, the grave question as to where justice lay in the great conflict between the Emperor and the Church. How is it, he asks, that the decline of the Empire is matched so closely by the rise of the Church?

Otto's world chronicle ends on a profoundly pessimistic note. But he lived to see the early ascendancy of his nephew, Frederick I, and in his *Gesta Frederici* hails him as the king and future emperor of peace, the born conciliator, the bringer of cosmic peace. 'Otto of Freising died during the illusory splendour of this new good fortune, in the first years of Barbarossa's reign. Had he lived only a few more years, say until he was fifty, he must have realized that the optimism . . . he voiced in his early enthusiasm for his nephew's gifts and energy was mistaken' (Werner Kaegi).

This sudden change of mood is uncannily German: deep pessimism (anyone who reads Otto of Freising attentively will note its undertones on every page), is followed by an effort to see the light – and the urge to hail a rising political personality as the saving leader. We meet this phenomenon in the Bismarck era and – at an ever lower level – in the years around 1933. Otto of Freising was a Cistercian, a bishop of the Empire and the son of a Babenberg duke in '*österreich*'.[1] His hopes and fears over the festering conflict between king, emperor and papal church, a conflict already genera-tions old, were genuine. They stemmed from the disturbance felt by a man who knew he had an obligation to both partners and that they were becoming each other's mortal enemies.

Anselm of Havelberg had personal experience of the Empire, of Rome, East Rome, the pagan lands in the east (only now being colonized by the Premonstratensians) and of the old south, a land of brimming culture. He went as Emperor Lothar's ambassador to Byzantium in 1135 and there disputed with Nicetas over the theologi-cal differences between the two churches. The spiritual richness and self-assurance he encountered in the east stirred Anselm to his depths. The west, however, with its many new orders and spiritual communities, each breaking fresh ground and each with its own new rules and habits, he found disquieting. This led him to question the reason for plurality in the church and in society, a matter which disturbed him as it disturbs German Catholics today: could God, who was Himself perfect unity and immutability, permit such diversity and contrariety in the world?

Anselm observed that the new orders were locked in violent conflict with one another, and not merely over verbal differences: his own Premonstratensians with the Cistercians, the old Benedictine monasticism with the Cluniacs, secular clergy with regular. His many travels, and countless conversations in Rome, Ravenna, East Rome and semi-pagan Havelberg (where he became bishop), convinced Anselm that change, progress, was the will of God.

Anselm collected his tentative and experimental thoughts in three books with the significant title *Dialogues*, in which he challenges the traditional, static and at bottom a-historical conviction held by most of his clerical contemporaries: namely, that *deus immutabilis*, God the immutable, rejects all innovations and change as wicked and unsound, a falling away from perfect unity. Anselm had come to see world history as a grandly-conceived educative work effected by the triune God, who teaches mankind through the truth which is Christ and through the Holy Spirit, 'the author and teacher of truth'. Anselm asserts emphatically and with great boldness that the church of the present is capable of grasping more than in the time of the Apostles. Such 'modernistic heresies' were repugnant to curial theologians even in the nine-teenth century. But Anselm argues that under the guidance of the Holy Ghost, Christendom experiences an unfolding of the faith which is present in the Gospel largely by implication. The councils of the church effected genuine advances into the interior, an actual evolution in dogma. The Holy Ghost educates mankind through diversity and differences, as in the case of the new orders, and through change which for the first time is here regarded as something positive. Through the Holy Ghost all christian peoples take part in this progress. The new is necessary precisely in order to sustain and develop what is valuable in the old. In new orders the church renews

[1] '*Österreich*' is the only German word to appear in Dante's *Divine Comedy*.

its youth like the eagle. It should surprise no one that the church looks and is different in the three ages of the world; this is her glory, that she is adorned with the variety of *diversarum religionum et actionum*.

From Anselm it would be natural to pass straight to Joachim of Flora. Joachim had connections with the Hohenstaufen court in Sicily and with the Hohenstaufen government in his native Greek southern Italy. Rupert of Deutz spent several years at Monte Cassino, Anselm of Havelberg died archbishop of Ravenna. Many complex strands, German-Italian, German-Roman, and Italian-Greek, come together in Joachim of Flora, abbot of Corazzo, and his work sheds a unique light on Otto of Freising's *gravis questio*, the conflict between Emperor and Pope. But before turning to Joachim we shall see how this conflict was reflected in the intellectual and literary activity of the German laity.

At first sight, the Holy Roman Empire seems to figure scarcely at all in their poetry, which makes it very different from the literature used directly or indirectly as propaganda by the Emperor and his publicists (for example, *Ligurinus*, the Tegernsee play of Antichrist, and some of the lays of minstrels and *minnesänger*). High German poetry draws its material from the west, from the British Isles and the Anglo-Norman kingdom, from Brittany, Provence and the Ile de France, from poetry derived from Celtic traditions and those of the Near East. This literature gives no prominence to the Emperor, who is passed over in silence or brushed aside, as in western annals and chronicles. King Arthur and the knights of his round table, Parsifal and the Grail, reflect the splendour, the glory and 'aspiration' of a hot-blooded and ambitious aristocracy which was not seldom in conflict with Rome, was frequently at odds with kings, and desired no truck with any emperor. The literary and cultural connections which linked the Welfs with England and the Hohenstaufen with the French made it all the easier for this material to penetrate into *minnesang*, courtly epic and verse romance.

The choice of this obviously 'western' material is itself of metapolitical significance. It was not only its richness and diversity that attracted the Germans. At first glance it would seem that men thus withdrawn into the inwardness of heart, spirit and eros wanted nothing to do with 'filthy politics'. When we look closer, however, we can see in this poetry an intense inner discontent with Empire and Church.

A poet of this school considered himself, and felt himself to be, an 'emperor'. His lady (Provençal *dompna*, Italian 'madonna') was his empress. For him 'the *regnum*' is love (*minne*), the relationship between the 'woman' and the 'man'. They administer the high sacrament of love to one another and need no church or 'parson'. This inner kingdom unmasks the sacraments, the divine tribunals and judgments, the 'pious slogans' of the old powers – Church and Empire – as delusions. The point is forcibly made by Gottfried of Strassburg in his *Tristan* (written probably at the court of the bishop of Strassburg during the critical years between 1205 and 1220): Mark, the canonically anointed and consecrated king, is sinful, foolish, hypocritical and depraved because he will not acknowledge the superior existential right of *minne*, the love relationship between his wife Isolde and Tristan. The religious-political fealty of the Holy Roman Empire bound the Emperor and his faithful, emperor and 'man'. Fealty likewise bound temporal and spiritual princes and 'all those who believe in Christ' to the Lord Pope in Rome. The new fealty of *Minne* actually nourishes Tristan and Isolde. This is true fealty, and exists uniquely and solely in their existential relationship with one another.

The two lovers are 'anointed by love'. They are themselves the new Christ, the anointed king and priest! They administer the sacrament of love to one another in their lovers' cave, which Gottfried makes appear heir to the Hohenstaufen *palatium* (its vault has a crown at its tip), a secular Gothic cathedral of light (heir to the cathedrals of the French monarchy), a 'Cistercian' castle of the Grail. To this inner kingdom, where the two lovers defy the old Empire, the old Church and the old courtly society, and tenderly dispense to each other the true communion, Mark, the 'sorrowing king', has no access.

And what of that other Christ, the Overlord of the Lord's anointed, and of anointed bishops (Otto of Freising celebrated king *and* bishop as *christus domini*)? Christ falls into place 'like a wind-blown sleeve' (an echo of contemporary fashion) and is pliant to the demands of love. In his divine judgment Christ finds for the two lovers, for their 'deception'. Attention has often been drawn to the 'nihilistic' tendencies in this greatest of all German love poems. This 'nihilism', in my view, should be interpreted as a sweeping aside of the Holy Empire and the old Church on the grounds of their 'nothingness', their pure nullity. We shall see that in a different yet covertly related sense German mysticism also brushes aside all the old sacral and political institutions as empty, inessential, unreal: they have no significance in the relationship between the loving heart and the 'non-habitual', formless, shapeless Godhead. Achieving 'tranquillity', becoming free from the drives, passions, cares and demands of the 'world' also means to become inwardly free from the pressure and oppressiveness of the old powers, which in their decadence are all the more terrifying.

Gottfried of Strassburg, the 'enlightened clerk', consciously presents the relationship between Tristan and Isolde as a model for the existential relationship between 'man' and 'woman'. He proclaims the sacramental significance of their life of love as an example all 'noble hearts' should follow.

> Their death, their life are our bread.
> Thus lives their life, thus lives their death.
> Thus they live still and yet are dead,
> And their death is the bread of the living.
>
> (Translated A.T. Hatto)

The gospel of the life, love, passion and death of the two great lovers, Tristan and Isolde is – when conned and accepted – communion for all lovers, for all 'noble hearts' in need of consolation and strengthening against attack from the wicked world. Here the wicked world is the old social order, the old Empire of anointed (until death) and impotent but dangerous kings and priests.

From Frederick I onward, the Hohenstaufen did all they could by military and political means to stave off the attack on their empire launched by popes and monks, by 'reguli' of east and west, miserable kinglets who were deficient in saving power. Now 'man' and 'woman' as two individuals face the challenge to their own empire, an empire which subsists 'merely' in their love-relationship; the challenge comes from powers they adjudicate powerless, the old Holy Empire and the old Holy Church.

Empire and papal church were themselves challenged in the teaching of Joachim of Flora. The work of this monk has been a subject of controversy from the twelfth century to the present day. Argument over its interpretation and true posterity, and the more recent debate over the authenticity of the writings attributed to Joachim, are an indication of the extent to which this personally humble man, who considered himself a very loyal son of the church (and was certified as such by Pope Honorius III) cast doubt upon, indeed 'removed' the old order: not through any will to do so, but at a much deeper, more subterranean level, through the substance of his thought. Joachim probably died in 1202. In the contest between Frederick Barbarossa and Alexander III he is likely to have sided with the pope. His challenge to the Empire appears a relatively simple matter. Italians of the nineteenth and twentieth centuries like to look on him as a forerunner of the Risorgimento. Joachim's *Italia* and *latinitas* correspond in fact to the regions of Italy (in the twelfth century there was no 'Italy' as such) and to a Latin-European Christendom which in Joachim's own southern Italy had to come to terms with the Greek cultural world. Joachim was not an enemy of the emperor on principle. Possibly he himself, and certainly some of his later adherents, had connections with the Hohenstaufen court and with Ghibelline circles. Charles the Great and the Ottonian emperors, whom he still regarded as Frankish, deserved respect. But with the 'German' emperors – Henry III, but especially Henry IV and Henry V – the emperors had started to play the role of antichrist. They behaved like Babylonians, persecuting the Roman Church and the true Christendom. Henry V was like Nebuchadnezzar, who defeated the Pharaoh Necho and led the Jews into the Babylonian captivity. In May 1184 Joachim spoke out briefly and to the point in the presence of Pope Lucius III, condemning Barbarossa's harsh treatment of the church. Frederick, he said, was a 'Prince of the Chaldees' and had made the leaders of the church his subjects.

Joachim was useful to monastic and other opponents of the regimes of Henry VI and of Frederick II and his sons and viceroys in Italy, who could invoke him in their defence of the 'poor peoples of Italy' against the overbearing and rapacious ambitions of the 'German barbarians'. But the other Joachim is the more significant. At the Lateran Council of 1215, which saw Innocent III at the height of his powers, a writing of Joachim's was condemned as heretical. As time went on, condemnations of writings attributed to Joachim and his spiritual successors accumulated, yet he soon became a great power in the church's underground. Thomas of Aquinas, who was blind to history since it had no place in his scheme of thinking, magisterially dismissed Joachim as 'unscholarly', and later schoolmen followed his lead. Dante sees Joachim shining in the circle of the sun in Paradise as a light of christian wisdom and one endowed with the truly prophetic spirit.

Joachim had no wish to revolutionize the Roman papal church. He was merely convinced that its days were numbered. Its empire, dominion, rites and rituals were being undermined, transformed, actively 'removed' by the 'New Gospel' into the empire of the Holy Ghost, under which men would become no longer literal believers but believers in the spirit. Through the Holy Ghost all things are made new. During the period of crisis immediately preceding the new age proper, a new order should form a nucleus of those already captured by its spirit. That time of crisis, Joachim declares, is now upon us: the time when believers in the spirit are persecuted, not least by the old believers, who persecute bearers of the spirit in every age.

The imperial diplomas, charters and manifestoes issued by the Hohenstaufen are addressed to 'all men', to all believers in Christ. The popes address themselves likewise. In his 'testamentary' letter of 1200 Joachim addresses himself, 'as in an encyclical', to 'all believers in Christ whom this letter may reach'. In it Joachim voices the great lament of all spiritually creative natures ('Let not the light of the spirit be extinguished'). 'Up to this present there are bound to be those who seek to extinguish the spirit and annihilate prophecy.'

This simple monk, who on his own interpretation was completely loyal to the church, was a prophet and saw himself as such: his words, his sermons, his pamphlets – 'on doves' feet', to use Nietzsche's expression – spread subversive ideas about the ending of the papal church and the beginning of the 'new age' at the very time when the popes, seconded by their allies, were annihilating the Hohenstaufen monarchy. These ideas made their way into monasteries and convents in Italy, southern France and Catalonia, and took hold among a dynamic element in the Franciscan order. At the Angevin court in Naples, in the Spain of Columbus – who cited Joachim – in monastic, aristocratic and bourgeois circles, Joachimite spirituality found an acceptance and radical development which Frederick I and Frederick II, not to mention the popes who took over their heresy laws, would have found almost unimaginable.

6

HABSBURG, LUXEMBURG, WITTLESBACH: THE EMPIRE FROM 1273 TO 1438

WHERE was the Empire? What was its centre? Changing dynasties and peripatetic emperors meant that the pole of the Empire was continually shifting. For Charles the Great, Aachen was the Empire's focal point. Under the Ottonian, Salian and Hohenstaufen emperors (apart from Frederick II, who had Palermo and Apulia in which to reside) the Empire had no centre, though individual emperors had their favourite places: Magdeburg in the case of Otto the Great, Rome and Aachen for Otto III, Bamberg for Henry II, Speyer, Goslar or Limburg for the later Salians. When Henry VI wanted to transport the imperial treasure and his Norman inheritance from Palermo to Germany for imperial celebrations at Trifels he needed a mule train of nearly two hundred. So far as the Italians were concerned, the Empire was migrating eastward. The only visible sign of the Empire's continuity was its insignia, the embodiment of the *rich*.[1] As men understood it, this was not only legally but quite literally so. To quote only one example, when Albert of Habsburg refused to hand over the insignia to Adolf of Nassau after the death of Rudolf he is said to have 'held on to the Empire'.

The Empire moved further east still, towards Prague and Vienna. With the extinction of the Hohenstaufen dynasty the partisans of the Přemyslid king of Bohemia, Ottokar II (1253–98) boasted that he was now 'the Hohenstaufen'. Ottokar, the 'iron and golden king', who was cupbearer of the Empire, was in fact a grandson of Philip of Swabia. Through his marriage to the widow of the last of the Babenbergs (killed fighting the Hungarians) Ottokar became Duke of Austria. He is the subject of a drama by Franz Grillparzer, the poet of the Habsburg Empire, entitled *König Ottokars Glück und Ende*, 'The fortune and death of King Ottokar'. King Ottokar was indeed fortunate: to his Bohemian possessions he added the Babenberg inheritance, Styria, Carinthia, Carniola, Istria, Aquileia and Pordenone. His power extended from the Adriatic to the Baltic. He was the founder of Königsberg in Prussia, giving it the name it kept until after the Second World War, when it was renamed Kaliningrad. In 1255 and again in 1267 Ottokar joined the Teutonic Order in its crusade against the Prussian pagans.

[1] 'rich' is the medieval form of 'Reich'.

But there came an end to this good fortune. At the election held at Frankfurt in 1273 Rudolf of Habsburg (that 'impoverished petty count', as Ottokar and his other enemies termed him) was elected king in preference to Ottokar, and on 24 October of the same year was crowned at Aachen [plate 58]. Rudolf immediately set about reclaiming for the Empire the rights and territories it had lost during the 'terrible time without an emperor'. King Ottokar, who stood to suffer most (and who had not taken part in the election, the Duke of Bavaria acting in his place), at first resisted. Later he gave way and agreed to a double marriage between his and Rudolf's children. Finally he allowed matters to come to a head in open conflict.

At the battle of the Marchfeld (not far from Vienna) fought on 26 August 1278 a dynasty was born: the House of Austria. King Ottokar's army included Poles, Silesians and Czechs, together with Germans from Brandenburg, Meissen, Thuringia, and Bavaria. The imperial force assembled by Rudolf (to fight against the king of Bohemia, an outlaw from the Empire) contained not only knights from Austria and Styria but also Rudolf's Swiss, Hungarian and Kumanian allies, who contributed substantially to the victory.

Ottokar's army entered the fray shouting 'Praha, Praha!' The troops fielded by the German king shouted 'Rome, Rome! Christus, Christus!' Rome and Vienna would battle for centuries over golden Prague. Before the fighting began there was chanting on both sides: Rudolf's men followed the bishop of Basel in singing the hymn, 'Holy Mary, mother and maid, all our need on thee be laid', while the Bohemians chanted 'Lord have mercy upon us'. King Ottokar was killed escaping from the field.

'I am the Rudolf of Habsburg of my line,' Napoleon once remarked – Napoleon who wanted men to regard him as the successor and heir of Charles the Great and who kept the pope beside him in Paris, as Charles would perhaps have liked to keep the pope in Aachen. Rudolf of Habsburg had the downfall of the Hohenstaufen before him as a warning, having lived through it and suffered from it as one of their supporters. He wanted peace with the pope and the church, and at a meeting with Gregory x in Lausanne confirmed the Roman Church in its privileges. Rudolf also wanted peace in the Empire; he revived Frederick II's *Landfrieden*, and succeeded in imposing it in Bavaria, Swabia, Franconia and along the Rhine.

The battle at the Marchfeld decided for the Habsburgs. As Adam von Wandruszka, a historian who is himself of Latin, Slav and German descent and whose father fell in the First World War has observed:

No other ruling family has been served down the centuries and to the end by such a conglomeration of European peoples, Germans, Netherlanders, Burgundians, Italians, Spaniards, Frenchmen, Irishmen, Scandinavians, most of the Slavonic peoples, Magyars, Greeks and Albanians. Even in the First World War, the emperor's army was still remarkable for its supranational character. Danish, Swedish and even French officers fought for the monarchy in its final battles.

Again, 'a history of the Habsburgs would in effect be a history of Europe . . . No other ruling house in Europe has been so "European", no other in the course of its career became to such an extent the embodiment and upholder of a universal, supranational ruling principle'. Everywhere the Habsburgs adapted themselves to the custom of the country, learned its language, attracted its native aristocracy to their court and into their service, and with a part of themselves became members of the lands and nations which they ruled. There are Tyrolean, Styrian, Hungarian and Italian Habsburgs to set beside the 'German' Maximilian, the 'Burgundian' Charles V and the Spanish Philip II.

Over the past six centuries the descent of the Habsburgs has been traced variously from the Romans, the Trojans and the Alamans. Even Francis Ferdinand, the heir to the throne assassinated at Sarajevo in 1914, still busied himself with genealogical problems connected with the origins of his dynasty, so anxious was he to establish a religious–political basis for his rule. Much ridicule has been heaped in recent centuries on these Habsburg attempts at demonstrating their kinship to personages from the ancient, Old Testament and early European worlds. The genealogies which purport to prove it were compiled relatively early, when their authors were ignorant of historical fact: on her mother's side, Maria Theresa was a direct descendant of the princes of the Asiatic steppes and numbered Ghengis Khan and Muhammed among her ancestors.

Rudolf of Habsburg might be an 'impoverished petty count' but he had Emperor Frederick II to stand sponsor at his baptism in 1218. The dynasty takes its name from 'Habichtsburg' ('goshawk's castle' – how often we find a cadet aristocracy playing the hawk and falcon to the lion and eagle of older dynasties), a castle which lies between the Aare and the Reuss (Canton Aargau) and is still jealously guarded by the Swiss (Emperor Francis Joseph wanted to buy it back). The Habsburgs were settled, that is, in the heart of Europe, in a region which had once formed part of the middle kingdom of Lotharingia. The first intimation of a Habsburg connection with the Danube region is to be found in a diploma of Emperor Henry V issued at Pressburg (Bratislava) in 1108, whilst he was campaigning against the king of Hungary. By the time Rudolf became king, the Habsburgs had acquired important possessions in the Sundgau, Aargau, Thurgau and Zürichgau, and as territorial counts in Upper Alsace were the lay administrators of several wealthy monastic houses. On 1 August 1291, as soon as they heard the news of Rudolf's death – it took seventeen days in coming – the three forest regions of Uri, Schwyz and Unterwalden came together and swore an oath to remain in permanent alliance. 'Urschweiz' had been born. The struggle against the Habsburgs and the Burgundians turned Switzerland into a Europe in miniature. August 1 is still the Swiss national day, celebrated with freedom bonfires on the mountains and countless other festivities. The Swiss cross (adopted by the Red Cross organization) and the Swiss national colours, red and white, are a living reminder of Switzerland's former connection with the Empire. After the collapse of the Danube monarchy, Switzerland hospitably welcomed as refugees the descendants of the dynasty which from the days of Rudolf had so often been its detested and dreaded enemy.

King Rudolf of Habsburg – he never achieved imperial coronation in Rome – made numerous concessions to the Rhineland electoral princes in order to win their support for himself and for his sons, Albert and Rudolf, who at the Diet of Augsburg, Christmas 1282, were enfeoffed with the Austrian duchies.

From the end of the twelfth century the right of electing the king, and hence the Emperor, had devolved exclusively on seven electoral princes: the archbishops of Mainz, Cologne and Trier, the Count Palatine of the Rhine, the duke of Saxony, the margrave of Prussia and the king of Bohemia. The three ecclesiastical electors played a key role. The archbishops saw the house of Habsburg as a threat to the territorial integrity of their sees and they therefore blocked Rudolf's plans for acquiring the German crown for his dynasty by forming themselves into an anti-Habsburg alliance, headed by Cologne. The archbishop of Mainz, Gerhard II Eppenstein (the fourth member of his family to occupy the see in the thirteenth century), with help from his archiepiscopal colleagues, then engineered the election of his own kinsman, Count Adolf of Nassau.

French crown jurists, holding a brief for their master, were keeping a close watch on events in Germany and the Empire at this period. They made much of the legal distinction between the emperor and the German king. It was French publicists, too, who first gave currency to the expressions 'king of Germany' (*rex Alamannie*) and 'king of Lombardy'.

Adolf of Nassau (1292–8) was a worthy knight, but as king was 'barren of constructive ideas'. Pope Boniface VIII poured contempt on him as 'the mercenary knight' of the English king, Adolf having conferred on Edward I the position (though not the title) of an imperial vicar in the Netherlands. When Adolf set about acquiring power for his own house, which meant seizing imperial property and any other estates he could lay hands on, the electors were soon disenchanted with him. The decision to depose Adolf was taken by an assembly of princes meeting at Vienna, after preliminary discussions at Prague. At Mainz on 23 June 1298 the electors declared Adolf deposed and elected Albert of Habsburg. Two weeks later Adolf was killed in a battle against Albert at Göllheim.

The victor, Albert I (1298–1308), owed his initial success to French support in face of opposition from the electors and from Boniface VIII, who declared his election invalid. In order to obtain the imperial crown Albert later submitted to the pope, but could do nothing to prevent the catastrophe which overtook Boniface at Anagni, when the French monarchy, admittedly in its own interests, avenged its Hohenstaufen allies of the early thirteenth century.

Papa judex ordinarius est omnium: the Pope is judge, lord, true emperor of the world. Such was the position upheld by Innocent IV against Frederick II. It followed that the Pope had the right to dispose of secular kingdoms. The judgments of the Pope were the judgments of God. As papal canonists expressed it, 'the Pope can lawfully do everything like God' (*omnia de jure potest, ut Deus*). Support was even forthcoming from Thomas Aquinas, 'prince of the schoolmen', who anticipated the claim put forward in Boniface VIII's much controverted bull *Unam Sanctam*: to save their souls men must be subject to the Roman see. Thomas was aiming at the Greeks; the popes' first target was the Germans, and after them the French.

At the beginning of his treatise *De translatione imperii* Alexander of Roes reproduces opinions he probably heard canvassed at the coronation banquet of Pope Martin IV in Orvieto (1281): if the imperial office could not remain with the Romans, it must on no account fall to the ill-bred and undisciplined Germans; only the French were worthy of it. Charles the Great was a Frenchman. The French deserved to take precedence over all other peoples. The Charles-myth was being fostered by the popes themselves, for example Urban IV. From King Louis VIII onwards (his mother was Elisabeth of Hennegau) the Capetians could again claim to be 'Carolingians' by blood.

1300 was celebrated as a Holy Year, the first of its kind, introduced by Boniface VIII to boost papal prestige. It was in this year that Pierre Dubois declared that the entire world ought for its salvation to be subject to the French king. His plan was for the Angevin Charles II of Sicily to secure the election of the French king as senator of Rome. As lord of the Papal State, he could then easily pay for the upkeep of the papacy. Until now, he said, the Papal State had been nothing but a hindrance to the Pope. In fighting for its interests by fair means or foul, the Pope had been obliged, like many other princes and their servants, to allow souls to be damned and go to Hell, instead of saving them from destruction. The Pope should be brought back to his proper task, that of spiritual leadership. The tone is one of biting irony, which soon became deadly earnest: to save his own soul, the Pope, 'God upon earth', should become the pensioner of the king of France and give up his terrestrial realm.

Boniface VIII (1293–1303) is a tragic figure [plate 59]. The magnitude of his claims, his consciousness of himself as pope and the interpretation he placed on his papal office, his isolation and helplessness, put one in mind of the last great embodiment of papal authoritarianism, Pius XII. The plan to honour the papacy in the Holy Year which was celebrated in 1950 – to signalize victory over the 'godless tyrants' – by making a film in which Boniface VIII was depicted as the reigning pope's illustrious exemplar was historically 'right'.[1]

Benedetto Gaetani came from Anagni, where he was also to meet his death. The Aragonese ambassador to the curia once reported to his master 'the pope has only three interests, and they absorb his entire attention: to live long, to amass money and to make his family richer and more important. And he wastes no thought on spiritual matters.' These biting words contain at least a germ of truth. Boniface – a peasant at heart, for all his legal education – was totally unintellectual and unspiritual and failed to read the signs of the times. He was as blind to the power of the university of Paris

[1] In the event the Austrian director, G. W. Pabst, had second thoughts and this interesting project came to nothing.

and the new generation of intellectuals as he was to that of the French monarchy. As cardinal he wrote insulting letters to the professors of Paris: 'I would have liked all the professors of Paris to be there, so their foolishness could have been shown up'; and again, 'you teachers of Paris, as in the past, are falling down on your jobs as teachers through your nonsense, with the result that you confuse the whole world, which you would never do if you recognized the position of the universal Church ... You fancy your credit with us is good and your prestige high. On the contrary, we see in you nothing but smoke and folly.'

On another, later, occasion he was reproached by Jean le Moine, who was a native of Picardy, for failing to consult the Sacred College. Boniface replied: 'Picard, Picard, you have a Picard skull, but by God I will pick it open, I shall do everything my way and no one, neither you nor anyone else here, shall stop me, since you might just as well all be donkeys.' King Charles II of Naples refused to sell him Gaeta, knowing that the pope wanted to bestow it on a nephew as a fief of the church: Boniface reviled him as a wicked scoundrel, whom the pope had been obliged to check lest the earth swallow him up. Boniface further inquired whether the king was really not aware that the pope could deprive him of his kingdom.

Albert I of Habsburg was aware, and submitted to the pope. Boniface had given him until 13 April 1301 to answer. By 30 April 1303, after protracted negotiations, matters were far enough advanced for the pope to recognize Albert as king in open consistory. He informed Albert's ambassadors that the Apostolic See had complete power to dispose of the imperial office and that the pope had entrusted the election to the electors. John of Zurich replied on Albert's behalf, extolling the high authority of the papacy and comparing the cardinals to eagles; the imperial eagle too was at the pope's service and at a nod from him would take wing, casting its gaze far and wide. By way of thanks the pope expressed the hope that King Albert would shatter Gallic pride. On 17 July 1303, at Nuremberg, Albert assented to the papal interpretation of the imperial office; he accepted that the Roman see had transferred the Roman Empire from the Greeks to the Germans in the person of Charles the Great and that the Emperor was subject to the Pope. Albert swore loyalty and obedience to St Peter and the pope and undertook to defend them. Because of the great harm done to the church by many of his predecessors, Albert also promised not to send imperial vicars into Lombardy and Tuscany without papal consent.

'It was an almost unprecedented moment of hierocratic triumph. The world seemed to lie at Boniface's feet' (Werner Goez). At times the aged pope would appear before the cardinals robed in imperial vestments; the imperial insignia he sported can still be seen in the cathedral at Anagni, among them a purple cloak embroidered with two-headed imperial eagles in circular fields.

Only forty days after Albert, king and presumptive emperor, had made this truly abject submission to the pope, the pope himself was a prisoner. He died on 16 October, broken in body, and was buried next day in St Peter's, to the accompaniment of a violent thunderstorm. The curial canonist Augustinus Triumphus (one of the most

redoubtable exponents of 'triumphalism', the ideology of the Church ever-triumphant)
praises Boniface to the skies as 'Christ's confessor and martyr'; manhandled by the
oppressors of the church, heaped with insults and injustices, had he not finally laid
down his life in defence of justice and for the preservation of the church's liberty?

The French pope John XXII, echoing a bogus letter of Philip IV, alludes to
Boniface VIII as 'that thick-head'. 'The Babylonian Captivity of the church began
with the assassination at Anagni' (F. Bock). The initiative, and the power to act on it,
had passed to Frenchmen; now that the papacy was at Avignon (and the popes were
French) it might be used to further the anti-imperial policy of the king in Paris.

Boniface had involuntarily dragged the papacy into this tragedy of European
dimensions (Englishmen, Italians, Germans, Czechs and others were united in their
dislike of the Avignon papacy) because of his belief that as pope he had the right,
indeed the obligation, to judge from his high throne the king of France. 'As king you
are like all other kings and stand beneath the Pope. Whoever maintains the contrary
is a fool and an unbeliever' (*Ausculta Fili*, 1301). The pope demanded from his 'very
beloved son', Philip, complete submission, and summoned all the French prelates to a
council at Rome, to open on 1 November 1302. But the 'very beloved son', King
Philip IV the Fair (1285–1314) was in a strong position, supported by the clergy, the
'intellectuals', an educated laity, the citizens of Paris and the Estates of his realm. In
France, as in England, the conflict with the Pope arose from the claim of these
western monarchs to full financial and legal sovereignty over their clergy; to the
pope this appeared as an attack on the sacred rights of the Roman Church. The king's
advisers prepared an edited version of the papal bull for publication in France (one is
reminded of Bismarck's treatment of the Ems telegram), a move calculated to stir up
nationalist feelings against the Italian pope. Two assemblies of barons, clergy and
bourgeois, meeting in Paris, upheld the independence of the realm and appealed to
the council to declare against the 'unworthy pope'. Boniface replied that while he
had a great affection for the French he was not blind to their failings; he knew how
French repute stood with the Germans and with the inhabitants of Languedoc and
Burgundy. St Bernard's remark about the Romans applied equally to the French:
they love no one and no one loves them.

The council duly took place. On 18 November 1302 the pope issued the bull
Unam Sanctam Ecclesiam. The pope sees himself as bearer of both swords, the spiritual
and the temporal. 'But we now declare, pronounce, establish and proclaim that it is
necessary to salvation for every human creature (*omni humanae creaturae*) to be
subjected to the Roman pontiff.'

In Paris the men determined to proceed against the pope were now ranged around
William Nogaret, who on the death of Pierre Flotte had become the king's trusted
adviser. Nogaret's father had been burned as a heretic. The pope's enemies included
the heads of the Florentine banking house of Francesci but above all members of the
Colonna family and their dependants. The Colonna had suffered at the hands of
members of the pope's family, the Gaetani, who with his backing had broken up

Colonna strongholds and confiscated their estates. The Colonna foregathered in Paris included Sciarra Colonna and the two cardinals, James and Peter Colonna; the latter were originally adherents of Boniface and had taken part in his election but in the clan warfare between the Colonna and the Gaetani they had been deprived of their dignities and declared heretics.

In Paris, the Colonna turned the screw tighter by accusing Boniface of heresy. The indictment, dated 13–14 June 1303 and promulgated at a solemn assembly of the Estates held in the Louvre, accuses Boniface of turning the whole of Christendom upside down merely because of his determination to destroy the French nation, which he accuses of being over-proud. Immediately afterwards royal messengers were dispatched throughout the territories of the French king to read out the charges against the pope and procure men's assent to a council. Hundreds of such agreements furnished by lay and ecclesiastical lords and town governments still survive. Anyone who refused assent was put in prison. We in our own day are not unfamiliar with 'spontaneous declarations' of this kind.

When he heard of the proceedings instigated by the Colonna, Boniface issued a further bull, *Nuper ad audientiam* (15 August 1303). Its mood is one of profound dejection. The French king's temerity surpassed even that of Frederick II in his revolt against Innocent.

The summer heat was unusually oppressive that year in Anagni, the pope's native city, to which he had withdrawn to be with his own people. In Rome he could no longer be sure of his life. It was at Anagni, and wearing his papal vestments, that he was captured in a surprise attack by Sciarra Colonna and Nogaret on 7 September. The attack itself, during which he was manhandled and abused and then kept for three days in custody, nearly cost him his life. He was set free however by the citizens of Anagni but only to die a few weeks later on 16 October 1303, killed by the humiliation he had suffered.

This unfortunate pope has been accused of doing untold harm and denounced for his 'overweening pride'. In reality he did nothing but take literally what all the popes since Innocent III, or indeed Gregory VII, had regarded as the sacred right of St Peter's successors, the right tersely alluded to by Thomas Aquinas, the greatest theologian of the church, when he says '*reges sunt ergo vassalles ecclesiae*': kings, including the 'king of Germany' were vassals of the church.

Albert I, the king who had acknowledged himself subject to Pope Boniface VIII, was murdered by a nephew on 1 May 1308, not far from the Habsburg. The clan now had many enemies, who wanted to see the Habsburgs reduced to their former position. King Philip of France, the recent victor over the pope, put forward his brother Charles of Valois as candidate for the imperial crown. This plan having failed, Archbishop Baldwin of Trier assumed the role of kingmaker and secured the crown for his brother Henry of Luxemburg, who after election at Rense reigned as Henry VII (1308–13). Baldwin subsequently made use of his ramified connections in France and Germany to help two further monarchs to the throne, Ludwig of Bavaria and his own great-nephew, Charles IV. A portrait of the archbishop done in wood carving can still be seen at St Gangolf's in Trier. His contemporary in the see of Mainz, Peter Aspelt, was also a kingmaker; he owed his own rise to the Habsburgs, but ended by supporting the Luxemburgs. On his tomb in Mainz cathedral this Lord Archbishop and Chancellor of the Empire stands out as a giant figure, dwarfing the three kinglets he 'created' [plate 60]. In the days of Rainald of Dassel the term 'kinglet' applied to foreign kings for whom an appropriate place had to be found within the hegemonial structure of the Hohenstaufen Holy Roman Empire. Now the tables were turned, and in the eyes of the French kings and the popes it was the German and non-German claimants and anti-kings who wrangled over the imperial crown who were the kinglets, and a powerful imperial bishop is content to see them so portrayed on his tombstone. As we have seen, the Luxemburgs were helped to the throne by their kinsmen; their next step was to enhance their dignity and that of the Empire by enlarging the scope of their authority.

With assistance from Peter Aspelt, Henry VII gained control of Bohemia, which on the extinction of the Přemyslids had passed to a weakling, Duke Henry of Carinthia. At the diet held at Frankfurt in 1310 Bohemia was transferred from Duke Henry to John, son of Henry VII: John married Elizabeth, daughter of Wenzel II, and successfully battled his way into Prague. His father meanwhile set out for the unhappy and feud-torn land of Italy, where his coming was awaited with high hopes as the advent of a prince of peace.

Henry VII fought his way through Italy to his goal of imperial coronation, which took place in the Lateran on 29 June 1312 (St Peter's was in enemy hands). The emperor's most dangerous foe in Italy was King Robert of Naples, an Angevin by descent and thus a scion of the royal house which had liquidated the Hohenstaufen. Henry opened his attack by staging a trial of Robert at Arezzo, conducted on inquisitorial lines, at which Robert was accused of disfealty as a vassal of the Empire. Sentence was passed on 26 April 1313 at Pisa, a city loyal to the emperor: Robert was formally dishonoured, outlawed from the Empire and condemned to death.

King Robert retaliated by sending out a circular to friendly towns in northern Italy calling for the abolition of the imperial office as a scandal and a public nuisance to the Pope, to France and to Italy. The *imperium* was immoral; conceived in violence and brigandage, acts of violence had continued to strew its path. Robert of Naples here gives a brief 'historical survey' of the Empire from Domitian to Henry VII, stressing the hostility shown by many emperors towards the church and the papacy and remarking on the burden placed on the Empire by the fact that its head had always to be chosen from the detested and undisciplined German people. Pierre Dubois, he says, had had the right idea when he advised the pope to deprive the electors of their right to elect and to make the French king emperor. The king of Naples goes even further; since it is a law that everything changes, with the beginning of the new age the *imperium* ought now to be superseded by the independent nation state. The Angevin had behind him Joachimite circles in Naples which assigned to his kingdom the salvation-bearing role of bringing in the 'new age' by reforming the church and assuming the functions which the Holy Empire had forfeited.

Many Ghibellines, and even Dante, a moderate Guelf, expected from Henry VII the settlement of a number of outstanding disputes. Henry's sudden death near Siena on 24 August 1313 was a profound shock to partisans of the Empire in Italy and Germany [plate 63]. The impact of this shock can still be felt in Dante's masterpiece.

Earlier writers – monks, chroniclers, bishops, political publicists, *minnesänger*, troubadours – register for us in some degree the tremors felt by contemporaries as they witnessed the struggle between Church and Empire, between pope and emperor. But it was only in the truly catastrophic situation of the years around 1300, when the line between apocalyptic hope and apocalyptic dread had worn very thin and was often blurred, that two men discovered a language capable of transmitting this shock to men of our own day: Dante, the great poet of the Catholic Middle Ages, and Meister Eckhart, the greatest of the mystics. The thought of both revolves about the Holy Empire, and both are inconceivable in the absence of that catastrophe which struck *sacerdotium* and *regnum* with equal force, if not always at the same time.

Many elements combined to produce the yearning and pain we find in Dante (who was as much an *émigré* as the many other *fuorisciti*, some of them our contemporaries, whose bitter experience of internal and external exile has fashioned some of the greatest Italian literature): a Franciscan 'spiritualism' buttressed by Joachimite hope; an education enriched by Arabic-Jewish culture, as was natural in an educated Italian layman; the Aristotelian scholasticism of Paris; an erotic mysticism which sprang originally from Albigensian Provence; and an anticurialism (not to be confused with anticlericalism, though the two are in many ways connected) whose roots were both political and spiritual and which was informed by a spirit of local patriotism.

One great target of Dante's anticurialism was what he himself describes as the 'she-wolf' of papal avarice. Individual popes, however, are indicted on several counts. Clement VI is consigned to Hell for having succumbed to the seductions of the western and infernal lust for power embodied in the French king, for having abandoned Holy Rome to cleave to the French, for his betrayal of noble Henry: the pope must bear responsibility for the treachery, warfare and bitter antagonisms which inevitably flowed from this Hell-inspired rejection of the lawful ruler. Boniface VIII is relegated to Hell as the 'black beast' and 'prince of Pharisees'. This pope's offence was doubtless all the more heinous in that he had planned to found a Tuscan kingdom for his family and to make Florence, Dante's loved and hated native city, its capital. Dante even banishes to Hell the hapless Celestine V, the pope Boniface displaced: his abdication made Celestine a cowardly traitor to the Holy Empire, since a true pope should unite with a true emperor in keeping joint watch over the twin paths which lie before every man as he journeys to his twin goals, salvation upon earth and salvation in Heaven.

In the letter Dante addressed to Henry he hails him in ecstatic terms as the coming emperor and prince of peace. The *De Monarchia*, the work in which Dante set out his programme, remained for centuries on the Index of prohibited books. The ban was only lifted in 1921, when the pacific Benedict XV (the pope frequently accused by the western Entente of showing partiality towards the Central Powers) issued his Dante Encyclical. With the disappearance from the scene of the last inheritor of the Holy Roman Empire it was at length safe for Dante's vision of empire to circulate freely.

Dante's thesis in the *De Monarchia* is that the western *imperium* owes nothing to any legal title in the pope's power to grant. The *imperium* derives directly from God. Its colour and saving sign is red, which is the colour of emperors and kings, the colour of joy and the Holy Spirit. *Romanum imperium de fonte nascitur pietatis*: the Roman Empire has its source in divine providence and divine compassion, which uses the Empire to educate men in *civilitas*, to make them civilized in their political, religious and civic lives. As *curator orbis*, as watchman over the world's salvation and its law, as the ruler compelling men to good, 'as the substitute for the world government which the Church, once purified, would assume' (Fritz Kern), the Emperor has the task of leading men upwards into that spiritual kingdom of humanity where the good pagan and the christian are united in spirit, culture, polity and love. This is the new community of saints, a community of men civilized in spirit, civilized by the Empire, in which the elect and good are at one and the same time 'Romans', 'Christians', 'Franciscans', 'Italians', members of the glorified Empire and the glorified Church.

John of Zurich, the envoy sent by Albert I to Boniface VIII, had demeaned the imperial eagle by speaking of its subservience to the cardinals and to the high and dazzling authority of the Lord Pope. Dante sees the imperial eagle in Paradise, roosting as the sun-bird on the tree of the world which is the tree of knowledge. From this tree the Cross was made, the Cross which became the shafts of the triumphal chariot of the church and caused the tree to blossom. But because the eagle deposits in the chariot the plumage of evil and greedy lesser birds of prey (standing for the western kings and the covetous nobility), the church has been turned into a monster. The Donation of Constantine made the church the whore of Babylon. This carnal and degenerate church could and would be delivered from itself by an angel pope of apostolic poverty and by the rightful emperor, the tyrant of Italy. The emperor rescues the world from its confusion, leads it into peace and freedom. All just emperors are holy. Dante finds the imperial eagle roosting not only in Paradise (the Earthly Paradise) but also in Heaven. In Heaven glorified souls combine to form an eagle, the primal golden imperial eagle, which is then further transfigured into the Johannine eagle, all holy fire, the community of redeemed souls. Another Italian admirer of Henry VII hails him as the cosmic emperor, in whom subsists the harmony of the planets, stars and elements.

> *Non aspettar mio dir più, nè mio cenno:*
> *Libero, dritto e sano è tuo arbitrio.*
> *E fallo fora no fare a suo senno:*
> *Perch' io te sopra te corono e mitrio.*
>
> (*Purg.*, XXVII, 139–42)

Expect no more
Sanction of warning voice or sign from me,
Free of thy own arbitrement to choose,
Discreet, judicious. To distrust thy sense
Were henceforth error. I invest thee then
With crown and mitre, sovereign o'er thyself.
(Translated H.F. Carey)

Having guided him as far as the Earthly Paradise, Virgil leaves Dante. The poet is to enter Heaven with his inward self set free. In effect Virgil is saying to Dante: 'Expect no more instruction from me. Your human and political will is free, lawful and wholesome. It would be unjust to deny you room in which to develop freely. I therefore crown you in your own right emperor and pope.' Charles Péguy, like Dante, was filled with a consuming anger when he saw the high powers of state and church failing in their responsibilities and in the years before the First World War openly denounced them. He was deeply troubled over what the future might hold for the state, France and the church. He had seen from the Dreyfus affair how a state could putrefy and die from committing a mortal sin, the murder of an innocent man through the courts. The church was corrupted by its inquisitorial system (that Bergson was placed on the Index proved the church's total lack of charity towards the 'poor'). The *res publica*, the common good of the whole human society, was being misappropriated and disgraced by those in authority. Péguy accuses Dante of visiting Hell like a tourist, inspired only by curiosity and without identifying himself with the damned. Péguy's own aim, like that of Victor Hugo, was to abolish Hell, and to set the damned free.

Péguy's accusation touches on something fundamental. The greatest Catholic poet of the Middle Ages *invented* his own Heaven, Hell and Purgatory. His infernal, purgatorial, paradisial and celestial landscapes are his own fabrication. What to contemporary believers in Church and Empire were completely objective facts, to Dante the poet were figments, creations of his political and religious imagination.

To find Heaven and Hell as the products of a creative ego, of an individual poet, is indeed quite extraordinary, and only possible and explicable as the wake of an infernal revolution on the historical plane such as had overtaken the historical Church and Empire. The German *minnesänger* sees himself as an 'emperor'. Dante has himself crowned pope and emperor by Virgil, the creative sacred genius who presided over Rome's public literature, not merely as the crowned bard on the Capitol but also in the only 'reality' which counted, in the realm of the creative imagination. Dante abolishes Heaven and Hell, 'liquidates' them in his poetry. In doing so he brings more to an end than just the Middle Ages.

'And I maintain: humanity is as complete in the poorest, the most despised of men, as in the pope or emperor; for humanity itself is dearer to me than the man whom I bear within me. May the truth I have spoken of help us to be equally united with God. Amen.' The words are the conclusion to a sermon by Meister Eckhart, the greatest of the European intellectual mystics, a man who fascinated Nicholas of Cusa, deeply influenced Hegel and Fichte, in our own day worked upon Heidegger and who appeals to Japanese Zen-Buddhists as a kindred spirit. In his mystical theology, his speculative thinking, his pastoral advice and his preaching, he abolishes Holy Roman Empire and Holy Roman Church no less sublimely than Dante.

Eckhart grew up in 'the terrible time without an emperor' and came to be the pastor of homeless spirits and intellects in Germany and in Bohemia. In his time it was not uncommon for towns on the Rhine to languish for years or even decades under an interdict. Neglect of souls was widespread, 'heresy' was rife: in Eckhart's day many heretics were burnt in the region between Strassburg and Cologne which was the scene of his chief activity. Eckhart was instructed by his order to accept a particular responsibility for nuns and other women religiously inclined. These were nobly-born women who found German mysticism a refuge; a list of them would include Kunigunde, sister of Rudolf of Habsburg, Margaret, sister of Henry VII, Margaret of Hungary, daughter of a Hungarian king, Elizabeth who was queen of Hungary and became a Dominican nun at Töss, Beatrice von Horn, Agnes von Ochenstein, Gertrud von Bruck, Anna von Vinneck, Gertrud von Jungholz.

One of Eckhart's best known tracts, the *Book of Divine Consolation* (1308–11), was written for Agnes, daughter of Albert I and widow of the Hungarian king. Agnes was often immersed in political activity; when her husband died young she lived with her mother Elizabeth in Vienna, acting as her secretary, adviser and deputy, and after her mother's death continued her activity on behalf of the country and its people from the convent Elizabeth had founded at Königsfelden, where Agnes spent the remaining fifty years of her life. Nothing could break her, though she suffered many blows – the death of her husband, the murder of her father, the defeat of her brother Frederick the Handsome in his fight to win the imperial crown (Agnes kept up her efforts on his behalf to the day of his death). The richest German princess of her day, she lived very simply, observing the spirit of the poverty movement to the full and lavishing gifts on churches, religious houses, towns and hermits. She also conducted an impressive peace campaign which was so successful that nearly all the arbitrations agreed to in the Swabian possessions of the house of Austria between 1314 and 1360 can be traced to her influence. Her master strokes were bringing to an end the war over Laupen (1340) and the conclusion of alliances for the house of Austria first with Berne (1341) and then with Strassburg, Basel and Freiburg (1350). Agnes is a key figure because she embodies three important characteristics of the age: the spiritually awakened woman, peacemaking by women, and the patronage of towns as areas of peace and freedom in the midst of much disorder. Such were the human and political co-ordinates within which Meister Eckhart worked.

The Empire, as an object in dispute, had no peace to offer; neither had the Church, the institutional 'church of walls' against which Eckhart preached, using a term first found in St Bernard and later seized upon by Luther, who found it in the anonymous *Theologia Teutsch*. Peace, says Eckhart, is to be found nowhere but in the soul, in the

Habsburgs, Luxemburgs, Wittelsbachs

58 Rudolf of Habsburg, in a window of the Stephansdom in Vienna. The Habsburgs were petty counts from Alsace and became masters of a world empire.

59 Pope Boniface VIII.

60 Archbishop Peter Aspelt of Mainz crowns kings of the Holy Roman Empire who are seen as 'kinglets', subservient to the Church.

63 (*opposite*) Emperor Henry VII, Dante's '*alto Arrigo*', seen on his tomb in Pisa, the city loyal to the emperor. Dante had high hopes of Henry as the prince of peace who would unite Ital

61 The city of Rome disputed over by popes, emperors, populace and aristocratic factions; the reverse side of a gold seal of Ludwig of Bavaria.

62 Gold coin of Ludwig of Bavaria, probably struck in the Netherlands by Edward III of England, who as imperial vicar assumed rights of coinage.

64, 65 Emperor Charles IV and his wife Blanche of Valois from the Stephansdom, Vienna. Rudolf IV of Habsburg (Charles' son-in-law) and the later Habsburgs regarded themselves as Charles' heirs both in Bohemia and in the Empire.

66 Emperor Charles IV and his son Wenzel with King Charles V of France at a state banquet in Paris, 1378.

67 An emperor at his coronation banquet attended by four electors, three ecclesiastical and one lay. From the copy of the Golden Bull (Charles IV's fundamental law for the Empire) made for Emperor Wenzel.

68 Initial from the magnificent Wenzel Bible, a product of the Luxemburg culture in Bohemia which sought to reconcile German and Czech traditions.

69 The stake is prepared in Constance for Jan Hus. This breach of faith (Hus had a letter of protection from the emperor) long blighted Czech relations with the Empire and the Germans.

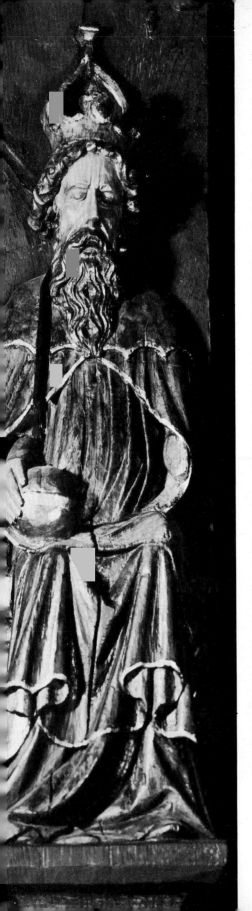

70 Figure of the emperor from the set of eight
(the remainder being the electors, embodying
the Empire) carved on beams supporting the
roof of the old Rathaus in the 'imperial city' of
Esslingen. The Holy Roman Empire was never an
absolutist 'state'; it was a federation.

71 Symbolic representation of the annual
renewal of the trading treaties between Nuremberg
and the Netherlands. During the fourteenth
and fifteenth centuries some south German towns
sustained a trade which in the sixteenth extended
to Spain, South America and India.

empire within, from which all that is hampering must be expelled. This explains why the soul 'should eject from itself all holy things'. But even this was not enough. The soul must also eject all images of God: then, and only then, will the cleansed and liberated soul, wholly immersed in the pure Godhead which is nothingness and more than nothingness, beyond all concepts, attain tranquillity. 'Every empire has its distinctive coat of arms. The Roman Empire has the golden eagle, the Franks have their lilies on a sky-blue ground. The sign of the kingdom of Heaven and of the Christian is the cross, which stands on no coloured ground but in light itself.' The soul must bear the cross and itself become the 'Son'. The soul itself must become God, must absorb into itself the fullness of the Trinity.

Because each claimed to be the terrestrial respresentative of Christ the King, pope and emperor had fought one another to the death. While men burned at the stake and the persecuted 'Poor Men of Christ' met their death by drowning in the Rhine, Eckhart was teaching that every christian man could and must become Christ, God. 'There is no difference between the begotten Son and the soul'. 'The soul is no different from our Lord Jesus Christ . . . and everything which can be said of our Lord Jesus Christ can also be said of the soul.' The Holy Trinity can be present in each soul.

The holy and undivided Trinity was the Empire's supreme patron and defence; the diplomas, the charters and the manifestos went out in its name. But Eckhart taught that the 'tranquil' soul gathers the Trinity into itself. 'The soul thus becomes a heavenly dwelling of the eternal Godhead, so that he accomplishes within it his divine work'. 'In the soul the heavenly Father begets the Son; the soul entices the Son for him out of the heart. In the soul these two, Father and Son, exhale the Holy Spirit.

'In this way, the soul receives the world as its own from the hand of the Father; and as the Son, holds the world; and in the Holy Spirit knows the world. And the soul which has thus entered into possession of the entire world attains to everlasting rest in God.' Eckhart takes seriously the Johannine text, 'the kingdom of God is within you'. The pope insists that he, and he alone, is in direct contact with God, that all roads to God lead through him. The Emperor allows men to proclaim that he too, as emperor, is in direct contact with God, the founder of the Empire. Eckhart preaches – and thousands, in all parts of Germany, pay heed – that every soul is in direct contact with God, and needs no pope or emperor for salvation. The walled church and the Empire totter and dissolve in smoke and ashes beneath the fires of red-hot love, as the loving soul absorbs the Godhead into itself. The soul is 'God's kinsman' and needs neither Rome nor imperial mediation for its canonization.

On 27 March 1329 Meister Eckhart was condemned in a papal bull issued by John XXII. An imperial edict of 17 June 1369, promulgated in the joint names of Pope Gregory XI and Emperor Charles IV, ordered the destruction of all books, writings and sermons in the vernacular, which meant that Eckhart's writings went with others to the stake. Each in his own fashion, pope and emperor had identified and acknowledged his great adversary.

72 Portrait of Emperor Sigismund, ascribed to Pisanello.

Jacques Duèse from Cahors had been chancellor to the Angevin kings Charles II and Robert of Naples before becoming pope. As John XXII (1316–34) this small, lean, bourgeois Frenchman fought the Germans, the German monarchy and Empire, with unremitting vigour. As chancellor of Naples he had probably drafted King Robert's memorandum on the *imperium*. Once he was pope he favoured the house of Anjou by canonizing Robert's brother, Louis of Toulouse, as patron saint of the projected Guelf 'empire' and by appointing Robert himself vicar-general of the Empire in Italy. The pope felt quite justified in disposing of this right of appointment which properly belonged to the Emperor, since in his view the imperial office was vacant. (In his charters this is baldly stated as a fact: *vacante imperio*.)

The pope could take this view because of the situation created by the disputed election which had followed the death of Henry VII. The votes of the electors were divided between two candidates, Frederick the Handsome of Austria and Ludwig of Bavaria, the one a Habsburg and the other a Wittelsbach. The result was an open confrontation between the two houses whose rivalry would endure for as long as the Empire itself. Although Frederick was defeated at Mühldorf in 1322 and became Ludwig's prisoner he was allowed to retain the title of king. Ludwig, whom the pope refused to acknowledge, turned his attention to Italy in the hope of winning the imperial title. In 1324 he was excommunicated; the pope's own candidate for the Empire was King Charles IV of France.

In his campaign against the Italian Ghibellines, who were Ludwig's ardent supporters, John did not scruple to use the heresy laws promulgated by Emperor Frederick II in 1220 and 1232. The special powers given to the cardinal legate Bertrand in 1320 to proceed not only against declared heretics but also against suspects and their aiders and abettors marks the opening of a decisive phase in John XXII's battle with his political enemies. By shifting his attack from political to religious and ecclesiastical ground he exposed his opponents to the sharper weapon of the Inquisition. This process of political inquisition was founded on imperial legislation, which was now being turned against the Empire and its loyalists. The pope appointed Cardinal Bertrand supreme judge of appeal in both ecclesiastical and secular causes, *auctoritate imperiale*, with imperial authority – an expression which crops up again and again in documents issued by the legate.

The victory secured in 1324 by the Ghibelline party in Italy was a bitter blow both to the pope and to Robert of Anjou, who with the pope's backing was building up his own empire in Italy. Their resentment centred on Ludwig, whom the pope accused of collaboration with the Lombard 'heretics', above all the Visconti. In fact the whole of Italy was riddled with 'heretics'. The word '*nobile*' had become a synonym for heretic. John XXII nevertheless reserved the accusing label 'heretic' for the political enemies he was so anxious to discredit and remove.

On 8 October 1323 a notice was affixed to the door of Avignon cathedral calling on Ludwig to renounce within three months his government of the Empire and to revoke whatever acts he had performed as king, pending formal approval of his fitness to rule by the Holy See. The pope freed all laymen and ecclesiastics from their oaths of loyalty to the king and forbade them to obey him. On 23 March 1324 Ludwig was excommunicated, the official reason being his support of the 'heretical' Visconti of Milan.

In this contest with the pope Ludwig was supported by the Ghibellines of northern Italy, by King Frederick of Aragon (who ruled part of Italy), by anti-papal Franciscan intellectuals and by a number of German towns. Taken together, they formed a broad band of opposition to the Avignon papacy and substantially prepared the way for the Reformation. It is significant that the imperial court was for a time the centre of a European opposition which included some of the most important minds in the intellectual and spiritual movements of the age. William of Ockham, an Englishman who had spent four years in an Avignon prison, and his fellow Franciscans Bonagratia of Bergamo and Michael of Cesena (General of the Order) took refuge with Ludwig at Pisa after Ockham and Cesena had signed a protest against Pope John's decree on poverty. John of Jandun and Marsilius of Padua had already sought and obtained imperial protection.

Ludwig's counter-polemics (which took the form of appeals against the pope) were composed at the courts of north Italian noblemen who favoured the Ghibelline cause; at the beginning of his difficult reign Ludwig had no chancery to speak of and not many intellectuals at his court. Under canon law there was only one indictment which could be levelled at a pope, that of heresy. In Ludwig's second appeal (known as the Appeal of Sachsenhausen, 24 May 1324), Ludwig accuses the pope of using religious weapons to destroy his enemies, that is by declaring them heretics. In so doing the pope had plunged Christendom into a schism and brought suspicion of heresy upon himself. This suspicion could only grow stronger when men considered how the pope had treated the Franciscans.

Part of the appeal is taken up with a long theological excursus emanating from Franciscan circles imbued with the ideas of Petrus Johannis Olivi. The pope, it is said, shows his contempt for the doctrine that Christ lived in poverty; he denies it both in his deeds and in his words, above all in his contention that the saviour and his disciples lived like members of the older religious orders, holding property in common. He refuses therefore to accept Franciscan poverty as apostolic and has stated before reliable witnesses that if he had been in power he would have dissolved the order of St Francis forty years ago and given it a rule enjoining the accumulation of property, as in the other orders. These views reveal the pope as a heretic of the deepest dye. It is tempting to see this Sachsenhausen excursus as the counterpart of the proposal put forward by Pierre Dubois that the pope should himself live in apostolic poverty. But this French suggestion was politically inspired and was designed to promote the interests of the French king. The spiritual intent of the Franciscan poverty movement, which looked to the emperor for support, went far deeper.

In the wider historical context it should be noted that St Francis, and those of his followers who obeyed his injunction to live in poverty and at peace, were very much in advance of their times. It has taken five centuries and two world wars to kindle the first faint beginnings of a Catholic peace movement (Pax Christi and other similar small groups), and even this failed to penetrate Vatican II. In the Avignon papacy the Franciscan poverty movement was faced with the most developed financial power in Europe, a power whose resources were devoted to wars and crusades in support of its political claims in Italy. The fact that Italy was an economic prize was certainly one reason why Henry VII and Ludwig of Bavaria came into conflict with the pope. Italy was far more prosperous than the German part of the Empire. The Romagna and the Marches were between three and four times more densely populated than Germany. During the period 1300–40 the population of Italy may have been eleven million, that of Germany fifteen million, that of France possibly twenty million.

The excommunicated Ludwig was crowned at Rome by a layman, Sciarra Colonna. The ancient rite of the imperial coronation order was used, the bishops of Castello and Almeria performing the ceremonies of consecration and anointing in place of the pope. In April of that same year (1328) Ludwig presided from a special throne set up in the forecourt of St Peter's (at that time still the resting-place of Otto II) over a solemn assembly at which three imperial decrees were promulgated. In the first Ludwig followed Frederick II's example and made heretics out of those who rebelled against the Empire. The second announced Ludwig's deposition of the pope. The decree describes Ludwig as steward and protector of the church and cites as precedent Otto I's deposition of another Pope John, John XII; it was solemnly proclaimed from the front of St Peter's basilica, thus virtually in the presence of St Peter himself [plate 61]. The author of this decree may well have been Marsilius of Padua, who in his great treatise *Defensor Pacis* insists that the clergy should limit themselves to strictly spiritual matters (administration of the sacraments, the ordering of divine worship), leaving all 'worldly' things to the state and the people; the church is more than the clerical church; it is the community (*universitas*) of all christian believers. The promulgation of the third decree, which prescribed that all future popes should reside in Rome, was made the occasion for a Roman carnival. Bonfires were lighted on which the 'false pope' was burnt in straw effigy, an indication that the Roman pope was perhaps nowhere more hated than in Rome itself. On Whitsunday Ludwig was again crowned emperor, this time by Nicholas V, the pope whose election he had meanwhile engineered.

At this point, while Michael of Cesena (elected General of the Franciscan Order for the second time in 1328) was marshalling Franciscan support for Ludwig from Pisa and polemics against John XXII were being posted by night on church doors in Paris, the Ghibellines gave the screw a further turn: the real vacancy, they claimed, was not in the imperial office but in the Roman see, whose bishop was non-resident. This line of policy did Ludwig little good. 'The installation of the anti-pope was a miscalculation of the first order and helped John XXII to a cheap victory.' The long-drawn-out struggle between emperor and pope did nothing to improve the state of affairs in

Germany. As one contemporary chronicler, Johann of Winterthur, remarks, 'we had reached the point where pope and emperor denounced each other as heretics and pilloried one another's errors.'

The pope, however, was now in danger of being ground down between two enemies, Paris as well as Munich. In Munich his chief enemies were still Marsilius and his followers, members of the Franciscan academy which was founded there after Ludwig's Roman expedition. They branded Jacques of Cahors (their name for the pope) as a heretic and denounced his current aspirations for a 'reconciliation' with the emperor as a sham whose only object was to avert his own posthumous condemnation by a General Council as a heretic (a fate Boniface VIII had only narrowly escaped). From Paris the pope was threatened by a change of policy by the French king, Philip VI, who had fallen out with Robert of Naples. To make sure the pope took his part, Philip charged John with heresy, just as Philip IV had charged Boniface VIII, and again with the compliance of the French clergy. The alleged heresy was contained in a sermon the pope preached on All Saints' Day 1331. His theme was the Beatific Vision, which he claimed would precede the resurrection of the body. The French Dominicans, who were very close to the king, took up the charge and for good measure waxed indignant over the reports that the pope was inclining towards a reconciliation with the emperor: the 'nationalistic' French Dominicans and the 'cosmopolitan' Franciscans of Munich had found a common cause, opposition to the 'erring' pope. A French national synod summoned by King Philip met at the palace of Vincennes on 19 December 1333 and denounced the papal thesis.

John XXII died on 12 December 1334, over ninety and a deeply embittered man. A German-hater on the grand scale, he had fought all his life to detach Italy from the Empire. Ludwig claimed that John welcomed the internal discord in Germany as a guarantee of peace and security for the papacy: had not John declared that the empire of the Germans was the brazen serpent he would bend all his efforts to destroy? The force of the pope's hatred also made a deep impression in Italy: 'he was a man of blood, no worthy servant of God'. At the last, when all his schemes were in danger of collapse, the truly mortal threat came from the French king, his erstwhile protector. It might be said that the last word in this particular phase of the struggle between Pope and Emperor was spoken by the German electors with their declaration in 1338 (the Declaration of Rense) that a king elected by a majority of their number needed no confirmation from the pope. The implication is that the imperial dignity derived not from the pope but directly from God and that John XXII's proceedings against the emperor were therefore null and void. The pope had no rights over the Empire.

In 1337 Ludwig (like Rudolf of Habsburg and Adolf of Nassau before him) concluded a short-lived alliance with England. During the twelfth and thirteenth centuries the Welf connection had maintained close links between Germany and the English court. Even so, from about the beginning of the thirteenth century, if not earlier, the English had lost that awareness of a common German-English descent, so strikingly expressed by certain Anglo-Saxon authors, and were increasingly disposed to regard the Germans as barbarians. English suspicions were first alerted by the imperial aims of Frederick Barbarossa and continued undiminished.

But England had a quarrel with France. To cut off one line of attack Pierre Dubois used scorched earth tactics to devastate the Netherlands. The ensuing great war between France and England for mastery in Europe was an all-out struggle fought with military, economic, financial, diplomatic and propagandist weapons.

The Avignon papacy gave financial support to the French king. The French higher clergy, until the time of the First World War a consistently chauvinistic body, identified itself wholeheartedly with royal policy. Late in July 1337 Archbishop Peter Roger of Rouen preached an inflammatory war sermon to a congregation which included King Philip and his ally King John of Bohemia. The religious-political ground Joan of Arc would tread had already been prepared.

In the late summer of 1338 King Edward III of England and Emperor Ludwig met on Niederwerth, an island in the Rhine. Details of the English expenditure on preparations for this journey are recorded in English treasury accounts still extant. Purchases include a special robe for the English king, fifteen tunics and cloaks as gifts for the emperor, the duke of Brabant and twelve notables from each of the two allied countries, and a further fifty scarlet cloaks with an oak-leaf border plus head coverings in blue material for the bowmen who formed the king's escort. Edward's outrageously expensive robe of state was embroidered with gold and silver leopards, the king's heraldic beast. Minstrels and entertainers accompanied the party.

The English court had set out for the meeting on 19 August, moving from Antwerp to the Rhine and proceeding thence upstream through Cologne and Bonn to Niederwerth, Archbishop Baldwin of Trier doing the honours. The emperor greeted his visitor by dispatching to him a live eagle, which was afterwards kept in the Tower of London menagerie. The Niederwerth meeting was followed by conversations at Coblenz and Frankfurt, where the English king took part in a diet. He was present in September at a solemn re-proclamation of an imperial edict of 6 August whereby Ludwig had confirmed the Declaration of Rense as a constitution of the Empire.

The emperor appointed the English king imperial vicar of the Netherlands. In the absence of the emperor Edward would rule as vicar-general of the Empire, an office transferred to the Netherlands from Italy. Edward promised huge sums in support of the emperor. He had coins minted [plate 62] with the double-headed imperial eagle and in keeping with his function as imperial vicar summoned diets in the Lower Rhineland.

In trusting Edward the emperor had been grossly deceived. The promised money was not forthcoming and Edward soon renounced the title of imperial vicar, whose assumption had earned him a stern reproof from Pope Benedict XII. The German-English alliance remains an episode. In 1346 the pope renewed the church's condemnation of Ludwig, who died the following year. The anti-king, Charles of Luxemburg, won general acceptance and became Emperor Charles IV [plate 64].

An English writer, Bede Jarrett, has described Charles as 'the most European of emperors', adding that he did more than any other ruler to create Europe's existing political order. (Jarrett was writing in 1935, four years before Hitler, with England's connivance, destroyed Czecho-Slovakia.) Konrad Burdach, a German and a specialist in German studies, claims Charles as one of the greatest statesmen the world has ever seen. Czech and German historians, in a tug-of-war which started in the eighteenth century, both claim him as their own. Czechs regard him as at once a great Czech king and one of the ablest, noblest, greatest rulers of any period and any nation (K. V. Zap). In 1937 the rector of the Czech university in Prague, at a ceremony held on the annual anniversary of its foundation, laid a wreath at the statue erected to Charles IV in 1348 which bore the inscription 'to a great Czech and European'.

Through his legislation as emperor Charles impressed on the Empire the structure it retained to the end. Charles saw the Empire as a state of states, 'a universal form of state with the faculty of over-arching all existing states', as the German-Bohemian historian Josef Pfitzner described it in 1938.[1] The social, political, intellectual and religious co-existence Charles IV aimed at for his peoples descended in the nineteenth century into a whirlpool of hatred and self-destruction. Charles meant to have a 'kingdom of God' in Bohemia, born of the fruitful co-existence of all 'Bohemians' whether of Czech or German descent, each retaining their own language and co-inhabiting a Prague at once German and Czech. Prague, Bohemia, became in fact the arena of silent underground battles between Czechs and Germans and later of volcanic eruptions which spilled over to engulf Spaniards and members of practically every European nation found in the emperor's service.

Praga caput regni: Prague 'is' Bohemia just as Paris 'is' France. In the east the Byzantine church and the Byzantine empire cast covetous eyes on Prague, and during the first century of its existence there was still doubt which way the decision would go. By about 1000, Prague had become definitely part of the west. Its legendary foundress and first queen was Libuscha, the subject of Grillparzer's great drama *Libussa* (1844): Prague was the threshold (*prah* in Czech) of her house in the virgin forest. Christianity only started to make headway among the people in the twelfth century, having previously been the affair of alien masters and the aristocracy. The first hymns written in Czech are petitions for mercy and deliverance, for peace and fruitfulness.

The Germans first came to the Prague region at the invitation of its indigenous territorial princes. From about 1178 they had their own mercantile quarter in Prague; the country as a whole offered the Germans great opportunity for enrichment through trade and mineworkings. Bohemian magnates took to building their castles after German models and gave them German names: Sternberg, Löwenberg, Riesenburg. The Přemyslid court maintained fruitful connections with the courts of the Hohenstaufen and the landgraves of Thuringia and many Bohemian noblemen

---

[1] During the Hitler regime in Prague Pfitzner became the city's chief burgomaster; he was afterwards publicly executed by the Czechs.

took German wives. German *minnesänger* at the court of Prague include Reinmar von Zweter and Ulrich von Türlin, who came from Carinthia and sang of King Ottokar II, living and dead, as his 'high and beloved lord'.

Wenzel (Charles IV) was a great-grandson of Rudolf of Habsburg. His childhood was overshadowed by the bitter antagonism between his parents which caused his Habsburg mother Elizabeth to live in banishment at the castle of Melnik. His father, King John of Bohemia, was usually absent on one of his chivalrous enterprises; it is possible that he was afraid of Prague. In 1323 the boy was sent to Paris to be brought up at the court of his uncle, King Charles IV of France, where the cult of the great Charles, Charlemagne, had been flourishing ever since the days of Philip the Fair. Wenzel Charles of Bohemia and Luxemburg was married off to Blanche of Valois [plate 65], niece of the French king, and his religious education taken in hand by Peter Roger, abbot of Fécamp. In his autobiography Charles IV relates that some years afterwards he met his old tutor again while on a visit to Avignon. Peter Roger, who had in the meantime become archbishop of Rouen and a cardinal, said to his former pupil, 'you will one day be King of the Romans', to which Charles replied, 'but before that you will be pope'. Both predictions came true.

Charles kept on amiable terms with the popes. In his imperial chancery, which he considerably expanded, he was surrounded by ecclesiastical advisers. His right-hand man was Ernst of Pardubitz, who as archbishop of Prague won the pope's backing for his plan to detach his see from Mainz and turn it into an independent archbishopric. The chancery was staffed by both German and Czech clerks, one hundred and thirty-eight in all. For fifteen years Charles was served as chancellor by Johann von Hohenmauth (otherwise Johann von Neumarkt), who was on visiting and letter-writing terms with Petrarch and Cola di Rienzo and belonged to the circle where *Der Ackermann und der Tod*, the Bohemian *Everyman*, was written. In Germany, where antipapal currents set up in the reign of Ludwig IV still flowed strongly, Charles IV was mocked by his enemies as 'the parson's king', 'the pope's errand boy'. Charles had a true piety of a soberly medieval kind. He intended to 'pursue the right', the rights belonging to his house and the Empire.

Charles' return to Bohemia followed two 'apprentice' years in Italy. He had to relearn his native tongue, but could now speak French, Lombard, German and Latin. He acted as regent in Bohemia during his father's absences.

We found this kingdom so neglected that on our travels we met with no castle which had not been mortgaged, and all its crown lands with it, so that there was no choice but to lodge in a house in the town, like any other citizen. Worst of all, the castle at Prague, deserted since the time of King Ottokar, had fallen into such rubble and ruin that it was beyond repair. We therefore caused to be built at great expense a fine new palace, the palace men see there today.

Charles invited to Prague two outstanding architects, Matthias of Arras, whom he had met at Avignon, and Peter Parler, then only twenty-three years old. His reign saw the building of the castle, the cathedral, the Charles Bridge, the Karlshof (for

Augustinian canons, an octagonal building modelled on Charlemagne's cathedral at Aachen) and sundry churches and monasteries. Karlstein on the Vltava became the 'Bohemian Escorial', a palace dedicated to the king's sacred ancestors and to housing the imperial treasures.

Charles IV, king and future emperor, at heart detested the knightly mode of life. This rejection is perhaps to be understood as a rejection of his father, whose character was so very different. Charles himself led a simple life, putting on outward pomp only when interests of state demanded it. He was a nervous, restless individual, never still. He always had to have something in his hands, he chipped away at pieces of wood (Jarrett remarks that today he would certainly have been a chain-smoker) and passed many sleepless nights in work and worry.

'Piously to see to what is right' was his motto. He wanted reconciliation between the Czechs and Germans in Bohemia. He invited to Bohemia monks from Croatia and founded for them the house of SS. Cosmas and Damian near Vyshehrad, whose function was to keep alive the Slavonic liturgy and the glagolitic script. Charles speaks in his charters of the sweet and wholesome habit of the native tongue, the noble idiom of the Slavs. In 1333–4 John of Dražič had founded at Raudnitz on the Elbe a house of Augustinian canons reserved exclusively for Czechs, an action he justifies in the foundation charter: experience has taught us that no good comes when two nations inhabit the same monastery; the Germans have enough monasteries already; Czechs fare ill under Germans; members of other nations who dare to enter the monastery should be excommunicated. In 1349 Ernst of Pardubitz, archbishop of Prague and a Bohemian Czech, removed the clauses restricting membership of the community to one nation.

One way of surmounting the national barrier was through education. Charles founded a reformed monastery (in all twenty-four religious houses were founded at Prague during his reign) and brought to Prague reforming preachers such as the Austrian Konrad Waldhauser. One of Waldhauser's pupils was John Milič, who could on occasion describe even the emperor as antichrist. In 1348 Charles founded the Empire's first university, Prague's famous Alma Mater Carolina. It was composed of four nations (the university of Vienna, founded in 1365 followed the same pattern): the Bohemian nation, which covered all indigenous students, German and Czech, and students from Hungary and Siebenbürgen; the Bavarian nation, embracing Austrians, Bavarians, Swabians, Franconians, Carinthians, Carniolans, Swiss, Tyrolese, Italians from imperial Italy, Hessians, Rhinelanders and Westphalians; the Polish nation, made up of German colonists in the east lands, Lithuanians, Prussians and Silesians; and the Saxon nation, composed of students from the remaining parts of north Germany and from northern Europe. Under the constitution each nation had a voice in important decisions and the rector was chosen from each nation in turn. Education and learning were also valuable as a means of communication. Charles brought the Dominicans to Prague, among them Meister Eckhart, who stayed for some years.

I   115

IV Charles IV and his wife, fresco in the Karlstein, the citadel Charles built to be his 'Escorial' long before the Escorial itself was thought of. Here he stakes his claim to be the true successor to Charles the Great.

The possibility of making economic development a binding force was not over-looked. Charles established trade routes throughout the Empire which converged on Prague, so that one could go via Prague from Venice to Hamburg or Bruges, and he promoted the development of Hamburg and the Hanse. Charles was in fact the first and last emperor after Otto IV to set foot on north German soil. His visit to Lübeck in 1375 struck even contemporaries as an unprecedented event. Charles had dynastic possessions in the Upper Palatinate which he developed into a kind of 'New Bohemia'. He devoted much attention to Nuremberg – in his own words 'the most eminent and best situated city of the Empire' – with the idea of making it another capital, second only to Prague.

Charles transformed the old Přemyslid coronation order (derived from a tenth-century German order) into the new coronation order used in 1347, which closely follows the French order of 1328. The gold and jewels from the old Přemyslid crown were reworked into a new royal crown similar to that of St Louis. It was subsequently placed on the head of St Wenzel [Wenceslas] and became the state crown.

The Habsburg formula – 'others may wage war, your good fortune is to marry' – applies equally to Charles as a dynastic politician. But he was not, as Maximilian I maliciously described him, an 'arch stepfather' to the Empire. His legislation for Bohemia certainly had the aim of turning the country into a state of the western stamp, but to the Empire he gave an imperial constitution (the Golden Bull of 1356) which reflected its nature as a unique federation [plate 67]. Charles deliberately rejected the uniformity which the centralized bureaucratic monarchies of France and England were steadily trying to impose. The Empire was a 'Commonwealth of Nations', an association which embraced bodies of greatly varying legal status and which in the narrower sense comprised the federation of the electors under the emperor.

In the Golden Bull Charles admonishes the electors to see that their sons learn the Italian and Slavonic (i.e. Czech) languages, as this would improve their handling of imperial business and lighten their task, 'since the fame of the Holy Roman Empire arises from the variety of customs, ways of life and language found in the various nations which compose it, and it requires laws and a form of government which pays heed to this variety'. This is the best 'definition' of the Empire there is, and even the greatest of the Habsburg rulers took it as their guide. Charles' autobiography, written as a 'Mirror of Princes' with the didactic purpose of showing how the christian prince ought to think, act and live, was held in high esteem at the court in Vienna. In 1527 the Estates of Bohemia presented it to Ferdinand I as a gift.

Charles' attitude to the towns was one of encouragement [plate 71], though he also regarded them with some suspicion as potential centres of unrest; at one time or another Aachen, Mainz and Speyer all turned against him. He issued many privileges to towns and sought to reconcile them with their bishops. He also encouraged leagues of towns, thus the Swabian League and the Hanse. Lübeck he honoured as an 'imperial city', and he promoted five cities, Lübeck, Rome, Venice, Pisa and Florence, to ducal rank.

Charles used his sacral-political position in the Empire to promote his policy of reconciliation. He looked to his two saints, Charles the Great and Wenzel, to bind the nations together, in particular the Germans and the Slavs. Wenzel, the saint who was at once his own baptismal patron and the patron saint of Bohemia, and who was buried in St Vitus' cathedral at Prague, was given a new liturgical office, for which Charles himself wrote the legend: not least among the legend's objects was to provide an edifying example for the Bohemian aristocracy to follow. Here, as in his auto-biography and in the Golden Bull, Charles can be seen sticking firmly to his maxim that the worst political sins are envy and ambition.

He also introduced the cult of St Wenzel into the Empire, founding chapels for him in the Marienkirche at Aachen, at Ingelheim and at Hamburg (where five altars in all were dedicated to him). He arranged for Aachen, Ingelheim, Sulzbach, Neustadt and Rottenburg to maintain Czech-speaking priests for the benefit of Czech pilgrims and Czech vassals performing their military service away from home. As a living survival of this symbiosis one can point to the service held in Czech each Sunday afternoon in St Peter's church in Vienna (a foundation which goes back to the time of Charles the Great).

Charles the Great was honoured by the building of the castle of Karlstein near Prague [colour plate IV] and by the attention Charles IV paid to the old Carolingian palaces, not forgetting Aachen. His visit to the grave of Charles' great enemy and victim, the Saxon duke Widukind, led to a further gesture of reconciliation, the restoration of the monument and the erection over it of the armorial bearings of Charles the Great and Bohemia: Charles IV hoped that by such means the 'unsubdued' past might be reversed and the ground prepared for the present and future reconcilia-tion of the peoples. Always concerned for the Czech-German balance in Bohemia, he ordered that all officials should be able to speak Czech (although the language of the court was mainly German, out of deference to his last three wives, who were German princesses). In districts of mixed population town governments had to be composed half of German and half of Czech councillors.

The Golden Bull of 1356, negotiated with the electors at diets in Nuremberg and Metz, remained to the end the Empire's basic and most important constitution. It provided for election of the emperor by seven electors meeting under the chairman-ship of the archbishop of Mainz, who was given the casting vote. Frankfurt was stipulated as the place of election, Aachen as the place of coronation, Nuremberg as the place where the first diet of a reign should be held.

Charles IV enlarged Bohemia through acquiring the Silesian duchies from the Poles and Brandenburg from the Wittelsbachs; he had himself crowned king of Burgundy at Arles, to offset the aggressions of the French king in this region. At Easter 1355 he was crowned emperor in Rome by a papal legate, the pope being resident in Avignon. Neither Petrarch nor Cola di Rienzo, who both visited Prague, could tempt him into an aggressively Ghibelline policy in Italy. For Charles the Empire's centre of gravity lay in Central Europe; he looked to Venice, Hamburg,

Nuremberg, and his ancestral Luxemburg, to the east and the south-east. His Rome was hundred-towered Prague.

Charles married his two daughters to Habsburg brothers, Rudolf IV and Albert IV and in 1364 concluded a succession treaty with them. Duke Rudolf IV of Austria tried to do in Vienna what his father-in-law had done in Prague: the Stephansdom, the new university, the so-called *Privilegium Maius* (a remarkable example of the forger's art), were intended as added lustre for the house of Habsburg, whose imperial and dynastic policies were in many ways similar to those of Charles IV.

The 'Wenzel' Bible (now in Vienna), a magnificent and elaborate manuscript with exquisite miniatures, was made about 1390 [plate 68] for presentation to King Wenzel IV by Prague's wealthiest German citizen, the judge and mint-master Martin Rotlöw. This showpiece can perhaps stand as a symbol of the problems facing the Luxemburg rulers who followed Charles IV. It was their fate to be caught up in the passionate revolt of the 'poor Czechs' against the 'rich Germans', the latter forming a large proportion of the higher clergy. The Hussite movement was the greatest religious-political revolution of the Middle Ages and its effects can still be felt today.

Charles IV provided for the future division of his lands and honours in advance of his death. His eldest son Wenzel was elected King of the Romans and received the Bohemian inheritance, the second son Sigismund (married to Maria, eldest daughter of the king of Hungary and Poland) received the mark of Brandenburg, the third and youngest son, John, was given the new duchy of Görlitz. Moravia went to Charles' nephews, Jobst and Prokop.

King Wenzel (1378–1400) was indolent and unstable, certainly not the man to turn the current schism in the church (Pope Urban VI at Avignon, Pope Clement VII in Rome) to the Empire's advantage. He never went to Rome for imperial coronation and was as incompetent in coping with German civil war as he was in ruling Bohemia. He is famous, or rather infamous, for an atrocity: the torture and subsequent drowning in the Vltava of Jan of Pomuk, vicar-general and archivist of the archbishop of Jenstein (with whom Wenzel had a quarrel). Three centuries later, to counteract the popularity of the Hussite martyrs, the Jesuits turned 'Jan Nepomuk' into a folk saint. In 1729 he was canonized and became a patron saint of bridges; thereafter his effigy greeted passers-by on countless bridges throughout imperial territory, telling them and the world that Bohemia and its people had been won back by the Counter-Reformation.

Wenzel was eventually taken into custody by his cousin Jobst and deposed. In 1400 the ecclesiastical electors meeting at Rense chose Rupert, the Elector Palatine, to be King of the Romans, but despite some initial successes he soon proved a spent force. He set out for Rome but was obliged to turn back at Padua, and in Germany failed disastrously against the League of Marbach. After his death (May 1410) he was succeeded as King of the Romans by Sigismund (1411–37), Charles IV's only surviving son [plate 72]. He already had Brandenburg, and as husband of Maria controlled the crown of Hungary. Since Wenzel was childless, he felt confident of inheriting

Bohemia as well. In addition he had a stalwart lieutenant in Frederick of Hohenzollern, the burggrave on whom he conferred the mark of Brandenburg, the rank of elector and the office of high chamberlain in the Holy Roman Empire.

Sigismund was broken by the Hussite movement, a religious-political force whose radicalism, social dynamism and militant energy spread alarm and havoc throughout eastern and western Europe. Czech communism and the Czech National Socialism of the last days of the Danube monarchy, in many ways the forerunner of German National Socialism, can be numbered among its descendants. It may be left an open question to what extent Hussite elements worked upon Hitler (whose name signifies Hüttler, i.e. serf, copy-holder of the monastery of Zwettl on the borderland between Austria and Bohemia, as his forebears are known to have been for nearly five centuries).

The movement had its beginnings in the Prague of Charles IV, who for all his personal orthodoxy had been a patron of non-conforming preachers such as Conrad Waldhauser, who occupied the pulpit of the Týn church, and of his successor Milič of Kromerize. Milič became vice-chancellor of the imperial court and founded 'Jerusalem in Prague', a place where priests and laymen lived together in a life devoted to inward meditation and the cultivation of their beloved native tongue. Milič may have been in contact with the *devotio moderna*, the great lay movement in western Europe whose founder, Geert Groote, possibly visited Prague during the 1360s. One of Milič's pupils was the Czech nobleman Thomas of Stitny, the first to plead for Czech as a literary and devotional language, who asked whether Czech was less pleasing to God than Latin. (Joan of Arc's theological judges asked whether God hated Englishmen). In 1391 Johan Ritter of Mühlheim had founded the Bethlehem Chapel in Prague's Altstadt, at which preaching was allowed only in Czech. In 1399 there were riots in the German Týn church when the priest tried to ban the singing of '*Buoh všemohuci*' ('God the Almighty') by Czech worshippers.

The Hussite movement is often considered as a merely anti-German movement. But this is a one-sided way of looking at it, since in fact Hussitism very soon spread into neighbouring German territories, in particular Thuringia and Saxony, and Hussite influences played their part in the German Reformation. As a young man, Luther was already conscious of his inheritance as a spiritual son of Jan Hus, and others who inherited the same spirit were later a strong influence on German revivalist movements.

Hus was for a time the confessor of Queen Sophia, a Bavarian princess, and long enjoyed the protection of the court. A modern public, amused and puzzled by Shakespeare's fairy-tale Bohemia set by the sea, might remember that Bohemia's tragedy is in many ways linked with England. Wyclif's teaching was brought to Bohemia by Czech students who went to Oxford in considerable numbers, partly in consequence of the close dynastic ties between England and Bohemia (Richard II of England had a Bohemian queen). Hus and Jerome of Prague were Wyclif's spiritual disciples, and indeed Hus has been described as one 'who preached Wyclif's doctrines in academically milder form'. Jan Hus from Husinec in southern Bohemia, a poor man's son, found supporters at court, among the Bohemian nobility and clergy, and not least at the university, from which in 1409 there was an exodus of Germans, repelled by the mounting tide of Czech nationalism. Some thousand professors, masters and students departed to pursue their studies in Leipzig and Erfurt.

In his sermons and writings Hus called on the Czechs to rouse themselves and seek deliverance – *On the deliverance of the faithful Czechs* is the title of one of his works. He and his companions composed Czech hymns in which religious and nationalist sentiments are characteristically blended. (Among small oppressed European minorities religious song is still an outlet for their feelings of revolt.)

Jerome of Prague, who fought alongside Hus, is an important figure in his own right. He studied in Prague and Oxford and was widely travelled, visiting Palestine, Paris (where he lectured in 1405), Heidelberg, Cologne, Poland and Lithuania to expound the 'new teaching'. He also paved the way for a religious and nationalistic 'panslavism', through the contacts he sought and obtained with Russian Orthodox churchmen. In due course some of Luther's friends and disciples, in search of allies against Rome, would seek similar contacts.

Professors, theologians, bishops, kings and popes closed their ranks against the new teaching. The words attributed to Hus as he went to the stake on 6 July 1415 – 'I die gladly for the Gospel I have proclaimed and taught' – need no authentication [plate 69]. Jerome of Prague followed not long after. The manner in which Jerome met his death – his brilliant speeches in his own defence, his unwavering calm – deeply impressed the Italian humanist Poggio Bracciolini, who describes the scene in a letter to Aretino in Italy.

Having no further faith in words, the Hussites took to arms. The years between 1420 and 1436 are ravaged by the Hussite wars, harbingers of the Thirty Years' War. The radical Hussites, the Taborites, made common cause with the more moderate Utraquists (whose chief demand was for the dispensation of the sacrament in both kinds, bread and wine, *utraque* . . . the chalice of the laity is still their symbol). Armies were put into the field by king and emperor, by German princes, by western noblemen, the pope lent his support, but nothing, it seemed, could stem the tide. In Jan Žižka, a knight from Trocnov, the Hussites had a military genius equal to the generals of the early French revolutionary armies. His successors, Prokop the Great and Prokop the Lesser, continued his victorious advances. Hussite swarms descended on German territories far from the Bohemian border. The German and western armies suffered a series of defeats, in 1420 (at Prague), in 1421 (at Saaz), in 1422 (at Deutsch-Brod) and finally in 1431, when a great crusading force commanded by Elector Frederick of Brandenburg and Giuliano Caesarini, the cardinal legate, was defeated at Taus.

This was the crusade of the fifteenth century, the era of the Maid of Orleans and the Hundred Years' War between England and France: a crusade against the 'Kingdom of God in Bohemia', a crusade against the Hussites. A few years later we find Giuliano

Caesarini, together with Nicholas of Cusa, emerging at the Council of Basel as leader of the moderate reform party.

In this period of intense confusion two councils of great significance in the evolution of European Catholicism – or more precisely of Roman Catholicism – took place on imperial territory: the Council of Constance (1414–18) and the Council of Basel (1431–49). Empire and church were suffering from profound disorders; each required a reform in head and members, neither achieved it. The Council of Constance did at least succeed in deposing three popes, John XXIII, Benedict XIII and Gregory XII. There was now only one pope, the newly elected Martin V, a member of the Colonna clan which had opposed Boniface VIII. The Council of Basel reached a compromise with the Hussites; after a military defeat this compromise was also accepted by the Taborites (1436). The church reform on which the educated laity and clergy, in particular the teachers in the universities, had set their hopes, made no headway. The conciliar epoch was the last heyday of the university of Paris; some of its theological representatives at the council arrived hotfoot from the trial of Joan of Arc.

Sigismund's prestige in the Empire had dramatically fallen as a result of the Hussite wars. He failed in his efforts to impose a general peace in the Empire and fought an unsuccessful war with the Poles, in consequence of which territory ruled by the Teutonic Knights was lost to the Empire and came under the suzerainty of the Polish crown. Before he died Sigismund had at least managed to secure the succession in Bohemia and Hungary for his son-in-law, Duke Albert of Austria, with whose reign the house of Austria began a rule which with brief interruptions and one revolution (1806) lasted until 1918. His own reign as Emperor Albert II lasted barely a year (1438–9).

7

THE RISE OF THE HOUSE OF HABSBURG
(1438–1519)

MAXIMILIAN I, 'the last knight', the emperor who through his Burgundian marriage became heir to Burgundy's European policy and the grandfather of Habsburg world power, seems already foreshadowed in the person of Rudolf the Founder, Charles IV's son-in-law. This Rudolf, a young man of burning ambition and great gifts who died childless at the age of twenty-six, had attempted to win a privileged position for his own house within the Empire. The claim he advanced in the so-called *Privilegium Maius* (a document forged by his chancellor) was rejected by Charles IV: if accepted, the privilege would have established the scions of the illustrious house of Habsburgs as 'archdukes', on a par with the electors as the first princes of the Empire; it would also have preserved the Habsburg lands as an indivisible unit. In Rudolf the dreams and ambitions born of a lively political imagination (a commodity not then in such short supply as it is with our modern statesman – the fault if any was on the side of excess) went hand in hand with sober realism, *Realpolitik*; and Rudolf resembled Maximilian in thinking that realism was at least as much concerned with realizing political fantasies as with haggling over treaties and rights. His flexible mind stood him in good stead during the troubled times he grew up in (a period of plague and schism). He acquired for his house not only the Tyrol but also, through his succession treaties, the prospect of succeeding to the crowns of Bohemia and Hungary and the countship of Görz.

After his death the house of Habsburg split into two branches, the Albertine and Leopoldine. Albert II, of the Albertine line, was the first to combine rule over the hereditary lands of Bohemia and Hungary with the imperial crown. Attempts at combining Bohemia, Hungary and the Austrian lands go back to the days of Ottokar II, the initiative coming now from Prague, now from Hungary, now from Vienna. The 'necessity' for such a union arose from the compelling consideration that only by their united strength ('*viribus unitis*' remained the device of the Danube monarchy down to 1918) could more powerful enemies be kept at bay. The Turkish invasion had been advancing on Europe unchecked for over a century, and like an avalanche gathered in momentum as it approached.

In 1396 Emperor Sigismund defeated the Turks at Turkopolis, in 1452 Frederick III was crowned in Rome, the last emperor to be crowned there, in the year before Constantinople fell. For three centuries, from the early fifteenth to the early eighteenth, the Emperor's task was to defend the Empire, the Church and the entire west against the Turks. In 1529 and 1683 the Turks stood at the gates of Vienna. Had Vienna fallen, the way into the Empire would have been open. Emperor Albert II died in Vienna on 27 October 1439, while preparing to wage war on the Turks. His son Ladislas was born posthumously. The intrigues of Helene Kottanerin, a middle-class Viennese, secured for him the crown of Hungary, while his guardian, Duke Frederick v of Inner Austria (of the Leopoldine line) was elected German king and, as Frederick III, German emperor [plate 73].

Few rulers have attracted so much indignant comment from later historians or such venomous contempt from contemporaries. He is attacked for his indolence, his inertia, his inactivity, his 'neglect of the interests of the Empire', his apparent reluctance to stand and fight his enemies, his acceptance of defeat upon defeat. Frederick III's first involvement in a dispute was with his brother, Albert VI, over the wardship of Ladislas Postumus. When Ladislas died in Prague (1457), his kingdoms of Bohemia and Hungary passed by election to national kings, George of Podiebrad and Matthias Corvinus. The citizens of Vienna (whose various quarrels with the Habsburgs went back to the days of Ottokar II) sided with the Styrian nobility in a revolt against Frederick. Turkish invasions of Styria started early in the 1460s. Corvinus occupied Austrian territories and made Vienna virtually his capital.

One cannot help speculating what was the matter with the sleepy giant – for physically Frederick was indeed a giant, of immense corpulence. In his old age he had a craving for fruit, the sweeter and more luscious the better, and he also drank heavily. This weakness was one of the causes of his death. His son Maximilian, though often incensed at his father's indolence, struck out the chapter in Grünpeck's *Historia Friderici III et Maximiliani I* which dealt with his father's death. Was the emperor quite oblivious to the famines, plagues, wars and Turkish dangers afflicting his peoples? The figure AEIOU first occurs among private jottings he made while still Archduke of Inner Austria. He may have found it in the *Convivio* of Dante, who in his musings on the pacific role of the world emperor hit upon a Latin verb composed solely of vowels, *'aueio'*, which he says means 'I bind all words together': *'veramente imaginare questa figura, AEIOU, la quale e figura di legame'* ('and whoso regards it rightly as AEIOU, sees it as the figure of a tie').

On one page of his notebook Frederick wrote down proverbs worth remembering, among them *Lieb ist laid* ('love is suffering'), *ego spero nescio quid – suspiro nescio quo* ('I hope for what I know not, I yearn for what I do not know'), *ubi amor, ibi oculus* ('where love is, there is insight, the eye sees only what it loves'), *Austriae est imperare orbi universo* ('all the world is subject to Austria'). So there we have it, the portentous device AEIOU which has been the subject of so much exegesis and is to be found on Frederick's dwellings and household objects. He was 'Frederick the Fat', who matched not at all the dream figure of that Frederick the Third for whom many men had yearned as the successor of the Hohenstaufen; he was deficient in all the qualities proper to an apocalyptical emperor, prince of world peace and saviour king. Yet this corpulent and drowsy Frederick III had unshakeable faith in the dignity of the imperial office and was not prepared to surrender a tittle of its rights. He was in no doubt that *Austriae est imperare orbi universo*, and that in concrete terms this meant that the German monarchy and the office of Roman emperor belonged by right to the house of Austria.

'Who is talking about victories? All that matters is to survive.' Rilke's well-known saying might have been Frederick's motto. He shared with many other Habsburgs a deep distrust of 'the luck of battle', and was persuaded into a campaign only against his will. Later Habsburgs had an instinctive preference for generals whose campaigns 'in the theatre of war' were conducted in such a way as to avoid pitched battles. Procrastinators, great and small, have always been popular in Vienna.

We shall come closer to understanding Frederick III, whose historical role as 'founder' of Habsburg world power was not fortuitous, if we consider his reign under the three aspects which make it noteworthy: the person of his secretary, Aeneas Silvius, his own descent into Italy, and his disagreements with his son Maximilian during the years of their joint rule, 1486–93.

Aeneas Silvius Piccolomini, who was born on 18 October 1405 in Pienza (originally Corsignano), was small in stature, round-headed, in later life somewhat stout, and accustomed to look on the world with an open eye. As a young man he was poor. Thomas Ebendorfer, the Austrian historian who was his contemporary, tells us that at the age of twenty-six, while earning his living as a secretary at the Council of Basel, he was always willing to fetch drinks for his friends from the nearest tavern. His youth, spent in the service of various ecclesiastics, was a restless, picaresque existence. He went to London disguised as a merchant and writes very candidly to his father about his relations with an English girl he met there. About this time he also wrote a love story, in which nothing is left to the imagination. Such was the 'poor worm' who addressed himself to Emperor Sigismund with the request that he take in hand the reform of the church.

Aeneas Silvius entered the employment of Frederick III in 1442. His belief in the emperor's mission was genuine and he would have liked to see him presiding over yet another Council. In an account he wrote of the Council of Basel he shows a definite conciliar bias, which later earned for the work a place on the Index, where it remained for several centuries. (No other work written by a pope can claim this distinction.) The interest Aeneas Silvius took in Germany is evident from his *Germania*: this account he wrote of Vienna and the German lands he visited in the service of the emperor contributed to the growth of German national consciousness during the fifteenth and sixteenth centuries and influenced the men around Maximilian.

Elected pope, Aeneas Silvius chose the programme name Pius II, which linked him both with the first Pope Pius and with Virgil's '*pius Aeneas*', founder of Rome. A reform-minded pope, he wanted to remain on friendly terms with the emperor in order to pursue their common struggle against the Turks. His draft proposals for reform can be found in *Pastor aeternus* (the nineteenth-century encyclical of the same title is conceived in a very different spirit), which incorporates important ideas derived from Nicholas of Cusa. It opens with a statement of what the pope believes to be his own obligations. He asks for brotherly correction in case of error and promises no one shall find him stiff-necked. He will be readily accessible to everyone, above all the poor. Pius kept the style of his court deliberately plain, even meagre, and its prevailing atmosphere was free, candid and self-critically humane.

At his accession in 1458 Pius was an avowed friend of the emperor, whose *Life* he had written, which did not endear him to countries such as Scotland, Denmark, Poland, France, Hungary and Cyprus, where his election was received with less than enthusiasm. There is a picture by Michael Wohlgemuth which shows pope and emperor, Pius II and Frederick III, side by side in fraternal harmony. This had been the Hohenstaufen vision in the twelfth century; it was reiterated by the compilers of the *Sachsenspiegel* and the *Schwabenspiegel* in the thirteenth, and was still the vision of the greatest theorizer about Church and State in the age of Frederick III, Cardinal Nicholas of Cusa.

In 1452 Aeneas Silvius Piccolimini had prepared the way for Frederick III's Roman expedition. The town chronicler of Siena (though at no time in the Middle Ages a 'city' of the Empire, Siena was always well-disposed towards it) in his account of Frederick's ceremonial entry on 7 February 1452 tells us that the Sienese went out to meet him at the fourth milestone. (When Frederick approached Rome the Milanese and Florentine ambassadors, to spite the Venetians by showing greater honour to the emperor, greeted him at the fifth milestone, the envoys of the curia at the third). The next part of the story is taken up by Aeneas Silvius himself. A band of splendidly accoutred young men, two hundred strong, went out to meet the emperor, at their head three mounted standard-bearers, the one in the centre carrying aloft the imperial eagle, black on a gold ground, those on either side the colours of Siena, silver and black in quartered shields. The imperial standard was delivered up to Frederick. At the gate of Siena he was met by a procession carrying olive branches, at their head the magistracy, then the clergy and the university, after them the townspeople and their children. All sang the hymn '*Veni creator spiritus*', after which Frederick, as rightful lord, was given the keys of the city. Frederick made reply through his interpreter, Aeneas Silvius, and the procession moved to the cathedral. The city was ablaze with torches and lights, the palaces lit to their eaves, singing children went through the streets with candles in their hands, celebration bonfires burned outside the walls.

These liturgies proper to the entry of the prince of peace are similar to those of the Palm Sunday procession which celebrates the entry of Christ the King. The Siena chronicler ends his account in the town's letter-book with a particularly fine flourish: '*Hac die serenissimus et gloriosissimus Dominus, Dominus Fredericus dei gratia Rex Romanorum intravit civitatem Serarum cum maxima pace et triumfo.*' ('On this day the all-gracious and glorious Lord Frederick, by God's grace King of the Romans, made his entry into the city of Siena, in great peace and triumph.') The King of the Romans made his entry as *Imperator Triumphans* pacing under the 'sky-canopy', while the people shouted '*Viva l'impero*'.

Two weeks later Frederick was joined by his bride, Eleanor of Portugal [plate 74]. She was the grand-daughter of Don João (John) I, who had captured Ceuta, the North African stronghold which subsequently became the starting-point for Portuguese explorations overseas. João was Grand Master of the Military Order of Aviz, the Portuguese branch of the Castilian Order of Calatrava. The Byzantine streak in Maximilian (he wanted to be a new Constantine) received strong encouragement from the Alexandrine aspiration of the house of Aviz to found a world empire in India. Maximilian's great-great-uncle was Don Fernando, Calderon's 'resolute prince' who died in a Moorish prison. One of his great uncles was the famous Henry the Navigator, who surrounded himself with learned advisers and thought and planned in continents: Maximilian's mother taught him to do the same. Her father, King Duarte (Edward) was a humanist and man of letters, as highly cultured as Alfonso el Sabio. His passion for writing books descended to his grandson Maximilian.

From his cradle Maximilian was marked out as the 'new Constantine' whose task was to save Christendom in the struggle against Islam. His mother, with papal consent, changed her name on marriage to Helena after the mother of Constantine the Great. In his autobiography Maximilian claims that this new Helena wanted her own son to be called Constantine, though his father preferred George, after the warrior saint who fought against pagans; Maximilian was decided upon in deference to the wishes of his Hungarian godfather, Nicholas of Ujlak, who found martyrdom while resisting the Turks in the Balkans.

Maximilian's other fore-ordained mission came to him through his Burgundian marriage, which made him heir to the anti-French system erected by Charles the Bold. This was a mission which the house of Habsburg, backed by France's 'natural and historic' enemies – England, Spain, Savoy – would shoulder for close on three centuries.

On 16 February 1468 the six electors (minus the king of Bohemia) elected the twenty-six-year-old Archduke Maximilian of Austria-Burgundy as King of the Romans. Emperor Frederick III disapproved of the election, since he had the worst possible opinion of his son and thought him unfit to succeed him in the Empire. The seven years' double rule which followed invites comparison with the last years of the reign of Maria Theresa, when she ruled jointly with Joseph II. In both cases two generations confronted one another, two confronted worlds which at bottom were closely akin.[1] Frederick III would treat his son and co-ruler like a schoolboy, leaving him to wait six hours for an audience. He was greatly annoyed when Maximilian

[1] This situation in which ruler and heir are in flagrant contrast is found for the last time with Emperor Francis Joseph and Crown Prince Rudolf (Schönbrunn and Belvedere), and Francis Joseph and Archduke Francis Ferdinand.

bargained his way out of Bruges by negotiating an agreement which Frederick regarded as contrary to all the best interests of the Empire; it was an 'eternal disgrace', and as such totally unacceptable. A prince should not allow himself to be blackmailed, and the undertakings Maximilian had given to the Flemish towns were therefore invalid.

Frederick III possessed a very strong sense of what was right; Maximilian showed at times 'a completely naïve amorality in political matters'. Frederick believed in the high responsibility of the office vested in him by God. For him the Emperor was the temporal head of Christendom, even at times when he lacked political power and prestige.

During the years of their joint rule father and son often pursued independent or conflicting policies. Yet at moments when relations between them seemed most strained a deep and genuinely human emotion would break through the old man's apparently impervious crust. A loving father then bestirred himself to charm his son with his own conception of the state and as time went on entrusted to him in increasing measure a share in the tasks of government, for example in the struggle with Hungary and France in 1489. From this year relations between Maximilian and his father show a fundamental improvement. In his Burgundian lands, Maximilian had come under the influence of western nationalism. His father trained him back in a hard school to the universalism of the imperial office. Much has been said of Maximilian's fickle, wayward and desultory handling of politics. But such behaviour merely reflects the great strain this re-education imposed. The inheritance from his ponderous father warred in him with the temperament he inherited from his mother, which was western, highly sensitive, nervous and flexible, a bequest from Portuguese, Burgundian and English forebears. (Eleanor was descended amongst others from Philippa of Lancaster, daughter of John of Gaunt.)

Furthermore Maximilian's childhood was by no means as idyllic as may appear from his own account. His tutor, Peter Engelbrecht, was so clumsy in his handling that the child suffered psychological disturbance and found difficulty in communicating. Wiener-Neustadt, where Maximilian grew up, was constantly receiving refugees from Hungary and Croatia whose tales of panic and of Turks who kidnapped men, women and children must have reached his ears. The harsh years in Burgundy which followed plunged the young prince out of the world of games and fantasies and into reality. His experiences with King Louis XI inflicted damage which went deep: 'there is no greater and more cowardly scoundrel in all the world' was his verdict on the king and it coloured his idea of France as a whole.

Maximilian was born on Maundy Thursday (22 March) 1459, at Wiener-Neustadt. Through his paternal grandmother, Cymburga of Masovia, he had Polish, Lithuanian and Russian blood in his veins. On his mother's side all his forebears apart from his English great-grandmother came from the Pyrenean monarchies. Among Maximilian's thirty-two immediate forebears, three were German, two French (both came from territories within the Empire or on its borders), four Italian, ten

Portuguese and Spanish (plus a further two who cannot be more closely identified), three English, three Polish, one Lithuanian and four Russian. Maximilian, who lives on in German folk memory, as 'The Emperor', was in truth a European.

Aeneas Silvius characterized his former master, Frederick III, as a man who wanted to conquer the world sitting down. Maximilian was pre-eminently mobile and in a very 'modern' manner. One can point to hundreds of villages and towns where he spent but a single night. The emperor was a man 'on the march' – a foreshadowing of his grandson, Charles V.

In *Weisskunig*, an account of his life which he intended as a pictorial and literary guide for the education of future princes, Maximilian sets down all the subjects he learned as a young man: reading, writing, the seven liberal arts, political science, star-gazing, the black art; 'love of history'; physic, the business of chanceries; the carpenter's trade, music, playing the lute; gastronomy; minting coins, mining; shooting with the crossbow, mounted and on foot; the use of weapons of all types; falconry, hunting the deer, chamois, ibex, wild boar and bear; fishing and fowling. The crowd of song-birds he carried about made such a din that it got on the nerves of his assistants.

At an early age he learned to paint and draw, and he stresses the usefulness of painting as a training for strategy. He tells us that as a child he deliberately sought the company of ordinary people, stove-keepers, sweepers, porters and the like, in order to learn the many different languages spoken in his future realm, for example 'Windish'. He ended up speaking seven languages. He was affability itself: young, of average proportions, with a radiant glance and engaging manner, he made it an unconcealed and genuine pleasure to meet men of 'the people'. He would dance cheerfully with the bourgeois wives of Nuremberg, he would chat with his mercenaries, with foundrymen about cannon, with his hunt servants, indeed with everyone he met, moved by a boundless curiosity. The first great and decisive experience of his life came to him when he went to Burgundy.

When Maximilian was young, Austria and Burgundy were two different worlds. Vienna and the Austrian lands were framed by their misery and bitter poverty, whereas Philip the Good of Burgundy had been the richest prince in Europe (only Venice was richer). Writing from the Netherlands, Maximilian exclaims over his discovery of twenty towns as large as Vienna and almost as many moated castles, all on a par with Laxenburg; he is awed to find that the duke has three thousand falcons and four thousand hunting dogs. The two worlds met for the first time when the 'poor emperor' and the 'rich duke' foregathered at Trier in 1473. Charles the Bold's dazzling entry into the city invited invidious comparisons with the emperor's own meagre retinue. One Burgundian courtier sniggeringly remarked that the emperor's forebears had very likely gone about in skins. Yet an emperor was always an emperor; the duke of Burgundy was what his military strength and the splendour of his court made him. Marriage plans between Austria and Burgundy had been in the air since the 1440s. Charles the Bold's price was his own election as King of the Romans, at which Frederick III demurred. Barely four years after this inconclusive meeting Charles' corpse, gnawed by wolves, was recovered from the frozen surface of a ditch and the Burgundian empire seemed to collapse overnight. But as in the fairy tales, a prince from far-off lands appeared to save the day: Maximilian seeking the hand of Mary.

Memories of this Burgundy have not vanished from a France in which men can still speak of 'Troyes en Bourgogne' and 'Sens en Bourgogne'. One modern scholar, Canon Maurice Chaume, made the study of Burgundian national sentiment from the time of the early Burgundians down to Charles the Bold a life's work. In the eleventh and twelfth centuries Burgundian artists produced distinctive romanesque work which was the match of any in Europe: one has only to mention Cluny, Autun, Vézelay and Auxerre. The Christ of the Vézelay tympanum [plate 38] is all judge, judge of the world. The mounted Christ of the Apocalypse in the crypt of Auxerre cathedral embodies with archaic force the immensity of the God of terror. Gothic art found a welcome in Burgundy and spread from there, enriched by Burgundian native tradition, throughout Europe.

The Carthusian abbey of Champmol, just outside Dijon, was erected by Philip the Bold to be the burial-place of this new Valois dynasty, the Burgundian Escorial. The nineteenth century turned it into a mad-house, and the funerary portraits of the dukes of Burgundy are now preserved in their former palace at Dijon. The human beauty of these dead figures is truly captivating. From the praying hands of Philip the Bold [plate 77] an invisible bridge reaches to the praying hands in the Escorial [plate 114]: this great gesture of supplication points forward to the *pietas* of Habsburg Madrid and Habsburg Vienna. The 'Spanish court ceremonial', which revolved round the cult of the dynasty and continued to be observed at Vienna down to the time of Francis Joseph, was first evolved in Burgundy.

At its height the Burgundian state embraced lands whose eastern frontiers started roughly from Guelders on the Zuiderzee, took in Amsterdam, Utrecht and Vanloo, Maastricht, Limburg, Luxemburg, Nancy, Schlettstadt and Kolmar, then went from the Black Forest to Waldshut, and from Rheinfelden up to Swiss territory just outside Basel. The western border ran along the English Channel from Flanders and Artois, passing through Ostend, Calais and Boulogne, as far as Eu and Dieppe, thus forming an important link with England, who found Burgundy useful as a continental ally. Burgundy in fact here bit deep into present-day France, almost up to Beauvais and St Quentin, embracing in addition Amiens and the Hennegau (which included Valenciennes).

The new Burgundian state had grown out of the old Lotharingia. In the eleventh century two successive emperors, Conrad II and Henry III, were crowned kings of Burgundy at the abbey of Payerne. The situation under these emperors was much what it was under Mary of Burgundy and Maximilian, that is, the link between Burgundy and the Empire was purely personal. This Burgundy bridged the connection between the Rhine–Moselle–Meuse and the Saône–Rhône waterways, making them 'the great arteries of the west' and strengthening the links between Romance and Germanic Europe. As a catalyst, Burgundy played an important part in the destiny of many nations – France, Germany, Austria, England, Italy, Portugal, Switzerland, Belgium and Holland.

'Unable to fulfil itself, Burgundy nevertheless helped many others to fulfilment, and may be said to have contributed as one of the component elements to the formation of Europe' (Gonzague de Reynold). The same could be said of two other historically remarkable structures, the Holy Roman Empire and Austria, whose disseminated influence acted as a catalyst and set up a wealth of counter-vailing influences. France, for example, took shape from her perpetual confrontation with the Empire, securing at the end of a protracted struggle the valuable prize of a large share in the Burgundian state.

Burgundy's sudden rise in the fifteenth century to the position of a European state was due to the energies of the ducal house of Valois. Some of the Burgundian lands were fiefs of the Empire, the rest being fiefs of the French crown. East of the Burgundian border at this period lay not one but several Germanies, 'des Allemagnes', to use Commynes' expression. Their union into an imperial confederacy occurred only after the collapse of Burgundy.

Burgundy as a whole was very wealthy. Half Europe dressed in Flemish cloth and a Florentine observer, Guicciardini, is forced to admit that the 'ports, fairs and markets' of the Burgundian Netherlands 'serve the whole of Europe'. Macaulay described Bruges, Ghent and Ypres as 'medieval Manchesters'. For a time Bruges was the banker of Europe. But since the towns were also riven by protracted struggles between 'rich' and 'poor', anyone wanting to dominate them needed prodigious energy and persistence. These were precisely the qualities Duke Charles possessed. As one of his biographers remarks, this 'dragon for work' worked as hard and as long as if he had to earn his living. Charles was a 'modern', a tormented solitary, always on the move, always working, always keeping track of his subordinates, down to the last entry in the ledgers of his finance officers. He found refreshment in music, which flourished greatly in the Burgundian lands. We first find Burgundian musicians employed at a Habsburg court in the time of Albert II, and again under Frederick III. In 1531 'Walloon Netherlanders' were members of the court chapel and Arnold of Brück (i.e. Bruges) was its director. Johannes of Revellis from Burgundy was arch-chaplain of the court chapel before becoming bishop of Vienna (1523–30), and in later days men and boys from the Netherlands were frequently employed as singers in the court chapel at Vienna.

The Burgundian ducal court 'shone brighter than the sun' and can compare only with the court of the sun-king, Louis XIV. The court travelled with the duke, taking with it as it moved to Bruges, Ghent or Brussels all the paraphernalia of a princely household, passing through the prosperous and troubled land like a giant caravan out of *The Thousand and One Nights*. It was the dukes of Burgundy who led the way as innovators of court etiquette and their ceremonial was later codified by Charles V,

V Scene from Maximilian I's *Tyrolese Hunt Book*. This passion for hunting was common among the great lords of old Europe down to and including Francis Joseph, who saw it as a truly imperial sport.

to become the pattern for all European courts down to the time of Louis XIV. This court ceremonial was of deep political significance. It exhibited the state, which was an incohesive and highly vulnerable artificial creation formed from mutually anta-gonistic lands and peoples and lacking inner coherence, as a work of art, an essay in celebration. For all their wealth and lustre, the dukes of Burgundy were regarded by the 'old' aristocracy as parvenues, and so had to insist daily, indeed hourly, upon their pre-eminence. Through their ceremonial they presented themselves to their peoples as 'kings'. The first to imitate this Burgundian model was Edward IV of England, which is not surprising since Charles the Bold had close connections with the great English houses, his mother being a Lancastrian and his second wife Margaret of York.

Burgundian ceremonial made of every action an act of state. The duke's daily routine followed a minutely prescribed ritual. At mealtimes the duke usually ate alone, except at festivals. Behind this exact apportionment of the daily programme and the stream of ceremonial – as behind all ritual and ceremonial – lay fear: fear of death, daily fear of insurrection, fear that the Burgundian state, that work of art, would collapse about its makers' ears.

The dukes' personal preference was for the simple life. But to impress the nobility and populace festal occasions were made an excuse for great displays. The sun-duke John showed no diffidence in inviting to Hesdin (both a castle and a palace) guests such as the emperor or the kings of France, England or Cyprus. Once arrived, the illustrious guest was treated to a display of magical contrivances.[1] Three statues unexpectedly spurted water at him, in one gallery a machine sprinkled him with flour, in another place he might be startled by thunder, lightning and rain or by a sudden plunge into a sackful of feathers. In the park there were bridges which gave way underfoot, waterfalls which played nasty tricks.

Under the Burgundian sun a miracle of art opened out; here is luxury, beauty and richness, a piety which delights in spectacle, taut faces framed by the pomp of robes: ecclesiastical and secular glory pressed into the service of the Burgundian state. Painters who worked in Burgundy include Claus Sluter, Van Eyck, Van der Weyden, Van der Goes, Dirk Bouts and Memling. Burgundian painting (a development from book illustration), Burgundian tapestry and Burgundian music: such were the arts which made the Burgundian court the pace-setter among fifteenth-century courts and caused it to outstrip the fourteenth-century leader, France. Burgundy's contribu-tion to the renewal of knighthood and chivalry was the Noble Order of the Golden Fleece [plate 76], inaugurated at the wedding of Duke Philip and Isabella of Portugal on 10 January 1430. The knights of the Golden Fleece were thought of as the duke's bodyguard and elite, surrounding him and his state with their own dignity and brilliance. Membership was initially restricted to thirty-one. Charles V increased it by

---

[1] This world of spine-chilling pleasures has a latter-day descendant (via baroque, with its harping on the mingling of terror and pleasure) in the Vienna Prater, with its grotto walks and mechanical popular attrac-tions.

twenty, Philip IV of Spain by a further ten. In 1794 the treasure of the order was removed to Vienna, where it still remains.

The Golden Fleece, the ceremonial world of the Burgundian court, the conception of politics as the interaction of diplomacy, war, religious-political festival and celebration – all this was given by Burgundy to the old Europe and helped to shape its destinies down to 1918. As we have seen, Charles the Bold went to his meeting with Frederick III at Trier in 1473 with a train intended to dazzle and overwhelm by its pomp the 'penurious emperor' and his retinue. He hoped at Trier to be designated Frederick's successor in the Empire. This dream had to be abandoned, but the duke nevertheless received the imperial vicariate over 'lower Germany', which carried the right of appointing to the imperial sees of Liège, Utrecht, Cambrai, Toul and Verdun. Burgundy was raised by the emperor to the rank of a 'kingdom'. Charles undertook to provide ten thousand men under his own command for the crusade against the Turks.

On a frosty night in January 1477 a small band of men with torches burst into Nancy. Among them was a Roman page of the house of Colonna, currently serving the duke of Burgundy. Frozen corpses lay about on the snow, the bodies of Swiss and Burgundian soldiers. The searchers went from one to another, until at last the page cried out, '*Hélas, voici mon bon seigneur*'. To his page, Charles was simply 'this good lord'; *Charles le Téméraire*, Charles the Bold, was the name given him by posterity. Dewez dubbed him the 'Napoleon of the Middle Ages'. He ruled over a fragmented realm, vulnerable on all fronts, defensible only through further expansion. Charles led a strenuous life, continually overworked and despite his abstemious eating and drinking a martyr to nervous indigestion. He lived under permanent threat from a great and dangerous foe, Louis XI of France. Charles wanted to found a great Lotharingian state to avoid the strangulation of Burgundy by France.

Louis XI was a master of economic warfare. The Burgundian lands were dependent on France for grain, and Louis hoped by stopping their supplies to create a famine. Louis perfected his technique only later, in his struggle against Mary of Burgundy and Maximilian, but he called for a blockade of the Burgundian lands as early as October 1470, at a conference held in Tours. Treaties Louis concluded with Switzerland contained clauses designed drastically to reduce Swiss trade with the Burgundian lands. Louis diverted English merchants from Burgundy and in truce negotiations with Charles the Bold sabotaged the promised lifting of the blockade. He encouraged privateering against the Burgundian fleet and tried to persuade the Hanse to cease using Bruges as their main staple in the west. He was behind *la guerre des foires*, a campaign to boycott Burgundy's fairs, and forbade his merchants to frequent the fair at Antwerp. He unilaterally devalued the Burgundian currency in France in the hope of strangling the detested Burgundians financially. He arranged with Lorenzo dei Medici (the Medici were bankers to both Charles the Bold and the French king) to cut off Charles' credit. Lorenzo's compliance led, however, to a split in the great banking house, since Tommaso Portinari, head of the Bruges branch, sided with Charles the Bold.

The duke of Burgundy knew his great enemy only too well, which was why he sought an alliance with England and the Empire and promised his daughter Mary to the son of Frederick III. The offensives of the apparently ultra-aggressive Charles the Bold were really defensive, thier object being to avoid encirclement by his enemies and strangulation.

Mary and Maximilian became acquainted by studying each other's portraits. The poirtrait he sent to her she looked at twenty times a day and reciprocated his gift with a l fe-size painting of herself. Was he not young, clever and brave? Had he not climbed to the topmost point of Ulm cathedral and in Munich prised open the jaws of a caged lion?

The catastrophe of Nancy was followed by revolts in the provinces 'de par deçà' (as they were known in Burgundian official terminology), in particular Flanders and Brabant. The chief aim of the towns was to revert to the situation as it had been two centuries earlier when the gilds had won control of town government after the Battle of the Spurs (Courtrai, 1302). Commynes perceived that the towns were wanting to establish a new world based on new relationships (à faire un monde neuf). The Estates-General sought to re-establish their old authority by means of the Grand Privilège they wrested from Mary in 1477. The clergy, still smarting from the taxes imposed on them by Charles the Bold, proclaimed his death as vengeance sent from God, divine punishment for his encroachment on the rights and possessions of the church. Louis XI felt that his hour had come. In his plans for winning all the territories of the duke of Burgundy a captive Mary, as a means of extortion, undoubtedly figured large.[1]

It was on 20 May 1477 that the eighteen-year-old Maximilian set out from poverty- and war-stricken Vienna to take the road for the golden west. The first Burgundian town he came to (at a time when the Burgundian state was apparently on the verge of dissolution) was Maastricht, which he reached on 5 August. At Louvain he was greeted by three thousand students who shoulted 'Vive Maximilien, Vive Bourgogne!' On 11 August he was in Brussels. Accompanied by seven hundred German knights of noble birth displaying on their breasts the red cross of Burgundy, himself accoutred in silver, Maximilian advanced 'like the archangel Michael' into regions where French was spoken but the French king feared. (Italians taking part in the Isonzo offensive during the First World War greeted the advancing Austrian troops with 'vengono i nostri', 'here come our own men', so tenacious was the memory of the Lombardo-Venetian kingdom.)

The contemporary Burgundian chronicler Molinet describes Maximilian's advent thus: 'Ainsy vient en nostre région le souverain des rois, l'honneur et la clarté de l'universelle fabricque du monde. Le peuple qui ambuloit en tenèbres fut souspris de grant lumière, laquelle

[1] Another French king, Charles VIII, actually succeeded in depriving Maximilian of a prospective bride in the person of Anne, the wealthy heiress to Brittany. Although the marriage had already been celebrated by proxy and Charles himself was betrothed to Maximilian's daughter Margaret, Charles forced Anne to become his wife. The talented Margaret (the future regent of the Netherlands) Charles kept in custody, intending to marry her usefully elsewhere in France. She wrote to her father that she was determined to escape from her abominable situation, even if it meant fleeing Paris in her nightgown.

illumina ceulx qui habitoyent en l'ombre de mort.' 'Thus there came into our land the sovereign of kings, the honour and glory of all the created world. The people who walked in darkness were surprised by the great light, which illumined all who dwelt in the shadow of death' [plate 81]. We are reminded of Frederick III's entry into Siena and of Charles V's entries yet to come: and of the festal entry of Augustus (prince of peace, surrogate for Christ) as it adorns the great doorway of the Vienna Hofburg leading from the inner court into the Michaelerplatz – *adventus domini, adventus Augusti.*

Maximilian entered Ghent, where the streets were decorated with streamers whose legend ran: '*Gloriosissime princeps, defende nos ne pereamus. Tu es dux et princeps noster, pugna proelium nostrum. Et omnia quae dixeris nobis faciemus.*' Maximilian is hailed as David, the saviour prince who will deliver his people. 'Defend us, lest we perish. You who are our prince, our leader, fight our battle. Everything you command we will perform.' In Ghent, his yet unseen bride awaited him. They stood together under torchlight in the Ten Walle castle, 'both as pale as death'. Neither knew the other's language, yet it was love at first sight.

At the first reception in the great hall of the castle in the presence of the Burgundian nobility, Margaret of York, Duke Charles' widow, and the Lady of Halewyn prompted Maximilian, telling him that his bride had about her person a carnation it behoved him to discover. Maximilian blushed and hesitated. The aged archbishop of Trier came to his rescue. 'Open the lady's bodice, perhaps you will find the flower there.' With trembling hand and to the delight of the entire court, he did as he was bid. The marriage was solemnized the next day in the castle chapel. The date was 18 August. At their marriage, the bridal pair were blessed by the papal legate. Maximilian placed the ring on Mary's index finger, as was then the custom, and the couple received communion in both kinds. The legate handed to Maximilian a morsel of bread and he partook of both this and the wine, together with his wife. This simple wedding of Mary and Maximilian was an occasion for deep emotion. The country was in mourning, it was threatened by the enemy, and there were grave struggles in prospect.

A modern Belgian historian, Luc Hommel, has described this August morning of 1477 as the real birthday of Belgium. The kingdom of Burgundy might have acted as a stabilizing element between France and Germany and prevented the great wars of the sixteenth to twentieth centuries. As it was, to quote the opinion this time of a Frenchman, Gabriel Hanatoux, the kingdom died too young to fulfil its destiny. In 1904 Kaiser Wilhelm II tried to buy the support of King Leopold II of the Belgians in the war he foresaw with Germany by offering to 'return the Flemish provinces unlawfully filched from the Belgians by the French. I will restore for you the duchy of Burgundy'. Charles V wanted to create a kingdom of Burgundy and bequeath it to the second son who was never born to him. In 1548 he established the Circle of Burgundy which retained its own special privileges and was linked to the Empire merely by its alliances.

Louis XI sent his troops through the Burgundian lands, plundering, burning and leaving famine in their wake. On 22 July 1478 the hoped-for heir was born at Bruges, Philip the Handsome. French agents spread the rumour that the baby was a girl. This rumour was scotched by the child's godmother, Margaret of York: as the christening party left the church of St Donat she undressed the baby and presented him to the crowd, an undoubted male. Eighteen months later Mary bore a daughter, Margaret, later to be known as 'la tante de l'Europe'.

Maximilian learned French from his wife [plate 82] and Flemish from the elderly Lady of Ravenstein. With his wife he joined in the festivals, weddings and amusements of the townspeople, when they were alone they played chess. They shared two sporting passions, skating and hunting. In the absence of chamois Maximilian coursed the hare, hunted the deer and rode out hawking. On a March day in 1482, when Maximilian and Mary were out hawking, Mary's falcon mounted the sky and plummeted; she lost her balance and fell from her horse. Mary was pregnant and her injuries fatal. She died at the Prinsenhof in Ghent on 27 March, at the age of twenty-five. 'La dame est morte': men wept for her in the streets.

The next years were hard ones for Maximilian, years he would never forget. French domination was fended off only with difficulty. The Netherlanders were unwilling to make him the guardian of his children Philip and Margaret, who were heirs to the Burgundian duchy. In 1488 he was taken prisoner by the citizens of Bruges and freed himself only through making far-reaching concessions which did not meet his father's approval. Frederick III wanted his son (King of the Romans since 1486) back in Austria, and to Austria Maximilian returned in 1489, having concluded the Peace of Montil les Tours with the Netherlanders. His field of vision shifted to take in east as well as west. From this time on his European policy describes two elliptical paths: in the east the struggle with the Turks, in the west the conflict with France.

Maximilian thought it better to arrive at alliances through treaties and marriages than to resort to war as a means of 'resolving' conflicts which military victory only provoked afresh. Cuspinian and other contemporaries assert he was willing to marry his sister Kunigunde to the Turkish sultan, so long as the bridegroom was converted to Christianity. He sent his little daughter Margaret to King Charles VIII of France as his prospective bride. In 1491 he concluded a defensive and offensive alliance with the great prince of Moscow against the Polish Jagellions, who were claiming Hungary. A further alliance with Moscow had the object of protecting the Teutonic Order against the Poles. Maximilian apparently hoped to reconcile the Russians and the Poles and is said to have written to the Grand Master of the Teutonic Order pointing out that Poland must be left inviolate for the sake of Europe as a whole and that the danger of Russia lay in its vastness. Fundamentally this was also the view of Maria Theresa, who died of grief at having consented to the partition of Poland.

Two marriage treaties concluded by Maximilian helped to determine the course of European politics down to the nineteenth century: the Spanish-Habsburg marriage treaty and alliance of 1495–6 and the marriage treaty with King Vladislav of Bohemia and Hungary, which resulted in a double wedding at Vienna in 1515.

The initiative for the Spanish marriage came from Spain. In 1474 Isabella of Castile and Ferdinand of Aragon, the 'Catholic kings', had united their two states in a personal union which withstood five years of war against the French and the Portuguese. The year 1492 saw the conquest of Granada, the last Moorish kingdom on Spanish soil, and the departure of Columbus whose commission from the Catholic kings was perhaps to seek out Prester John in India and prepare the way for a global alliance against Islam. Unified, Spain could embark on the offensive against Islam in North Africa, but its own coasts were under continual threat from French, Portuguese and Moorish privateers; there was also the fear that the Moors in the south of the country would give active support to any Islamic attempt at reconquest. Threatened from within and without, the Spain of the Catholic kings expelled first the Jews, in 1492, and ten years later the Moors.

Ferdinand wanted the Spanish-Austrian double marriage, which he proposed to follow up with an Anglo-Spanish marriage alliance, as a protection against France. When Charles VIII of France invaded Italy in 1494 the other powers were alerted to the danger he presented. The Apennine world of little states was already familiar with the policy of 'balance', which it had evolved to suit the Italian conditions of the fifteenth century. The tactic was now to be applied to western Europe as a whole. At Venice in 1495, on Spanish initiative, a 'Holy League' of European powers was formed in order to check the ambitious Charles VIII, whose aim in Italy, so the pope declared, was to become emperor.

The Holy League of 1495 brought Spain the support of Maximilian, Pope Alexander VI and Ludovico Moro, ruler of Milan and Venice; a year later the League was joined by Henry VII of England. Charles was at once forced to abandon his Italian conquests. Spain's need for security in face of French aggressiveness was most opportune for Maximilian, whose hostility to the French stemmed from his experiences in Burgundy and his more recent experience of the cynical behaviour of Charles VIII towards his daughter Margaret. The marriage policy of Ferdinand and Maximilian resulted in two weddings: Joanna, second daughter of Ferdinand and Isabella, married Philip, son of Maximilian and Mary of Burgundy, while Juan, the only son of the 'Catholic kings', married Maximilian's daughter Margaret. Three untimely deaths in the space of the three years 1497–1500 (those of Juan himself, of Isabella, eldest daughter of Ferdinand and Isabella, and of Miguel, her only child) made Joanna and Philip heirs to the Spanish kingdoms. Their son Charles, the future Emperor Charles V, who was born in 1500, would unite the Spanish dominions with the hereditary possessions in the Netherlands and in Austria. When Queen Isabella died, Philip the Handsome acted as regent for Prince Charles in Castile. King Ferdinand managed to drive the French out of Naples, which from 1504 was ruled by a viceroy from Spain. To secure the safety of this Spanish kingdom in the Mediterranean Ferdinand entered into an alliance with Maximilian and Henry VIII of

England. In 1515, because of the growing Turkish threat in the Mediterranean, he also persuaded the French to join the pact.

The Turks were also the involuntary cause of a meeting between the rulers of Poland and Hungary and Emperor Maximilian at Vienna in 1515 which resulted in another double wedding. This meeting was arranged by the Viennese humanist Johannes Cuspinian (Johann Spiessheimer of Schweinfurt), a diplomat and scholar in Maximilian's service, who has also left us an account of it. Despite careful preparation, the meeting nearly never took place: as so often, Maximilian was short of money (the Italians dubbed him 'Massimiliano senza denaro', 'Maximilian the penniless') and postponed the congress because he could not receive the kings with proper ceremony. Jacob Fugger in Augsburg was reluctant to advance yet more money in the absence of adequate guarantees. The centre of negotiations accordingly shifted to Augsburg and eventually the Fuggers agreed to a loan of 54,000 guldens, not least because they were afraid that without the projected alliance they might lose their rich mine-workings in Upper Hungary, whose protection against the Turks demanded the maintenance of good relations between Austria and Hungary.

A great fire at Pressburg in the late spring of 1515 had reduced a third of the town to ashes and the rendezvous of the three rulers was transferred to the Hartmannsfeld, an open space at a crossing of the Leitha in the neighbourhood of the village of Trautmannsdorf. Seated in a horse-litter, flanked by five hundred knights, Maximilian received first the royal children, Louis and Anna, then King Vladislav, also in a horse-litter, and finally King Sigismund of Poland, mounted on a charger. On 17 July the whole train moved to Vienna. The days until 29 July were filled with speeches, tournaments, banquets, theatrical presentations and balls. There followed four days of talks at Neustadt. On 22 August the double betrothal was celebrated in the Stephansdom: Louis, the nine-year-old king of Bohemia and Hungary was betrothed to Maximilian's grand-daughter the Infanta Maria, while the elderly emperor was betrothed to twelve-year-old Anna of Hungary. This latter union was to become void if within a year either of Maximilian's grandsons, Ferdinand or Charles, was united with Anna per verba de praesenti, otherwise Maximilian was to complete the marriage within three months. The necessity then arose, however, for removing the impediment to a marriage between Anna and Ferdinand created by her prior betrothal to his grand-father, for which a papal dispensation was necessary. Because of the time these acts of state took to complete, the actual marriages were only concluded in 1521, Ferdinand marrying Anna of Hungary.

In 1515 Maximilian had ceremoniously admitted the little prince Louis into the league of the house of Habsburg, adopting him as his son, appointing him vicar-general of the Empire and naming him his rightful successor in the imperial office. King Louis II was killed fighting the Turks at Mohacz on 29 August 1526. Sultan Suleiman entered Buda and there kept the feast of Bayram. The Turks remained in occupation of central Hungary for the next century and a half; once in Buda(-Pest) their objectives were enlarged to include Vienna, whose 'golden orb' surmounting the Stephansdom they coveted as the jewel of the western Empire. In their own estimation the Sultans were the legitimate successors of the East Roman emperors.

The chilling cry '*Kruziturken*' ('Kuruzi and Turks!') still has currency in Austrian dialect speech, an echo of the time when alarm bells were perpetually sounding for a Turkish attack. During the last decades of the fifteenth century roving Osmanli bands spread constant terror and confusion by their raids on Carniola, Croatia, Bosnia and Styria. Maximilian cherished the lifelong dream of winning the imperial crown of East Rome. He sketched out campaigns against the Turks with his own hand, confident that he knew their ways and likely routes of advance. His thoughts were occupied with the Turkish war from his youth to the day of his death, his aim being, as he wrote to Willibald Pirkheimer in 1514, the recovery of the Eastern Empire, *recuperation illius imperii*.

This goal was the star which guided his policy as emperor: it was his duty as protector of the church and of Christendom to expel from Europe its hereditary enemy Islam – the Turks. For this purpose the Empire itself had to be organized as a zone of peace, given a coherent legal structure and made into an economic unit capable of bearing the heavy costs of the Turkish war and the other campaigns this war entailed (against the French, for example, who were allies of the Turks).

For all his high hopes and high ideals, Maximilian knew very well that in practice the Empire was a league of princes with the Emperor as its figurehead. He was a modest man, always ready to listen to the advice and opinions of others, capable of extracting humour from even the most unpalatable of facts. This humorous trait, and his willingness to take the blame for difficult situations, is often commented upon by contemporaries. In jest he called himself 'king of kings', which indeed he was, since the Germans gave him no obedience but aspired to be kings themselves. In this he betrays a thoroughly 'modern' outlook, far removed from the medieval conception which saw in earthly majesty the bodying forth of the God of terror.

Led by Berthold of Henneberg, archbishop of Mainz, the electors were ready for a reform of the Empire in a sense which would accept the dualism of 'Empire and Emperor' and strengthen the imperial constitution as against the emperor. At the Diet of Worms of 1495 Maximilian persuaded the Estates to assent to an imperial tax, the 'Common Penny'. But at the same time the Estates saw to it that they were systematically incorporated into the Empire's new bureaucratic offices. The *Ewige Landfriede*, the *Reichskammergericht* (the Empire's permanent court of appeal, set up initially at Regensburg in 1507 but later moved to Worms), the fixing on the Estates of military burdens to be assumed on behalf of the Empire – all these had their beginnings under Maximilian and laid the foundations on which the Empire's bureaucratic institutions and division into circles would rest for centuries to come, in fact down to the end.

In 1500 the electors insisted on the establishment of a standing commission formed from the Estates as a kind of executive council for the Empire; they were afraid that the emperor was about to involve the Empire in private and unnecessary wars (with the Swiss and in Italy) and wanted to see that within the Empire he was kept in check. In his hereditary dominions he could do as he pleased – as the electors did in their own territories. Maximilian nevertheless started to build up a central administration on the western model, which was familiar to him from his days in Burgundy.

At Hagenau, once a palace of Charles the Great and Frederick I, the king of France became in 1505 a vassal of the Empire, or rather of the king of the Romans, with Milan as his fief. The fair appearance of the act belied its crucial content, namely that Maximilian had been forced to recognize the French seizure of Milan in 1500. He had hoped that his own marriage in 1494 to Bianca Maria Sforza, niece of the Milanese duke Ludovico Moro, would lead to more concrete measures to counteract French expansion in Italy. Maximilian's object in Italy was to prevent the French king from reaching Rome and grasping the imperial crown. In 1506 Maximilian lost by death his only son, Philip the Handsome. Despite many hindrances, by 1507 Maximilian was ready to set out for Rome for his imperial coronation when Venice put a fresh obstacle in his way by refusing him transit. Acting on impulse, Maximilian decided on an imperial coronation on German soil, a plan he had had in mind since the previous December. On 6 February 1508 he assumed in Trent cathedral the title 'Roman Emperor Elect' and then sent a message to the 'Empire' (i.e. the Estates) regarding future modes of address: in writing he was to be Roman Emperor Elect; in speaking, for convenience sake, Roman Emperor. But the last imperial coronation – with one unique exception – had already taken place.

Pope Julius II recognized Maximilian's proclamation of his new title. This was not, however, the limit of Maximilian's aspirations. As he disclosed in a letter to his daughter Margaret, his trusted confidante, he had thoughts of seeking the papal tiara for himself when the Roman see next became vacant (a notion which has caused some surprise in more recent times). There were solid enough reasons for the fantasy. Maximilian took seriously the emperor's traditional responsibility for reforming the Church. He wanted to have the council summoned to meet at Pisa in 1511-12 transferred to a city on imperial soil, either Constance or Verona. At times Maximilian thought hopefully of deposing Pope Julius II, the *papa terribile*. Erasmus describes Julius as a 'christian Mars', having witnessed him riding into Bologna at the head of his troops, intent on war against the Florentines if they refused to surrender Michaelangelo, who had sought asylum among them from himself.

Following French precedent, Maximilian also wanted to make the Church's wealth in money and land available to the imperial treasury. With Julius deposed, imperial rule might be restored in Italy, though this would now have to be on a shared basis with France.

From the churchman's point of view Maximilian – like Joseph II after him – was a 'wicked unbeliever' (Cardinal Raimund of Gurk). Concealed within Maximilian was a bearer of 'enlightenment', in the best sense of the word; he took a lively interest in religious problems, and wanted to bring real help to the common people, whose religious education had been either neglected or distorted. He conceived a plan – which he discussed with Peutinger – for publishing good religious texts which everyone could understand so that the people might be brought closer to their faith. He suggested to the curia a revision of the regulations about fasting which would make it easier for poorer communities to observe their obligations; thus the forty days of Lent would have been split up and some allowance made for climatic conditions.

Maximilian had lengthy conferences with the folk preacher and reformer Geiler of Kaiserberg and the learned abbot Trithemius, at which the talk turned on questions relating to the boundary between faith and knowledge. Why does God require from man only belief in him and not knowledge of him, as he does from the angels? Can non-Christians attain felicity? Is it possible to prove a divine ordering of the world? What is the attitude of the 'righteous God' to the corruption of the innocent? Maximilian took delight in conversing at length with scholars, 'intellectuals'. (The leading statesmen of our own time have not so far been distinguished for their interest in intellectual discussion. John F. Kennedy was an exception.) Maximilian turned the decaying university of Vienna into one of the most sought-after universities within the imperial orbit. His literary circle followed him even on campaign. Maximilian, hailed by Jacob Spiegel as 'father of the scholars', had no use for merely time-killing diversions. His agents travelling in Germany, France and Italy had instructions to seek out records, historical writings, coins, inscriptions, armorial bearings, portraits in church windows and similar objects. Informed of the discovery of a 'pagan stone', he asked for details of the place where it was found and entered them in his notebooks. He commissioned abstracts and translations of historical sources, for example Pirkheimer's translation of the *Chronicle* of Johannes Monachos, a Byzantine historian contemporary with Justin the Younger, which Cuspinian had discovered at Ofen: in this way the Greek Empire and the deeds of its rulers would have a living memorial.

All Maximilian's thought and action can be traced back to three essential and basic components: his thoroughly 'modern' spirit of enquiry, his conception of an *imperium orbis* and his religious-political belief in the mission of his house.

The spirit of enquiry comes out in his lively interest in the arts and sciences, his desire to be a Maecenas, his endeavours to attract to his court the best artists of his day and his cultivation of the leading German humanists. Maximilian was open to the world and hungry for what it had to offer. All living things were of interest, yet for all his specifically Catholic pleasure in life he was never unmindful of death. For years he carried his coffin about with him.

Maximilian's idea of Empire meant an *imperium orbis*, the Empire as it had been under Charles the Great, Otto the Great and Frederick II. It was for this that he needed to win back Italy and Arelate Burgundy. Künigseck, his captain in the field, once told the emperor that the prospect of making a military contribution to the assertion of his *imperium* over 'Europe, Africa and Asia' was all that gave point to his own declining years. But in Maximilian the old imperial idea is combined with the intellectual and political tradition of Portugal [plate 79], and thus looks also to the future, to the ideas of Empire current under Charles V. Maximilian's idea of a universal rule leans heavily on the formulations of later medieval reformers, for example Alexander of Roes and Dietrich of Nieheim (who in turn look back to Otto of Freising and the ideologies of the Hohenstaufen and Ottonian eras). It was this tradition that Gattinara handed on to Charles V.

Maximilian's concern for the *Imperium Romanum* inspired his plans for rebuilding the neglected imperial vault at Speyer, a project which clerical opposition, lack of money and loss of interest on the part of Valkenhauer, the sculptor, forced him to abandon. Maximilian encouraged scholars to edit works connected with the history of the Empire. Cuspinian's edition of the two great theoretical treatises on the history of the German Middle Ages, Otto of Freising's *History of the Two Cities* and his *Deeds of Frederick I*, was published under imperial auspices. This sumptuous work, which appeared at Strassburg in 1515, is prefaced by a woodcut by Urs Graf showing Emperor Maximilian enthroned between the two archdukes, Charles and Ferdinand.

The Maximilian who was so modern that he had to save time by doing business over his meals [plate 95], who dictated to several secretaries simultaneously, was at the same time thoroughly atavistic in his belief concerning the antiquity and descent of his house [plate 92]. Roman descent was not enough; he wanted to claim for his house descent from the Franks, the Trojans, the Old Testament patriarchs. The sources of this sense of election, as we find it in the early Habsburgs, are still not clear, but we already find traces of it in circles round Rudolph I's queen, Gertrude Anna, and in Agnes, whom we have encountered as the daughter of Albert I. The splendour and force of Maximilian's own personality must also be taken into account: '*Ego possum ferre labores – volo etiam honores*', 'I, Maximilian, can take upon my shoulders Herculean labours – likewise I long for honours'.

From *Kayser Maximilians besonder buch, genannt der Zaiger*, completed by Jacob Mennel in 1518, we discover that the Habsburgs rise on three ladders – part of the great Habsburg cosmic theatre. A silver ladder leads the house's secular rulers, from landgrave to emperor, to the lunar heaven; a golden ladder conducts clerical Habsburgs, from hermit to pope, to the solar heaven; a third ladder, composed of precious stones, is trodden by the saints of the dynasty and leads them, like Jacob's ladder, to the highest heaven [plate 86].

Mennel, who was also Maximilian's genealogist, belonged to the circle of scholars surrounding the emperor which also included Cuspinian, Suntham, Stabius and Peutinger, his 'historical oracle'. Mennel's *Fürstliche Chronick genannt kayser Maximilians Geburtsspiegel* (compiled 1512–17) runs to six volumes. The first volume deals with the 'Hebrew line' (it gives the genealogy of Christ and a list of the popes), the 'Greek line', which goes back to Hector, and the Latin genealogy from Aeneas. The second volume traces the generations from Clovis to Archduke Charles (the future Emperor Charles v). The third and fourth volumes deal with collateral branches and with families related to the Habsburgs by marriage. The last two volumes are devoted to legends of the saints of the dynasty (forty-seven beatified, one hundred and twenty-three canonized). Convinced that he represented in his own flesh and blood the entire human race, Maximilian was equally convinced that God had called him through his 'two houses of Austria and Burgundy' to defend the Empire against East and West, against the Turks and the French.

In about 1515 Mennel was asked by the emperor to compose a memorandum for the guidance of Maximilian's grandson and heir, the future Charles v. Addressed to the '*tres puissant seigneur et prince Charles, futur roy de Castille et de Hongerie, archiduc d'Austrice, duc de Bourgoigne, de Brabant, etc.*', the memorandum admonishes the future ruler to pay particular heed to two connections, the connection between Hungary and Constantinople and the connection between Burgundy and Austria.

Hungary had occupied an important place in Maximilian's thoughts ever since 1490, when he had won a victory at Stuhlweissenburg over a rival king, Vladislav. He had subsequently taken the title of a king of Hungary, confirmed by Vladislav in the peace of Pressburg (7 November 1491) which also made Maximilian joint ruler of western Hungary. Hungary was important as the bridge to Constantinople; Maximilian's aspiration to the Byzantine crown is confirmed by an entry in his *Wappen-Puech* (*c.* 1507) which shows him displaying the armorial bearings of the East Roman emperor – 'King Max or his successor hope shortly to take Constantinople'. Moreover, Maximilian fulfilled the requirements of the old imperial tradition: *homo, genere Grecus, imperio Romanus*, Greek by birth, his Empire was Roman. Mennel's memorandum was intended to direct the interests of the thoroughly western-minded prince Charles (he had been admitted to the Order of the Golden Fleece when only a year old) towards the east. Europe was narrower in 1955, when Augsburg celebrated the thousandth anniversary of the battle at the Lech and cast the Huns of 955 as the prototype of the wicked enemy from the east. At Maximilian's bidding, Mennel expounds for the young Duke of Burgundy and Archduke of Austria the following version of Hungarian history. The Trojans and the Huns were descended from Noah (Maximilian was ignorant of the true descent from Muhammed and Ghengis Khan). After the destruction of Troy, Hector's son Francio (Francus) fled to Hungary, to which he gave the name Sicambria. The Huns, a noble people, ruled over Europe and hence over a 'third of the world'. The Huns had equally noble successors in the Tatars, who gave Lower Pannonia the name Hungary. Upper Pannonia was converted to Christianity thanks to 'Marquis Rudolf d'Austrasie', who lived in Alsace and called the new christian country Austria after his Austrasian fatherland.[1]

The close verbal resemblance of 'Austria' and 'Austrasia', and the 'close relation-ship' it suggested between Austria and Burgundy fascinated Maximilian. All the noble blood of Europe, indeed the blood of all the great dynasties of the ancient world

[1] Austrasia was the heartland of the Carolingian Empire, lying between the Rhine and the Meuse. [T]

flowed in the veins of the Habsburgs: the 'invention' of their ancestors took place in a subconscious deeply rooted in the archaic.[1]

Maximilian was a political propagandist of the first rank. He wanted all his literary projects to be published by the use of wood engraving, so that through this cheap medium a wide public could become acquainted with his aims and programmes. (Wood engraving was also of enormous importance later, in spreading propaganda for the Reformation.) The master publicist gathered in Augsburg, Nuremberg and Strassburg all the great graphic artists of the day: Albert Dürer, Dürer's pupils Schäufelein, Springinklee and Wolf Traut, the Augsburg artists Burgkmair and Beck and the Regensburg artist Altdorfer, all of whom were employed on drawings and wood-engravings. Baldung, Breu and Cranach contributed to the emperor's Book of Prayers.

Maximilian's Nuremberg, the Nuremberg of the *Meistersinger*, was destroyed by bombs in the Second World War, as was the Augsburg of the Fuggers, his financiers. Both were fine and ancient cities, whose splendour, richness and European reputation derived at least in part from the artists assembled there by Maximilian. He was the last emperor to accord Nuremberg pre-eminence over the other imperial cities and the last to regard it as the intellectual centre of the Holy Roman Empire. Under him Nuremberg became the seat of the first centralized institutions the Empire ever had, the *Reichsregiment* or 'imperial executive'. The age of Maximilian was the time of Nuremberg's last flowering, just as it was also the time of the last flowering of the old Empire. Maximilian was on friendly terms with Nurembergers such as Willibald Pirkheimer, the great humanist, Albert Dürer, and the Pfinzing brothers; we know that he enjoyed dancing with the Nuremberg wives (in August 1489 he stayed there a day longer on their account) and that on occasion he joined the journeymen in their sports. At Nuremberg he fitted himself out with good weapons and armour and refurbished his horse-troopers, for which he received a loan of three thousand guldens from the town council.

Maximilian's close connections with the bourgeois families of Nuremberg and Augsburg underline the political importance of the German imperial cities at this period of their economic and cultural heyday. In no other country of Europe were there so many communes of comparable size and independence.[2] Maximilian – and in this he resembled the arch-chancellor of the Empire and the electors – was no great friend and patron of urban political independence as such. The imperial cities were valued as a source of taxation. Some of the smaller ones were mortgaged by Maximilian. Others, threatened by disturbance from within or without, received an imperial captain (*capitaneus imperatorio nomine*), whose task was to restore order, direct defensive operations, initiate negotiations for a peaceful settlement and avert an

---

[1] There is a parallel in Russian history. In the time of Ivan 'the Lord of the Terror of God' ('the Terrible' is a mistranslation), the descent of the ruling house of Rurik was traced back first to Prus ('Prussia'), the brother of Emperor Augustus, and thence to Alexander the Great, Nebuchadnezzar and Noah.

[2] The Flemish and Italian towns in their cultural and economic heyday were virtually independent states.

armed clash by making the imperial presence felt. As 'defender' of the town committed to his charge, the captain's role was to represent the Empire and assume military, diplomatic and executive responsibility on behalf of the Empire and of the town in question, as for example happened in 1495 at Weissenburg in Alsace.

The political status of the German towns within the imperial constitution was still not clear. Until 1648 no agreement could be reached on whether non-mediatized[1] towns had a seat and voice in the imperial diet. This uncertainty remained even though the issue appeared to have been settled by a measure proposed at Worms in 1495 by Archbishop Berthold of Mainz, as part of the movement for imperial reform. Under this proposal, the imperial towns would have been summoned to the imperial diets and allowed to take part in their deliberations. The influential 'big cities' (Cologne, Augsburg, Nuremberg, Ulm, Strassburg, Lübeck, Frankfurt, and so on) much courted by the princes as sources of finance and as potential military or economic allies, and these big cities often had their cluster of small client towns.

Many of Maximilian's undertakings were financed by the Fuggers, who also bore the cost of the imperial election of his grandson, Charles v. The cost of producing Maximilian's literary works was borne by the artists and craftsmen of the south German cities: thus *Freydal* (which describes tourneys, combats, 'masquerades', mock battles and tournaments) [plate 83], *Theuerdank* (a verse epic describing Maximilian's journey to claim Mary of Burgundy as his bride) [plate 85], and *Weisskunig*, an autobiographical work composed between 1505 and 1516 [plate 82]. The 'white king' is Maximilian, from the accoutrements he wore in the tourney and in battle; the king of France is the blue king, the king of Hungary the green. *Weisskunig*, which Maximilian dictated to his private secretary, Marx Treitzsaurwein, is a prose work, illustrated with 251 wood engravings. *Weisskunig* was not published until 1775. *Theuerdank* was originally intended to form part of it, and Maximilian meant the whole work, a few presentation copies excepted, to be kept in a trunk and issued only after his death. *Lyber laudis post mortem*, 'praise comes only after death', he wrote above a picture in Grünpeck's biography of Frederick and Maximilian depicting him in the tourney. Another picture in the same book, in which the death of Frederick III is shown accompanied by portents, he scored through thrice, noting 'Friedrich Nyt' in the margin. His father was not to be shown in this light.

It was proper that the fame due to the arch-house and its sacred kindred should come to it only after death. Maximilian started planning his mausoleum as early as 1502: the thought of death was the Habsburgs' familiar.[2] As he planned it, the dead emperor would rest in the company of his ancestors and predecessors – forty monumental standing bronze figures of his forebears, thirty-four busts of his ancient Roman predecessors and a hundred statuettes of saints from his own and kindred clans. The

---

[1] Non-mediatized towns are those which remained directly dependent on the Empire and had no lord close at hand [T].

[2] Archduke Francis Ferdinand started to plan his own mausoleum at Artstetten near Melk in 1910, four years before his assassination at Sarajevo.

place destined for its reception was the church of St George in Wiener-Neustadt: his Order of St George had the struggle against the Turks as its special charge.

In the event the monument was neither as large nor as impressive as the emperor intended. It was completed only towards the end of the sixteenth century and can be seen today in the Hofkirche at Innsbruck. On 9 October 1515 the English ambassador Wingfield sent back a report from Innsbruck criticizing the heavy outlay on the statues. King Arthur, resurrected in the twelfth century as one of the illustrious forebears of the English kings, appears in the Maximilian monument as the supremely handsome prototype of great princes and noble knights, and as Maximilian's 'kinsman'. As a bronze statue it is one of the finest in the world; it was cast by Peter Visscher in 1515, probably from a sketch by Dürer [plate 91].

Power, intellect, art, learning and technology united under the patronage of the emperor was the dream of the contemporary humanists. It is explicitly formulated in the programme Conrad Celtes, 'prince of humanists', drew up for the Society he founded at Vienna. In 1507 Hans Burgkmair translated the scheme into visual form with his double-headed eagle shown accompanied by the emblems of the Celtes Society [plate 87]. The emperor is seen at the eagle's neck, seated on a tripod, flanked by standard-bearers displaying the arms of the Empire and the cross of Jerusalem on either side; at his feet rises the spring of the Muses, with the Muses themselves seated in the basin of the fountain; below them we see Philosophy with the seven liberal arts; and lower still a Judgement of Paris. The arc formed by the eagle's tail feathers has seven medallions on either side, showing on the left the days of the Creation, on the right the seven mechanical arts. Bottom left and right are the arms of the German monarchy and of Austria.

The funeral celebrations for Frederick III included Maximilian's coronation of Cuspinian as poet, a ceremony which took place on 7 December 1493. Schiller might mock, but to the Habsburgs and the Viennese splendid obsequies were a high feast day, a piece of state theatre, a sacral-political act, a spectacle of death and a festival of the living. In October 1500, on the nomination of the faculty of medicine, Cuspinian was elected rector of the university of Vienna; he was then barely twenty-seven. Maximilian subsequently had reason to be grateful to Cuspinian for his services as a diplomat, which led to the succession treaty concluded at Vienna in 1515. Bernhardin Strigel made a painting of Maximilian and his family to mark the occasion [plate 89], and in particular the adoption of little Louis of Hungary into the Habsburg family. Maximilian – who had the magnanimity and liberality which from the days of his earliest forebears men expected of a ruler – gave the picture to Cuspinian.

Cuspinian turned his beloved 'imperial family' into a 'holy family', that is to say, he incorporated the picture into a side altar he built for the chapel of his house on the Singer-Strasse (not far from the Stephansdom). In 1520 Cuspinian commissioned Strigel to paint on the back of the first picture a true Holy Family, including John the Baptist. Cuspinian had his own family painted at the same time [plate 90] and the two panels were hinged together to form a diptych. The addition of appropriate inscriptions changed Cuspinian and his family into the family of Zebedee, the Galilean fisherman whose sons James (the Less) and John were numbered among the apostles. Maximilian, his son Philip the Handsome, his daughter Margaret and his grandsons, Charles and Ferdinand, were given names from the genealogy of Christ. We know from a collector's mark that this picture was later acquired by Charles I of England. In 1913 it came back to Vienna by way of Berlin and was purchased by Count Wilczek for his castle at Kreuzenstein.

In the interval between the painting of Strigel's two 'holy families', times already had changed in Europe. The emperor as *christus domini*, the anointed of Christ the King, had been under attack from Rome for the past four centuries and more; now the imperial office stood in jeopardy within the Empire itself. On the evening of 17 April 1521, the day on which he first came face to face with the emperor and the Empire, Martin Luther wrote a letter to Cuspinian. 'I have just stood up before the emperor and the princes of the Empire and was asked whether I would withdraw my books . . . as Christ is gracious to me, I never will in all eternity renounce so much as a tittle of them. My good wishes, dearest Cuspinian. Worms, Wednesday after Quasimodo geniti, 1521.' In his haste Luther made a mistake over the date.

Cuspinian could not follow Luther. The humanist from Schweinfurt had settled in Vienna, where he witnessed the Turkish war, the Peasants' war and the uprisings in the Empire from the emperor's standpoint. After the battle of Mohacz (1526), the battle which cost King Louis his kingdom and his life and brought the Turks close to Vienna (three years later they were at its gates), Cuspinian appealed to the German princes to come to the rescue of the Empire and Christendom. He puts his finger on dipsomania as the disease which was crippling the Germans.

The sons of the great humanist took no interest in his work. Sebastian (who dropped the Cuspinian and reverted to his German name of Spiessheimer) was an energetic businessman. He managed his father's estates and for a time held the concession for transport services in Vienna. After his father's death he was more than willing to sell his priceless collection of books, which included treasures from the Bibliotheca Corviniana. This unique collection of manuscripts and books had been assembled at untold expense by the Hungarian king Matthias Corvinus, only to be dispersed and plundered after his death. Some of the manuscripts are said to have been brought to England by Christopher Urswick, the English ambassador who afterwards became archbishop of York. Cuspinian's second son, Nicholas Chrysostomus (his name reflects the Greek aspirations of Maximilian and his Viennese circle) was skilled in pyrotechnics and through his knowledge helped to defend Vienna against the Turks.

In June 1518 a total eclipse of the sun was observed at Vienna, which in Cuspinian's circle was taken to portend the death of the emperor; Georg Tannstetter, astronomer-astrologer[1] and doctor of medicine, had placed this interpretation on the eclipse when it was first predicted six years earlier. In the autumn of the same year the emperor's

[1] Astrology and astronomy continued bound up with each other until well after the time of Kepler.

The Rise of the
House of
Habsburg

73 Emperor Frederick III
on his tomb in the Vienna
Stephansdom. Despite
defeats and political
débâcles he retained an
unshakeable belief in the
world-wide mission of
his house.

74 (*left*) Frederick III
meets his bride, Eleanor
of Portugal, from whom
their son Maximilian I
inherited the Portuguese
ambition of mounting a
crusade against Islam.

75 Christ crucified on an
imperial eagle; below,
the Estates of the Empire.
A woodcut made in
1487, a time when
numerous plans for
imperial reform were
current.

Ce commence le second livre de la thoison d'or

tresexcellent prince
et tresreluisant en
puissance et vertu
et mon tresredoubte
te seigneur monsr

Charles par la grace de dieu duc de
bourgongne de lotrich et de bra
bant de lembourg et de luxen
bourg, Conte de flandres, dar
tois et de bourgongne palatin

76 Chapter meeting of the Order of the Golden Fleece. The courtly civilization of late medieval Burgundy was the basis of the court ceremonial adopted by the Spanish Habsburgs.

77 (*opposite*) Philip the Bold, from the tombs of the Dukes of Burgundy in Dijon. This highly gifted and 'modern' prince ruled a realm poised between France and Germany.

82 Maximilian and Mary learn each other's languages – German, French, Flemish.

Opposite
78 (*top left*) A calendar of the mid-fifteenth century depicts the sun (Sol) as an emperor on horseback. The imperial structure is seen as part of the natural order of the universe.
79 (*top right*) The young Maximilian kneels at the feet of St Sebastian, patron of Portugal as a world power.
80 (*bottom left*) The histories of Maximilian's reign emanating from his circle describe the portents observed on his accession to the Empire, an event visibly approved by the heavenly powers.
81 (*bottom right*) The banners of Maximilian and Mary flying from the towers of Antwerp in honour of their marriage.

83, 85 The three books most closely associated with Maximilian himself, *Weisskunig*, *Freydal* and *Theuerdank*, interpret the history of his earlier life as a quest for the hand of Mary of Burgundy. Burgkmair's engraving from *Weisskunig* (*previous page*) shows Maximilian and Mary together; in the drawing from *Freydal* (*opposite*) Maximilian is seen taking part in a *Mummerei* he has arranged in honour of his bride; and *Theuerdank* (*right*) concentrates on the warlike achievements of the 'Last Knight' and the treacherous enemies he defeats on his quest.

84 (*opposite*) *Le revers du jeu des suysses, c.* 1499. Caricature of the policies of Louis XII of France, whose aim was to divert the Burgundian inheritance of Maximilian to himself: he plays cards with the Doge of Venice and the 'Schweizer', the other European powers looking on.

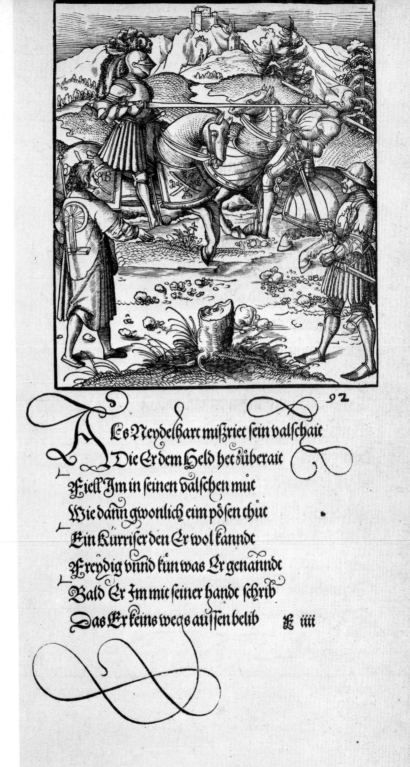

Als Neydelhart misriet sein valschait
Die Er dem Held het zuberait
Fiell Im in seinen valschen mut
Wie dann gwonlich ein pösen thut
Ein Kurriser den Er wol kannde
Freydig vnnd kun was Er genanndt
Bald Er Jm mit seiner hande schrib
Das Er keins wegs aussen belib   E iiii

86 (*above*) Maximilian and his kinsmen on the heavenward ladder. Emperor Maximilian set great store by religious-political genealogies which demonstrated his kinship with Romans, Greeks and Huns. Noble Huns like Attila were as acceptable as ancient heroes and Christian saints.

87 (*right*) The imperial eagle used by the Celtes Society. The figure symbolizes Maximilian's aspiration to gather all the arts and sciences under the wing of imperial patronage.

88 Dürer, *The Feast of the Rose Garlands*. Emperor and pope kneel before the Virgin, in a tribute by the greatest of the artists to enjoy Maximilian's patronage.

OPHAS FRATER CARNALIS IO= HI MARITI DIVAE VIRG MARIAE

I
JACOBVS MINOR EPVS MARIA CLEOPHAE HIEROSOLIMITANVS VIRG MAR PVTATIV TERTERA D

III
IOSEPH IVSTVS SIMON ZELOTES CONSO= BRINVS DNI NRI

89 Bernhardin Strigel, *The Family of Emperor Maximilian I*; see p. 145.

90 Bernhardin Strigel, *Johannes Cuspinianus and his Family*.

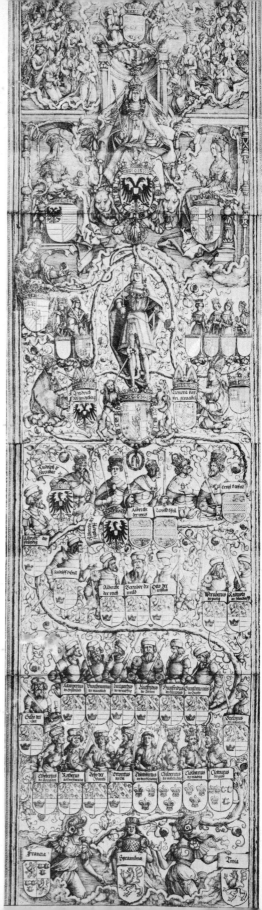

91 (*above*) King Arthur by Peter
Visscher, one of the noblest representations of knighthood in European art.
Statue from the cenotaph of Maximilian
in Innsbruck: a mythical English king
is numbered among Maximilian's
forebears.

92 (*right*) Gate of Honour designed by
Dürer. It shows Maximilian's ancestors
back to Clovis, the first Frankish king.

94 (*above*) Jakob Fugger with his book-
keeper, Matthias Schwarz. The development
of the Fugger's trading house into an economic enterprise on the world scale was achieved
through close collaboration with the house
of Habsburg.

93 (*top left*) Habsburg Castle, Switzerland.
Illustration from a history of the house of
Habsburg by Johann Jakob Fugger.

95 (*left*) Maximilian carries out business
over a meal, a situation typical of the
emperor's ceaseless activity in every sphere
of his life.

96 Emperor Maximilian on his death-bed. Like most of the Habsburgs, Maximilian made a cult of death and of respect for the dead.

97 *Memento mori*, 1505, by Dürer. Death rides through lands laid waste by war, pestilence and famine.

health began to fail. Tanstetter was one of the doctors summoned to attend the emperor, but his astrological certainty tied his hands.

Maximilian bore his sufferings with patience, resigned to the will of God. He passed his sleepless nights in conversation with his doctors, who were also his friends. He had read to him legends of the canonized and beatified members of his dynasty, penitential psalms, the history of Christ's passion and the sermons of St Brigitte. For the past five years he had unobtrusively carried his coffin about with him; his entourage took it for a treasure chest or a book press and one of his servants is said to have stored papers in it. On 12 January 1519 Maximilian, 'the last knight', died at Wels [plate 96]. Many Germans look on him as the last emperor of the Holy Roman Empire.

8

THE EMPIRE ON WHICH THE SUN
NEVER SET

IN OUR own day two contrasting views of Charles v are put forward. One sees him as the 'figurehead on the galleon of the European movement',[1] the other as the hero of '*Hispanidad*', a Spanish Latin-American cultural and political union. Both are beside the point, since Charles v was above all European and emperor. The most significant verdict is that of the French language, with its *Charles-Quint*: Charles v is the only emperor, apart from Charlemagne, to be known by a French soubriquet. Again, although Shakespeare has little good to say of 'Charles the emperor',[2] in matters of self-display the English royal house owed much to Charles and his presentation of the imperial office. Furthermore, every Englishman who could read could see his name in any church, since Erasmus of Rotterdam's *Paraphrases of the New Testament*, with its dedications to Charles v, Archduke Ferdinand of Austria, Francis i of France and Henry viii, was one of the two books every church in the land was required, from the time of Edward vi, to have on view. 'Keyser Karl' is still a favourite in the folk tradition of Flanders (when he was in the Netherlands Charles liked to mingle with the people, drinking beer with them and joining with them in archery) and in conflicts between Flemings and Walloons he is often invoked as a national hero.

Charles reigned for thirty-eight years (1519–56) and spent a quarter of them in transit. Between the time of his first departure from the Netherlands and his abdication he paid nine visits to the Empire, seven to Spain, seven to Italy, four to France, two to England and two to North Africa. He spent twenty-eight years in the Netherlands, eighteen in Spain, eight in the Empire, two and a half in Italy, seven months in France, four and a half months in North Africa and seven weeks in England. He slept in well over three thousand different beds, not to mention the occasions when he carried his own bed with him. This great traveller moved within a polygon bounded by Wittenberg, Vienna, Messina, Argel, Seville, Corunna and London. Charles never saw the Adriatic, Prague, Buda or the Habsburg; he was in Vienna only once. And despite his frail health, he was driven on by a tireless energy; most of the wars fought during his time were conducted by him in person.

[1] This view is attacked by Peter Rassow in his *Karl V. Der letzte Kaiser des Mittelalters*, Göttingen 1957.
[2] *Henry VIII*, I, i.

Charles was small and sparely built [colour plate vi]; in his veins flowed the blood of Europe. His ancestry was Europe itself: he was Spanish, Portuguese, French-Burgundian, Netherlander, Plantagenet; he had a little German blood; among his forebears were Greeks, Italians, Slavs and Lithuanians, as also Spanish Muslims and Jews. Pope Paul iv, enemy both of Charles v and Philip ii, described the Spanish as a brood of infidels and Jews. There was in fact Moorish blood in the old Spanish kings. Alphonso v was called Adfunch-Ibn-Barbarya, 'Alfonso, son of the Berber woman'. Don Hernando Alonso de Toledo, baptized Alfonso vi after the fall of Toledo, contributed his blood to Charles v through the Enriquez and Pachecos. The Jew Ruy Capón and his beautiful and wealthy daughter Maria Roiz brought Jewish blood into the higher aristocracy of Spain and Portugal and thus to Charles v. A tract entitled *El Tizón de la Nobleza* (the taint of the aristocracy), current about 1560, accused all the grandees of Spain of possessing Jewish and Moorish ancestors. The author was probably Cardinal Mendoza (in his full name Don Fransisco, Cardinal de Mendoza y Bobadilla, Bishop of Burgos), an uncle of that Count Chinchón, also a Bobadilla, who was refused admittance to one of the great orders of chivalry on account of the 'impurity of his blood'.

The royal and princely titles of Charles v (they come to over sixty) and the lands which conferred on him his many and various rights may be read in the preamble to the Edict of Worms of 1521 and to the *Landfrieden* of 1548. He was *king in Germany*; that is, Charles was the elected supreme head of the German Empire, suzerain-in-chief of a historical entity which had already fallen apart into petty states; he exercised few direct powers, was bound by his electoral concessions, by the imperial diet and by the *Reichsregiment*, and in later years was represented in Germany by the German king Ferdinand. Even so, his office was still more than that of a president. He was *Archduke of Austria, etc.*, in other words territorial ruler of a complex of German petty states whose past evolution had been determined by the dynastic policy of individual princes (basing themselves on feudal law) but was now a possession secured by hereditary, dynastic, and constitutional right. He was *Duke of Burgundy, etc.*, which meant that Charles enjoyed in Burgundy and the Netherlands ruling rights he inherited ultimately from Charles the Bold. He was *King of Castile, Aragon, etc.*, exercising the crown rights of his Spanish mother *vis-à-vis* the Cortés of the various historically separate realms: he was thus the successor in law to the monarchs who through the *reconquista* and their dynastic marriages had created a Spain which extended on the one hand to Aragonese southern Italy (Naples and Sicily) and on the other to the New World opened up by Castile. He was *King of Hungary, etc.*; his brother Ferdinand's Jagellon marriage involved the Habsburgs in claims to kingdoms on the upper Elbe, on the Danube and in Dalmatia, which meant exposure to the Turks and assumption of the burdens brought by crowns which had already long been tossed to and fro between dynasties alien to the countries concerned.

Charles was born on 24 February 1500 at the Prinsenhof in Ghent where his grandmother Mary of Burgundy had died; all that remains is a low arched doorway and a fragment of wall. He grew up virtually an orphan. His father, Philip the Handsome, died in 1506; his mother Joanna ('the Mad') lived out a twilight existence in Spain where she died in 1555, only shortly before her son's abdication. Charles' childhood was spent in the care first of Margaret of York, widow of Charles the Bold, who told him many tales of the English Wars of the Roses, and then of Margaret of Austria, Maximilian's favourite daughter. The place of a father in his life was filled by Guillaume de Croy, Sieur de Chièvres, who tried to bring him up as a complete Burgundian. The mind of the young duke was nourished on chivalrous romances, aristocratic 'romanticism' and the missionary ideals of Burgundy.

When Charles came to Spain in 1517 to take possession of his inheritance he spoke not a word of Spanish. His Burgundian entourage and Burgundian regime gave offence. The 'tyranny' of this arrogant young foreigner who gave leading positions to his Burgundians, disregarded the rights of the provinces and their estates and set up central organs of government, was met with opposition: from the Cortés of Castile and Aragon, from the Comuneros, a group of towns which with support from a section of the nobility mounted a revolt which lasted two years (1520–22), from the gildsmen, townsmen and country folk of Valencia and Mallorca. The Spaniards who at first resented him and took no interest in the Empire became Charles' truest imperial subjects; conversely, Charles himself became a 'Spaniard' with Spanish as his second mother tongue. It was a later Spanish boast that Charles spoke French with his ambassadors, Italian with his wives, German with his grooms but Spanish with God.

The French, to discredit him in the Empire, spread the tale that Charles was hostile to the Germans long before the charge was taken up by 'Protestants'. Francis I declared himself a candidate for the imperial crown as early as 1516 (Maximilian only died in 1519!) He was not the first French monarch to compete for the imperial crown: Philip III had done so in secret, Philip VI quite openly. The French king's agents who canvassed for him in Germany appear to have stressed that Charles the Great had been both a German and a Frenchman.

Expenditure on Charles' imperial election amounted to 852,000 Rhenish guldens, representing rather more than two tons of fine gold. This man who placed an archaic trust in the saving strength of his ancestors knew also how to win the confidence of the great European capitalists, Jakob Fugger and Bartolomäus Welser of Augsburg, Filippo Gualterotti of Florence, Benedetto Fornari and Lorenzo de Vivaldi of Genoa. These credits were followed by others, and the close financial ties thus established led to profitable openings in the markets and ports of Germany, Spain, Italy and America. The emperor's perpetual financial embarrassment contributed in its own way to the establishment of the first European common market.

Charles V, the unanimous choice of the electors, was crowned at Aachen on 23 October 1520. The setting was Charles the Great's octagonal church, lit by the chandelier of Frederick Barbarossa, whose twelve shining turrets stood for the Celestial City, the eternal Jerusalem. First Charles twice kissed the cross of the Empire which had belonged to Lothar. Then he prostrated himself. The coronation mass was the mass for the Epiphany, which has as its Epistle *'surge illuminare Jerusalem . . .'* ('rise and shine, O Jerusalem, for the prince of peace is come'). The Elector of Cologne put the prescribed six questions to the young ruler, to which his answering *'volo'* ('I will') came with a seriousness which made all his future destinies, and with them those of Europe, a foregone conclusion. 'Wilt thou hold and guard by all proper means the sacred faith as handed down to Catholic men?' 'Wilt thou be the faithful shield and protector of Holy Church and her servants?' 'Wilt thou uphold and recover those rights of the realm and possessions of the Empire which have been unlawfully usurped?' (Charles' policy of *'recuperatio'* rested on his unswerving conviction that the Empire and Burgundy should be reinstated in all their former rights and possessions.) 'Wilt thou protect the poor, the fatherless and the widowed?' 'Wilt thou pay due submission to the Roman pontiff and the Holy Roman Church?' After he had made answer, the spiritual electors handed to him the sword of Charles the Great. Cologne, assisted by Trier and Mainz, then placed the crown on his head. Charles took his place on the throne of Charles the Great and at the communion received both bread and wine.

The Diet of Worms brought the twenty-one-year-old emperor face to face with Martin Luther, sixteen years his senior. Charles had his profession of faith ready, written out in his own hand. 'I am descended from the christian emperors of the noble German nation, from the Catholic kings of Spain, from the archdukes of Austria, from the dukes of Burgundy, all of whom remained until death the faithful sons of the Roman Church and constant defenders of the Catholic Faith.' This is at once communion and communication, and archaic on either count. What Charles is affirming is that the faith is the faith of his fathers and forefathers and he is therefore obliged to defend it. Friend and foe are left in no doubt that he would lose all his realms and territories rather than sacrifice that faith.

In Luther and Charles v two reformers were confronted; their aim was identical – the reform of the Church in head and members – but they thought to achieve it by entirely different means. Christendom as a whole, the One Holy Church, was as much the concern of the German Augustinian monk turned professor as it was of the emperor.

Some naïve historians (principally German historians) have wistfully supposed, even into quite modern times, that Germany might have been saved if the new emperor had been not a foreigner but a kind of young Maximilian (as people expected him to be) who would have placed himself at the head of the Reformation. But this is wishful thinking and ignores the reality. Luther was a revolutionary. His concept of the Church virtually abolished fifteen centuries of christian tradition and of the Church's understanding of itself. His declaration that the Pope, the clergy and all the Church's rights and possessions were by definition null and useless, indeed wicked and poisonous, did not stop with them: he was also condemning the order which had obtained for a thousand years, the cosmic household in which God, the saints, men and beasts dwelt under the same roof. For this radical son of the radical Augustine and the German mystics there was but one issue: the relation of the soul to the unfathomable God who is wrath, fire, volcano, terrifying rage and who condescends – with what incomprehensible grace! – to wipe out the sinfulness of wicked man. In the storm and stress of his youth Luther was anarchical and nihilistic (religiously anarchical and nihilistic). He discarded all secular and ecclesiastical establishments. But he was later horrified when his radical friends probed his religious revolution deeper and drew from it social and political conclusions. This second revolution was one Luther rejected.

Dr Martin Luther, monk (he was always a monk at heart) and professor, handed the despairing people, whom he despised, over to the princes for 'punishment'. He had no taste for dialogues and discussions, sought no debates, whether with Baptists, Enthusiasts, the dissident Swiss theologians (Zwingli and others) or with fellow Germans such as the radical Müntzer or the quietistic Sebastian Franck. The German princes became the spokesmen for German protestantism. Their power and influence was on the increase, since the estates and jurisdictions confiscated from the church were added to their own. The independent congregations thrown up by the Reformation were soon taken over by the princes and regimented into regional churches under their own control. They appointed their own church officials to supervise clerical education and discipline, men they had educated in their own universities and schools, where the teachers were men of the Reformation, trained in humanistic and legal studies.

At its first eruption the Reformation had already shattered the old images and forms and the old intellectual and ecclesiastical structures and orders; as it gathered strength it turned into a European revolution. The Anabaptist regime set up in Münster in 1535 was only the first of many proletarian religious revolts to break out in the western part of the Empire and the Netherlands. During Charles' lifetime there was no political revolt against him in the Netherlands, despite the growing economic hardships many individuals had to suffer; radical revolution started there only in 1566, with the revolt against images. But there is no mistaking that Luther was a firebrand, a revolutionary who left no stone standing of the Great Order he demolished, a big gun who shattered the 'walled church' and brought the old Holy Roman Empire crashing with it to the ground. Anyone who doubts it has only to read with proper attention the flysheets, pamphlets and woodcuts inspired by the German Lutheran revolution, not to mention Luther's own writings against the pope and his manifold denunciations of peasants, common folk, young people, Baptists, Enthusiasts, Papalists, the Devil, and the Devil in human form.

There is, however, another and constructive side to German protestantism. Here the leading figure is Melanchthon, who retained a lifelong attachment to Erasmus of Rotterdam (thunderingly denounced by Luther as a man lacking in piety). Led by Melanchthon, a band of theologians educated in the schools and universities of the Protestant princes painstakingly gathered the shattered fragments together and used them as a base on which to construct a Lutheran scholasticism, a Lutheran dogmatic, a Lutheran doctrine of the church and a Lutheran church discipline. These reformers enjoyed the protection of Protestant princes who were afraid of the chaos which would result from a struggle of all against all and were therefore willing to reach a political compromise with the emperor. They perceived the danger which lurked behind the mounting demands of some of the great figures, just as they feared the possibility of revolution from below. Very few, and they were to be found among Luther's most ardent early disciples, had grasped that the Reformation had effected a permanent revolution.

Charles v was faced with an insoluble problem, inasmuch as great conflicts do not as a rule allow themselves to be 'solved'. Despite much good will on both sides, the gulf between Catholicism and Protestantism still remains unbridgeable, because each side starts with such totally different assumptions.

The manner in which Charles v failed to resolve this irresolvable conflict reveals him as one of the great figures of world history. His failure had tragic implications for both Catholicism and Protestantism, but it also had some very fruitful results. Without Charles v the Council of Trent, which was a happening of world importance, is 'unthinkable': two scholars of contrasting backgrounds, Jacob Burckhardt (humanist and liberal Protestant, in later life a non-christian), and Hubert Jedin (a Jesuit) are here in agreement. In the course of the negotiations which so repeatedly broke down, the emperor's theologians won the respect of their German Protestant opponents, who in turn emerged from these religious dialogues equipped with the moderation and self-discipline which made possible the development of a Protestant corpus and its integration into the Empire.

One man who spent his life trying to build bridges and to initiate negotiations between the two embattled camps was Erasmus of Rotterdam, who was as harshly attacked for his pains by Luther as by Roman Catholic monks and theologians. As he put it himself, 'my fate is to be stoned from both sides'. In his battles to preserve the Empire and secure a Catholic reform, Charles was faced with four foes; the papacy, the German Protestant princes, the king of France and a militant religious-political Catholic party. At critical moments all four were in practice against him.

Charles v, the most Catholic emperor the world has ever seen, found in the popes his most formidable adversaries.[1] At first, however, the situation promised well. Adrian Dedel Floriszoon, son of an artisan, was the protégé of his aunt, Margaret of Austria, the regent of the Netherlands, who was a woman of distinction and education (she wrote French poetry and could speak Latin and Spanish). She discovered the young man's talents, made him court preacher at Mecheln and appointed him vice-chancellor and tutor to the young Charles v. Adrian, a humanist of the *devotio*

---

[1] In 1945, when the papacy was uncertainly feeling its way towards an understanding with the western democracies, the papal stamp issued to commemorate the four hundredth anniversary of the opening of the Council of Trent carried the head of Charles V. This belated 'reparation' may be compared with the Dante Encyclical of 1921.

moderna school, was anxious to work for peace, for a reconciled Europe and a reform of the church. Charles had already obtained a cardinalate for Adrian before carrying through his election as Pope Hadrian VI [plate 105]. For what it achieved, his short pontificate (from 9 January 1522 to 14 August 1523) can only be compared with that of John XXIII. Hadrian cut down the establishment of the papal court, embarked on a reform of the curia and sent his legate Chieragati to the Diet of Nuremberg to make confession of the guilt of the Roman Church: 'We have all sinned, and the sin starts with the head of the church . . .' This 'untimely' confession (it continued to be considered untimely down to the time of John XXIII) called down on the pope the wrath not only of the Catholic party, which saw its front 'weakened', but also of Luther, who 'replied' with a pamphlet. The pope also attracted the mockery of the Romans, who reviled him even in his grave. He died in the middle of the hot Roman summer, worn down by the heavy burdens of his office (he referred to the papal throne as 'this chair of misery').

Hadrian was succeeded by a Medici pope, Clement VII (1523–34): as Jedin remarks, 'a personally irreproachable pope', who 'fell into the grave error of supposing that the schism which increasingly threatened to engulf him could be checked by political means, by the application of clever diplomacy'. As Jedin adds, Clement is known to have detested and feared the idea of a council. In his reminiscences (written for his son Philip in 1550), Charles stresses that from 1529 he himself constantly pressed for the summoning of a general council. For us, the emperor's conciliar policy is the guiding thread in his relation with the popes. At first he hoped a council would decide the controversy over the faith; latterly, as the Lutheran movement continued to spread, that it would undertake the reform of the Church in head and members, a reform of the clergy and the cure of souls.

The beginning of his reign finds Clement VII apparently well-disposed toward the emperor and at the same time attempting to negotiate a hostile alliance with Francis I of France. Warned that the pope was playing this double game, Charles accused him of it openly; Clement tried to steer a middle course, but still the tensions mounted. The thunder cloud broke over Rome on 6 May 1527, when the emperor's troops stormed into the city. Their captain, Charles of Bourbon, was killed, leaving his men – Spaniards and German-Lutheran mercenaries – to roam at will, murdering and plundering as they went. The pope fled, but fell into the emperor's hands and remained his captive until the following December.

This was the *sacco di Roma* [plate 103]. It signified, as others have pointed out, the end of the Renaissance, the end in Rome of a Catholicism eager for life, warm-blooded, exhilarating, the end of the Rome Nietzsche[1] so much admired, the renaissance city whose splendours and heady delights were compounded from archaic, antique, popular-'pagan' and christian elements. It took centuries for papal Rome to recover from the shock, whose tremors could still be felt in the nineteenth and early twentieth

[1] Nietzsche indeed accuses Luther of having destroyed this Catholicism by a barbarous reversion to the Middle Ages.

centuries. Under Clement VII's successors Rome became the Rome of the Counter-Reformation and the Inquisition, the seat of a harsh and apprehensive regime administered by a great curial bureaucracy.

Papal propaganda denounced the emperor as 'Luther's robber chief', 'worse than Luther himself'. Imperial supporters in Spain, for example the two Valdes brothers, spread the idea that the *sacco di Roma* was a divine punishment inflicted on curial Rome for its corruption, deceits and blasphemings. Clement VII describes his grief at the sight of the eternal city in a letter to the emperor on his return in 1528: 'We saw before our eyes a miserable dismembered corpse'. Though secretly still hostile, he now became the emperor's ally.

The Great Peace so ardently desired by Erasmus and the emperor's humanists seemed on the point of realization. The year 1529 saw the conclusion of three peaces: in June between the emperor and the pope at Barcelona, in August between the implacable Francis I of France and the emperor at Cambrai (the 'ladies' Peace, negotiated by Margaret of Austria and Francis' mother, Louise of Savoy), in December between the emperor, his brother Ferdinand I of Austria, the pope and some of the Italian states, at Bologna. On 22 February 1530 Charles was crowned with the iron crown of the Lombard kingdom; two days later he was crowned emperor by the pope at Bologna. This was the last time an emperor was crowned by a pope, the last occasion on which Christendom saw emperor and pope united in the high splendour of their offices. The pope crowned the emperor and handed to him the ring, sword and orb. After mass the emperor swore to defend and increase the holy christian faith.

As though to underline the universal character of this festival of peace, heralds came to it displaying the arms of England, France, Hungary, Savoy and Lorraine and ambassadors were sent by many christian kings and princes. The college of cardinals was led by Boniface Palaeologus, a member of the Byzantine imperial dynasty, who was accorded this prominence because he was regarded as a symbolical link with Constantinople; many of Charles V's supporters saw the emperor as a new Constantine. The only representative of the German princes was Philip of Bavaria, the Count Palatine, who carried the orb.

The year of his imperial coronation saw Charles V at the height of his power in Italy and marked the beginning of that Habsburg rule in Italy which endured until the French Revolution and after. The *trionfo* of Bologna – the solemn entry of pope and emperor and the festivities and ceremonies accompanying the imperial corona-tion – was a magnificent spectacle, designed to impress upon the world that Christendom was united and at peace [plate 104]. Yet only a short while before the pope had been the emperor's prisoner; and not long after he resumed his political flirtation with Francis I, which resulted on 12 October 1533 in the betrothal of Clement's grand-niece, Catherine dei Medici, to the future Henry II of France. Francis I made this his opportunity to open talks with the pope about an alliance with the Turks against the emperor.

Clement always found ways of circumventing the emperor's pleas and demands for the council he so much desired. Clement's successor was the Farnese pope, Paul III (1534–49). Paul III had four children. His eldest son Pier Luigi Farnese, like Cesare Borgia one of nature's despots, was appointed gonfalonier of the Church, and three of his grandsons became cardinals while they were still in their middle teens. Yet this pope so given to nepotism introduced into the Sacred College the pious Gasparo Contarini, a devout layman, and a number of Erasmian-educated clerics whose office was to prepare the way for a council.

Meanwhile Charles V was trying to persuade the pope to take common action with him against the Turks and their French ally Francis I. In 1535 the emperor campaigned against Tunis. In the following year the Turks invaded Apulia, as part of a plan concerted with the French who were supposed to attack simultaneously from the north; in the event of victory the French king was probably to have kept Rome, while the Osmanlis (as heirs to the East Roman emperors) took over the former Byzantine possessions in southern Italy. On 8 February 1538 a Holy Alliance was concluded against the Turks at Rome, the signatories being the pope (against his will), Ferdinand I of Austria, and Venice. In June of the same year the pope was busy at Nice arranging a ten-year truce between the emperor and the French king; he had hopes of a dynastic alliance with the emperor and proposed that his grandson Ottaviano Farnese should marry Margaret, an illegitimate daughter of Charles V.

The wrangling over summoning a council continued, attended by much bitterness. Francis I threatened the pope with a defection on the scale already achieved by Henry VIII of England. Charles V, Henry's ally, made it clear to the pope that he could suffer the same fate as Clement VII. The peace reached between Francis I and Charles V at Crespy in 1544 at last made it possible to summon the Council of Trent to meet on 13 December 1545 (after an attempted summons for 1542 had failed).

The Council of Trent [plate 116] marks the beginning of the Counter-Reformation and of a new epoch in the history of Roman Catholicism which lasted into the decades following the Second World War. The Roman Church now saw itself as a religious-political army; operating through its priests, reforming orders and bishops as a continental power, it would deploy all possible military and diplomatic means to win back, step by step, the European territory lost to the Reformation. The Counter-Reformation pursued its irredentist policy in the grand manner, so much so that similar efforts on the part of a Charles V or a Louis XIV appear mere episodes by comparison. In 1542 Pope Paul III instituted the Holy Office (the Inquisition) to combat heresy. It has had a long life; in Spain and the Papal State it was revived even after the French Revolution. An archbishop at the Second Vatican Council in 1962 at long last demanded a 'sancta inquisitio sanctissimae inquisitionis', a pious and sober inquisition into the work of the Inquisition: Roman Catholicism has received more harm from the arbitrary, legalistic and bureaucratic procedures of the Holy Office, which has so often condemned truly religious and learned priests and theologians, than it ever did from papal nepotists.

Paul III appointed as first president of the Council of Trent Cardinal del Monte, who would succeed him as Julius III, though only to disappoint the many hopes men placed in him. The five years of his pontificate (1550–55) were given over to sensuous enjoyment. The cardinals he created included two of his nephews and his former monkey-minder, a dubious guttersnipe of seventeen. He also fought a long war against Ottaviano Farnese, the grandson for whom Paul III had obtained the duchies of Camerino and Castro. The next pope, Marcellus II, was the scholar Marcello Cervini, who in his blameless life resembled Hadrian VI; but he died within three weeks (1 May 1555). Marcellus' successor was Paul IV, whose head, all that remains of a colossal statue he had set up in the Capitol during his own lifetime, may still be seen at Castel Sant'Angelo. The statue itself suffered the fate common to great tyrants and their monuments (Stalin is only the most recent example): after the pope's death the Romans smashed it to bits and threw the pieces into the Tiber, from which the giant stone head was later recovered.

Pope Paul IV (1555–9), so a nephew of his boasted, would conclude an alliance against Charles V with the Turks, the French and the Devil. As Gian Pietro Carafa he had been papal nuncio to Ferdinand the Catholic in Madrid, and hated the Spanish, including Charles V and Philip II. While a cardinal he had been the driving force in the Inquisition, vowing that if his own father were a heretic he would himself gather wood for the stake. The changes which took place in the Inquisition as it evolved at this period are summed up by Cardinal Seripando: 'At first it was a moderate, merciful tribunal, in keeping with the character of Paul III; but later, particularly in consequence of Carafa's inhuman severity, it acquired such a reputation that men grew convinced no more fearful and terrible judgments were passed anywhere upon earth'. The most important of the reforming cardinals created by Paul III now found themselves languishing in the prisons of the Inquisition.

Paul IV compiled the first Roman Index of prohibited books. St Peter Canisius described the Index as a stumbling-block, Cardinal Michele Ghislieri (afterwards Pope Pius V), who presided over the Roman Inquisition, remarked that people who prohibited Ariosto's *Orlando Furioso* and other jewels of Italian literature only made themselves ridiculous. In setting up the Index Paul IV prepared the way for that monstrous denunciation of human creativity which would later, in the spirit of this particular Counter-Reformation, place the great poets of Europe under censorship.

This monkish zealot, who prized above all else the 'purity of the Church' and the 'purity of the sacred doctrines', was a reckless nepotist (he made his criminal nephew, the condottiere Carlo Carafa, cardinal-secretary of state) and persecuted Charles V beyond the grave. Within a few months of the religious peace of Augsburg (25 September 1555), which for half a century and more enabled Lutherans and Catholics to live tolerably at peace within the Empire, Paul IV had made an alliance with Henry II of France. Henry, who was already in league with German Protestant princes and the Turks, was even then pushing the Empire into the position which led eventually to the Thirty Years' War. For Paul IV all means were justified when it came to fighting the emperor and the detested Spanish, and he had no scruples about employing Huguenot mercenaries. He refused to make peace until forced into it by Philip II.

This hatred of Paul IV for everything Spanish brings to our notice a matter of great significance. In the sixteenth century (and even in the seventeenth) the curia often had a greater dread of the Spanish than of Luther and the Protestants. The anti-Spanish reaction at Rome in the latter half of the sixteenth century was responsible for a momentous change within the Society of Jesus, the order founded by the Spanish Loyola. The Spaniards of the first and second generation, many of them men of great gifts who had been close to Loyola, were pushed aside in favour of Italians. An 'Aryan clause' directed against the Spanish[1] was brought into operation, to remain in force down to 1945. At Rome men were very ready to believe that Spaniard-Jew-Moor=agitator-denier-of-the-Trinity, but they were equally alarmed by the serious convictions Charles V and Philip II showed in their religious policy. The curia's hatred of Spain contained an important political element. The popes of the sixteenth century felt as much encircled by Charles V and the Spanish as their predecessors had by Henry VI and Frederick II. From Sicily and Naples on one side and from Milan on the other, imperial and Spanish forces could hold Rome in a pincer grip. If this was a lethal threat to the papacy – and especially to a politically self-conscious papacy, ready to use all the military and political resources of the age to defend its own territories and those of its nepotic dukes – it also pin-pointed the lethal dangers inherent in the emperor's policy. As Luis Vives, the great Spanish humanist, observed, all crises began in Italy.

In Italy imperial policy had overreached itself. There were differences, substantial as well as personal, between Charles' closest advisers and collaborators. The chief matter in dispute was whether a single power could hold and defend both Milan and the Netherlands. Spanish resentment over the costly policy of retaining Milan came to a head in 1544, when the aged Cardinal of Toledo, Juan Pardo y Tavera, spoke out against it; conversely, the young Duke of Alba was for relinquishing the Netherlands, Spain's running sore. But from the imperial standpoint Milan was by far the more important. Its access to the Alpine passes made it the key to Charles' empire as the port and entrepôt for Germany and Flanders. Without Milan – and Genoa – the Empire had no hope of establishing its power in the Mediterranean. Furthermore, the trio Milan, Naples, Sicily, complemented the old Mediterranean-slanted Catalan and Aragonese policy, which in consequence of Columbus' discoveries had now expanded into a 'battle for the Atlantic'. Charles' flotillas in the Atlantic and Mediterranean were constantly preyed upon by French, Turkish and Moorish ships. Since 1521 the Spanish had resorted to a convoy system, reinforced by ships which regularly patrolled the coasts between Gibraltar and Cape St Vincent and the Azores. Armed speed-boats were kept in readiness to give chase to pirates, in particular French

[1] Ignatius had encouraged Spanish Jews to come to Rome and accepted them into the order.

pirates, who lay in wait for the silver fleets. Jean Fleury, the Normandy pirate who in 1522 plundered the treasure of Montezuma, ended his life on the gallows, condemned to death by Charles v.

The emperor relied on this American treasure to help finance his policy in Europe. It is time to investigate exactly what were the aims of this slight, ailing man who was Roman Emperor, King of Spain and Duke of Burgundy, and in particular to discover what interpretation he placed upon 'Empire' and on the obligations arising from his various offices.

In his political testament (dated 18 January 1548), Charles v charged his son Philip II never to forget Burgundy, '*nuestra patria*', 'our fatherland': hence the struggle against the French king, who wanted Burgundy back. But this clinging to Burgundy also visibly contains an element of 'Empire romanticism' and of the universalist imperial ideology associated with Dante. When Charles asserts that world peace can be achieved only through the existence of the emperor as a supreme sovereign he places himself in line with Dante and with the idea of Empire current at the Hohenstaufen-Sicilian court of Frederick II. In this view the *imperium*, the Holy Roman Empire, is the only guarantee of world peace, the sole protector of the church and Christendom. It is not surprising to discover that in his youth Charles was in close contact with many Dante admirers, in particular Mercurino Gattinara, his political tutor and lifelong adviser, who was related to Dante and a proponent of his *De Monarchia*. Erasmus was asked, for purposes of imperial propaganda, to bring out a new edition of this paradigmatic exposition of the Roman-Italian-imperial ideology, but refused.

As well as Burgundians, the chief spokesmen for this imperial ideology at Charles' court were Italian and Spanish humanists with Erasmian leanings. The concept of Rome as the agent of world peace has its roots in the Stoicism of Marcus Aurelius, the emperor who died in Vienna. Titian painted Charles v as the new Marcus Aurelius, Ariosto, in *Orlando Furioso*, hails him as heir and successor to Charlemagne's christian chivalry. Ariosto adapts for application to Charles v the Johannine text usually reserved for Christ or the pope: '*E vuol che sotto a questo imperatore – Solo un ovile sia, solo un pastore*'. When one emperor rules (Charles v), then dawns the age of peace; one flock, one shepherd.

This ideological 'imperialism' had a great influence in both England and France. The Tudors relied on the Carolingian-Ottonian-Hohenstaufen imperial tradition, recently revived by Charles v, in their struggle with the Pope. Queen Elizabeth is celebrated as Astraea, the virgin ushering in the golden age. In the *Faerie Queene* Spenser appropriates Ariosto's gospel of peace, which he had addressed to Charles v, and applies it directly to Elizabeth. A contemporary woodcut shows the queen between two pillars: these are the Pillars of Hercules, overstepped by Charles v in his device '*Plus Ultra*'. One strand of English imperialism can thus be traced to the religious-political imperialism of the circle round Charles v.

French publicists (Dubois, Postel, Bruno, Campanella) proclaimed the 'all-christian king' as the true successor of Charles the Great: he was the *dominus mundi* called to rule over Christendom. Sixteenth-century Italians thus had two imperial saviours to choose from, the emperor and his French imitator. Luigi Alamanni transferred Ariosto's celebration of the emperor to the French king (in *Girone il Cortese*, which he dedicated first to Francis I and then to Henry II). The influence in France of ideas and tendencies current at the court of Charles V has received little scholarly investigation, but the main pointers to it are clear enough: the numerous imperial symbols in evidence at the solemn entry of Charles IX into Paris in 1571, Ronsard's *Franciade*, in which he presents Charles IX as a new Augustus, Charles IX's adaptation of the two imperial pillars for use in his own device [plate 108]. Tommaso Campanella, a Dominican of heterodox views who spent many anguished years in a prison in Spanish Naples, put forward the pope as his choice for the role of universal monarch; later he shifted his preference to the Spanish king and finally, having escaped to France, to the French. Campanella's youth coincided with the rise of Spanish domination over Europe; shortly before he died a child was born in whom Campanella greeted the future sun king. The infant was indeed Louis XIV, by descent far more Spanish than French.

Ideas about Empire current in circles round Charles V profoundly affected Europe and the two Americas. But what did Charles himself think? Modern scholarship has made it clear that in framing his policies he did not simply underwrite the ideas and theories of Gattinara and the Italian and Spanish humanists.

The device *plus ultra* which the young Charles chose for himself in 1517 [plate 106] may appear antithetical to the *ne plus ultra* of antiquity. In the antique world men who ventured beyond the Pillars of Hercules turned their back on the Mediterranean, the ancient cradle of civilized man which he had ringed about with his gods and artifacts; beyond the Pillars lay death and demons. In 1552 Lopez de Gomara dedicated to the emperor the first history of America, his *Historia General de las Indias*, in which he hails the discovery of the New Indies (America) as the greatest achievement since the creation and the incarnation. It is likely that when Charles chose his device, thirty-five years before this book was published, he did so in a spirit of knightly endeavour. His was a spirit far removed from the 'New World' and equally far removed from the ideology, later so richly elaborated, which presented him as a new Hercules, an emperor capable of subduing the monsters let loose by his times and (in the stoical-christian tradition) himself. This last principle, self-conquest, was one the emperor did take seriously. But the imperialist principle was one he spurned; he had no wish to be or to become a world monarch on a global scale, still less the tyrannical master of enslaved peoples.

'*La monarquia universal es tirannia*' ('universal monarchy signifies tyranny'). But the idea of a universal monarchy had already gripped Ferdinand the Catholic, and was expounded for the benefit of young Charles in the *Testament* of the Catholic Kings, and even more plainly in the *Relación del ideario político de Fernando* composed by Ferdinand's minister Pedro de Quintana. Central to these expositions is the idea that peace must be created among Christians so that they may carry on the war against the infidel. Ferdinand and his collaborators accuse the French of aspiring to a universal monarchy for themselves.

Under Charles v Bishop Mota and his circle upheld the view that the supreme authority of the Holy Roman Empire was exercised only over separate, individually autonomous, realms and territories. There was no question of multiplying the Empire's possessions by a policy of expansion but rather of respecting and maintaining what it already held and of recovering by lawful means and in a just war any rights and possessions it had lost. In an address to the *Consejo Real* delivered in Madrid in 1528 Charles characterizes princes who seek foreign conquests as tyrants. He himself was about to set out for Italy, but not to oppress other peoples ('*tyrannizar los pueblos*'), and with no intention of annexing foreign territory. In November 1529 the emperor had a significant conversation with the great Venetian ambassador Gasparo Contarini, in which there was mention of the rumours circulating that he aimed at universal monarchy. This, he said, was a slander whose falsity he intended to prove. In the following April, hard on his return from his successful campaign against Tunis, he remarked to the pope: 'Some people say I want to be monarch of the world. My ideas and my achievements prove the contrary: my intention is to fight not Christians but the infidel, and to see Italy and Christendom living at peace, each man possessing his own.'

'To each his own' was the ideal that drove Charles to make war on Francis 1 and kept him for the rest of his life revolving in the fatal treadmill of the French wars. How could he do otherwise when the French king wanted to deprive him of his old Burgundian inheritance and refused to surrender lands which by right belonged to the Holy Roman Empire?

Among the various writings Erasmus dedicated to Charles v probably the most significant is his *Paraphrases of the Gospel of St Matthew*, which contains an exposition of the emperor's duty. This consists, according to Erasmus, in pursuing a christian policy by which the religion of the Gospels may be protected, promoted and *reformed*. Martial popes and expansionist princes are equally abhorrent.[1] In the strongest possible terms, first in 1516 and again in 1522, Erasmus urged Charles to renounce some of the Empire's old rights rather than embroil all its former territories in a policy of military *recuperatio* (today we would call it reunification).

Charles had too great an atavistic involvement with his ancestors to be capable of following this advice from the greatest humanist of his realm. On 16 January 1523 he informs his brother Ferdinand of his intention to place 'our enemy King Francis' under the ban of the Empire and to demand from him all the old imperial territories he had occupied: the kingdom of Arles, the Dauphiné, the counties of Valence and Provence, the principality of Orange, Montélimar, and so on. The duchy of Burgundy is presented as the rightful claimant not only to the whole of the former Lorraine but also to still older rights the Empire had once possessed in south-eastern

---

[1] Thus in 1518 he writes 'they are turning Frenchmen into Germans', and again, 'now they are making Flanders into a Germany'. The parallel with 1914 and 1940 is irresistible.

France. Charles' preoccupation with 'the old rights of the Empire' was still with him when he came to draw up his testament in 1548.

To the French monarchy, expansionist and aiming at Empire (the Italian campaigns of Charles VIII and Louis XII must be seen in this light), Charles was a formidable enemy. He surrounded France from all sides – Spain, Italy, Germany, the Netherlands, England and Burgundy. Francis I aimed to break out of the circle through allying himself with the pope, with other Italian rulers, with the Turks and with German protestants.

Relations between the two brothers-in-law, Charles V and Francis I, were poisoned by mutual misunderstanding. The emperor, enmeshed in the courtly code of honour, attempted to dispose of the great clash of interests as though it were a personal contest between knights. He several times challenged Francis I to a duel and was bitterly disappointed when the French king neither accepted the challenge nor adhered to his sworn agreements. There was, too, the hurt inflicted on Charles by the fate of his beloved sister Eleanor: it was known throughout Europe that Francis I had infected his wife with syphilis[1] and then abandoned her, stout, ailing and miserable, to take his pleasure with comely courtesans. The emperor was blind to the fact that no duel, marriage, or forced treaty could resolve or banish from the world the great conflict which had already dominated European politics for a century and a half, a conflict in which France and the Spanish-Habsburg world monarchy stood genuinely opposed.

The wars between Charles V and Francis I were protracted. The Italian wars were even given a fresh impetus by Charles' defeat and capture of his enemy at Pavia in 1525, since under the subsequent treaty of Madrid Francis was made to renounce not only Milan, Genoa, and Naples but also Flanders and Artois and even Burgundy – the old Burgundy.

Brantôme, the great French strategist who was as brilliant with the pen as with the sword, is generous in his admiration of Charles V. In his *Grands Capitaines* he describes him as the greatest emperor since Julius Caesar and Charles the Great and an unparalleled master in the art of war. The age of Charles V saw important developments in the art of conducting war in a 'theatre' (even Clausewitz retains this concept). Machiavelli's *Arte della guerra* (1518–20) was only one of several works on the subject to appear about 1520. Crack troops, such as the Swiss mercenary corps formed by Maximilian I on the model of the Spanish *tercero* and the French artillery and cavalry, were famous throughout Europe. Mines were first used around 1495 and perfected by a Spaniard, Pedro Navarro, who deserted to the French. The supreme weapon was infantry (as it continued to be down to the First World War) in which the Spanish were pre-eminent. They fought in tightly compact square formations six-thousand strong, each man armed with a seventeen-foot pike.

In the age of Charles V the great practitioners of war as an art abhorred large-scale battles and sought to avoid them. They were not worth risking if a war might be won

[1] The fact is mentioned, for example, in a letter from Danticus to the king of Poland, dated 19 May 1531.

VI In this bust of the youthful Charles V by Conrad Meit the future 'Charles of Europe' appears as a radiant young prince of the house of Burgundy.

more economically by tactical means. Great battles were a rarity and took place only by mutual agreement. Only seven such took place in Europe in the space of forty years: La Bicogne (1522), Pavia (1525), Mohacs (1526, a crushing victory for the Turks), Cérisoles (1544), Mühlberg (1547), Saint Quentin (1557) and Gravelines (1558). Siege warfare, starving out and out-manoeuvring the enemy, economic and diplomatic negotiations all played an important part. A good stratagem was to spin out a campaign until the opposing army disbanded from lack of money. *Pecunia nervus belli*: money was the sinew of war. The highest bidder, who could entice away his opponent's mercenaries, stood the best chance of victory. These methods were supplemented by a '*stratégie logoratrice*' (Piero Pieri), in other words devastation of the enemy's country to the point at which he was forced to surrender. In this the French became past-masters.

Charles v, a military genius, was greatly loved by his soldiers precisely because he deployed his art in aiming at victories achieved without great bloodshed. He always rode with his men, and when he was plagued by gout had himself tied to his saddle with one leg in a sling. He never gloated over his triumphs and was at great pains not to humiliate defeated enemies. The emperor ordered alterations to be made in a picture which showed the French running away at the battle of Renty (1554): it was not so, they had 'made an honourable withdrawal'.

A picture of the battle of Pavia, painted by an unknown artist soon after the event, hangs at Hampton Court. Mühlberg, Charles' greatest victory, we see through the eyes of Titian. The two men first met in January 1533. Five months later the painter was already proudly styling himself *Titianus, eques Caesaris* – Titian, Count Palatine and Knight of the Golden Spurs (only Rubens rose so high). Titian's incomparable *Emperor Charles at Mühlberg* [plate 98] is no narrative but a painted equestrian monument in celebration of the victory. Charles may have remembered that his grandfather Maximilian had planned an equestrian statue for the choir of SS. Udalrich and Afra at Augsburg. With this picture Titian created a genre which retained its potency down to the time of David's *Napoleon crossing the St Bernard*.

After the battle Charles is said to have echoed Julius Caesar's '*veni, vidi, vici*'. In his memoirs (1549), Avila compares the battle of Mühlberg with Caesar's crossing of the Rubicon – only the Rubicon was now the Elbe. Maximilian shared with his grandson Charles v a war-mysticism in which St George, champion of Christendom in the fight against the infidel, merges into the christian knight, *miles christianus*, and both into the emperor. *Sant Jago España, Sante Jorge imperio* (St James the Moorslayer, the saint venerated at Santiago de Compostela, and St George, champion of the Empire), was the battle cry at Mühlberg, fought on St George's day in 1547. The lance the emperor carried into battle was a short one, but Titian has painted him with the long imperial lance which from the time of Otto the Great had been one of the Empire's most venerated insignia. Equestrian portraits of Constantine the Great show him with the great lance, and Titian may well have seen Giulio Romano's fresco in the Sala di Costantino in the Vatican.

Supporters of Charles extolled him as a new Constantine, victor over the Turks, future conqueror of Constantinople. Inside the Empire proper, however, the new Constantine was expected to vanquish and coerce the Protestant 'rebels'. Mühlberg delivered the leader of the Protestant princes, John Frederick, the Saxon elector, into his hand. Philip of Hesse surrendered voluntarily and became Charles' prisoner. The emperor's victory in Germany seemed complete. At the 'armed' Diet of Augsburg in 1547–8 he imposed the 'Augsburg Interim', under which, pending the decision of a general council, Protestants were conceded communion in both kinds and clerical marriage, in return for a resumption of their Catholic obedience.

The emperor had demonstrated his military superiority, but at the expense of rousing not only the Protestant but also the Catholic princes of the Empire against him. It was feared that Germany would become Spanish – under a Spanish army of occupation and a Spanish emperor. Charles had thoughts of promoting his son Philip II of Spain instead of his brother Ferdinand of Austria as the next imperial candidate. It was at this juncture that the emperor was deserted by his brilliant Protestant general, Maurice of Saxony. Thanks to this defection, a league of German princes, in alliance with Henry II of France,[1] was able in 1552 to drive the emperor from the German part of the Empire as a fugitive. On his way into Italy he remarked to Schwendi, his chief captain: 'I meant well by Germany, but neither side is grateful to me. The Catholics are not, since they would be content only if I had Maurice beheaded and left no castle in Germany standing; I have earned no gratitude from the Lutherans. I therefore commend them to God, that he may make it good.'

The religious peace reached at Augsburg on 25 September 1555 brought the internal conflicts to an end. In the following year the emperor abdicated. All through his reign Charles had fought fairly over the Empire and the German Protestants. His meeting with Luther at Worms on 17 April 1521 remained the only personal encounter between the two. In the decades which followed this meeting, however, Charles realized for himself that the 'heretics' could not simply be 'annihilated' and 'exterminated' at will, as the hard-core Catholic party in Rome, Spain, France and the Empire demanded. There remained only one other path to try, that *via media* of Erasmus and the humanist theologians which both Luther and Rome viewed with such scorn and suspicion. The aim was to reach a viable compromise with the Protestants through a series of religious conferences, to be followed by a General Council which would pronounce the final solution. This council would be a great reforming council, reforming everything in sight – Rome, the imperial church, the Catholics and the Protestants.

Between 1531 and 1547 the emperor was the focus of all moves towards unity, as of all religious conferences (Speyer, Hagenau, Worms, Regensburg) which came close to achieving the grand compromise. The efforts of Catholics such as Gropper and

---

[1] Under the peace of Chambord (1552) France received the imperial vicariate over the imperial cities of Metz, Tull-Toul, Virten-Verdun, Cammerich–Cambrai, which henceforth figure in the annals of war under their French names.

Veltwyk (a Jewish convert and Hebrew scholar who was professor at Louvain), who acted as the emperor's theological intermediaries, and of Protestants such as Buer and Capito, with Melancthon in the background, did much to narrow the gap. In their willingness to create a favourable climate Catholic spokesmen kept to the Erasmian precepts of moderation, courtesy, charity. Men should first agree on one or two points and leave the rest to time and the future to resolve.

The wisest and calmest heads in the Protestant camp recognized the patience and religious sincerity the emperor's representatives brought to the dialogue. But hopes of the grand compromise were wrecked by the intransigence of Luther, the anxieties of Rome and the political opposition to the emperor building up inside Germany.

The emperor took great pains with the Protestant princes and tried to persuade them to take part in a council. He was undeterred by personal humiliation, even of the kind he experienced in his talks at Speyer in March 1546 with Philip of Hesse, the brains behind the League of Schmalkalden. Three times more he implored Philip to come to the great religious conferences at Speyer, where the diet was in session, and was three times refused. The Religious Peace of Augsburg was actually concluded between Ferdinand, the emperor's brother, the electors and the princes. This compromise, which Rome fiercely attacked and refused to recognize, contained the germs of new conflicts, but it also laid the foundations (built on after the Thirty Years' War) for the grand compromise which would make the Holy Roman Empire unique in Europe as the one large political arena in which opposing christian confessions could live lawfully side by side. This situation, with all its attendant stresses, made possible the flowering and richness of German intellectual life in the late eighteenth century, which in turn paved the way for Germany's world importance and scientific achievement in the nineteenth.

Augsburg fixed Roman Catholicism and Lutheranism, on equal terms, as the Empire's two poles, replacing that old duality of pope and emperor which had been reflected in the double choir arrangement of imperial cathedrals. Other sects (soon to include Calvinism) were excluded: German Lutherans tended to fear other Protestants more than the Devil himself. Furthermore, choice of religion was conferred only on the Estates of the Empire, i.e. the princes, on the non-princely nobility (the *Reichsritterschaft*) and on the imperial cities. Subjects had to follow the religious profession of their territorial rulers: *cuius regio ejus et religio*. But subjects were at least allowed the right to emigrate, a precious right, which in the twentieth century has often been withheld. Ecclesiastical princes might decide personally in favour of Protestantism, in which case they were no longer allowed to rule their territories, which had to remain Catholic. This was the Ecclesiastical Reservation clause, a source of much future trouble. In Austria the *declaratio Ferdinandea* (based on precedents from Inner Austria) gave confessional freedom to the Protestant subjects of ecclesiastical rulers.

Charles' formal act of abdication as ruler of the Netherlands is dated Brussels, 25 October 1555; the imperial crown he relinquished on 23 August 1556. Before leaving Brussels Charles v formally gave account of his reign. 'I sought the imperial crown, not that I might rule over more realms but to provide for the well-being of Germany and my other kingdoms, to create and preserve peace and harmony throughout Christendom and to bend its forces against the Turks. My many treaties have been broken through the passions of unpeaceable men. On errands of war and peace, I have therefore had to travel nine times to Germany, six times to Spain, seven times to Italy, ten times to the Netherlands, four times to France, twice to England and twice to Africa. God is our God, thanks be to Him, even in misfortune.'

'Nine times to Germany, six times to Spain.' Charles had spent a lifetime trying to reform the empire.[1] He wanted to preserve its federal structure and hoped to establish an imperial league as the new form of organization regulating relations between the king and the princes as also between the princes themselves. Leagues were nothing new in Germany. In Charles' time they fell into two broad categories, those which could be said to be working towards unity in the Empire and those which encouraged its fragmentation. In the first group there were three types: leagues such as the Rhenish League which aimed at a federation in which the king would be merely an equal partner with the other Estates; leagues of Estates with whom the king, as ruler, formed a coalition; and leagues which wanted the king to have no powers of any kind.

The Swabian League, founded in 1512 during the reign of Maximilian, occupied an important role in Charles' plans for reform. In 1519, the year Maximilian died, the Swabian League alone possessed any real power which spilled over into the individual territories, and Charles was always hoping it might revive. On the other hand was the *Reichsregiment*, which figured in the plans of the leading princes to turn the Empire into an aristocratic republic. As the council of the emperor and the Holy Roman Empire, it ought, they maintained, to exercise the emperor's powers in his presence as in his absence, and advise and decide on all matters affecting the Empire. It should consist of the emperor (in his absence a president) and twenty-two members working in harmony. This plan Charles found unacceptable, but a compromise was reached at the Diet of Worms in 1521 under which the *Reichsregiment* would act only in the absence of the emperor and would represent the supreme governmental authority in the Empire. The emperor was to nominate four out of its twenty-two members, together with a viceroy as its head; and the *Reichsregiment* would enter into no alliances with foreign powers without the emperor's consent.

In the decades that followed the *Reichsregiment* disintegrated, as did the Swabian League, despite Charles' repeated efforts during the thirties and forties to revive it. The Swabian League had brought together the more 'democratic' elements among the towns and petty nobility of south-west Germany. Charles' brother, Ferdinand of Austria, was more inclined to favour the *Reichsregiment*, since he thought the great princes, with their superior power, would be more effective in checking the Turks. Early in 1547 there are signs that Charles was planning a new organization

[1] Charles' plans for the reform of the Empire have been sympathetically studied in our own day by Martti Salomies, son of a Finnish Lutheran archbishop (see bibliography).

designed to ensure lasting peace within the Empire, and negotiations over this new imperial league took place in 1547–8 at Augsburg. As late as 1552–3 Charles was still trying to form a league (the *Memminger Bund*) which would embrace the whole of Germany and unite all the territories belonging to the Empire with the Netherlands.

A memorandum Charles asked Sigismund Seld, his vice-chancellor, to draw up in 1554 is aptly described by Brandi as 'a political testament for Germany'. Its main propositions reflect the views of the emperor himself. Imperial authority has declined; the princes are more independent than formerly; the power of the Emperor rests on his hereditary possessions, constantly under attack from outside enemies. The system of *Landfrieden* is useless since they cannot be enforced: the two available sanctions, proclamation of outlawry and the obligation on members to provide mutual assistance, are totally inadequate, since anyone attacked is finished off before 'help' arrives. Yet either from inertia or stupidity, there are still plenty of people who will speak up in the diet for these outmoded, useless weapons. As in the past, the only hope lies in the creation of leagues on the model of the old Swabian league.

Charles v's plans for reform were wrecked not merely by the overweening egotism of the princes but also by the conflicting aims of Habsburg policy in the Empire. On the one hand the Habsburgs wanted to rebuild the Empire on a firmer foundation, on the other they wanted the strongest possible support for a specifically Habsburg policy, which the princes regarded as the emperor's 'private affair'. Even so, it is probably still true that the only chance for unification in the sixteenth century lay in the direction of developing and organizing the Empire as a confederation. That task had still not been accomplished by the time our present century dawned. Only as a confederation could the Empire hope to fend off the danger, assailing it from within and without, of becoming a tyrant and 'that monstrous thing, a universal monarchy'.

'. . . six times to Spain.' In his abdication address Charles begged forgiveness for any injustices he had unwittingly committed during his reign. He then departed to Spain, for the house at San Geronimo de Yuste which had been built for him in imitation of his birthplace, the Prinsenhof at Ghent.

No people (or rather peoples, since the peoples united under the Spanish monarchy were very conscious of their separate identities) had resisted Charles so passionately as the Spanish: it is their boast that they have never submitted to imperial authority, not even that of Charles v. Under Charles v and his son Philip ii (his preferred successor in the Empire) Spaniards served the Empire on all the battlefields of Europe, while other Spaniards, in America, presented him with a new idea of Empire. Cortés, the conqueror of Mexico, writes to Charles v: 'Your Highness can call yourself emperor under the new title of Emperor of New Spain, and with no less right and profit than you call yourself Emperor of Germany' [plate 110]. Charles was not to be tempted by an independent *imperium* in the New World (not even by an *imperium* independent of the Pope and the Germans). When Vitoria launched his attack on the legality of the *conquista* in America he based it explicitly on the existing rights of the western Empire. Charles' imperial eagle, the *aguila de Austria*, can still be seen in South America as a subject of native Indian art, reminding us that it was once the sacred symbol which sanctioned the freedoms Charles proclaimed for the Indians, just as the dollar sign reminds us of Charles' device *plus ultra*.

The extent to which American silver and gold helped to finance the policies and wars of Charles v in Europe is a matter of controversy. But the 'Empire on which the sun never set' belongs to world history. Starting with Charles v and his brother Ferdinand, the old double eagle of the Empire, in the form of the double eagle of the House of Austria, took up residence in both Madrid and Vienna. For close on two centuries the history of the Holy Roman Empire and the destinies of the Spanish Empire are closely interwoven.

Cortés was not alone in suggesting to Charles that he assume the title 'Emperor of America' (*Emperador de Indias*). The idea was also put forward by Niklas de Witte, a Netherlander, and Mototolinia, an Italian. Thoughts of an overseas, Mexican, secundogeniture for the House of Austria were thus already in the air. Charles v was not an 'imperialist'. Nor was he a singleminded ruler in the fashion of his son, Philip II. How he appeared in men's estimation can be judged from the widespread report, which originated in the entourage of the viceroy, that for reasons of conscience he even contemplated giving Peru back to the Incas. The permanent conflict of conscience which troubled him as he faced the tremendous problems opened up by the New World sheds light on his policy in Europe, where he felt himself just as responsible for Protestants as for Catholics. He was torn between two poles: on one side was his '*real concienca*', the religious and ethical duty he had assumed with the crown, which obliged him to care for his Indian subjects; on the other was his '*real servicio*', his duty towards the economic necessities of the crown, which obliged him to exploit the 'Indies' to the uttermost in order to finance the crown's policies in Europe.

The enthusiasm of the early Spaniards who first voyaged to the Americas was stirred and sustained by mythological and eschatological speculation, by hopes of finding Paradise, by fantasies of mounting a global crusade against Islam (Columbus set out to find Prester John in his fastness in the east and enlist him in a crusade which would catch the Islamic lands of Africa and the Mediterranean in a trap). The soldiers of Cortés saw St James the Moorslayer fighting at their side (the same 'Sant' Jago' who was invoked against the Protestants at Mühlberg). The conquest of America thus presented itself as an extension of the *reconquista*, an extension of the war against Islam and paganism. A lust for gold spurred men on in the adventure, but at a killing cost in suffering and deprivation as the small Spanish force fought its way through the vast and alien worlds of the South American continent. Disenchantment and bitterness soon followed. What sense was there in undergoing such sufferings and making such sacrifices? Who was to profit from them? Murmurings of this kind gave rise to disagreements, some of them quite acute, between the Spanish 'colonists' and the far distant crown. Charles v, perpetually short of money, neither would nor could support the cost of opening up the overseas territories. He therefore delegated royal rights to private interests under a form of contract known as *capitulación*: the state was unwilling to bear the great financial risk involved in South America, but was ready to share in the profit. This practice led to the development of a dualist colonial administration in which royal officials on the one hand confronted conquistadors and private entrepreneurs on the other. In the viceroyalty of Nueva Espana the split became in essence a split between *letrados* ('academics' – many officials had been formed in the Erasmian humanist tradition) and *hombres de experiencia*, men of practical experience who knew 'how to get the best out of the natives'.

Charles v was anxious to protect the natives from exploitation and extermination. This he sought to do by settling Indians in their own reserves, isolated from the Spanish colonists and their pernicious influence. Hence it became necessary to eliminate the private jurisdictions granted to the *encomenderos* who used native labour to work their own estates and those ceded to them by the crown and resented outside interference. Their resentment is understandable. European Spain was confronted by many enemies, military, political, economic, intellectual and religious. The Spanish peninsula itself was not proof against the corruption of Spanish orthodoxy and 'racial purity' by Moors, Moriscos and Jews and the many hererodoxies and heresies now flowing into Spain from Europe. In self-defence against this open Europe, with its exorbitant and exhausting demands, the Spanish attempted to make their America a closed Spanish-Catholic state, an *Estado catolico cerrado*, in which no 'foreigner', whether pope, emperor, German, Fleming, Frenchman, Portuguese or Italian had any business to interfere.

In a letter he wrote to Charles v in 1518 the jurist Zuazo tells the tale of how Pope Alexander vi, himself a Spaniard, in 1493 divided the earth like an orange between the king of Portugal and the grandfathers of his present majesty. In America, the Spanish half, the Spanish king was overlord of the church and its bishops and clergy were his royal officials. Foreign missionaries and foreign businessmen were not allowed to penetrate.

The legal code the Spanish devised for the New World was based on these maxims. That it was harsh is proved by the repeated exemptions granted by Charles v. The first to agitate against it were the Flemings, who wanted the young emperor to create bishoprics for them in the New World. Next German soldiers and merchants appeared on the scene, as the Fuggers and Welsers started to show an interest in the overseas empire. The ensuing clashes were serious, since the Spanish would not recognize special agreements entered into by the emperor. By January 1535 Bishop Bastidas of Venezuela was writing to the emperor imploring him not to allow any more Germans into the country: some who had already arrived were persons of low degree and tainted with the views of the heretic Martin Luther. In 1538 German trade was totally excluded in favour of Spanish. After 1540 aliens could no longer obtain residence permits. Under Philip ii the colonial regime would become still more exclusive and Spanish-nationalist in character.

On 9 November 1530 a law was promulgated which was to be a cause of much religious grievance in Latin America and whose after-effects are still apparent there today. This was the law forbidding all 'foreigners' to set up missions in the Spanish empire. The 'foreigners' chiefly affected were the Franciscans. Under Charles v the legislation against foreign missionaries was harsher than against foreign traders and businessmen, although Charles himself made a few exemptions on behalf of individual foreigners who were members of religious orders.

In their overseas territories, the Spanish (in contrast with the Portuguese, who practised an 'open' economy), were erecting a closed Spanish state. The economy, the church, the police, the army, the schools, the legal system, were all supervised by the royal government, working through its secular and religious officials and tribunals. Is it then surprising that there was a growing temptation to create a closed Spanish Europe in the image of this closed America?

It was precisely this prospect, which played on the fears of popes, German Catholics and Protestants, Netherlanders and all non-Spaniards, that finally produced the great conflagration of the Thirty Years' War. With Spanish troops, Spanish strongholds, Spanish statesmen, Spanish religious and Spanish allies planted everywhere in Europe, the day would surely come when Europe would become a closed Europe, on the model of the 'closed Catholic state'. In time it gradually dawned on people that there was a remarkable parallelism between the unprecedented events taking place simultaneously in Europe and America. The 'discovery' of that inner world in which every soul has direct access to God was the European 'counterpart' to the discovery of the New World. Luther and the great Spanish conquerors of America belong roughly to the same generation. 1517, the year when Luther nailed his theses to the church door in Wittenberg, was also the year when the first expedition under Francisco Hernandez de Córdoba set sail for the conquest of Mexico. Luther died in 1546, Cortés the year after.

The drama of European history and in particular of the Holy Roman Empire, in whose secular, ecclesiastical and political shape and future the Spanish were now starting to show an interest, is further underlined by a fact often overlooked by contemporary and later observers, namely that there were two Spains. These two Spains cannot be separated from one another and not infrequently carried on their great debate within the mind and heart of the same man. The world public was made aware of this conflict through the disputation between Las Casas and Sepulveda which took place at Valladolid in the presence of the emperor in 1550.

The 'other Spain', the reverse side of the closed national system, probably drew its sustenance from very ancient themes of individual liberty and the freedom of the ego. Spaniards of the nineteenth century described themselves as a nation of twenty-two million kings. An age-old thirst for freedom, above all for freedom to think and know and to form independent judgments, was reinforced in the sixteenth century by a Spanish neo-scholasticism open to reality, by the development of a similarly orientated jurisprudence, and by numerous other elements which had found their way into Spain through the Erasmian movement.

98 Titian, *Emperor Charles V at the battle of Mühlberg*. Mühlberg saw the emperor at the height of his power in Germany. The subsequent fall was swift and steep.

100 (*above*) Fortune smiles on Margaret of
Austria. The court of this great Habsburg
princess was a model for its patronage of
art and learning.

101 (*right*) The submission of Ghent to
Charles v in 1540. The proud and prosperous towns of Burgundy and the
Netherlands were constantly in revolt
against their princes.

99 (*left*) *Au juste poids véritable balance*
(detail), anonymous painting, early
sixteenth century. An allegory of the
balance of power in Europe at the
accession of Charles v (on the extreme left
of the illustration).

102 Petitioners from all ranks of society crowd round the young Charles V, seeking from their ruler the protection subjects regarded as their age-old right.

103 *Sacco di Roma*, 1527. In Protestant Germany and Catholic Spain the capture and plunder of Rome by imperial troops was interpreted as divine vengeance.

104 The coronation procession of Charles V in Bologna, the last occasion on which a Holy Roman Emperor was crowned by the pope (Clement VII).

105 Pope Hadrian VI's entry into Rome as shown on his tomb in the German church at Rome, S. Maria dell'Anima. During the all-too-short reign of this Netherlandish pope, who collaborated with Charles V, the cardinal-legate to the Diet of Worms made a unique confession of papal guilt.

HENRIC COMES ANASSAV ARCHIEPS BARREN EPSCAVRIEN EPVSBRIXIEN NIC L PERNOT· MICHAELMAIVS INNVMERICANONVM LEGVMQVE DOCTORES VIR

106, 108, 109 Emblems of Charles v, (*left*) which Charles ix of France and other European rulers adapted for their own use (*centre*). The emblem of the Pillars of Hercules with the over-arching crown and bands (*plus ultra*) was used on Spanish-Habsburg coins (*far right*) struck for South America and eventually became the sign for the dollar.

107 Charles v with allegorical figures, 1550. The portrait stands between renaissance and baroque – it has been said with justice that baroque begins with the *sacco di Roma* in 1527.

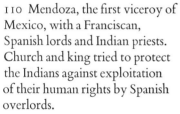

110 Mendoza, the first viceroy of
Mexico, with a Franciscan,
Spanish lords and Indian priests.
Church and king tried to protect
the Indians against exploitation
of their human rights by Spanish
overlords.

111 Death-ship of Charles v, 1559.
Reminiscences of the death-ship which bore
Celtic heroes to the Isles of the Blessed are
here combined with the barque of the Church
and the ceremonial barges and galleys of
Pharaonic Egypt and imperial Rome.

La Chapelle ardante

Francisco de Vitoria (1483/5–1546) was the father of international law in Europe; as a theological writer he was prepared to give an unprejudiced linguistic exposition of difficult expressions occurring even in such highly suspect authors as Valla, Erasmus and Melanchthon. Vitoria, who attracted audiences of over a thousand students, early in 1539 took the subject 'De Indis' as his theme for a special lecture, justifying his choice with the reflection that the murder, expropriation and exploitation of so many innocent people made it a matter not only for jurists but also for theologians to investigate. The argument of his lecture is as follows: the Indios were the lawful and peaceful proprietors of their lands. No pope or emperor had any right to allow these lands to be seized by force merely on the grounds that the proprietors were not Christians. Even if they refused to accept the christian faith when it was offered them, that was still no legitimate ground for making war on them. Furthermore, there was no evidence he knew of to prove that the faith had been demonstrated to the Indios, over a suitably long period, through the example of a properly christian mode of life or through the testimony of miracles. In any case, since the Indios were not Christians they were not subject to the spiritual authority of the pope. Neither the pope nor the emperor had any inherent right to universal dominion. There was no 'natural right' of conquest in the name of a higher civilization or a superior faith. No one had the right to make forcible conversions. The Spanish king, however, did bear responsibility for the deeds, misdeeds and cruelties perpetrated by his subjects in America.

One can imagine what would have happened to any Catholic theologian and university professor who as a member of the Catholic Church in Germany lectured with such frankness say in 1935. Even today, criticism of the regime and its taboos only half so outspoken, if voiced in Spain or the German Bundesrepublik, would lead at the very least to disciplinary measures. Vitoria's lectures on the New World certainly caused an unprecedented commotion and he was condemned on all sides for doing damage to the papacy, the emperor and to Spain. The letter Charles v wrote in his own hand to Vitoria's religious superior comes close to being a warrant for his house-imprisonment. He did not, however, demand Vitoria's dismissal from his chair, and in 1539 and 1540 Vitoria delivered two more famous lectures, De iure belli (on international law) and De magia, a critique of the ancient world: the idea that pagan states have as good a title as christian ones is basic to his thinking. Charles v wanted Vitoria to be one of his representatives at the Council of Trent, but he died in 1546, only a year after the Council opened. But his candour, and his concern for universal justice, lived on in some eminent disciples.

Sixty theologians from Vitoria's school at Salamanca sat at the Council of Trent, at which Melchor Cano, who succeeded Vitoria in his chair, played a leading role. Cano, like many Spanish theologians of the emperor's party, was a bitter enemy of the Jesuits, whom he described as forerunners of antichrist. The preacher on the first Sunday in Advent which immediately preceded the opening of the council was Domingo de Soto, who had been Vitoria's pupil. The Gospel for that day deals with the Last Judgment; Domingo de Soto applied it to the Council, to bring home to the

112 The Chapelle Ardente constructed for the obsequies of Charles v, whose Habsburg cult of death and the tomb was inherited from the Burgundian dukes. An age which believed steadfastly in the passage through death to immortality made death and funerals an occasion for visible triumph.

fathers their terrifying responsibility. They were answerable for Christendom, the Council was under judgment. On the subject of the *Indios*, he declared that neither their serious offences against the natural moral code – sodomy, cannibalism and idolatry – nor their resistance to conversion to Christianity gave the Spanish the right to attack and subjugate them, since they were not subjects of the pope or of any christian rulers; he does, however, make an exception in the case of *Indios* actively hostile towards Christians. It was quite impossible to impose the faith by force. Tales of infants of heathen parents being baptized in their thousands by people who could give no guarantee that they would be brought up as Christians – tales he had heard from the perpetrators themselves – only filled him with horror. There could scarcely be any greater sacrilege. We may here detect a tacit and embittered allusion to the forced baptisms of Jews and Moors which took place in Spain between the fourteenth and sixteenth centuries.

It was Domingo de Soto (in 1548–9 the emperor's confessor) who took the chair in the debates between Las Casas and Sepulveda which took place between August 1550 and May 1551 at Valladolid. It is not surprising that contemporary Spanish historians are engaged in rehabilitating Sepulveda, whose authoritarianism is in keeping with the authoritarian aims of the present regime, or that Las Casas, his open-minded opponent, is regarded in Spain as a sinister, dangerous, 'decadent' figure.

In these debates two Andalusians confronted one another as spokesmen for the 'two Spains'. Las Casas knew the cruel hardships and miseries of the New World from personal experience as a colonist and had taken careful note of what he saw. Sepulveda, sixteen years his junior, had been a student at Alcala, Sigueunza and Bologna. He had never been 'out there' but knew it all better than Las Casas – from the pages of Aristotle. Sepulveda uses Aristotelian arguments in defence of total colonialism, that is of the right to rule over 'inferior' peoples: men and peoples are by nature unequal; the more highly developed have a right to rule the culturally backward; serfdom and slavery are the natural and just conditions of those who by nature are unfitted to rule themselves by the dictates of reason. The Spanish conquest was justified because the *Indios* were idolaters and practised human sacrifice. The first duty had been to subdue them by force, the second to evangelize them. Augustine's opinion that it was just to wage war on heretics applied equally to the barbarian *Indios*.

When Las Casas came to speak he enumerated, for the world to hear, all the atrocities committed beyond the seas, and in so doing brought down the rage of his fellow Spaniards on his head. Spain's political and religious enemies down the centuries have seized on Las Casas as a crown-witness against Spain and the Spanish world mission, fabricating from his testimony the '*leyenda negra*' – the black legend – which makes Spain out to be a monster. It was used to good effect by the maritime Protestant powers in their struggle against Spain. Yet those who denigrate Spain – and they have their descendants in the modern Anglo-Saxon world – deserve to be reminded of the counter-charge made by Immanuel Kant, himself of Scottish Protestant descent. Kant attacked the utter lawlessness of the maritime powers in their colonial wars and pointed to its fruit, 'the cruellest and most calculated form of slavery', a slavery brought about by 'powers who out of piety perform many works, and, while drinking injustice like water, are happy to know they are numbered among the elect by reason of the rightness of their belief'. The blackening of Spain's record in world history on account of her deeds in Mexico and Latin America was part of a carefully calculated design to expose Spain as unholy and to enfeeble Spanish might both in Europe and overseas. No less unjust is the *leyenda rosa*, so carefully cultivated in our own time, which brands Las Casas as a dangerous fanatic, probably a psychopath, virtually a crypto-communist. What good could there be in a man who 'soiled his own nest'?

Las Casas stuck to his principles. The *Indios* were born free, and papal consent to the Spanish rule in America did not abolish their freedom: the Spanish regime would have a just title only if the *Indios* freely consented to Spanish overlordship and rule. Missionary work is only possible in conditions of peace and freedom. Christ can only be preached effectively to men who are free. All men are created equal by God, there are no inferior and superior races, no inferior and superior nations. The only evangelism justifiable in the eyes of God and the world is peaceable evangelism which works through love and a good example (*paz, amor y buen ejemplo*).

His 'royal conscience' made Charles v increasingly aware of the crown's impotence beyond the seas, where viceroys, settlers and royal officials increasingly did precisely as they pleased. But the crown did not relax its efforts to protect the *Indios* and see that they received justice.

Realization of his impotence in the great struggle taking place in the Empire weighed on the emperor's mind long before his abdication in 1555. He told the Portuguese ambassador in 1542 that the thought of abdication first occurred to him in 1535, when he was returning from Tunis, and later admitted to the same confidant that he ought to have abdicated in 1547, after his victory over the Lutheran princes at Mühlberg. Again, had Philip shown himself more adroit in the conduct of affairs in the Netherlands when he made his debut there in 1549, Charles would probably have seized that as the occasion for handing over the crown.

Before taking leave of this restless, truly European emperor, we shall do well to follow him into the most alien of his worlds, London and Paris. On his arrival in London in 1522 the young emperor was given a magnificent reception. A living tableau mounted at Gracechurch by the London branch of the Hanse showed Charles the Great seated between Charles v and Henry viii and investing both with a sword and a crown. In the winter of 1539–40 Charles v made a three-months' progress through France, the land of his greatest enemy, and received a triumphal welcome. Setting out from Spain, he travelled by way of Bayonne, Bordeaux, Poitiers, Loches, Blois and Orleans, reaching Paris on 1 January 1540; six days later he left for Ghent. The impression made by this progress, which had 'Peace' as its motto and throughout which king and emperor rode side by side, was quite extraordinary. French propaganda had admittedly helped to pave the way, but the many odes composed to welcome the emperor and the demonstrations of the populace point to something further. It seems that anti-imperial France retained an awareness of its own 'imperial' tradition, which was actually intensified by this 'counter-propaganda'. The history of the French monarchy from the twelfth century down to the age of Versailles and the Sun King, indeed down to Napoleon, has to be interpreted in the light of this inner, dialectical involvement with the Holy Roman Empire.

French-speaking poets who were also Burgundians were used to singing the emperor's praises; they had celebrated his victory at Pavia as a victory over the king in Paris. Champier, it is true, at one time took issue with Aeneas Silvius and the German humanists Wimpfeling and Sebastian Brand over the descent of Charles the Great, asserting that he was of French nationality and the king of France, therefore far superior to the emperor.[1] But in a little work published at Paris in 1544 Champier now declared that it was for the Empire and the Emperor to give and dispense justice to the whole world: in a dispute between two neighbouring kings, for example, it was for the Emperor to adjudicate; if they refused, he was entitled to confiscate their kingdoms.

This unusual homage was offered three years after the entry of Emperor Charles into Paris. A century and a half earlier Charles IV and Sigismund had merely visited the French king. As Charles V progressed through France he was hailed as *pax nostra* (at Poitiers on 9 December 1539). In accordance with an ancient tradition, on his entry into each French town Charles had the prisoners set free, a ritual proper to the prince of peace, the peace-bringer. For his solemn entry into Paris the emperor, attired wholly in black, was mounted on a black horse; the banner of the French king was carried by a herald in white armour. One is reminded of those gatherings before the First World War to which the monarchs of Europe came attired in the uniforms of each other's regiments. In that dying world ceremony, blood sports and war as drama were closely linked. The last and greatest gathering of the 'European family', the funeral of King Edward VII at Windsor on 19 May 1910, was attended by sixty princes, together with detachments from the many foreign regiments (German, French, Russian, Austrian, and so on) in which Edward VII had held honorary rank or command.

The great drama Charles V had staged for Europe ended at San Geronimo de Yuste. The widespread rumour that the emperor had become a monk was not unfounded, since he appears to have gone through some ritual of admission to the Hieronymite order; he was, however, excused from the necessity of proving his blue blood (*sangre azul*) free from the Jewish and Moorish taint. Plagued by gout, he remained in seclusion at his country house at Yuste.

During these last months, and in his dying hour, the emperor's gaze constantly rested (to the consternation of his doctors, so Figueroa relates) on Titian's *Gloria* [colour plate VII]. This picture, completed in 1554, was the last work the artist

---

[1] Relying on Old Testament authority, Champier had previously noted that the office of kingship was older than that of emperor. Emperors were made by human election, but kingship was hereditary, that is to say kings were made by God.

executed for the emperor. Titian himself named the picture *Trinity*; in the codicil to Charles' will (1558) it is described as a *Last Judgment*. It was Philip II, deeply dedicated to the cult of his father, who named it *Gloria*. The emperor is shown kneeling and dressed in his shroud; close by is the imperial crown which, like the emperor in the twelfth-century *Play of Antichrist*, he has now discarded. Beside him are the kneeling figures of Isabella, his favourite wife, long since dead, and his sister, Mary of Hungary. Below are Philip II and his daughter Joanna, and a little lower still an old man (probably Titian himself). The young woman in the picture represents the Church, for whom Charles fought a lifelong battle. The turbanned figure on the eagle is Ezechiel, herald of divine judgment and the prophet who proclaimed the restoration of God's people. In his testament of 6 June 1554 Charles had prayed that God would receive his soul 'into his divine glory'. In Titian's picture his prayer is on the point of being granted.

9

THE MADRID–VIENNA AXIS

THREE rulers – two future emperors and a king – grew up in and under the shadow of Charles V: his brother Ferdinand I, Ferdinand's son Maximilian II, and Charles' son Philip II. King Philip of Spain was formed and fettered for life by his cult of his father, from which he drew deep personal satisfaction. Maximilian grew up at the court of Charles V, who was fond of him and allowed him to perform vice-regal duties; but once he left Spain Maximilian did everything he could to rid himself of the Spanish influences which had moulded his early years. Charles' brother Ferdinand was recognized as ruler of the hereditary Austrian possessions under the treaties concluded at Cologne, Worms and Brussels in 1521-2 which had also confirmed the 'major' privileges of the house of Austria allegedly secured by Rudolf IV; in 1531 Ferdinand was elected King of the Romans and on the abdication of his brother succeeded him as emperor. In character Ferdinand differed fundamentally from Charles; he found the Spanish and the superior weight of Spanish power a burden. This sense of Spanish oppressiveness determined many of the actions of the Vienna Habsburgs during the next century and a half and continued to weigh on them even after Spanish power in Europe had declined.

It was in any case in the nature of things that the Madrid-Vienna axis should be subject to frequent and severe strain. The interests of Vienna were concentrated chiefly on Buda(-pest), Belgrade, Siebenbürgen, Prague, the German parts of the Empire and northern Italy; in some places – in the Empire, Italy and the Netherlands – they often ran directly counter to those of Madrid. For Madrid, anything that happened in Paris, Rome, Brussels, on the European and African shores of the Mediterranean, in England or in America was of central importance. In view of these global interests and concerns, not to mention the tensions set up within the east-west Habsburg conflict by the increasing number of Habsburg burdens and the steady expansion of the battle fronts, one can only marvel that the axis survived so many storms and lasted as long as it did.

When Ferdinand, the brother of Charles V, came to Austria as a young man in 1521 he spoke Spanish and Flemish and understood Italian. He brought with him two Spanish poets and a great fondness for French poetry, a taste soon shared by the Austrian nobility. Once arrived in Austria, he started to learn German. In adapting himself so well to the situation he found in Vienna Ferdinand displayed to the full a quality for which the Habsburgs are famous. He is sometimes charged with being too accommodating and it is alleged that because of the Turkish danger and the strength of Protestantism in his Austrian possessions he allowed himself to make greater concessions to the Protestants of the Empire than his stronger brother would have approved. This judgment does little justice to the wider scope of Ferdinand's political aims. Erasmus saw Ferdinand as a type of John the Evangelist and dedicated to him his *Introduction to the Gospel of St John*. Ferdinand was an Erasmian to the core and during his reign the ideas of the great humanist made headway in Austria. The Erasmian virtues of reconciliation, mediation, compromise, self-control and forbearance, which Grillparzer brings out so well in the scene between Emperor Rudolf II and the Protestant Julius of Brunswick in his *Bruderzwist in Habsburg*, and which Maximilian II, Ferdinand's much-traduced son, tried to promote through his policies, were already present in Ferdinand.

For centuries Austrian Habsburgs were educated according to 'Mirrors of Princes' which followed Erasmian principles. There were Erasmians in Ferdinand's immediate circle: his chancellor, Bernhard of Cles (later cardinal of Trent) and two bishops of Vienna, Johannes Faber and Friedrich Nausea. Faber, who tried to persuade Erasmus to come to Vienna, favoured close cultural relations between the Netherlands, Burgundy and Austria. Nausea described Erasmus in an obituary as a writer who wrote in collaboration with the Holy Spirit and a teacher whose teachings had taught men once again to be worthy of the creator: he deserved to be a saint (1536). This view, expressed by the bishop of Vienna, was not shared by the Roman Catholic militants in Cologne, Louvain, Valladolid and Rome, who were currently denouncing Erasmus as the patriarch who had spawned Luther and his heresy. Their call for a great war to 'exterminate' the 'heretics' won no response from Ferdinand, who was afraid that such a war would ruin the Empire and cause the collapse of the triangular Bohemian-Austrian-Hungarian defence system which barred the Turkish advance into the heart of Central Europe.

In 1521 Ferdinand married Anna, sister to Louis of Hungary. After his brother-in-law's death at the battle of Mohacs, Ferdinand contested the succession to the crowns of Bohemia and Hungary for himself. His election to Bohemia in 1526 was unanimous, but his bid for Hungary split the country. The offer of St Stephen's crown came from only a minority of the magnates, meeting in a diet at Pressburg on 15 December 1526; the majority, meeting at Stuhlweissenburg, elected Johann Zaplya, the voivod of Siebenbürgen. It was this split that helped to bring the greater part of Hungary under Turkish rule.

The visit Ferdinand paid to Prague in 1526 signalled the reopening of the Bohemian lands, after their devastation during the Hussite wars, to the house of Habsburg, Rome and the Latin west. Ferdinand brought the Renaissance to Prague, importing Italian architects and masons to build a summer palace (the Belvedere) for his wife Anna on the hill opposite the Hradčany palace. He aimed, however, less to impose an alien veneer on the sadly damaged country than to conquer it from within. In 1543

Prague witnessed what a contemporary Czech writer, Bohdan Chudoba, describes as 'one of the most astonishing spectacles of the century', the meeting between Ferdinand, the king brought up in the spirit of Erasmus[1] and Mystopol, the regent of the Hussite consistory at Prague, at which Ferdinand ordered Mystopol to countermand a Hussite decree forbidding celebration of a Hus festival. The prohibition had been the result of growing pressure on the part of a radical purist and puritanical group within the Hussite church.

The compacts and treaties with the Protestants of the Empire (culminating in the agreements made at Passau in 1552 and at Augsburg in 1555), which from the Roman and hard-core Catholic point of view were 'impossible', would never have come about without the energetic collaboration of Ferdinand and his son Maximilian; the latter was appointed by Charles V to preside over the Diet of Augsburg. Both as representatives of Charles V and as rulers in their own right, Ferdinand and Maximilian made a significant contribution to the rebuilding of the Holy Roman Empire (which by virtue of its foundation and institutions was a Roman Catholic Empire, endowed with a protectorate over the Roman Church) as a community to which both Catholics and Protestants could legally belong. This extraordinary achievement was something which until the nineteenth or even the twentieth century no state in Europe believed possible.

This revolution – and it was a revolution – began in 1521 at the Diet of Worms. The fact that the diet concerned itself with the religious question at all was revolutionary, as Konrad Repgen points out, since a synod would have been competent to deal with Luther as a 'heretic'. On 25 July 1532 the Elector of Mainz and the Elector Palatine in the name of the emperor concluded the 'Religious Peace of Nuremberg' with the Protestant princes. By concluding this treaty with 'heretics' the emperor severed the law of the Empire from Catholic canon law at a vital point. The year 1532 marks the end of a chapter in the history of ecclesiastical law within the Empire and a watershed between 'medieval' and 'modern' times. It saw in effect the first introduction into the Empire of a religious code which was confessionally neutral. The seed of future settlements – in 1555, 1635, not to mention 1648 – had already been planted.

The popes tried to ignore what had happened. Clement VII, alarmed by the Turkish danger, approved the emperor's efforts at reaching a compromise with the Lutherans in 1532: they were after all Christians (as Pius IV was to remark in 1565 with reference to Siebenbürgen, 'heretics are after all Christians'). We find Cardinal García de Loaysia, a former general of the Dominican order and Charles V's confessor, advocating political compromise with the Protestants as early as 1530. Since he thought the existence of the schism no reason for jeopardizing the stability of the state, he had no qualms over the negotiations with the League of Schmalkalden and advised

---

[1] Ferdinand had moreover been permanently influenced during his Spanish youth by Juan de Palomar who had met Bohemian Hussites in Prague and at the Council of Basel, and by Cardinal Juan de Torquemada.

VII Titian's *Gloria*, the picture the dying Charles V liked to feast his eyes on to keep present in his mind the glory of Heaven, which, as he firmly believed, he would shortly share.

Charles v to postpone discussion of Lutheran errors, which he thought it best to dissemble.

In giving this last piece of advice Loaysia uses the word '*dissimular*', one of the commonest words in the Spanish political vocabulary of the sixteenth century. It can have a variety of meanings, depending on the outlook of whoever is using it. With some it is the equivalent of 'all in due time', meaning that the speaker is only waiting for a favourable opportunity to inflict military and political defeat on his enemies. But it can also have the Erasmian sense of an appeal to 'truth, the daughter of time': the full truth only time will reveal, for time will judge between the religious parties who at present are blinded by the dust of battle. True solutions will be reached only when distance affords a better view. In the case of Ferdinand and Maximilian II '*dissimular*' has this positive meaning. In their efforts to achieve compromises they were grateful for any co-operation, whatever its motives. At first, however, their efforts looked like failing. The pope insisted that an imperial diet – especially a diet which had heretics among its members – was not the proper forum for debating questions which affected religion and the church. God had entrusted the disposition of ecclesiastical property to the church alone. There must be no more glossing over, because that was forbidden. In a famous admonition dated 24 August 1544 the pope called on the emperor to annul all existing agreements or run the risk of punishment. The Roman drafters of this document had in mind those great conflicts which had engaged the popes and emperors of the past, from the time of Henry IV to Ludwig of Bavaria. This famous admonition remained a scrap of paper, thanks to a change in the pope's attitude when he realized how great was the resistance in the imperial and royal camp and how complicated the politics of Europe had become.

The Religious Peace of Augsburg of 1555, although not formally recognized by the pope, at least seems to have had his tacit agreement. In 1955, looking at it in a very different light, Pius XII described the Peace as a great contribution to the 'common weal' of Church and Empire, and an act which had saved the Empire. (Pius no doubt had his own 'Turks' in mind, the present-day Communists.) In the last year of the sixteenth century a jurist named Joachim Stephani coined the formula '*Cuius regio ejus religio*', which usefully summarizes what Augsburg had achieved. For all its provisional character, the Religious Peace came to take its place with the Golden Bull of Charles IV, the imperial *Landfrieden* and the imperial electoral promises ('the capitulations') as a piece of fundamental law, indeed as the very basis of the Holy Roman Empire. In imperial propaganda of the early seventeenth century it is celebrated as the Empire's most sacred constitution.

Pope Paul IV (1555–9), the fanatically anti-Spanish and anti-Habsburg pope, was long credited with having rejected the Religious Peace, but this is not borne out by the evidence. It seems, however, that in 1558 Paul contemplated deposing Ferdinand for condoning heresy. Paul took advice in the matter from the future Pope Pius V, who during his own reign threatened Ferdinand's son Maximilian with deposition as a full-blown heretic. The Roman Church and curia in theory made no surrender of their claims, even though these claims were now superseded; in practice, however, the church started to adapt itself to the situation. 'And in this contradictory state of *sic et non* is foreshadowed a good part of papal and church history in centuries to come, in fact down to our own time.' Nearly a century would pass before the Holy See, on 18 April 1641, made an attempt to resolve the latent contradiction.

In the meantime the compromise of 1555 was consolidated. The Lutheran Estates had a legitimate status within the Holy Roman Empire and the renewal of German Catholicism from within could make headway under the legal protection afforded by the Religious Peace of Augsburg. In virtue of the *Jus reformandi* of 1555 Catholic territories retained the right, only removed by the Peace of Westphalia, to impose Catholicism.

Ferdinand's dealings with Protestants in the hereditary Austrian lands, in Bohemia and inside the Empire, were harassed by constant espionage and sniping on the part of the curia, and by uncertainty over whether Charles V and the Spanish would agree to his arrangements. This friction with the other Habsburg branch was inherited by Ferdinand's son Maximilian II.

Ferdinand endeavoured to ease things for his eldest son by dividing the Habsburg territories he had himself inherited, but this in fact did nothing to lighten Maximilian's load. Maximilian (since 1562 King of the Romans and of Hungary and Bohemia) received the Bohemian lands, the surviving fragment of Hungary and Austria above and below the Enns (present-day Lower and Upper Austria). His brother Charles received Inner Austria (Styria, Carinthia and Carniola), with Graz as his residence, while a third brother, Ferdinand (who was married to Phillippine Welser, daughter of an Augsburg patrician), was given the hereditary possessions in the Swabian Rhineland, Tyrol and the Vorarlberg.

This division created problems of its own, made all the greater by the fact that headship of the house was held to lie not with Maximilian but with Philip II of Spain, who was born in the same year. The two cousins represented different worlds. The observant eye of the Venetian ambassador to the imperial court noted the different ruling styles of the two lines. In Vienna was Maximilian II, all charm and affability, proficient in German, Latin, Italian, French, Spanish, Czech and Hungarian and tolerant of men of different faiths. He had to allow his sons Rudolf (II) and Ernst to be educated in Spain, where they were taught to be proud and reserved. Philip II hedged himself about with barriers intended to create an aura of divine awe, terror and majesty round the untouchable person of the king: 'there was a certain line which even the most trusted confidant did not cross, because if he did he fell flat on his nose' (Baltasar Porreño).

'My brother Ferdinand, strive like a good knight of Christ, be faithful to your Lord till death,' Cithard, his confessor, could address the emperor thus informally and without title, having been commanded to do so a few months previously by Ferdinand himself. Ferdinand died on 22 July 1564, resigned to the will of God and with no death struggle, the Erasmian 'pious knight of Christ'. 'He went out like a little light in a hanging lamp' reports one observer, and Maximilian was at his bedside.

Ferdinand's last years had been darkened by serious conflicts with Rome. He sent representatives to the third session of the Council of Trent (1561) to demand communion in both kinds for the laity: if laymen and priests could live united in one body in the Eucharist, Catholicism would no longer be split between laicism and clericalism. Acceptance of Ferdinand's second demand, the removal of clerical celibacy, would probably have meant the end of separate Lutheran communions in the Empire. There were Lutheran pastors in plenty who were ready to return with wife and child to a reformed Catholic Church. Hence Ferdinand's third demand, for a genuine reform of the church and not least of the church's properties and possessions.

In June 1562 Ferdinand submitted a formal letter to the Council which made plain his utter lack of confidence in the curia; he describes it as hostile to reform and unfitted to carry it out. Later, on the intervention of Delfino, who was nuncio in Vienna, he withdrew the memorandum. Ferdinand knew that the first two sessions of the Council (1545–7, 1551–2) had been a great disappointment to his brother Charles. Philip II's only concern was to bring the whole thing to an end. In general he had little use for the Council of Trent and allowed its decrees to be published in Spain with the proviso that they were only valid 'so long as they did not infringe the rights of the Spanish crown'.

It was in Spain that the young Maximilian grew up. He was born on 1 August 1527 (the year of the *sacco di Roma*) and passed his infancy and childhood in Innsbruck, Maximilian's first tutor known to us by name was Wolfgang Schiefer, a native of Alsace and a former pupil and table companion of Luther. Charles V, who had a high opinion of Maximilian, brought him to his court when he was only seventeen and married him, against his will, to his daughter Mary. She remained a Spaniard throughout her life, but was a faithful wife and their five children were born of a happy marriage. Maximilian was present with Charles at the battle of Mühlberg (1547) which saw imperial power in Germany at its peak. Among those captured on that day was the Elector John Frederick of Saxony, whose Lutheran Bible, a magnificent piece hand-bound in black velvet, also fell into imperial hands. It later came into the possession of Maximilian, who studied it assiduously.

Maximilian came to Spain in 1548; his suite consisted of two Czechs, Vratislav Pernštyn and Jaroslav Smiřicky, and an Austrian, Adam Dietrichstein. But he was repelled by the pomp, harshness and exclusiveness of the Spanish mode of life, and never felt at home. Anxious letters came to him from Bohemians, who implored him not to forget their language. His cousin Philip, sent by Charles V to Brussels to prepare himself for his future responsibilities, found himself equally uneasy. When in pious *imitatio* of Christ the King, Philip and his Spaniards escorted an ass through the streets on Palm Sunday, the Flemings only laughed. His efforts in the summer of 1550 to join in the drunken celebrations of the German nobility lacked conviction. His drinking partners took him for a 'weakling', which is not surprising; the excessive drinking which took place among German noblemen and students was partly due to the reputation it had acquired as a sure sign of virility.

On his way home from Spain Maximilian fell seriously ill at Wasserburg on the Inn. He was afterwards convinced that the German Catholics, working through Cardinal Christoph Madruzzo, who had entertained him in Trent, had tried to poison him. Ferdinand devoted much care to the religious formation of his son. He summoned to Vienna a pastor inclined to Lutheranism, Johann Sebastian Pfauser, who remodelled the court services on 'evangelical' lines. Pfauser said of himself, and there is no reason to doubt him, that he was neither Lutheran nor Papalist. Maximilian took the same line. He once said to Hosius, the papal nuncio, 'I am neither Catholic nor Protestant but a Christian'. Maximilian, like the adherents of the *devotio moderna*, the reformed Czech Catholics and Utraquists and the moderate Hussites, wanted communion to be administered in both kinds. There were always Czech noblemen in his retinue, and they had an influence over their elected king. Maximilian was courted as the 'friend of Gospel truth' by Czechs and Germans alike, and the Bohemian Brethren, the forerunners of the Moravians, sent him their confession of faith and asked him to intercede for them with Ferdinand. Maximilian refused to have his children educated by Jesuits and entrusted them instead to the suspect Georg Muschler, a professor at Vienna university. His private correspondence with Augustus of Saxony is written in cipher and with invisible ink. 'Under persecution at Vienna' he reports on 2 April 1556, for he himself was aware of being persecuted and spied upon at his father's court, so much so that he refused to take part in the Corpus Christi procession.

Paul IV reproved Ferdinand severely for the Religious Peace of Augsburg and the 'heretical education' of his son. He attacks the heir to the throne as a 'wicked heretic', a Lutheran who possessed a Lutheran library, employed a Lutheran preacher and made common cause with Lutheran princes. Nor was Spanish criticism lacking. The Spanish ambassador urged Mary to leave Maximilian, but she stood by her husband.

The pressure on Ferdinand was so great that he accused his son of turning all his subjects into heretics and offered him the choice of submission or disinheritance. Maximilian turned for help to the German Protestant princes, who with many pious and edifying phrases left him in the lurch. They had no wish to break with the emperor, nor did they believe it was possible to make the Holy Roman Empire '*evangelisch*'. The episode had a lasting effect on Maximilian, and from now on he was careful to keep religion and politics apart. In February 1562, at Prague, in the presence of his brothers Charles and Ferdinand, Maximilian placed his hands between his father's and swore to live and die within the Catholic Church.

Maximilian nevertheless stayed true to his inner conviction, with the result that when he lay dying at the Diet of Regensburg one last battle, over the last sacrament, developed round his head. The Spaniards urged him, his wife besought him on her knees to receive it from the hand of the court chaplain. But the dying emperor replied that his chaplain was in heaven. He resisted even the pleas of his sister, the

Duchess Anna, declaring that he surrendered himself to the will of God, conscious of having fulfilled his duty towards his creator.

There was unfeigned sorrow in both camps of the Empire at the death of Maximilian. Protestants and Catholics mourned him as 'father' and 'brother'. He had taken as his motto *'da pacem patriae'* ('give peace to the fatherland'). His perception was just; in an epoch of continuing war, both cold and hot, the task of the statesman was to *give* peace, not to be continually demanding it from others.

In Maximilian's eyes his supreme duty as a ruler was to compose the serious and political conflicts within his territories and reconcile the peoples. He was also interested in reforming Catholicism, and regarded any effort in that direction as part of his duty. He conceived a plan for giving his Protestant subjects an independent ecclesiastical order and invited Chytraeus, a professor from Rostock, to work out the details. An agreement made in 1571 secured to the Estates of Lower Austria freedom of religion on their own properties and in their own castles. Maximilian's brother Charles, although in sympathy with the spirit of the Counter-Reformation, was persuaded by the example of Vienna and fear of the Turks to accept similar arrangements for his own territories. Lutheran and Calvinist visitors from Germany were astonished and disturbed at the 'unbridled freedom' prevailing in the Austrian territories, a freedom which had made them a magnet for religious non-conformists of every description.

Yet before the century was out the Counter-Reformation had conquered; it left deep wounds, especially in Styria and Upper Austria, which even in the twentieth century have not completely healed: it is no coincidence that the *Los-von-Rom* movement ('Separate from Rome' movement) and National Socialism both took such hold in Austria, a land where men's hearts were clouded by crypto-Protestantism and three centuries of resistance to the Habsburg-Rome axis.

As emperor, and as a man well aware of the horrifying threat of religious-political civil war, Maximilian had to take a stand over two of the most appalling events in European history: Spain's brutal suppression of the revolt in the Netherlands and the massacre of St Bartholomew. An outburst of violence in the Netherlands which raged for five days (14–19 August 1566) wrecked hundreds of churches and monasteries and thousands of art treasures. The Spanish sent Alva to revenge them [plate 117]. Letters from the imperial court at Vienna implore the Spanish in Madrid and Brussels to act with clemency, since harsh treatment could only end in total destruction. Maximilian wrote to his cousin Philip II on 9 July 1567, pleading that clemency alone could avert 'the destruction of fair and good lands and the devastation of great and highly prosperous trading centres;' clemency, he claimed was more in keeping with 'the eternal omnipotence of God' than 'arrogant severity.'

The court in Vienna was dismayed to learn of the arrest of Egmont and Hoorn. In this situation Maximilian called on one or two outstanding diplomats he could count on to act as mediators and conciliators. Among them was Count Hoogstaten, a close friend of William of Orange, who was in touch with Maximilian through Vratislav Pernštyn. Pernštyn was a knight of the Order of the Golden Fleece (elected at

Antwerp in 1566) and was accepted as a friend not only by the Netherlanders but also by Spanish noblemen. Pernštyn, like Erasmus, was able to cross back and forth between two separated worlds. He represented Maximilian in Madrid on the occasion of Philip II's third marriage to Maximilian's daughter and then went on to interview Francis II of France at Blois.

Philip had informants among the Czech nobility who kept him in close touch with the political and religious situation in Bohemia. The pressure he applied to Maximilian, already his brother-in-law and now his father-in-law, to impose the Counter-Reformation in Bohemia might well have caused the Thirty Years' War to break out there and then. But Maximilian withstood this pressure, all the more stoutly since his feelings and those of his whole court were outraged by news of the arrest and imprisonment of the Spanish crown prince, Don Carlos, and of the executions of Egmont and Hoorn, despite the emperor's repeated pleas for mercy. It seems that Don Carlos had been planning to flee from Spain, probably to take refuge at the court in Vienna, since he was betrothed to the emperor's daughter Anna. In his perturbation Maximilian debated whether he ought not to go in person to Philip to plead for Don Carlos and the Netherlands. Just how Don Carlos met his death, whether by murder or execution, is an open question. Nor do we know whether, as is rumoured, he was in fact accused of plotting with the Netherlanders and the French Protestants. His fate was a common tragedy of crown princes. The French ambassador Fourquevaux wrote on 12 September 1567, 'the father hates his son no less than the son hates his father'. For Philip II, who venerated his own father Charles V as a saint, it was a particular tragedy and the death of his son weighed on him for the rest of his life. Two plays written in the sunset glow of the Holy Roman Empire, Schiller's *Don Carlos* and Goethe's *Egmont*, give dramatic shape to these two tragedies Maximilian did his best to avert. A performance of *Don Carlos* under an absolutist, semi-absolutist or totalitarian regime makes the audience aware that the plea for freedom of thought Schiller puts into the mouth of the Marquis de Posa, '*Sire, geben Sie Gedankenfreiheit*,' must be their own rallying cry to freedom.

The emperor was no less appalled by the news of the massacre of the Huguenots in Paris and throughout France which took place in August 1572, the massacre of St Bartholomew. Spain and Rome were jubilant at this annihilating blow to the 'heretics'. This jubilation, and the retrospective jubilation of some nineteenth-century Catholics over the event, goaded the English historian Lord Acton (himself a Catholic) into remarking, 'when a mob murders, that is murder; when a king murders, that is murder; when a pope murders, that is murder'. Maximilian found it painful that the 'murderous gang' were among his kinsmen, and in a letter in his own hand to the Elector of Saxony, dated 13 December 1572, characterizes the massacre as an infamy the French would have bitter cause to regret. The widow of the hapless Charles IX who was the nominal ruler of France (the real ruler was his mother, Catherine de Medici) in later life took up residence in the Hradčany palace at Prague, where she built the All Souls' chapel. In reparation for the massacre she founded a house of Dorothean nuns in the heart of Vienna. Emperor Joseph II handed over the buildings to the Protestants and it remains to this day the spiritual centre of Austrian Protestantism.

'The course of the world runs contrary to all reason', as Maximilian remarked to Micheli, the Venetian ambassador. The emperor steadfastly advocated policies of moderation and peace through negotiation, but his counsels fell everywhere on deaf ears, not least in Germany. What alarmed him most was that the two major Counter-Reformation powers, Rome and Spain, attached more importance to the crushing of heretics than to repelling the Turks. As his vice-chancellor Zasius bitterly remarked, the pope (Pius v) contributed not a cent from the Turkish tax he had been granted but used the money to build a house for the Inquisition. All the pope raised was 'unnecessary uproar' in Germany and in Christendom.

Maximilian hoped he might lead the 'impudent Bishop of Rome' (as he described him at an interview with the English ambassador at the Diet of Speyer) back to the apostolic path. At Rome there were even fears that this nephew of Charles v was planning a second *sacco di Roma*. Although Rome and Spain rejected his policy of reconciliation with the Protestants in the Empire, he persevered with it in his own territories. He reprimanded Georg Eder, imperial *Reichshofrat* and university professor, for his *Evangelische Inquisition* (1573), a lampoon against the Protestants and 'court Christians' (the theological 'fence-sitters' at court, who wanted to be neither Lutherans nor papists but 'merely' Christians) and had the work suppressed. The emperor defended his married confessor and his own practice of taking communion in both kinds – matters of standing reproof from Spain – with the argument that his father Ferdinand had fought for both concessions at the Council of Trent.

The major concern in Eastern Europe was the struggle against the Turks, and here Madrid and Vienna were again at loggerheads. Maximilian preferred to have the Poles as his allies, while Philip II looked for an alliance with Russia, and perhaps ultimately with Persia. Philip sent Fajardo as his envoy to Russia; on his way back he was detained by Maximilian at Prague (1571–2). Ivan IV, 'Lord of the terror of God', was meanwhile making overtures to the Turks, and the Poles accordingly warned Spanish and German arms manufacturers not to export German weapons to Russia. The Russo-German connection presented a great danger to Poland, as it would many centuries later when Seeckt, the general of the Weimar Republic who wanted Poland destroyed, attempted to join up with the Red Army. Maximilian's dealings with Poland represent one link in the chain of an Austrian policy towards Poland which Maria Theresa still thought a good policy for Europe. King Sigismund II of Poland had two Habsburg wives in succession. On his death in 1572 Maximilian tried to win the Polish crown for himself, but the Poles elected Charles of Anjou. For Paris this election was an important stage along the road to converting France into a 'European monarchy' and winning for France the imperial crown.

Maximilian hoped through his treaties, compromises, dynastic marriages and negotiations to prevent European politics from running wild. He wanted men to be so hedged about that they might be restrained from self-destructive madness. The gardens of Kaiser-Ebersdorf and Schönbrunn, and the Prater in Vienna, which have often been allowed to lapse into wilderness, are his fitting memorial. He was a patron of art and science and brought to Vienna distinguished scholars of the calibre of the botanist Karl Clusius (Charles de l'Escluse) and the physician Johann Crato von Kraftsheim, both of them Protestants. His interest in the natural sciences and horticulture gave Maximilian some welcome relaxation, taking his mind off the spectre of religious strife. At Ebersdorf – his 'Tusculum' – he experimented with new plants; among the animals in his menagerie was an elephant, a rarity at that time. Like Maximilian I, he strove to make Vienna a truly 'imperial' city, a centre of European intellectual life. He was a patron of music and like his predecessors invited musicians from the Netherlands to Vienna; but he also cast his net wider, and tried to tempt Palestrina away from Rome. His court librarian was a Netherlander, Hugo Blotius.

In 1576 Clusius planted in the palace gardens at Schönbrunn and Laxenburg specimens of the red horse-chestnut which the emperor's envoy David Ungnad had brought back from Constantinople. These were the first horse-chestnuts to grow on European soil. The potato, introduced into Europe from America by the Spanish, came to Vienna by way of Belgium. Augerius Ghislain de Busbeck, a Netherlander who belonged to the court academy at Vienna and was employed by Maximilian as tutor to his sons, went as his envoy to Constantinople and sent back old manuscripts and coins to Vienna; among the plants he brought back from the famous Byzantine gardens were the tulip and Maximilian's own favourite, the lilac: the first of the Vienna lilacs blossomed in the May of 1569, in the garden in front of Busbeck's house. In this way, as in others, Maximilian followed the precept of the Greek fathers to let a hundred flowers bloom. He agreed with Erasmus: Europe should not dissolve into ashes but burst into flower.

But what of the blight that threatened the flowering in the Netherlands? In his agitated correspondence with Philip II, Maximilian implored his cousin to make some concessions to the Protestants which would effectively counter the risk of rebellion and the break-up of his realms. Philip's reaction may be judged from the terms of a message he sent to Rome: 'And so His Holiness can rest assured that I would rather lose all my territories and sacrifice my life a hundred times over than allow even the slightest impairment to religion and the divine liturgy. I have no thought or desire to be the ruler of heretics. I will endeavour to compose the religious strife in the Netherlands without resort to arms, if that be possible. But if I cannot without resort to force restore everything there as I should wish, I am resolved to take up arms.' In his concern for his cousin's salvation Philip sent to him the learned theologian Gallo, who dogged his footsteps from Vienna to Regensburg. These two cousins, who differed so greatly in disposition, were each concerned over the other's policy for the salvation of Christendom and of the world, though their immediate concern was whether those policies made them for the moment partners or enemies.

For this reason, if for no other, a survey of Europe and the Holy Roman Empire

113 Tomb of Charles v by Pompeo Leoni in the Escorial. The emperor is seen with his wife Isabella, Eleanor, Queen of Portugal and France, Mary of Hungary, widow of King Louis II, who died at the battle of Mohacs, and Mary, wife of Maximilian II of Austria.

FILIPE SEGVNDO REY DE ESPAÑA.

Suma ratio pro Religione.

114 (*left*) Façade of the Escorial basilica. The Cortile de los Reyes stresses the close kinship between the kings of the Old Testament and the anointed king in Spain.

115 Philip II of Spain, seen as the champion of the Catholic faith. His watchword was *summa ratio pro religione*, and he dedicated all his political authority and state-craft to the defence of the faith. The divine citadel of the Escorial is seen lying between him and his enemies.

116 The Council of Trent, which laid the groundwork of ecclesiastical, political and social structures retained by Roman Catholicism until the Second Vatican Council.

117 (*overleaf*) Peter Brueghel the Elder, *Massacre of the Innocents*. Comparable with Picasso's *Guernica* as a work of protest, it was directed against Spanish atrocities in the Netherlands. Protests also came from the emperor in Vienna, where the picture hangs today (it formed part of the collection of Emperor Rudolf II!).

CONCILE DE TRENTE Par Vargas.

118 (*top*) Fighting in the streets of Prague in 1611. Unrest in Bohemia was not eased by the political vacillation of Rudolf II, and in 1618 led to the outbreak of a European war.
119 (*bottom*) Archduke Ferdinand investing Emperor Rudolf II with the chain of the Order of the Golden Fleece.

120 (*top left*) Emperor Rudolf II with the seven electors. South German enamelled beaker, 1592.

121 (*above*) Tycho Brahe, one of the many scholars and scientists attracted to Rudolf II's court at Prague, seen in his observatory.

122 *Celsae graviore casu decidunt*, 'the highest things fall the furthest'. Emblem from Juan de Borja's *Empresas Morales* which appeared in Prague in 1581.

123 Emblem from the title-page of Melchior Goldasts' *Monarchia Sancti Romani Imperii*, 1611; see p. 201.

124 Coronation of the emperor and the festal ball held in honour of the empress on the occasion of the coronation of Emperor Matthias I in Frankfurt, 1612.

would be incomplete without a character sketch of Philip II. This son of Charles V was the living embodiment of Spanish policy, of Spanish preoccupation with religion and of that Spanish will to rule which helped to plunge Europe into the Thirty Years' War. There were also traits which made a substantial contribution to the shaping of Counter-Reformation Europe. Spanishness was an important ingredient in the Catholic Europe which was formed by mannerism, baroque and the humanism of the Counter-Reformation, and remained so down to 1918. It appears at its most impressive and distinctive in the person of the *Rey del mundo*, Philip II, King of the World.

The *leyenda negra* has made of Felipe Segundo a monster, though in Spain itself he is valued and admired even by some who reject the former monarchy. Philip did not, like his cousin, learn to speak seven languages. He spoke only Spanish, that is Castilian, and when he wrote it made spelling mistakes; he knew a little Latin and French, but not enough to speak them with assurance. The blame for his lack of education lies with his tutor, Juan Martinez. Charles V wanted to engage Viglio, the celebrated Flemish humanist, but he declined the position.

But it should not be thought that Philip grew up in blinkers. His entourage always included clerics under suspicion of heresy; he himself read the writings of Erasmus and was impressed by the pictures of Hieronymus Bosch, which from the viewpoint of the church were dubious in the extreme. Intellectual narrowness, and bigotry of the nineteenth-century stamp were foreign to his nature. His strain of harshness had different roots. As a young man he took pleasure in sports, hunting and dancing. He could show great tenderness towards his adolescent daughters, as we know from a correspondence unearthed in 1867 by the Belgian historian Gachard in the archives at Turin. The publication of these letters in 1884 caused something of a sensation. Traits of Philip's character were revealed which no one (not even members of certain nineteenth-century circles who fancied themselves in the van) had previously suspected in such a 'monster'. Philip followed the sacrosanct precepts of his father to the letter. His social legislation, for example, through which he tried to protect the labour force in South America, has an astonishingly modern ring.[1]

Philip saw himself as responsible for the spiritual and physical well-being of twenty nations [plate 115]. It was this sense of responsibility that chained him to the desk at which he spent eight hours a day and turned him into a *rey burocrata*, the first man, as one writer put it, 'to attempt to guide the course of the world from a writing-desk' (Alexander von Randa). He would fall asleep at his work and be found slumped over it in the morning.

But the king had no right to sleep or to make things easy for himself. Philip was in sympathy with Teresa of Avila, and with her attempt to rouse Spain from apathy with the urgent warning, 'Cease your slumbers, the world is in flames!' The papal nuncio wanted the great mystic put away as a madwoman, but Philip defied him and gave her his protection. He abandoned the sports and favourite pastimes of his youth,

---

[1] Philip prescribed an eight-hour day for workers employed on building fortifications and in factories.

but retained his love of art, music and painting. His reign saw the establishment of the first Spanish academy of sciences. The system he devised for the Escorial library (which was open to all who could profit from it) became a model for future librarians, and it was he who started the practice of requiring the deposit of every newly published book. The famous botanical garden which still bears his name was created under his supervision, for he was a passionate flower-lover. He may never have asked himself in so many words what was the right way to cultivate men, but his answer is written into his life's work: by retaining the tightest possible control and acting only out of the deepest concern for the spiritual well-being of one's subjects. Both maxims imposed an excessive strain, on king and subjects alike. Philip saw himself first and last as the servant of his peoples. As he instructed one of his viceroys: 'The people do not exist for the ruler, the ruler exists for the people. He must work for the people committed to his charge, take care for their tranquillity and peace, arrange their lives with order and justice. This is his first and highest duty, for which he will one day have to render an account.' Philip's thoughts were obsessed night and day by the account he would have to give both at the Last Judgment and to his father, whom he felt as a living presence. One of Charles v's bequests to him was a gigantic load of debt. '*Si no falta el dinero*' ('if there is enough money') became one of Philip's most characteristic utterances. This made it all the more imperative to subject everything to the king's painstaking and minute control. By the end of his reign the government of the Spanish world empire was organized through twelve great councils with the king at their head. Within the councils criticism was freely invited and was freely forthcoming. But all decisions rested with the king alone. Of particular importance was the Council of State (which dealt with foreign affairs and other large issues) and the Council of the Indies. Philip expected from his servants complete objectivity and impartiality, to the exclusion of all personal considerations. His agents were ordered to carry out his instructions to the letter and he preferred them not to know of each other's activities.

'I am resolved to sacrifice my own flesh and blood to God, since I place service to Him and to the general good above all human considerations.' This was the light in which Philip saw the sacrifice of his son, Don Carlos, whom he regarded as a danger to the state and to all his subjects. Philip was prepared to play Abraham to his son's Isaac.[1]

Philip felt personally responsible for all his subjects, past, present and future, indeed for all Europeans, the Bohemians not excepted. All had to be saved from the final condemnation of the Last Judgment. Despite his precarious health and chronic shortage of money, Philip bestirred himself to buy up as many relics of German saints as he could, to keep them out of the hands of reformers to whom they were nothing but bones. Seven thousand such relics, conveyed in carefully sealed chests,

---

[1] Kierkegaard, who was dominated by his father, admired this Abraham who was prepared to sacrifice his son to God. Unamuno admired Kierkegaard, learned Danish for his sake and as a Spanish devotee of Kierkegaard introduced 'existentialism' into the vocabulary of modern European literature.

found their way to the Escorial. Philip liked to visit them, convincing himself that anyone who thus possessed Germany's past had a stake in the battle for Germany's future. The Catholic territories of Germany would be won back by Spanish soldiers. Did not the Spanish poet Ramón de Basterras boast that 'the world was a forest of Spanish lances'? A barrage of Spanish prayer should be sent up to save a world in peril of annihilation, a peril incurred by the innovators' physical attacks on churches. 'I can never express to you,' Philip writes to Cardinal Granvelle, 'how wounded I feel by the sacking and destruction of the churches in Flanders; no personal loss could ever be so great a sorrow as the least insult or disrespect offered to Our Lord and His likenesses, whose honour and service I rank above everything in this life.'

King Philip sent his half-brother, Don John of Austria, the victor in the sea battle against the Turks at Lepanto in 1572, to suppress the rebellious Netherlands. Don John had at his disposal six thousand Spaniards, four thousand Frenchmen (supplied by the Guise), two thousand Walloons and two thousand Lorrainers. At Gembloux in 1578 his troops went into battle led by the cross and under standards bearing the device, '*In hoc signo vici turcos, in hoc vincam haereticos*' ('Under this sign I defeated the Turks, under this sign I will defeat the heretics'). Don John was no ideologist, nor was he a politician. 'I have no wish to be a politician, I am a captain in search of a war.' This campaign in fact cost him his life, not on the battlefield but from an illness he caught while visiting sick troops. His body had to be smuggled back to Spain carved up into four pieces and was given burial by Philip in the Escorial.

Work started on the monastery-palace of the Escorial [plate 114] just at the time the Council of Trent was ending (1563). Philip intended the Escorial as the visible and potent centre of Spanish might and Spanish dedication to duty. It was to receive the bones of his father, transferred by Philip from San Yuste, and the coffins of his Spanish ancestors [plate 113]. These assembled relics of his holy forebears, the saints of Europe, should radiate from the Escorial a purifying influence to the benefit of rebellious and heresy-stricken Europe (and not least of Spain itself). Immured with his monks inside the Escorial, companioned by his books, his art treasures and his gardens, Philip watched and waited for the coming Catholic rebirth of Europe. The Escorial was the first true centre of the Counter Reformation. If Rome was the second, it owed the fact to the work of another Spaniard, Ignatius of Loyola. Once the Viennese Habsburgs had succeeded in restoring peace in their Catholic provinces they built their own Escorial outside the gates of Vienna at Klosterneuburg, once the property of the Babenbergs.

In 1576 Francisco de Sande, the Spanish governor of the Philippines, proposed to the king that he should undertake the conquest of China. The royal council were of the opinion that the vast size of China made crusading notions of this kind mere fantasy and in his answer to the great soldier Philip temporized. 'It appears to me that at the present time we can do no more than to seek to establish friendly relations with China.' He wrote in the same sense to the Ming Emperor Shen-Tsung, signing the letter with his full titles right down to Archduke of Austria, Count of Habsburg,

Flanders and Tyrol (1580). In 1583 a governor of Manila again proposed the conquest of China, asserting that this was a better prospect than the Flemish war.

Spain had before her a choice between carrying on the war in Europe and building up a world empire which reached out beyond the Philippines to China and Japan. Philip showed much interest, particularly after the union of Spain with Portugal (which, as Ludwig Pfandl remarks, made the whole of Spain a 'second Escorial'), in plans for a world-wide trading and customs union. Trade and traffic on the high seas would be safeguarded and regulated by the Spanish and Portuguese navies, working from Spanish and Portuguese ports. German 'capitalists' would play a leading role. (It was Philip who gave the Fuggers and the Welsers their monopoly in the Caribbean spice trade.) The year 1584 saw the arrival of Japanese ambassadors at Madrid. In 1585, in the interests of peace-keeping, Philip prohibited all un-authorized missionary expeditions to China. We know only too well what lasting harm was done in China, after the liquidation of the heroic early Jesuit mission, by totally misconceived missionary activity which appeared to be the lackey of powerful political and economic interests. Philip prohibited the use of the word 'conquista' in Spanish America. America was to be won not through crusades or by conquest but by missions and good positive government, through Spanish colleges and universities.

Despite the enormous possibilities which seemed to be opening up in other con-tinents[1] Spain preferred to concentrate all her might on Europe. One factor which determined the decision to stay in Europe was Philip's long and fruitless rivalry with the England of Elizabeth I. The seas were already swarming with English ships, the property of noblemen and great London merchants, which made 'piratical' attacks on Spanish ships wherever they found them, whether in American waters, off the coast of Flanders or in the Channel. Philip stood out for the freedom of the seas, asserting in 1564 through Guzmán de Silva, the Spanish ambassador in London, that this was 'the main issue as regards maintaining peace and friendship with England'. The increasing successes of the English freebooters led in the end to Philip's plan for a Spanish invasion of England and the debacle of the Armada.

Spain saw herself, however, primarily as a continental power. Step by step, Europe was to be reconquered for the church. Philip II looked towards Prague, where the new emperor, Rudolf II (1576–1612), who was the son of his sister Mary, had taken up his residence [plate 120]. For years letters passed to and fro between Madrid and Prague as with tireless patience Philip courted Rudolf on behalf of his daughter Isabella. At length, only a year before Philip's death, a marriage was arranged between Isabella and Rudolf's brother Albert; as part of the bargain the Netherlands were declared 'independent', with Albert as Regent. Rudolf himself remained a life-long bachelor, like many of his artist friends. As his long reign wore on, he became increasingly incompetent as a ruler. He was wasting away and seemed prepared to

---

[1] To give only one example from the period about 1580, Spanish horses were being exported both to Kyushu in Japan and to Lipizza in Austria. Both strains are still flourishing.

let the wickedness of the world take its wicked course, as though there were malign stars whose decree man could not alter. The prestige of the emperor and of the house of Habsburg fell sharply. Rudolf had neither the will nor the authority to carry out the tasks confronting him. He did nothing to keep the Estates, above all the higher nobility, within bounds; he was not of the calibre to fight the Turks or to take action against either Protestants or Catholics; he was too weak to stand up against his brothers and close relatives, who wanted to depose him. When Rudolf II died in 1612 Europe was already preparing for the great conflict which would break out a bare seven years later and become the Thirty Years' War.

The powerlessness of Emperor Rudolf II has many facets. The times were out of joint. It had only now become evident what lay behind Luther's revolution, the Peasant Wars and the rise of the Estates, namely that men were searching for new forms and new paths, and this because they could no longer find their way in the old household of God or among the old orders of God-King, emperors and kings. Art, and the arts in general, quickly got wind of this terrifying fact and started to make it known. There is a 'puzzle picture' which at first sight appears composed of random lines and strokes but which when tilted and held at eye level reveals hidden among the splodges and swirls a 'portrait' of Charles V, Ferdinand I, Pope Paul III and Francis I. The author of this 'liquidation' of the highest powers in Christendom was Erhard Schön. His picture was painted about 1535; round about 1630 another artist, Desiderio Monsù, who was born about 1593 in the old imperial city of Metz, painted an 'Exploding Church'. For many Europeans of the period, not least those who lived on imperial territory, all churches were exploding, or indeed had already long since burst asunder: such was the conviction, for example, of men like Sebastian Franck and Paracelsus.

G. R. Hocke remarks that 'the artists living between 1520 and 1650, like those who were born between 1880 and 1890, were haunted by visions of the end of all things.' He further reminds us that Leonardo was already painting apocalyptical pictures of diluvian catastrophes and other cataclysms which describe the end of the world with horrifying precision. Then there is Dürer's disturbingly modern 'Dream vision', which resembles the mushroom cloud of an atomic explosion. Raphael's decidedly mannerist, almost abstract, *Great Flood*, which is among the frescoes to the galleries in the Vatican, was painted before 1520. 'One has the impression', says Hocke, 'that men were not only tormented by anxiety, but were also in a state of complete bewilderment'. These qualities of fear and incomprehension 'are most strikingly expressed in the portrayal of the damned in Michaelangelo's *Last Judgment*.'

Looking back on the catastrophes and self-inflicted wounds of the Thirty Years' War the great German baroque poet Andreas Gryphius wrote:

> Die Herrlichkeit der Erden
> Muss Rauch and Asche werden
> Was wir für ewig schätzen
> Wird als ein leichter Traum vergehen.

(The splendours of our earthly home
Dust and ashes must become
What we take for lasting treasure
Passes like a dream of pleasure.)

Emperor Rudolf II dealt with the external world – the rebellions, the petitions and demands which came pressing in on him from all sides – by shutting himself up in his castle at Prague and refusing to hear them mentioned. He was a man of sensibility, deeply interested in art and learning. The process of decomposition had gone so far and so deep in Europe that it very likely occurred to him that all this frenzied activity within the labyrinth in whose exitless mazes God and man seemed to have shut one another up for good was merely childish. His passivity did not shield the emperor from unpleasantness. The first problem was the imposition of the Counter-Reformation on Lower Austria, a land unsettled by peasant revolts and the Turkish menace. When the governor of Lower Austria died, Archduke Matthias, the emperor's brother, tried to unite the Austrian Habsburgs in action against the inactive emperor in Prague. A thirteen years' war with the Turks was concluded in 1606 by a peace which left the emperor's followers with the two Hungarian counties of Waitzen and Nograd and the Turks with Erlau and Kanitza, together with a war indemnity. But this peace had its positive side, since it meant that the Empire and the Habsburgs were able to face the terrible years which now followed without having their hands perpetually tied in the east by the Turks.

The open feud between the emperor and his brother – the *Bruderzwist in Habsburg* – was exploited for their own purposes by the Estates of Hungary, Austria and Bohemia [plate 118]; they emerged as the victors, in the first place over the emperor, and as things turned out over Matthias as well. In 1608 the Hungarian Estates elected Matthias as their king and Rudolf ceded Moravia to him in the same year. In 1609 the emperor was forced to issue the Letter of Majesty which made such far-reaching concessions to the Bohemian Estates (riddled with Protestantism) that they set up what was in practice their own regime. In 1611, one year before his death, the emperor had to accept the coronation of his brother as king of Bohemia. Some of his supporters expected from Matthias a great burst of activity, but he remained in effect the captive of the Estates. In the seven years of his reign as emperor (20 January 1612 – 20 March 1619), Matthias never became the effective ruler even of his own territories. In the Empire he was opposed both by the union of Protestant princes and by the Catholic League headed by Vienna's great rival, the Duke of Bavaria. Ferdinand of Inner Austria was crowned king of Bohemia and recognized by the Hungarian Diet as king of Hungary in Matthias' own lifetime. This Ferdinand II, who was emperor during the Thirty Years' War, amongst his many other pressing problems in the Empire and his own hereditary possessions had to pay for Philip III's recognition of himself as king of Bohemia by surrendering to the Spanish Habsburgs the reversionary right over the family's possessions on the left bank of the Rhine.

It was Spaniards who pushed the enfeebled Habsburgs of Prague and Vienna into the Thirty Years' War. The Prague of this period is inconceivable without its Spanish party and its hispanized Czechs. Juan Borja [plate 122], who was appointed Spanish ambassador to Rudolf in 1578, had a Czech daughter-in-law; his interest in eastern Europe was such that he commissioned Froben of Basel to print a small Latin-Spanish-Czech dictionary for the use of the Spanish colony at Prague. He was also a keen observer of the emperor, reporting to Madrid on his want of decision, his fits of melancholy and the night terrors which made him repeatedly call out for his valets. Among the first generation of hispanized Czechs was Vratislav Pernštyn, whose death near Linz in 1592 was mourned in Spain like the death of a Spanish grandee. His beautiful daughter Polyxena married Vilem Rožmberk (Rosenberg), head of one of the richest houses in Europe, who was the agent of the Habsburgs in Poland and himself aspired to the Polish crown. As her second husband Polyxena married in 1603 Zdeněk Vojtěch Lobkovic (Lobkowitz), who since 1599 had been chancellor of the Crown of Bohemia. Lobkovic was a frequent visitor to Italy and Spain and on several occasions acted as the emperor's special envoy to Madrid. His marriage marked him out as the leader of the Spanish group in Bohemia and his castle at Raudnitz became a centre of Spanish cultural, religious and political influence; his Spanish library can still be seen there today.

As the new century dawned even the most basic foundations of the European order seemed to be crumbling while Emperor Rudolf wasted away in the castle at Prague. Spanish thoughts turned once again to active resumption of leadership in the house of Habsburg and there was some idea that Philip III, Philip II's feeble successor, might become king of Bohemia. By the time of Pope Clement VIII (1592–1605) there were even people in Rome willing to contemplate a Spaniard as candidate for the imperial crown. Three outstanding ambassadors to Prague, S. Clemente, Zuñiga and Oñate, were responsible for bringing the struggle over the Empire into the mainstream of seventeenth-century history. Guillén de S. Clemente, whose presence was welcomed by the hispanized Czechs, became the centre of the Spanish party in Prague. When news came that he was dying, Madrid at once dispatched Zuñiga to replace him. Baltasar Zuñiga was an experienced diplomat who took an interest in the affairs of the Empire as a whole. His circle included Lobkovic and his wife Polyxena and others of the Czech nobility, notably Karel Liechtenstein, a former Bohemian Brother who had been converted to Catholicism.

In his determination to salvage Bohemia at any price for the Spanish, Zuñiga sided with Matthias against Rudolf (who was fanatically anti-Spanish). Ambrosio Spinola, a wealthy Milanese who was a volunteer commander with the Spanish army in the Netherlands, even suggested that Philip III should declare himself Rudolf's successor in Bohemia. Zuñiga built up the Catholic League within the Empire (in his reports to Madrid he differentiates sharply between the lands of the Austrian Habsburgs – Austria, Bohemia, Hungary – and the parts of the Empire in which the emperor's authority was only nominal). After eight years in his post at Prague Zuñiga returned to Madrid. As a member of the Council of State he was soon a significant figure in the direction of Spanish foreign policy. One aim of this policy was to fashion the League of Catholic Princes into an instrument for furthering Spanish designs over the Empire. Zuñiga's successor at Prague was Oñate, who was obsessed by the idea of enlarging and consolidating Spanish power, though for him Spanish power wore a different face than it had for Charles V or even Philip II. It was Oñate who engineered the dispute over Bohemia which was the immediate cause of the Thirty Years' War.

Rudolf II must have regarded the superior strength of the Spanish and their allies as a formidable threat to 'his' Bohemia. These power politicians and their associates, the leaders of a militaristic religious-political party all too conscious of its goals, filled him with the worst forebodings. His reaction to the threatened outbreak of a great war, the first European war (as the Thirty Years' War has with justice been called), was to follow the example of the ancient Roman emperor Hadrian by attempting to build up round himself a world which was a harmony of opposites, *discordia concors*. As O. Schürer remarks, Rudolf aimed at 'the intellectual-political conciliation of the "disparates" in his threatened Empire'. Rudolf knew he inhabited a pluralistic Europe (pluralistic in nationality, religion, religious denomination, race and so on), but hoped it might still find an overriding unity in the intellectual reconciliation of all its opposites.

Rudolf's Prague was in many ways the counterpart of Elizabeth's England and Medici Paris, as Schürer has pointed out. But Prague was under the greatest pressure, for on Prague were gathering all the forces of 'revolution' and 'counter-revolution' – from Rome, Madrid, Wittenberg, Geneva (Calvin's city), Munich and Vienna – as they prepared for the great battle. Rudolf was twenty-four when he came to Prague and found in it the landscape of his soul. A dreamer by nature, he created there for himself an art world full of mysteries as an antidote to humdrum reality. In his early years at Prague he still took pleasure in the glittering festivities of the court. He had Italians and Germans as well as famous Netherlanders in his *hofkapelle*. Sweet music soothed and relaxed the emperor, who scented the murder that lay in the air. Art too was a consolation: hence his collections of Dürer and Brueghel [plate 117] and his appointment of the scurrilous painter Guiseppe Arcimboldi as a Count of the Empire. Rudolf brought to Prague artists from all over Europe, though none from hated Spain. He also assembled many famous craftsmen, medal-makers, collectors and portrait painters and laid the foundations of some vast collections. He had, too, a penchant for 'marvels', sending his court painter Savery to the Tyrol to sketch the grotesque shapes of mountains. Rudolf wanted all the wonders of the world to be assembled at Prague, to keep terror, death and annihilation at bay.

Where other powers sent out agents to glean political and military intelligence, Rudolf was concerned only with tracking down great works of art. Conscious of the mounting iconoclastic storm which since its first onslaught in 1525 had destroyed so much that was priceless, he was bent on salvaging what he could for his own treasure houses. Acquiring works of art seemed in fact the greatest stimulus to his flagging energies and he could conduct lengthy negotiations with Nuremberg over the purchase of Dürer's *Adoration of the Trinity*. In 1601 strong men actually carried

Durer's *Feast of the Rose Garlands* [plate 88] slung from poles all the way from Venice over the Alps to Prague, to avoid damaging the picture. The circle of artists Rudolf gathered round him became his confidants. A privilege issued for the painters' gild at Prague on 27 April 1595 ordains that in future their work is to be qualified not as 'craftwork' but as 'painter's art' (*malkunst*). The emperor himself enjoyed working with his hands, for example as a stone-cutter. Exact and artistically demanding manual work was a means of keeping his pulverizing thoughts at bay. He looked to the works of art and nature to provide the meaning he could no longer find in churches or in the world of power. His strong interest in the natural sciences links him with men of other periods in which scientific knowledge has been similarly invoked to fill the terrible vacuum left by the death of earlier belief.

In his flight from death and madness (though madness claimed him in the end), Rudolf immersed himself in the natural sciences, in particular the study of the stars. He brought Tycho Brahe to Prague [plate 121] and on his recommendation appointed Johannes Kepler court astronomer; Kepler's *Tabulae Rudolphinae*, compiled at Prague, are dedicated to the emperor. Kepler, whose mother was persecuted as a witch, in 1608 drew the horoscope of Albrecht von Waldstein, otherwise known as Wallenstein: a reminder that the line between astrology and astronomy was still no clearer than that between chemistry and alchemy. In his role as the new 'Hermes trismegistos' the emperor formed what was virtually an alchemists' academy. Macabre figures such as the Polish Sendivoy and the English Doctor Dee became his familiars. In Catholic and hispanized Czech circles this company was viewed with the deepest distrust.

We should not overlook the pathological traits of this imperial Vertumnus. (Arcimboldi painted Rudolf as Vertumnus, the god of autumn and of change.) He was very sensitive to what was in the air, the smell of burning, the whiff of corpses, his beautiful Prague plundered and reduced to ashes, the world of old Europe, rich in images, done to death. The manner in which such of Rudolf's treasures as survived the Swedes and other plunderers were finally destroyed in the late eighteenth century is symbolic of the ending of the old Empire which Rudolf had already foreseen. On the orders of Emperor Joseph II the castle of Prague was converted in 1781 into an artillery barracks. The cellars, hollowed out of rock, were needed for bomb-proof powder magazines. Artillery officers searching the vaults with commendable zeal and conscientiousness discovered there pile upon pile of Rudolf's treasures, many of them damaged, which had been stowed away in haste when the thunder of the Prussian cannon aroused fears that the city would be sacked. On 13 and 14 May 1782 this 'junk', which included busts, vases, statues, 'heathen images', wood and ivory carvings, sculptures, old musical instruments and armour, was put up to public auction.

The gems, crammed together in little boxes, were listed merely according to their colour, for example the lapis lazuli as blue, the chrysoprase as green, the topaz as yellow, all under the simple designation 'stones'. The gold and silver bulls and wax seals were torn from the diplomas and entered separately in the ledger, while the charters and privileges were put into the sale simply as so much parchment and old paper . . .

The Ilioneus statue, which had lost its head and arms in the cellar and had become an unrecognizable and crumbling torso, figured in the catalogue as 'kneeling male figure in white marble, head broken-off' and in another description bluntly as a 'corner-stone in marble', while Heintzen's copy of Corregio's *Leda* is described as 'naked female figure being bitten by a vicious goose'!

The Ilioneus statue was purchased for 51 kreuzers by an antique dealer named Helfer, a baptized Jew who was known by the nickname 'Laudon' (his favourite expression: it was the name of a famous general who commanded the armies of Maria Theresa). The reserve price was 50 kreuzers; when Hans von Aachen bought it for Rudolf II in Rome he had paid 34,000 ducats. Helfer sold it for four guldens to a stone-mason called Malnisky, whose widow sold it for six '*siebzehner*' to a Viennese collector of antiquities named Barth; with the head of the statue, which had been sent on by the auctioneers much later, the widow Malnisky started up a head factory. In 1815 the future Ludwig I of Bavaria saw the statue when he was in Vienna for the Congress and purchased it for 6,000 ducats, which is how the statue comes to be in the Glyptothek at Munich.

The ultimate fate of Rudolf II's treasure house (a few pieces found purchasers in Saxony, St Petersburg and Vienna) in a prosaic, puritanically bureaucratic age, deficient in images and colour, stands out as symbolic of all the iconoclastic revolts against the worlds of images, colours and forms which made up the old Europe. This devastation of men's inner landscape, which is also the landscape of the soul, began in the age of the Reformation; the wave of destruction was borne along by the iconoclastic frenzy of radical Baptists and Enthusiasts in the Netherlands and in Lutheran and Calvinist states – whose soldiers carried it into other countries – and by the time of Rudolf II was already at its first peak. Then came the Thirty Years' War, which over wide areas of the Empire destroyed much that in France vanished only with the Revolution and in Russia only under the iconoclasm of the early days of Bolshevism. Baroque, the last and most continuous formal expression of the culture of the Holy Roman Empire – in a sense the only one it ever had – represents a strenuous endeavour, crowned by some great achievements, at undoing the ruin which had overtaken the old world of forms, at positively displacing it. The beginnings of this attempt can be found even in the midst of the Thirty Years' War.

IO

FROM THE GREAT WAR TO THE GREAT PEACE

IN 1619 the 'Winter King', Frederick the Elector Palatine, whom the Bohemian Estates had elected in defiance of the house of Habsburg, purged Prague cathedral of its art treasures to make it fit for the conduct of a 'purified' divine service following the German-Calvinist rite. His reign ended the following year, with the defeat at the White Mountain on 8 November 1620 [plate 125]. Next day the imperial forces were already in the city. In solemn procession, Domenico Ruzzola conducted into the cathedral a portrait of the Virgin he had found in a church sacked by the Protestants at Strakonice in southern Bohemia. The scene was made the subject of a fresco in the Carmelite Church of Santa Maria della Vittoria in Rome, a church built in honour of the victory at the White Mountain and dedicated to Our Lady of Victories, patroness of the victorious armies of Counter-Reformation Europe.

On the evening of 20 June 1621 Prague witnessed a religious-political ceremony which before long figured on flysheets distributed throughout Europe by Protestants and Catholics in an effort to fix the great spectacle on men's minds [plate 126]. The scene as great companies of monks, priests and soldiers filed into the square outside the city hall resembled a Corpus Christi procession (introduced by the victorious Counter-Reformation into the lands it reconquered). The square was dominated by a scaffold three feet high, ready for death to take the stage.[1]

Catholic and Protestant clergy stayed with the prisoners until the last moment, preparing them for death. Colonel Wallenstein's soldiers kept the city quiet. The first to mount the scaffold was a German, Count Schlick, who did so 'with a cheerful countenance', clad in black velvet, a book in his hand. He was followed in turn by the sexagenarian Wenzel Budowetz, Freiherr von Budow, who was a devout member of the Bohemian Brethren, Christoph Harant, Freiherr von Polžic and a connoisseur of art, and the octogenarian Kaspar Kaplíř, Ritter von Sulewitz, who disdained to plead for the mercy he had been promised. After him came Dionys von Czernin (a Czernin would be the last Foreign Minister to serve the Danube monarchy) whose brother Hermann from his high seat on the balcony could observe how well and with

---

[1] Baroque combines the art of dying, *ars moriendi,* the art of living, *ars vivendi,* and the art of loving, ***ars amandi.***

what dignity he met his death. Then Dr Jessenius, anatomist, physician and philosopher, mounted the steps leading to the scaffold, accompanied by all four German preachers. Prior to execution, he had his tongue cut out, because he had 'sinned' with it through acting as the spokesman for the Estates. While the executions were taking place the Emperor Ferdinand II was at Mariazell, on his knees before the altar of the Virgin, praying for the souls of the executed with whom he felt himself bound in the *communio sanctorum*.

In 1936 the young and puritanical Albert Camus was on his way home to France from Prague by way of Vienna. The baroque of Prague had affected him deeply and unpleasantly. Probably what hurt him even more than all the pomp was the whiff of death, always inseparable from high baroque. In the address he gave on accepting his Nobel Prize in 1957, two years before his own death, he called for the total abolition of capital punishment: in the battle against death men should stand shoulder to shoulder. In baroque, however, this solidarity lies in the bestowal and acceptance of death as the common lot of all mankind.

The scaffold erected in Prague in 1621 was the beacon heralding the Thirty Years' War. Twenty-seven eminent men met their deaths on it. Many confiscations of land followed, and much of this property went to Liechtenstein and Wallenstein. Soon Wallenstein had built himself a new palace, to which the nobility of Europe flocked in droves to share in its bizarre festivities. The magnificent bronzes which stood in the garden were later looted by the Swedes and are today in the grounds of the Baroque Theatre Museum at Drottningholm. It was at this time, too, that a great spate of emigrants left Bohemia. The Bohemians of this migration found their way to France (where their name later became attached to the easy-going artist population of nineteenth-century Paris immortalized in Puccini's opera), to Holland, Brandenburg, Poland, Scandinavia, Siebenbürgen and Turkey.[1] Among their number was Amos Comenius (Komensky), the great thinker and perhaps the greatest educationist Europe has so far produced.

The Church of the Holy Trinity in Prague's *mala strana*, which had been in the hands of the German Lutherans, was handed over in 1624 to the Discalced Carmelites and its dedication changed to Maria Victoria. Following this example churches dedicated to the victoress of the White Mountain sprouted all over Catholic Europe. From Italy, Spain and the Netherlands, religious orders new and old trooped into conquered Prague, Scottish Franciscans (known as Irish), Carmelites, Servites, Capuchins, Cyriacs and Theatines. A new Prague grew up, at once old and new, Romanized-Bohemian.

Ferdinand's ill-fated Edict of Restitution of 6 March 1629 has to be seen against the background of the great victory of the imperial forces at the White Mountain, the

---

[1] They were allowed to sell their goods and chattels but had to purchase their pardons and hand over a certain percentage of the proceeds to settle their account with the state. The sufferings of the Bohemian exiles and their wide dispersal contributed in the nineteenth and early twentieth century to the growth of anti-Habsburg feeling in Paris, St Petersburg, London and America.

Prague executions, the triumph of the Catholic League and Ferdinand's own Spanish cast of conscience, which required him to 'reinstate' Catholicism in his territories and in the Empire. This attempt at reverting to the territorial religious boundaries as drawn in 1552 and 1555 (when Calvinism had been excluded) threw the Protestant Estates of the Empire into a panic. Did the emperor then intend to set up the dreaded 'universal monarchy'? Against this danger the Protestants allied themselves with the Swedes, the Danes and the French, all the emperor's enemies in Christendom, and even with the Turks. The Thirty Years' War broke out with the full force of a conflagration and brought the Empire to the edge of the abyss.

Despite this catastrophic development, which in the minds of many induced, if it did not indeed create, a profound alienation from the Empire, it should not be forgotten that on the eve of the great war there were also 'interests' alert to preserve the Empire.

The election and coronation of Emperor Matthias at Frankfurt in 1612 is depicted for us in a sequence of fourteen episodes by Johann Theodor de Bry [plate 124].

In 1366 Charles iv had granted the request of the city of Frankfurt for a copy of the Golden Bull sealed with the same seal as the copies prepared for the electors. Amongst its other provisions, the Bull laid down that on the death of an emperor the archbishop of Mainz was to invite the other electors to appear at Frankfurt within three months, either in person or through a plenipotentiary. The electors or their proxies were restricted to a mounted escort of two hundred (only fifty of whom were to be armed), the burghers of Frankfurt undertaking full responsibility for their security. Maximilian ii had been both elected and crowned at Frankfurt, because of the sudden death of the archbishop of Cologne who by rights should have presided over his coronation at Aachen; this set a precedent, and thereafter both ceremonies took place at Frankfurt. The election ceremony took place in the Church of St Bartholomew, where the electors first attended a mass of the Holy Spirit, during which they prayed for illumination. The new King of the Romans, kneeling in readiness at the altar, was hoisted onto it by the electors and from this same electoral chapel proclaimed as emperor.

There followed the ceremonies of the coronation day. Early in the morning the envoys from Nuremberg and Aachen met the electors in the cathedral and handed over the imperial insignia, which were then placed on the nave altar. The lay electors went to fetch the king and conduct him to the church, where he was met at the door by the spiritual electors. In the course of the mass (just before the Gospel) the King of the Romans took the coronation oath, swearing to protect the Church, to ensure justice and to be what the words of his title proclaimed him, a 'perpetual augmenter of the Empire', *auctor imperii*, '*allzeit Mehrer des Reichs*'. He also swore to protect widows and orphans and to honour the pope. Next came the anointing, on head, neck, breast, right arm and hands. The anointing made him emperor, turned him into an ecclesiastic (precisely in what sense, however, had been a matter of controversy ever since the eleventh century). Having moved into the chancel, the emperor was invested with the imperial robes and received the sword of Charles the Great, the ring, the sceptre and the orb. The three archbishops, Mainz, Trier and Cologne, then placed on his head the imperial crown. After a second oath, reaffirming the emperor's obligations to Church and Empire, the mass was concluded. One further ceremony remained, the enthronement on the chair of Charles the Great, which was placed on an elevated rostrum in the south transept. The proceedings ended with a *Te Deum*. The emperor next received congratulatory good wishes, dubbed a batch of new knights, and was enrolled by two emissaries from the chapter of Aachen as a canon of their cathedral.

After the ceremonies in the cathedral the procession set off for the city hall, the Römer, the King of the Romans walking beneath the 'sky-canopy', which was borne aloft by the city councillors. The great officers of state discharged their duties, the elector of Saxony as chief marshal by riding to a heap of oats and taking a silver measureful for the emperor's horses, the elector of Brandenburg as great chamberlain by holding a filled silver ewer and basin and a towel in readiness for the emperor. This theatrical display of the Empire and its majesty was also a festival for the people. Coronation day was a time for popular carnivals in the old market-place and on the Römerberg. As Lord High Steward of the Empire, the Elector Palatine betook himself to a makeshift kitchen hard by St Nicholas' church; here a slice from the gigantic ox roasting on the spit was conveyed on a silver platter to the emperor. The elector of Bohemia, in his capacity as chief butler, offered the emperor wine and water in silver vessels. The people got their share of the coronation oats and meat, red and white wine flowed from the fountain on the Römerberg.

At the coronation banquet in the Römer's *Kaisersaal* each of the great lords had a table to himself, and if one of the electors was absent his table was left empty. All the lesser lords, together with representatives from the cities of Aachen, Frankfurt, Cologne and Nuremberg, dined in the next room. The emperor sat completely alone. In the evening there was a great firework display, during which an artificial castle on the Main was set ablaze and rockets lit up the night sky.

The coronation of the Emperor Matthias, recorded for us in pictures by Johann Theodor de Bry and in writing by the emperor himself, in his carefully kept diary, was followed not long after by fireworks which sent the whole Empire up in flames.

The formality and ritual observed in the election and coronation suggested that nothing was changed, that Emperor and Church, Roman Empire and Roman Catholic Church, were still inseparably linked. Without this particular church, without the Pope, had the Roman Empire any meaning? Could the Holy Roman Empire declare itself 'protestant'? Evidence on this burning topic is to be found in the monumental *Monarchia S. Romani Imperii*, a treatise written by Melchior Goldast which appeared in three volumes between 1611 and 1614.[1] In the first volume, dedicated to Johann Sigismund, Margrave of Brandenburg, Electoral Prince and Great Chamberlain of the Holy Roman Empire, Duke of Prussia, etc., Burgrave of

[1] Re-issued at Prague in facsimile in 1960.

Nuremberg, etc., Goldast asserts that the present contest over the majesty of the Empire is a re-enactment of the great conflicts of the past. On the one hand he sees the emperor, the kings, the electors, the princes, on the other the pope, with his cardinals and bishops. 'But', he protests, 'the Emperor is the supreme bishop' (*imperator est pontifex maximus* – like Constantine the Great), the Emperor is 'bishop and overseer of the church in its outward aspect' and as such has a duty to defend and regulate the church. It falls on the Emperor to call councils and synods, to confirm ecclesiastical laws and ordinances and to amend religious observances. It is the Emperor's duty to suppress superstitious and idolatrous (mis)uses, to oversee the moral conduct of the clergy, to punish clerics who fall short, to appoint and remove the church's servants. The Pope is bishop as regards the internal affairs of the church, and in these matters the Emperor is subject to the Pope; but in the external affairs of the church the Pope ought to be subject to the Emperor. Former popes, he says, are witness to the truth of his sayings, but now – *o tempora o mores!* – the mother (church) has strangled and devoured her first-born son the emperor (we are reminded of Goya's painting of the evil arch-patriarch, strangling his sons on the ramparts of reaction). The popes and other spiritual servants of the church are no longer subject to the Emperor, as in the days of Gelasius and Leo IV. The bishops have ceased to obey the Emperor: witness the complaints of Frederick III and Maximilian I. The curia shamelessly asserts that the Pope is absolute monarch on earth, *vicedeus*, a Deputy-God. This is what Bellarmine and many other canonists teach, 'a brood come straight from Hell to swarm over Europe'.

To defend the Holy Roman Empire and the dignity and majesty of the emperor in Christendom and the church Goldast summons up witnesses from all periods of christian history. They range from Agobard of Lyons and Hincmar of Rheims to Innocent III, from Michael of Cesena to Aeneas Silvius Piccolomini; they include conciliar decrees from Constance, Basel and Pisa, Pico della Mirandola's defence of Savanarola and many Italian and French authors who had rejected the immoderacy of papal claims. Writing on the eve of the great war, Goldast has assembled this powerful array to prove to the world that the monstrous arrogance of the pope was a threat not only to the emperor but to all rulers, secular and spiritual, and to all men, laity and clergy alike. The Roman pontiff was no longer a good shepherd but a ravening wolf. Had there been no Roman emperor, there would have been no pope. Had there been no pope, the Roman Empire would still be flourishing. Goldast hoped through this great mass of documentation, which was published under imperial licence, to rally the Catholic and other Estates, the princes, scholars, clergy and laity of the Holy Roman Empire, to its defence. *Tua res agitor, paries cum proximus ardet.* All are threatened when a neighbour's house is on fire. A vignette on the title-page to the first volume depicts the double-eagle surmounted by the imperial crown with above it the motto *Renovabitur*: the empire will be renewed [plate 123]. The imperial eagle is perching on a new branch which has grown from the stump of the tree. We shall do well to interpret this picture, as indeed the great work itself, as a manifestation of that unique patriotism which although invisible, and often overlooked, ensured the continuity of the Empire in both Catholic and Protestant territories and 'carried' it through all the crises and catastrophes of the seventeenth and eighteenth centuries: the object of this patriotism was not a state, had no army of its own, levied no general taxes; it was a league of states which sided now with and now against the emperor – at its best moments it was 'Emperor and Empire' – and it was now threatened with a lapse into a permanent state of war, which at one time or another seemed to bring every Estate in conflict with the rest.

Two events were of such exceptional moment in together determining the destinies of the Empire down to the Peace of Westphalia that they deserve particular attention: the battle at the White Mountain and its preliminaries, and the Edict of Restitution.

The first link in the chain was the Defenestration of Prague; on 23 May 1618 representatives of the Bohemian Estates forced their way into the castle at Prague and threw Ferdinand's Catholic councillors out of the window. They fell more than fifty feet into the castle ditch; none was killed, although one was seriously injured. The sensational news of the 'collapse' of Ferdinand's 'government' as it spread about Europe on flysheets shocked enemies and went to the heads of friends, as with the storming of the Bastille which unleashed the French Revolution: it had all the quality of a symbolic event, and the 'insolence' of the insurgents in Prague and throughout Bohemia took fire from it. The Bohemian Estates elected as their king the Elector Frederick v, the Count Palatine, and crowned him in St Vitus' cathedral. This was followed by a 'cleansing' of the cathedral and the other churches of Prague at the hands of radical Calvinists who had come with Frederick to Prague. They threw out all the altars, pictures and statues, an act of image-breaking which horrified even the Lutherans. Frederick's queen, the proud Elizabeth Stuart, objected to the crucifix on the Charles' bridge as 'a naked bather', offensive to her eyes, and ordered its removal; it was thrown into the Vltava.

It was really the Spaniards who took charge over the struggle for Bohemia, Zuñiga and above all Oñate (who has been described as 'the architect of the Great War'). There was opposition to their energetic policy in certain circles in Madrid (men like the duke of Feria, the new governor of Milan, saw the plan to encircle and destroy the king of Bohemia as a threat to the peace of Europe), but this only spurred them on. Both sides were arming for the conflict. King Frederick hoped the English crown, the English Church (he was in touch with Archbishop Abbott of Canterbury) and wealthy English merchants and noblemen would provide him with money, troops and support. James I read with interest the partisan literature, which both sides distributed in London, but did little to help his son-in-law. He only bestirred himself when the Spanish threatened to invade the Palatinate, which James regarded as his daughter's personal property. Frederick's representative in London, Count Achaz Dohna, now found it easier to raise money; the seventeen thousand pounds he collected was used to fit out an expeditionary force which was sent to Rotterdam. King James, deeply committed to what today we would call the 'conservative' cause in

Europe, tried his hand as a mediator: through his agents, Francis Nethersole in the Netherlands and Henry Wolton in Vienna, he proposed that Frederick should retain the title of a king of Bohemia during his lifetime, that all the privileges of the nobility should be confirmed and the country recognized as an elective monarchy.

Oñate, however, was determined to push the emperor into war. We find Ferdinand telling the Spanish ambassador in London that Frederick 'is already beginning to feel the wrath of God'. The 'wrath' was principally that of Oñate. In the first half of 1620 the budget of the Spanish embassy to the imperial court rose to 555,000 guldens, nearly all of which was used for armaments. In England there were fears that the Spanish would capture Nuremberg, the main source of finance for the Bohemian rebels. The Bohemian nobility were well aware that Spain presented the greatest threat. One of their number, speaking at a banquet in honour of the Turkish envoy Mehmed Aga and of Bethlem of Transylvania (who had sent Frederick a detachment of eight thousand cavalry) roundly declared that the Habsburgs had sold the kingdom of Bohemia to Spain, transforming its freedom into slavery and its free citizens into slaves. The insurgents were adroit enough to spread their anti-Spanish propaganda throughout Europe, distributing woodcuts showing non-Spanish towns and regions dominated by Spanish fortresses.[1]

In Frederick's camp indiscipline, frivolity and cupidity prevailed, a state of affairs which so discouraged Jiři Nachod, who commanded the twelve thousand strong force of the Moravian nobility, that he left his troops in Western Moravia.

On the night of 7 to 8 November 1620 Frederick's army, part of which had come from Lower Austria,[2] arrived tired out at a plain within five miles of Prague which is known as the 'White Mountain', because it lies higher than the city itself. The supreme command was vested in Thurn, who had two other German immigrants as his deputies, Anhalt and Hohenlohe. German soldiers made up the bulk of the infantry, and the cavalry had a strong Hungarian contingent.

Ferdinand had only a few Germans and Czechs under his imperial banner; over three-quarters of his force was made up of Italians from Milan and Naples, 'Burgundian' Frenchmen from Lorraine and the Netherlands, and Netherlanders. His chaplain-in-chief was the Spanish Carmelite Domenico Ruzzola, most of whose preaching was done in French and Italian. Among those who heard him was a young officer with the imperial force, René Descartes, whose crucial vision came to him one night at Ulm. With his Cartesian order grounded in a French reason he would in due course attempt through lucidity and rationalism to surmount the chaos, doubts, and disorder of mankind. The troops of the German Catholic League who fought on the side of the emperor were commanded by Johann Tserclaes de Tilly, a Netherlander. The leader of the imperial force was Bucquoy, under whom Wallenstein served.

---

[1] Balanced by the maps distributed by Poles after World War Two showing the battlefields all over Europe which in modern times have claimed the lives of Polish soldiers fighting for other countries' freedom.

[2] A plan for a combined German and Bohemian force to march on Vienna having failed.

At the moment battle was engaged, Frederick was in Prague, entertaining the English envoys Conway and Weston at one of his banquets in which the drink flowed so freely. He made haste to the battlefield, only to flee overwhelmingly defeated. His first place of refuge was Silesia.

The battle at the White Mountain had serious consequences, whose after-effects are with us to this day. Emperor Ferdinand treated Bohemia as a rebel country which his forces had conquered. The Prague executions, the Catholicization of the country, and the confiscations of rebels' estates have already been touched on. The 'Revised Constitution' of 10 May 1627 converted Bohemia into a hereditary dominion of the Habsburgs, governed through the Bohemian chancery in Vienna. All the Habsburgs down to Joseph II had themselves crowned king of Bohemia at Prague. Resistance from the Austrian Estates and from Austrian Protestantism was also suppressed. Under a patent issued in 1627–8 the Protestant landed nobility were given the choice between turning Catholic and emigrating. Thus in the name of the Counter-Reformation the Emperor Ferdinand had combined the Habsburg lands into one huge and impressive power complex: the result was a Catholic, baroque and Habsburg Central Europe which stretched from Silesia to Habsburg Hungary and took in Bohemia, Moravia and the united provinces of Inner and Lower Austria. The specifically 'Austrian' sphere of influence which down to 1918 extended deep into Polish and White Russian territory, into Siebenbürgen and Rumania and into the Catholic parts of the Balkans, was created by the military forces of the emperor, the religious orders of the Counter-Reformation and the reconstituted universities[1] acting in concert with a new popular culture which was grounded in preaching, spectacle, music, liturgical observance and the feasts of the church.

In his own dominions Ferdinand exploited the victory at the White Mountain to the full. He planned to unite all the lands governed by his house into an indivisible and hereditary monarchy. In his absence government would be exercised by a centralized *Geheimratscollegium* to which both Bohemia and Hungary were also made subject. He divided the court chancery, making one chancery for the Empire and another for Austria. He intended all his own dominions to be under the control of a centralized bureaucracy, the only exceptions being the Tyrol and the old hereditary possessions in the Empire, which were given a separate governor in the person of Archduke Leopold, Ferdinand's youngest brother.

At the promptings perhaps of Lamornani, his Spanish confessor and adviser, and certainly of his own imperial conscience, Ferdinand now succumbed to the temptation of pressing on towards the re-catholicization of the Empire. On 6 March 1629 he published the fateful Edict of Restitution which decreed in effect that church lands appropriated by Protestant princes since the treaty of Passau (1552) were to be restored in accordance with the Ecclesiastical Reservation clause which was annexed

---

[1] In Prague the Utraquist Charles University was amalgamated with the Jesuit University to become the Carolina-Ferdinandea; in 1620 Archbishop Markus Sitticus of Hohenhems established a university at Salzburg, while Bishop Peter Páznány was similarly active in Hungary.

to the Religious Peace of Augsburg. Only those who acknowledged the Augsburg confession (and this meant the Lutherans) had the right to practise their religion freely; all other sects – including the Calvinists – were to be eliminated. Commissars were appointed by the emperor for the express purpose of implementing and enforcing the decree.

The political implications of the edict are usefully summarized by Repgen:

> If a stroke of the pen was to determine the confessional status and ownership of church property in two archbishoprics and in at least three, probably seven, and perhaps as many as thirteen bishoprics, the vital political interests of nearly all the great Protestant houses in the Empire were bound to be affected; and the reintroduction of enclaves of church property – over five hundred monastic and other foundations were involved – was in some regions a basic threat to the internal development of territorial sovereignty, . . . to say nothing of the ecclesiastical and religious aspects.

Those Protestant Estates which were still neutral or were allied to the emperor or the Catholic League were driven to unite in resistance. The Edict presented a direct threat to the archbishoprics of Bremen and Magdeburg and to the bishoprics of Halberstadt, Minden and Verden; indirectly threatened were Lübeck, Ratzeburg, Schwerin, Kammin. The North German Protestant princes under the lead of King Christian IV of Denmark[1] found it increasingly difficult to hold their own against Wallenstein as he set about imposing the imperial policy of restitution. It was in these circumstances that Gustavus Adolphus of Sweden offered himself as the saviour of the Empire, with the thought that eventually he might become emperor.

Albrecht von Waldestein – Wallenstein – (born 1583) belonged to the 'petty' Protestant nobility of Bohemia. His loyalty to Ferdinand (1619–20) laid the foundations of his fortune in landed property and Ferdinand gave him the title Prince of Friedland. Wallenstein was a great organizer; he conjured armies out of the ground and ran his own estates on the basis of a war economy, acting as his own minister for the army and for war. Wallenstein created an army for the emperor, something he had never had before. Through the occupation and ruthless exploitation of enemy territory the war could be self-supporting. Since the war was intended to beget further wars it was important to fight as few great battles as possible, since these were too costly.

'Provocation' for the Swedish intervention was provided by the foundation of the first imperial-German navy and the manifestation of imperial power on the German shore of the Baltic. Looking back on this stage of his career in after years, Gustavus Adolphus remarked to Oxenstierna 'things had come to such a pass that all wars being waged in Europe were mixed up together and became one war'. If the Thirty Years' War was the first European 'world war' it was also, as we shall discover from the wrangling over the peace in 1648, the first civil war of European dimensions.

One of Spain's vital interests was to reduce the threat to her trade from the

---

[1] Christian of Denmark possessed the duchy of Holstein, which lay within the Empire [T].

dangerous competition of the Netherlands. Olivarez, who in practice controlled Spanish foreign policy, suggested a trading treaty which would bind the Hanseatic towns firmly to Spain and so cut out the Netherlanders. Spain also wanted a naval base and took steps to gain possession of the county of East Friesland. These Spanish designs in the Baltic alerted Wallenstein, who probably never knew that the Spain he found so uncongenial harboured his most ardent admirers. However, he was united with Madrid in his opposition to the elector of Bavaria, leader of the Catholic League, who in his turn was the enemy of Vienna and Madrid.

The years between 1626 and 1629 held out bright prospects for Wallenstein and the imperial power. Wallenstein had a plan: if Philip IV dispatched a fleet to the North Sea, the emperor would set about creating a joint Austrian and Spanish fleet in the Baltic; the two fleets could then be linked by a canal between the North Sea and the Baltic which would be built by Wallenstein himself. There was nothing new in a Bohemian statesman showing an interest in the north and north-east. Ottokar had founded Königsberg, Charles IV had been a patron of the Hanse and the last emperor to visit the northern parts of the Empire. Wallenstein in fact envisaged the creation of a single unified trading area stretching from the Danube or the Adriatic through Bohemia and Silesia to the Baltic. The Hanse towns, though 'good Empire loyalists', had no wish to enter engagements which would expose them to military and political action. The imperialists wanted as their naval base the town of Wismar, which in 1626 had made itself militarily independent of its own territorial ruler. In 1627 Wallenstein occupied Jutland, in 1628 he was appointed 'General of the Baltic and the North Sea' and in 1629 was invested with the duchy of Mecklenburg, which its dukes had forfeited for taking sides with Christian of Denmark.

Wallenstein wanted to give the Empire a navy. But for this he needed the help of the Hanseatic towns, which had long been weak and disunited. When the proposition was put to the December meeting of the six Wendish towns (Lübeck, Hamburg, Rostock, Lüneburg and Stralsund) held at Lübeck in 1627 the reply was an amicably worded refusal. The towns were not prepared to ruin themselves on anyone else's account. The decision was to some extent influenced by anti-Spanish feeling. The Hanseatic towns complained of the ill-treatment offered to their seamen in Spanish ports; nor was there any wish to see Hanseatic towns under Spanish occupation. In 1628 the Hanseatic diet meeting at Lübeck again refused the emperor's demand for ships. Wallenstein's failed attempt on Stralsund in the following year, which was foiled by the support given to the town by Denmark and Sweden, sealed the fate of imperial designs to control the Baltic. Wallenstein, 'Imperial General of the Baltic and North Sea', was left without a navy, high and dry. At the Diet of Regensburg in July 1630 the Catholic princes, who were jealous of Wallenstein and the emperor, prevailed on Ferdinand to dismiss Wallenstein and reduce the imperial army to a force of forty thousand.

On 6 July 1630 King Gustavus Adolphus of Sweden landed with a small army in Pomerania, ostensibly as the watchdog of Lutheran freedom which was threatened by the Edict of Restitution, in fact to safeguard the Baltic, by now virtually a Swedish lake.[1] Gustavus Adolphus was devoid of any religious scruple. Not long before he had asked the Infante in Brussels what hopes there were that Spain would conclude a commercial treaty with Sweden. Philip IV was unwilling to desert his Polish allies and refused the overture. The Viennese took the affair lightly, dismissing Gustavus Adolphus, whom they dubbed the 'snow king', as 'one more little enemy'. But Ferdinand too made the serious mistake of underestimating the Swedish king. In 1631 Gustavus concluded a treaty with France which guaranteed a French subsidy for his Swedish troops, and the literally devastating forays which swept the Swedes to the gates of Prague and Vienna began in grim earnest. The alarm cry, 'the Swedes are coming' was soon an even more chilling sound than 'Kruzitürken'.

That Sweden was able to enter the Empire as a combatant was due to the tragic presumption of the Catholic League. The Protestant princes did not everywhere receive Gustavus Adolphus with open arms. In spite of everything, they still felt themselves part of the Empire, even though events had caused a temporary disruption of the attachment. Furthermore, rulers like the elector of Brandenburg were quite naturally afraid that the Swedes would annex territories to which they themselves laid claim (Pomerania and Prussia). The event which made Brandenburg and Saxony throw in their lot with Gustavus Adolphus was Tilly's capture and sack of Magdeburg in May 1631, an atrocity committed in the course of imposing the Edict of Restitution. In September of the same year the imperial forces suffered a crushing defeat at Breitenfeld near Leipzig. This battle marks the turning point in the Thirty Years' War. Gustavus immediately set about the occupation of southern Germany, and after a battle at the Lech on 15 April 1632 entered Munich. In this emergency Ferdinand recalled Wallenstein and appointed him supreme commander, with almost unlimited powers. Wallenstein chased the Saxons out of Bohemia, dug himself in against Gustavus Adolphus before Nuremberg and then drew him off into Saxony. On 16 November 1632 Gustavus was killed at the battle of Lützen. Thereafter Wallenstein busied himself with politics rather than war. He allowed the Swedes to plunder the lands of the Catholic princes, entered into repeated negotiations with them, and plotted the downfall of the emperor. The history of König Ottokars Glück und Ende seemed to be repeating itself in the career of this petty Bohemian nobleman who had risen to be one of the richest, most powerful, most feared and envied men in Europe.[2] It looked not impossible that he would end as king of Bohemia, perhaps even as emperor. Yet his fall was inescapable, and a secret tribunal meeting in Vienna condemned him to death. The emperor succeeded in persuading the bulk of Wallenstein's

---

[1] In the nineteenth and early twentieth century 'Gustav Adolf' societies, named for this hero of Protestantism, took as their aim the reconversion of Catholic Germany and Austria and the recovery of ground conquered from Protestantism by the Counter-Reformation.

[2] Schiller's Wallenstein trilogy, composed in the Empire's last declining years, glorifies the rebels. This support for rebels is a noticeable feature of German literature from the Middle Ages onward: it is for Herzog Ernst and Wilhelm Tell.

officers to break their oath of unconditional obedience to their commander and on 26 February 1634 Wallenstein was assassinated at Eger. Command of the imperial forces was assumed by the emperor's son, Ferdinand III. In September 1634 the Swedes were defeated at Nördlingen. In May of the following year John George of Saxony and the emperor concluded the treaty of Prague, to which the majority of the Protestant princes later subscribed. The next aim was to raise a powerful imperial force and drive the foreigners from the Empire.

This could have been the end of the war. All the participants, not least the Swedes, were weary of it. But Cardinal Richelieu now decided on direct intervention. He wanted to see the emperor and the Spanish beaten to their knees, but would have preferred to keep the war going by subsidizing their enemies. The battle-weariness of the Swedes made this course less practicable than formerly and on 28 April 1635 he agreed with the Swedes to a joint conduct of the war. On 19 May Richelieu declared war on Spain and engaged Bernhard of Weimar to command his forces. The entry of the French into the war prolonged it by another thirteen years. The regions worst affected by French and Swedish depradations were the south-western parts of the Empire, Bavaria, Bohemia and the hereditary Habsburg lands. The Swedish advance along the Danube brought them almost to Vienna.

The war became more savage and so did the men who waged it. The principal victim of the plundering and murdering gangs of a soldiery run wild was the defence-less peasantry. Many small towns were completely destroyed. Literature composed against the background of the Thirty Years' War takes up the cry of complaint and gives shape to the suffering and outrage. This is noticeable above all in the Catholic and Protestant lyric poetry of the period, in which a deep pessimism may wrestle with an almost despairing trust in God. The distress the people in the Empire suffered from the many kinds of violence inflicted on them by the Thirty Years' War has been brought home to our own generation through Berthold Brecht's *Mother Courage*. Brecht's play is based on a work by the great Hans Jacob Christoffel von Grimmelshausen (*c.* 1622–76), who was also the author of that portrayal of the people in their misery, *Simplicius Simplicissimus*. In a memorable episode from this novel a madman sees in a vision the dream-figure of an emperor of peace, bringing healing to the desolated world and desolate mankind.

Emperor Ferdinand III (1637–57) knew well enough that the Emperor's first and last duty was to make peace, keep peace, give peace. He summoned the Estates to a diet at Regensburg in 1640, the first full diet since 1613. At this diet the emperor's representatives perhaps stood a good chance of persuading the German princes to accept a peace. But Richelieu's agent, a Capuchin father named Joseph (born Joseph le Clerc du Tremblay, Baron de Maffliers) adroitly sowed confusion among the German princes, playing them off against each other: as Ferdinand said of him, he carried the electors' hats back to France under his hood. Father Joseph was at once a harsh and unprincipled 'real-politician' and the spiritual director of high-born ladies (in which capacity he wrote over eleven hundred letters to Antoinette d'Orleans). Many years before (at Memmingen, in November 1619) Wallenstein had confided to him his dream of founding his own kingdom in Germany and recapturing Constantinople – once the goal of Maximilian I and until 1917 of the Tsars.

The war therefore continued, although Brandenburg and Saxony made a separate peace with the Swedes. During the last years of the war Bavaria, the main sufferer, was terribly ravaged by the Swedes and the French. The end came at last in 1648. The Peace of Westphalia, which concluded the Thirty Years' War, fixed the political and religious landscape of Europe and of the Empire down to 1806 and after, in some respects down to the First World War.

Cardinals Richelieu and Mazarin bear a large share in the guilt for the disintegration of the Holy Roman Empire in the Thirty Years' War. But part of the responsibility lies at the door of certain popes who left the emperor in the lurch and gave the Catholics in the Empire either the bare minimum of support or none at all. The catastrophe in the Empire began during the pontificate of Paul V (1605–21), the pope who presided over the completion of St Peter's. This Borghese pope was occupied with dreams of bringing Russia to the Roman obedience. (He was in close contact with the false tsar, Demetrius.) For the Empire he seems to have had no policy at all.

After the short rule of Pope Gregory XV (1621–3) the papacy passed to Urban VIII, whose pontificate (1623–44) largely coincided with the period of the Thirty Years' War. Born Maffeo Barberini, he chose his papal name in honour of the French pope who preached the First Crusade and occupied the first years of his reign mainly with quite unrealistic crusading projects of his own. He had the bones of Mathilda of Tuscany, Gregory VII's protectress in his struggle with Henry IV, brought to Rome and erected a tomb for her in St Peter's. On 18 November 1626 he performed with due pomp the consecration of St Peter's, the church it had taken nearly two centuries and twenty pontificates to build. Whenever Father Joseph, Richelieu's agent was in Rome, the pope would receive him in three to four hour long audiences at least two or three times a week. In 1628–9, the year of the Edict of Restitution, Rome presented a double face to the world: what was apparently right for France (the pope approved Richelieu's policy towards the Huguenots) was right for the Habsburgs only with reservations. This pope, as Repgen observes, had only one real political interest at heart, the Papal State and the Barberini family. To the Catholic League he offered nothing but fine words. He was at bottom opposed to the Habsburgs and irresolute in his attitude to the election of Ferdinand III, which he did not accept as binding. He spent enormous sums on lavish establishments for his nephews and on his wars, but had nothing for the Catholic League.

The emperor and his Catholic theologians debated anxiously the cardinal question how far the protector of the Roman Church ought to go in meeting heretics. From an instruction he gave to his nuncio, Rocci, it seems that Urban VIII was in favour of 'dissembling' – he would observe the forms but would neither accept nor openly reject what the emperor agreed with the Protestants.

Some people thought Urban might excommunicate the emperor. Wallenstein believed there was a chance of it in the spring of 1632, when there were negotiations with John George of Saxony: 'when the pope hears that the imperial edict (of Restitution) has been quashed, the emperor will at once be placed under the ban'. In the next year this vain and touchy pope sowed the seeds of a scandal which occupies Catholicism to this day. Fancying that Galileo had done him a personal injury, he brought the old man to trial at Rome, and allowed the Inquisition to threaten him with the rack. One result of Galileo's condemnation was a migration of natural scientists from Catholic into Protestant Europe (Heidelberg, Holland, England).

'After 1630, and certainly after Breitenfeld, there could no longer be any compromise without the abandonment of some Catholic positions in the empire, no true peace inside Germany without the surrender of some of Catholicism's legal titles.' At the Diet of Regensburg of 1640–41, the pope at last showed open opposition to the conclusion of peace between the emperor and the Protestants. For the first time since the beginning of the Reformation, Rome registered an official protest against a decree of the imperial diet. With the rejection of the amnesty decree (whose exact terms were still unpublished), the pope threw off the dissembling mask he had kept in place even at the time of the Edict of Restitution (1629) and the Peace of Prague (1635). The Diet of Regensburg met for the first time on 13 September 1640 in the presence of the emperor and under the presidency of the only lay elector to put in an appearance, Margrave William of Baden. Prospects for a settlement seemed good. The great problem for debate was 'how the Holy Empire might be restored to its former undivided and flourishing state and perpetually maintained therein'. The papal protest was signed by his representative Caspar Mattei on 18 April 1641 and conveyed to the emperor. Its purport was to urge and warn the emperor:

As shield and protector of the Roman Catholic Church, that Your Majesty, walking in the footsteps of your forefathers and as befits your Majesty's piety, is to defend the inviolability, untouchability and impugnability (*indemnitas*) of the Catholic religion, of church property of whatever description and of all clerics, and Your Majesty is neither to allow nor condone any other state of affairs. If Your Majesty acts otherwise I shall resist, and declare the resistance of His Holiness and of the Apostolic See.

In this document pope and nuncio turned their back on the future. They were clinging to the legal position of a (falsely interpreted) past, remote from the living realities of the world. They had themselves 'blocked the road by which Rome might once again have helped to shape political events'. The emperor made no reply to the pope's protest and behaved as though nothing had happened.

The Peace of Westphalia of 1648 [plate 129], by placing the confessions on an equal legal footing and providing for the 'perpetual' alienation of church lands after a standard lapse of one year binding on both parties, ratified the break with canon law and with the law governing the church within the Empire. The pope of the day – who protested against the greatest peacemaking effort in European history and never

VIII Pereda, *Vanity*. The transitoriness of all empires, above all world-empires, was the constant preoccupation of later Holy Roman Emperors (starting with Charles v, if not before). Spectacle, ceremonial, war, the daily routine were to be daily reminders of the emperor's mortality.

recognized the Treaty of Westphalia – was the feeble Innocent X, who reigned from 1644 to 1655. The papacy, which for over a thousand years had been the prop and stay of 'Frankish' western Christendom and a partner with the Empire and the Emperor, was not among the partners whose treaty gave a new shape to Europe.

The impressive painting by Gerard ter Borch entitled *The Conclusion of the Peace of Münster* now hangs in the National Gallery in London [plate 130]. It shows the ratification of the treaty between Spain and the Netherlands which took place in the town hall at Münster on 15 May 1648. The artist was an eye-witness and painted the scene with careful exactness. The Spanish wear magnificent court dress, the Dutch the black clothes of the bourgeoisie. Peñarandas the Spaniard has his arm round the Calvinist Barthold van Gent.

The great assemblage, which would have no equal in Europe until the Congress of Vienna in 1815, met at Münster and Osnabrück, two small episcopal cities in Westphalia. Both were predominantly rural: herds going to pasture were driven through the town, hens and pigs roamed freely, harvest wagons rattled over the rutted streets. Among the houses of the poor rose up a few statelier edifices, residences of the cathedral canons and town houses of the nobility, which were used as conference houses. The surrounding countryside was waste and desolate as a result of the war. Count Trauttmansdorff, who headed the imperial deputation, dated one of his first dispatches, 'from Münster, behind the pig-sty', a querulous Frenchman described Münster as '*la ville aux cochons*' ('swines-ville'). Frenchmen, Spaniards and Italians fancied they were seeing for themselves the primitive Germania described by Caesar and Tacitus.

From Münster dispatches took fifteen days to reach Vienna, ten to reach Paris (six by express courier), four weeks and more to reach Madrid; to Stockholm (from Osnabrück) they took sixteen days, to Dresden between five and six. It was a congress of ambassadors: in all 148 were present, 37 of them foreigners and the rest Germans, 10 of whom represented the house of Austria and the remainder the Estates of the Empire.

The papal nuncio, Fabio Chigi (later Pope Alexander VII), was a highly cultivated and good-humoured man, respected even by the Protestants. However, he had instructions from Rome to treat only with the Catholic powers and not with the 'heretics', and he was well aware of the delicacy of his position. Aloisi Contarini, the Venetian who acted as intermediary between the parties, had been ambassador in London, Paris, Rome and Constantinople, but 'the most considerable man at the congress was Maximilian, Count von Trauttmansdorff' (F. Dickmann). Trauttmansdorf can be given the credit as the architect of the peace. Born a Lutheran like most of his colleagues in the imperial delegation, he had been converted to Catholicism in his youth and spent many years in the imperial service. As a negotiator he was quite capable of toughness and decision, but preferred to act the part of a comfortable, jovial Austrian (the princes' delegates sometimes referred to him as 'father'). 'Now run away and be nice good children' was his advice on one occasion to the Protestant delegates. His integrity and distinction won him the respect of all parties except the Spanish, who hated him.

The peace congress took place against a background of lavish display, gross banquets, drinking bouts and general debauchery and venality. Yet despite the corruption, and despite the mutual lack of sympathy which existed even among members of the same delegation (the Swedes and the French are cases in point), many of the delegates had a genuine awareness of the responsibility and magnitude of their task. Brienne, the French secretary of state, expresses this awareness in a letter he wrote to Münster. 'Laid on us is the greatest task there has been for centuries. We have to make peace not only between two crowns but for the whole of Europe, and establish it so securely that any aspiration of disturbing it must remain vain.' Nineteenth- and twentieth-century historians of the German nationalist school are often harsh in their judgment of the Peace of Westphalia. Hitler declared his aim was to demolish the French system of 1648. The most recent historian of the peace, F. Dickmann, said in Münster in 1959: 'Let it be emphasized once again. For our people the peace signified a national disaster and for the Holy Roman Empire, the form in which the German people had hitherto found their state, it signified the onset of the malady to which it eventually succumbed.'

'The year 1648 is one of the great years of catastrophe in our history': but Dickmann stresses too that Münster saw the beginning of a new order. In the past the conflict between powers whose life-styles and history were so different (Protestants, Catholics, etc.) had been dominated by their intense hatred for one another. Truces were always of short duration, a pause after which the enemies fell on one another with renewed vigour. After 1648 a new and rational manner of thinking began to make headway as the fundamental principle of modern Europe. 'This new order, as is made plain for the first time by the Peace of Westphalia, rests primarily on the enforced coexistence of the different sovereignties and powers.' One feature of the peace is of overriding significance for the European society of states: 'in place of the former unity of church and faith there was now a community of sovereign states. It was through this community that the unity of Europe would in future express itself.' '*Pax sit Christiana, universalis, perpetua veraque et sincera amicitia.*' Christians of very different confessions had the task of creating between them a true and lasting peace in a spirit of amity and mutual trust.

Trust depended on the ability to forgive and forget and reach a genuine reconciliation, on the will to allow a 'permanent obliteration of the past'. '*In amnestia consistit substantia pacis*': 'amnesty' implied a constructive 'forgetting and forgiving' of the terrible acts of carnage the parties had perpetrated against each other.

'The Peace of Westphalia is the last and most important fundamental law of the old Empire.' Down to 1648 the constitution of the Empire was governed chiefly by customary law, which because it was living could go on developing. Custom was now very largely replaced by constitutional law.

As late as the nineteenth century the English historian Gardiner considered that the religious provisions of the Peace outweighed in importance the rest. It marked the breakthrough which set European thought on the road towards a toleration which meant something more than the temporary condonation of unfamiliar beliefs.

If before the war every German territorial ruler, not always without reason, saw subjects who entertained different beliefs from his own as potential traitors, after the Peace he could rest assured if a portion of them professed a different belief. . . . Toleration could now be observed without any danger to the state. If in Germany freedom of belief and of conscience were established at a very early date, this was due not least to the Peace of Westphalia.

The Peace of Westphalia ensured the continuance of the Emperor and the Empire. The Empire was not a monarchical state but a league of states formed from the Estates. The peace treaty confirmed the full sovereignty of the Estates and bound the emperor to obtain consent from the diet to his legislation. The right of deciding on peace or war which the emperor had removed from the Estates by the treaty of Prague was restored to them, together with the right of federation and the right of military command. There was nothing new in these developments, now legally ratified: even medieval emperors enjoyed nothing greater than the right of supreme command over an army already assembled in the field; they had no undisputed right to levy an army – that was a matter for the territorial princes. Down to 1918 the German imperial army was never a unitary fighting force but was composed of contingents supplied by the German princes. Supreme power over the army belonged not to the Empire but to the princes and attempts to alter the situation (under Charles v and Ferdinand ii) ended in failure.

The right to make alliances with other powers made the princes, in practice, sovereign. But this right of making political treaties had already been foreshadowed by feudal compacts German vassals concluded with alien lords in the Middle Ages, of which there are examples in the western part of the Empire as early as the thirteenth century. In the fourteenth century the right of princes in the north-western part of the Empire to form their own alliances was fully developed. And at Chambord in 1552 we find German princes entering into a formal alliance with a foreign power against the emperor.

Before 1648 the emperor's right to make laws and interpret them gave him significant privileges as compared with the competence of the Estates. No clear division had ever been made between the competence of the *Reichskammergericht* and that of the *Reichshofrat*. The Emperor's jurisdiction over the Estates (he had no longer any to speak of over his subjects) gave him the weapon of the imperial ban. Because it belonged to the Emperor alone, the ban was enforced by imperial commissars. Wallenstein did so in masterly fashion – through war. This method made it possible to 'eliminate' whole principalities, that is to say, Estates.

At the peace congress the antagonism between the electors and the other princes came out much more strongly than the antagonism between the emperor and the Estates or between the emperor and the electors. In the sixteenth century there had been several hundred princes of the Empire, but the process by which the larger secular princes swallowed up the smaller was already under way and gathering strength. The ecclesiastical princes, such potent factors in medieval king- and emperor-making, found their political importance dwindling (especially now that they no longer had many troops at their disposal). This is true even of the three ecclesiastical electors. Cologne was virtually the preserve of second sons of the house of Bavaria. Mainz had lost many of its great possessions, temporarily as booty to the Swedes and permanently to France. The elector of Trier had veered between the French and the Spanish; his fortress of Ehrenbreitstein was the first place in Germany to receive a French garrison. In 1635 the Spanish invested Trier and handed the elector over to the emperor, who kept him in confinement at Vienna for ten years as a traitor to the Empire.

The two secular electors, Brandenburg and Electoral Saxony, had supported the emperor. Brandenburg inherited eastern Pomerania and was given the sees of Cammin, Halberstadt and Minden and reversionary rights over Magdeburg. Western Pomerania, Rügen, Stettin, Wismar and the sees of Bremen and Verden were given to Sweden, although they remained fiefs of the Empire. John George of Saxony received Lausitz. The partner who presented the greatest problem to the Habsburg emperor (as to his non-Bavarian predecessors in the Middle Ages) was Bavaria. At the beginning of March 1647 Trauttmansdorff painted the situation in the gloomiest colours: Bavaria would ally with France against the emperor and carry the Rhenish, Franconian, Swabian, Bavarian and Westphalian circles with him, turning them into French protectorates; the imperial office would be abolished or transferred to France. 'He had, as it were, a vision of what would come to pass a century and a half later'. Richelieu had spared no effort in promoting the idea of a Bavarian emperor. His aim had been an imperial office reconstituted on purely elective lines – a return to the Golden Bull. In all matters important to the Empire the Emperor ought to be bound by the general voice of the Estates and by his recognition of the Estates as structures within the law of nations, in particular as regards their right to make alliances. A French flysheet current in 1618 pointedly remarks: 'the imperial office is a nullity and means nothing by itself, but any other number it can increase tenfold.' Duke Maximilian of Bavaria knew what pressure he could apply to this 'nullity' and applied it to the limit. He kept the title of Elector Palatine (awarded to him in 1623) and received the Upper Palatinate. An eighth electorate was created to compensate the son of the 'Winter King' – displaced for a second time – for the loss of the Palatinate.

In the Protestant parts of the Empire, doubts about the imperial office were concerned more with its theoretical than its practical aspects. Down to the end of the sixteenth century the old doctrine still prevailed: the Empire was the continuation of the Roman Empire, in law the Emperor possessed all the powers of the Roman *princeps*, taken over in full from Roman law *ratione imperii*. The territorial sovereignty of the princes was interpreted as a power conferred on them by reason of their office. The doctrines that the Empire was an aristocracy ruled by the princes and that they possessed the right of resistance grew up on Lutheran soil. Philip of Hesse gave the

Lutheran princes their political education. A writing by a pastor of Magdeburg, inspired by his city's resistance to the emperor when the Interim was in force, set a precedent for the French Calvinists. This work was read by French opponents of monarchy, for example Franz Hotman, and through such channels influenced theories of resistance in both Europe and America. In 1603 Johann Althusius propounded the theory that the princes of the Empire exercised a double office: a particular office (*officium speciale*) as territorial ruler acting on behalf of the Empire and a general office (*officium generale*) as an Estate of the Empire acting in the name of the people. As individuals they were subordinate to the Emperor, as a totality they were his superior. The Emperor, as the people's highest official, was bound to observe the promises contained in his contract on assuming office, his electoral capitulations.

Bogislav Philipp von Chemnitz (otherwise Hippolithus a Lapide, the name under which he issued his writings) published in 1640, two years before he entered service with the Swedes, a work which attracted widespread attention, *De ratione status in Imperio nostro Romano-Germanico*. The Empire, he asserts, is an aristocracy ruled by the princes, and the house of Habsburg has no indigenous rights in Germany. He would like to see the office of Emperor either completely abolished, or at least never remaining too long in the same house. No law could withstand the demands of harsh necessity. The Emperor should be given only the outward trappings of dignity and majesty, and certainly no share of real power.

In the concluding section of his work, which he himself later regretted, Chemnitz calls on the French and Swedes to assist in expelling the Habsburgs from the Empire: their territories should be confiscated and added to the Empire and the new emperor elected in accordance with a fundamental law stipulating that no more than two emperors would be elected from a single house. Sweden and France, the Empire's two most formidable enemies, carried away from the Peace of Westphalia rich booty in the form of imperial territory. The Swedish acquisitions entrenched them firmly in northern Germany and gave them control of the Baltic. By their descent on the Empire in 1630 the Swedes had overstrained the resources of a country with only a million inhabitants and over-estimated their power. In 1648 they demanded compensation for their material and human losses, and a permanently altered situation in Germany as security for their gains.

France, under the Peace of Westphalia, was assigned the imperial cities she had held since 1552 and was confirmed in the possession of lands belonging to the bishoprics of Metz, Toul and Verdun she had occupied since that date. In addition France received the Habsburg counties in Alsace and jurisdiction over ten Alsatian towns of the Empire and the right to maintain garrisons in Philippsburg and Breisach on the right bank of the Rhine. The legal position over these towns was intentionally left vague, which made it possible for Louis xiv to embark on his later wars of aggression. Cardinal Richelieu's role in the Thirty Years' War had initially been that of a silent collaborator in all anti-Habsburg coalitions. He regarded it as a dynastic struggle between France and the Habsburgs which did not directly affect the Empire. 'Down to the middle of the seventeenth century there was no national antagonism between the German and French peoples, neither was there any serious political conflict between France and the Empire.' But French aggression in the latter part of the Thirty Years' War and above all under Louis XIV sowed the seeds of the fatal Franco-German discord which grew steadily throughout the nineteenth and early twentieth centuries and led directly to the First World War. Richelieu himself began it, and his war outlasted him. He died on 4 December 1642, to be succeeded by Mazarin, his self-avowed disciple. But Mazarin introduced a new element of brashness into French policy and the effect of Richelieu's careful and discreet manipulations (he was the first European statesman to advocate the idea of all-round mutual security agreements) was cancelled out by a new 'imperialism'.

The Spanish and the emperor, Madrid and Vienna, met at the Peace Congress as ancient allies and enemies. The signature of the Peace of Westphalia (14–24 October 1648) between the emperor, France and Sweden marked the dissolution of the Spanish-Austrian alliance. Philip IV of Spain realized that the emperor had no choice but to make peace, since otherwise he would have fallen. But Spain remained at war with France for eleven more years. The Infanta Maria Theresa married Louis XIV, who hoped to inherit Spain [plate 134]. Louis was himself half-Spanish (he was the son of the Infanta Anna, daughter of Philip III and Margaret of Styria); his wife was the daughter of Philip IV and sister of Charles II of Spain and of Margaret Theresa, who married Emperor Leopold II; and he became the greatest foe of the house of Habsburg and of Spain.

The first treaty to be signed at the Congress in Münster–Osnabrück was between the Spanish and the Netherlanders. The struggle between them had lasted eighty years, but it was the Spanish who were the first at Münster to accord European status to the Netherlands, by ascribing to the rebel state they had never recognized the rank of a sovereign power.

The Spanish court of the seventeenth century still stood on its dignity. The imperial ambassador in Madrid did not succeed in having himself addressed as 'Excellency' as his master desired. From the time of Philip II this title was reserved for Spanish grandees and the ambassador had to be content with 'Illustrissimus'. (This did not prevent the title 'Excellency' making its triumphal way into Germany, where to the chagrin of the imperial government it was used by electoral delegates to meetings of the electoral college and the imperial diet.)

During the Thirty Years' War and for the remainder of the seventeenth century relations between the courts of Madrid and Vienna were often strained to say the least; that they did not break was largely due to the efforts of some outstanding ambassadors. Seventeenth-century Spain was a miserable country, justifying Philip II's lament that God had given him so many realms to rule but no son capable of ruling them. Spanish claims, however, were still grandiose: a book by Gerónimo de Cevallos entitled *The Royal art of ruling well* is dedicated to Philip IV, 'Emperor of all the Spanish'. But Philip II's successors – Philip III, 1598–1621, and Philip IV, 1621–65 –

were weaklings, incapable of guiding the reins of government for themselves. Favourites 'reigned' in Madrid. Philip iv's particular favourite, Olivarez, exclaimed to the king, 'The trouble with us, sir, is that we have no heads!' Spain was an exhausted country [plate 131], which by the mid-seventeenth century had no first-rate minds capable of mastering the taxing demands of a struggle in so many arenas – Italy, the Empire, the Netherlands, England and the high seas of the world.

From the activities of Oñate, the 'architect of the great war', and from Spain's sombre reputation in the Empire, it would be pardonable to suppose that Spanish influence in Vienna was wholly malign. But not all Spaniards were warmongers and fanatics, and at certain critical moments their advice tended the other way. Spanish advisers counselled against implementation of the Edict of Restitution, fearing it would try the patience of the German Protestants beyond endurance. In sharp contrast with the Jesuits, who were considered wholehearted supporters of religious wars, Spanish theologians were on the side of political moderation and compromise. Quiroga, a Capuchin who came to Vienna as the confessor of a Spanish infanta, surprised everyone by favouring peace with the German Lutherans.

During the Thirty Years' War Spain raised vast sums of money for the emperor, money which admittedly often arrived too late. These monies came from the kingdom of Naples and Sicily; the American money was needed for Spain itself. 'But if the emperor had depended on Spain for money, in due course the exhausted world empire would depend for men on the more populous regions of Germany' (G. Neceneseffy). Olivares demanded ten thousand German veterans for service in Italy.

The tension between Madrid and Vienna during the Thirty Years' War and after was to some extent alleviated by a carefully contrived system of intermarriages. Emperor Ferdinand iii (1636–57) married the Infanta Maria, sister to Philip iv of Spain and also to the Queen of France. Maria has been described as 'one of the most attractive figures of her age'. At seventeen she had been wooed in knight errant style by the future Charles i of England; but this projected marriage to a 'heretic' failed to materialize. The Infanta's marriage to Ferdinand (1631) was the master-stroke of Franz Christoph, Count Khevenhüller, imperial ambassador to Madrid.

The marriage was a very happy one. When Ferdinand went away to command his troops in person, which was not uncommon, he sometimes left Maria as his regent. But in 1646 she died suddenly at Linz, and the entire country was plunged into gloom. At the time relations between Madrid and Vienna were under exceptional strain. After his defeats of 1636–40 the emperor had been forced to mortgage his own estates and put his wife's jewels in pledge. Catholic positions everywhere were under overwhelming pressure from the Swedes, the French and the Protestants. All the princes, even the Catholics, were against the Spanish. But whatever the temptation to abandon it, the Spanish alliance still held.

In March 1645, the emperor found himself in a hopeless position. 'I have no money, no men, and no generals.' It seemed likely Vienna would fall. The Swedes were at Krems on the Danube, Rakoczy was on the march from Siebenbürgen and making for Vienna. In this emergency the thoughts of men in Vienna and Madrid turned to a political marriage. The emperor in fact had two marriages in mind: between his daughter Maria Anna and the Infante Baltasar Carlos,[1] and between his son Archduke Ferdinand and the Infanta Maria Theresa. Unbeknown to Vienna, however, plans were afoot in Madrid for a French marriage, and Maria Theresa became the bride of Louis xiv.

At the peace negotiations in Münster and Osnabrück Count Trauttmansdorff found the Spanish representatives, Peñarandas and Terranovas, hard men to deal with. The Spanish-Austrian alliance was dissolved, although connections were maintained. The imperial city of Vienna and the baroque culture of the Empire are inconceivable without this Spanish influence.

---

[1] When the six-year-old Spanish prince Baltasar Carlos learned in 1635 of the birth of Archduchess Maria Anna, he complacently remarked on the good news that the queen of Hungary had given him a wife.

II

THE EMPIRE IN THE BAROQUE AGE
(1657–1740)

On a day in 1665, Mehmed Pasha (Ahmed Köprülü), the grand emissary of the Turks, rode into Vienna on a mettlesome white horse, escorted by mounted knights in armour who had gone out to meet him. The music of brass cymbals, drums and shawms preceded the procession. Four standards with waving horse-tails symbolized the military might of the Turks. This important visitor, whom the emperor had generously allowed to make this impressive entry, was conducted to his lodgings at the Golden Lamb by the court chamberlain, the burgomaster and leading gildsmen, the highest dignitaries of court and city.

In August 1664 a compromise peace had been concluded between the emperor and the Turks at Vasvar in Hungary. It was followed by the exchange of complimentary embassies. But the Turks recognized no peace with 'infidels' and for them the treaty was only a truce. It followed a successful action at St Gotthard in the Raab valley on 1 August, when Count Raymund Montecuccoli, with a force made up of Austrian and imperial contingents halted the Turkish invasion of Styria. Among those who accompanied Mehmed Pasha to Vienna was Evliya Çelebi, son of a goldsmith from Istanbul, scholar, traveller and poet, who has left us his account of this 'remarkable journey into non-Mohammedan country and to the city and fortress of Vienna in the year 1665'. Çelebi is an acute observer (he notices for example the difference between Germans and Hungarians), and is complimentary about Viennese shopkeepers, doctors, workmen, artists, women and handsome young men. He is impressed by the Stephansdom with its organ and gigantic tower, from the top of which shone the 'Goldene Apfel', the imperial orb. This 'Goldene Apfel' loomed large in the religious-political fantasies of the Turks as the glittering symbol of world dominion which invited them to achieve this goal through conquering the lands of the 'Giaours', the unbelievers. Most of the Turkish armies whose aim was conquest were really engaged in a counter-crusade, directed from Constantinople, the holy city and second Rome, and actively supported by the 'christian Soliman', King Louis xiv. Çelebi could appreciate the ideal which made the 'German emperor' as king of kings bear sway over 'all the peoples of Christendom'. Being nurtured in the Byzantine-Osmanli tradition, he avoids using the expressions 'Roman emperor' and 'Roman Empire' when speaking of the West. The Turkish embassy stayed nine months in Vienna, during which time there was ample opportunity to study and measure the city's fortifications. Çelebi decided the magnificent fortress was impregnable.

Kara Mustafa, 'the Turkish Wallenstein', thought otherwise: in 1683 he stood before the gates of Vienna. The reigning emperor, Leopold I (1657–1705), had been destined for the church and his natural piety and scholarly and artistic leanings were in fact chacteristic of the type of cultivated cleric. The premature death of his elder brother (Ferdinand IV) in 1654 left Leopold to become head of the Viennese branch of his house. His election as King of the Romans and then as emperor was only achieved after extraordinary exertions and in face of obstruction from Brandenburg, Sweden and France.

Leopold [plate 139], physically slight of stature, was forced by Louis XIV and the Turks to wage permanent war in both east and west. He held his own and was eventually able to take the offensive by bringing three weapons into play: the mercantilist policy he followed in his hereditary dominions and in the Empire, his alliances with the European enemies of the Sun King, backed up later by the appointment of Prince Eugen to supreme command of the imperial forces, and the upsurge of intellectual-political religious and cultural activity which found its medium in imperial baroque.

Wide areas of the empire had been ravaged by the Thirty Years' War. In some regions – interspersed by others the war had barely touched – population losses amounted to sixty per cent of the population. The overall decline in the rural population of Germany is reckoned at forty per cent, while town populations are considered to have fallen by a third. Into this devastated and industrially underdeveloped country came a flood of goods from France, the first European country to industrialize. Leopold wanted to unite the Empire economically. He envisaged his plan for the Empire's economic defence against France as 'a knife placed at the root of all her revenues and commercial dealings'. Joint colonial projects with Brandenburg and Spain started to be considered as early as 1660–61.

The way in which politics and economics were intertwined with religion in the seventeenth and early eighteenth centuries is illustrated by the career of Cristobal de Rojas y Spinola. Of Spanish descent, he became a Franciscan and during the 1650s spent some time in Cologne, where he held classes for potential converts and succeeded in winning over some influential people (including a future cardinal). Spinola first went to Vienna about 1660, in response to an invitation from the emperor's first minister to act as his confessor; during the Turkish wars Spinola was entrusted with a number of diplomatic missions. He invited to Vienna his friend J. J. Becher, the leading exponent of mercantilist policies in the Empire. Spinola favoured the reunion of the two churches as a means of bringing peace to the Empire and also advocated the acquisition of colonies, hoping that the spirit of reconciliation would thrive better on virgin soil than on ground laid waste by the Thirty Years' War.[1] In 1665 he put

[1] The plans of nineteenth-century Russian reformers such as Muravev for making Siberia a new Russia were inspired by similar motives.

forward the idea of a customs union. Ten years later he was denounced by France (which had every reason to fear him) as a heretic and was obliged to defend himself in Rome. In 1677 the emperor sent him round the Empire on a threefold mission: to win consent for the formation of a permanent imperial treasury which would be fed from an inheritance tax levied throughout the Empire; to advise princes and towns on ways of developing their economies; and to attempt through mediation to bridge over some of the differences between the confessions. A further charge was to win support for a standing army for the Empire, which was in fact set up in 1681.

The 'resurrection of the Empire' after the Thirty Years' War was due to Louis XIV, whose expansionist policy overstepped all the limits Richelieu had set for himself and for France. In the War of Devolution (1667–8) Louis conquered part of the Spanish Netherlands, having bought the co-operation of princes in the south-west and north-east of the Empire, notably that of the Elector of Cologne (Peace of Aachen, 1668). During Louis' Dutch War of 1672–8 (which the Sun King started by a surprise attack) a mutual defensive alliance was concluded in 1673 between the emperor, Lorraine, the Netherlands and Spain. In the following year the Empire declared war on Louis XIV. At this period the propaganda campaign against the 'new Soliman' was at its height. Europe was in an uproar over Louis and Protestants hailed Emperor Leopold as the new saviour of the Empire.

Louis brought the Swedes, the Poles (the French candidate, John Sobieski, won the election to the Polish throne in 1674), the Hungarian rebels and the Turks into play. The anti-French coalition collapsed and under the Peace of Nymwegen (1679) Leopold was forced to accept most of France's conquests. Now that Lorraine was under French occupation French diplomats and troops poured into the western regions of the Empire (1679–84): Alsace and the counties of Saarbrücken and Zweibrücken were occupied and Strassburg and Luxemburg turned into fortresses whose purpose was at once to defend expansionist France and to provide a launching-place for further conquests. Louis' political activities in the south-east were also bearing fruit: the great Turkish offensive grew out of the Magyar revolt in which the Hungarian rebels allied with the Porte against the Habsburg. In July 1683 Vienna was cut off by the Turks, and the imperial court forced to take refuge in Passau. This success on the part of the Sun King, whose engineers and sappers accompanied Kara Mustafa's army, produced an unexpected reaction which led to the arrival before Vienna of a German and Polish force collected by Duke Charles V of Lorraine and King John Sobieski of Poland which effected the relief of the city. This was the turning-point. After 1683 it was possible to set in motion the great counter-attack which in the eighteenth and nineteenth centuries drove the Turks back into south-east Europe.

The resources of the emperor would not stretch to a war on two fronts. In order to continue his struggle against the Turks he concluded with Louis in 1684 the Truce of Regensburg, which guaranteed France the 'free and undisturbed possession' of all imperial territories acquired before 1 August 1681. But in 1688, the year when

Belgrade, the gateway to the Balkans, was captured from the Turks, Louis embarked on the third of his wars of conquest by invading the Palatinate (the War of the League of Augsburg, 1688–97). His pretext was the (disputed) claim of his brother's wife to inherit the Palatinate from the childless elector, who had died in 1685. The Sun King was now confronted by the 'Grand Alliance': the League of Augsburg, composed of the emperor, Sweden, Spain and some princes of the Empire, was now joined by the England of William of Orange and subsequently by Spain and Savoy. Louis' persecution of the Huguenots impelled the Elector of Brandenburg to transfer his allegiance from Paris to Vienna.

In 1689 the armies of Louis xiv systematically laid waste the lands of the Palatinate on both banks of the Rhine: Mannheim, Speyer, Worms, Oppenheim and the castle at Heidelberg all fell victim. Under the Peace of Ryswijk (1697) France retained Alsace and Strassburg but Lorraine was handed back. In this same year supreme command of the imperial forces was assumed by a short and slim-built young man whose services Louis xiv had already rejected: Prince Eugen. His victories over the Turks gave the emperor control over Hungary and Siebenbürgen (Peace of Karlowitz, 1699). In the War of the Spanish Succession (1701–14) the emperor, together with England, Holland and Brandenburg (whose elector on 18 January 1701 declared himself 'King in Prussia') fought the armies of the Sun King on battlefields in western Europe, southern Germany, and Italy. Louis had as his allies two Wittelsbachs, Max Emanuel of Bavaria and Archbishop Joseph Clemens of Cologne. The most significant victory of the great coalition was won by Marlborough and Prince Eugen at Blenheim in August 1704. The death of Emperor Leopold in 1705 was followed by the brief reign of his son Joseph I (1705–11), who died of smallpox. The fact that his heir, Charles VI, was also heir to Spain wrought a transformation in European politics. England led the way by concluding a peace with Paris whose purpose was to frustrate the development of Spanish-Austrian ascendancy in the Empire and in Europe.

We can now return to the period of Leopold's arduous beginnings and to his economic policy. Economic warfare as a means of bringing pressure to bear on an enemy was not completely unknown in the Empire. In 1412 King Sigismund had embarked on an economic war against Venice which lasted over twenty years. In 1597 Emperor Rudolf II expelled the English Merchant Adventurers from the Empire for political reasons (he wanted to show his support for Spain). The economic policy of Leopold I was directed chiefly against the French. On 7 May 1676 he issued a decree, based on expert advice, forbidding 'the importation of any French merchandise into the Empire'. This was because the French had been flooding the German market. Leibniz hazarded the guess that about a tenth of total German production seeped away to France in payment for French goods. Becher put the French turnover in Germany at about four million *taler*. The prohibition was aimed at luxuries, fashionable clothing and household articles; medicaments and similar articles were exempt. The decree was given very thorough consideration by the three houses of the imperial diet meeting at Regensburg. It was published at Nuremberg on no less than sixty-one occasions, and was even proclaimed in Basel and Zurich. In the imperial towns the decree was greeted with consternation. In November 1676 the money-changers of Frankfurt protested to the town council, asserting that at no time, whether in peace or war, had christian or barbarian peoples suffered any such restriction. The most vehement opposition came from the ruler of Bavaria, who was unwilling to abandon his ties with France. Full implementation of the law was held up by the incompetence of imperial officials and their lack of systematic guidance. In 1677, therefore, Becher was instructed as imperial commissar to enforce the Empire's first serious interdict – a fresh ban on the importation of French goods.

The economic life of the Empire in general, and the efforts being made to weld it into a self-contained trading area, received a powerful new stimulus from the Sun King's aggressions and his revocation of the Edict of Nantes (1685): forty thousand French Huguenots (out of the three hundred thousand odd who emigrated) took refuge in imperial territory. With an unusual unanimity, inspired by Louis' reign of terror, the Empire assented on 7 June 1689 to a draft law proposed by the emperor which forbade 'all trading and trafficking, all exchanges and correspondence, in short any form of commerce whatsoever, whether by land or water, with the enemies of the Empire'. Hamburg and the Spanish Netherlands ignored the imperial edict, and French goods continued to enter the Empire by way of the 'green frontiers' between the Netherlands and France and between the Empire and Switzerland. This contraband traffic led to a form of economic warfare between the Empire and some of the Swiss cantons.

An edict for the regulation of trade issued in 1705 (drafted under Leopold but published over the signature of Emperor Joseph) remained in force down to 1806. It represented a moderate attempt at providing the Empire with an economic policy. It has been said that the age of Leopold I can be regarded as the 'first laboratory for testing the problems of the industrial epoch, the period during which the rational part of men's minds underwent development' (J. Bog).

Nevertheless, it would be a mistake to suppose that the 'economy' of the baroque Empire was dictated by purely economic considerations; current political-religious opinions and the prevailing outlook on the world also played their part. At the beginning of the eighteenth century Leibniz (in 1674 a pupil of Colbert in Paris) was busy with plans for an all-German 'Intelligence Agency' and a 'National Workhouse'. He wanted to see Germany transformed into a manufacturing and exporting state which could beat France in the economic field. In 1670 he had called on the emperor to conclude an alliance with the princes and so keep the Empire together. All reforms depended on the restoration of 'traditional, forthright German trust'.

In Leibniz's vision of a *Reich Europa* the 'Freedom of Europe', in which the potentialities of all the nations come to their fullest flowering, is a stylized image of the Holy Roman Empire. He saw the Empire as a corporate body, a protective union which existed for the sake of its members and was present in each. Each country was thus 'the Empire', each ruler had the task of 'representing' imperial authority.

Gottfried Wilhelem Leibniz was the greatest philosopher of the Holy Roman Empire. He stands with Meister Eckhart, Nicholas of Cusa, Erasmus and Goethe. Leibniz was born two years before the end of the Thirty Years' War, on 1 July 1646, and died on 14 November 1716. He was small of stature, never lost his childhood timidity, suffered from a speech defect and was always ailing. From his twenties he affected a full-bottomed wig, in order to conceal a swelling on his neck the size of a pigeon's egg. As a writer he was indefatigable, but his output was in papers and letters rather than books – seventy-five thousand papers and fifteen thousand letters, never less than three hundred letters a year, some of them treatises in themselves. The fabric of his thoughts was 'open' on all sides – like the open system of the Empire. Of his great rival Newton it has been said that his picture of the cosmos reflects the constitutional monarchy and aristocratic government of the England of his day. Newton's God is a supreme ruler who discreetly refrains from interference with the government of the universe, except at times of exceptional crisis. The picture of the world presented by Leibniz, his outlook on the world and the entire body of his religious and philosophical thinking, whether he knew it or not, is a eulogy of the Holy Roman Empire: his universe is one of a pre-established harmony, sustained by a regulated but voluntary co-operation of the 'monads' (an expression he borrowed from Theresa of Avila). Just as in the Holy Roman Empire – as Leibniz saw it – the princes, the imperial towns and all the other groups and individuals who were centred on the Emperor were supposed to work together in free and orderly fashion, so did faith and reason, God and man, nature and the supernatural, the smallest objects and the greatest, work together in the cosmos.

For Leibniz the historian the idea of Empire had found its ideal realization in the Ottonian system, the elliptical co-operation of Emperor and bishops in the tenth and early eleventh centuries. Emperor and Pope guiding Christendom as brothers, the *Sacrum Imperium* as preached and striven for under the Salian and Hohenstaufen emperors – this Holy Roman Empire, Leibniz maintained, was a model for the free ordering of human society.

'The Empire is but a chimera and a skeleton.' Many in Europe shared this opinion of the Dutch statesman Jan de Witt, which he voiced in 1664. But it was countered by the young Leibniz: 'Germany is the centre of Europe'. His feeling for the Empire was 'German'-centred, but in a universal sense, in the way that the circle round Schiller, Hölderlin and the young Schlegel still thought of 'German': as serving the universal, moulding man in dignity and responsible liberty.

The world he grew up in made Leibniz acutely aware of the disintegration caused in the Empire and Europe by generations of political and religious conflict. He never lost his admiration for the French scholars and thinkers he acknowledged as his masters and friends, but was in no doubt that the storm-centre of Europe lay in France, at the court of Louis XIV. Leibniz discerned beneath the evident miseries of the disintegrating Empire the basic structures which had endured a thousand years, and tried to revitalize them in the service of a new political spirit and theory and as agents of diplomacy. When he looked at France, beneath the apparent brilliance of the Sun King's regime he discerned the *Mala Franciae*, the wretchedness of France: while Paris enjoyed a false flowering, the provinces were drained dry. 'To outward appearance all is fair, but within is crippled and deformed.' Mismanagement on the part of government and exploitation of the non-privileged grew unchecked, while the king and the high nobility lived a life of luxury.

Leibniz perceived that the Sun King's aggressions were provoked by unadmitted fears. In a memorandum entitled *Consilium Aegyptiacum*, which he addressed to Louis XIV in 1672, Leibniz advises the French king to abandon his plans for attacking Holland and the Empire and to turn his attention to Egypt – 'the Holland of the East' – as a more attractive goal. Napoleon would take this road, but the Sun King, continental to the core, stayed in Europe. In 1683, the year the Turks besieged Vienna, Leibniz published an exposé of Louis' designs for the conquest and dismemberment of Europe under the title *Mars Christianissimus*, which echoes Erasmus' description of Pope Julius II. Leibniz was familiar with the work of the 'third force', political thinkers and theologians in the circle of Charles V and Ferdinand I, and continued where they left off.

The political unification of Europe – which as a good European Leibniz could not conceive of without France – presupposed a religious conciliation. In his philosophical essays (all of them 'occasional pieces')[1] Leibniz is concerned to draw all essential ideas (traditional Catholic, Lutheran, Calvinist, enlightened, non-christian, 'pantheist') about the *one* reality of God and the world into his own thought. In this undertaking mathematics and an unblinkered reason became for him the measure and central point of a rational and mystical union of all elements of reality.

Leibniz conceived thought as a sympathetic exercise which took into account all the possibilities open to the opponent. He thought himself into the minds not only of Newton, Spinoza, Descartes and Bayle but also of theologians of different types, Calvinist, Roman Catholic (Spanish and Italian), German Lutheran and enlightened. Political thinking, as a preparation for action, entailed envisaging all the possibilities open to Europe. Between 1671 and 1707 Leibniz did all he could to support the political negotiations over ecclesiastical reunion taking place between Rome, Vienna, Hanover and Paris. But where Emperor Leopold I and Popes Innocent XI and Clement XI thought in terms of negotiating to restore Protestantism to the bosom of the Roman Church, Leibniz hoped for something further-reaching, an effort by Rome, Wittenberg and Geneva to reform themselves: a genuinely fruitful encounter could arise only from profound self-criticism and a renewal of each confession on its own original principles. Leibniz carried on an extensive correspondence with Landgrave Ernest von Hessen-Rheinfels (1680–93), a Catholic brought up as a Calvinist, who was sincerely anxious to see the Roman Church reformed from within and the two Europes (Catholic and Protestant) reconciled. This correspondence, and

---

[1] It is wrong to accuse Leibniz of being the creator of a system; he leaves everything 'open', his hypotheses are models, a demonstration of possibilities.

his own experiences in Hanover, made Leibniz particularly conscious of something often lost sight of, namely that the Holy Roman Empire had survived the Thirty Years' War not only in the southern and south-eastern Catholic territories but also in the Protestant north and centre.

The centre from which Leibniz conducted his political and metapolitical operations was Hanover, whose ruling house (descended from the Welfs) he served from 1676 until his death in 1716. As an expert on legal and constitutional matters, Leibniz produced opinions in support of Hanoverian claims (for example, to an electorate, to possession of Celle, and in defence of the Hanoverian succession to the English throne).

The ladies of this house did more than the males to create for Leibniz the atmosphere his spirit needed if it was not to stifle. Indeed, his first close woman friend was the Duchess (afterwards Electress) Sophia, 'the cleverest woman of her time', ancestress of the ruling houses of Prussia, England and Hanover and a daughter of the Winter King of Bohemia and Elizabeth Stuart. Sophia's sister was the Elizabeth of the Palatinate to whom Descartes dedicated his *Principia philosophica*. Her brother Karl Ludwig was a friend of Spinoza. Leibniz provided the link, too often lacking, between an enlightened Protestant and Catholic-Latin Europe. This world of feminine culture passed in the next generation from the 'Court of the Muses' at Herrenhausen near Hanover to the courts of Sophia's descendants, the Charlottenburg of her daughter Sophia Charlotte, the Monijou of Sophia Dorothea, the Brunswick-Wolfenbüttel of Philippina Charlotte, and the Weimar of Anna Amalia. Goethe's Weimar sublimated and transformed the symbiotic elements which made the Empire appear so much a 'monarchy of opposites' that some saw it as an impossible monstrosity, others as a mine of living experience.

Leibniz discerned in Austria (as Goethe would in Bohemia) the lineaments of the old Europe and the old Empire. 'When the empire began to fail, God roused up a new power in Austria.' When Leopold I died of a dropsy in 1705 Leibniz composed a Latin distich as his elegy: 'Habsburg, to thy eternal glory, Leopold, thou hast shown us how to be holy and great; continue to be both.' The voice is not merely that of a court humanist but of a man affirming an unshaken belief in the two poles of the Ottonian Empire, its 'sanctity' and its secular greatness. The Leibniz who declared, 'Leopold forced even the most sceptical and suspicious to acknowledge that he had the good of the fatherland at heart', was also spokesman for those other Protestants of northern and central Germany who even after the Thirty Years' War still recognized the emperor, Leopold I, as their Emperor.

Even so, the unique phenomenon of the house of Austria, with its seat in imperial Vienna, acting as the leading power in the Empire and as the emblem of Europe itself,[1] may well strike us as unthinkable without the contribution of one slight man who came to Vienna penniless: Prince Eugen.

---

[1] As late as the mid-eighteenth century, the figure of Maria Theresa with imperial crown, tiara and sceptre was used in the monastery church of Birnau on Lake Constance to emblemize Europe.

125 The conflict between Frederick the Elector Palatine and Emperor Ferdinand II is diagrammatically expounded in allegorical terms as the battle between the eagle and the lion, with allusions to the Bloody Assize of Prague and the battle at the White Mountain. The crown in dispute is that of Bohemia, where the Thirty Years' War, Europe's first world war, was sparked off, to be fought with the full panoply of propagandist and terrorist techniques.

126 The Bloody Assize of Prague, 21 June 1621. A deliberate exercise in political terrorism, this execution of highly placed and highly regarded noblemen produced horror and indignation throughout Europe, England included.

127 Flysheet publicizing the cruelties of the Turks. The flysheet was the most effective medium of propaganda available and was used against the Turks and as a weapon in the conflict between Protestant and Catholic Europe.

128 From *A peasant 'Our Father' against the merciless soldiery.* The peasants in general had much to suffer in their exposed and unprotected villages and hamlets from the constant depradations of a soldiery run wild.

129 A courier broadcasting news of the conclusion of the Peace of Westphalia to Vienna, Paris and Stockholm. He rides past graves and over broken weapons.

130 Ter Borch's justly famous painting *The Peace of Münster*. The Calvinist Dutch and the ultra-Catholic Spanish, the two enemies most radically opposed, are the first to shake hands and make peace. The Peace of Westphalia determined the shape of Europe down to the time of Napoleon, and in essence down to 1918. Hitler and Goebbels proclaimed their intention of giving Europe a different foundation.

131 '*French luxury Victorious over Spanish pride*'. Louis Testelin has used the favourite medieval theme of the battle between the virtues and the vices to illustrate for propaganda purposes the French struggle against fears of Spanish encirclement, France's dominant preoccupation during the Thirty Years' War.

132 Entry of the Infant Ferdinand, Archduke of Austria, into Antwerp, 1635. In renaissance and baroque Europe triumphal entries were propaganda demonstrations designed to enhance the ruler's power and strike terror into his enemies. During the Thirty Years' War Antwerp was the most unpredictable of cities.

133 The Estates pay homage to Emperor Ferdinand III, 1652. The homage of the nobility to the territorial ruler on his accession signalized his actual assumption of power. In the case of Ferdinand III it meant that in his own territories he remained victor in the Thirty Years' War; all his Catholic and Protestant subjects here submit to him.

Durchleuchtig[st] Infantin der Himmel gibt Euch /nur   Vnd Ihr bleibt. Grosser Printz Mein König für Vnd Für

134 Louis XIV with his family and his bride, Infanta Maria Theresa. Their marriage, which was to cement the Treaty of the Pyrenees between France and Spain, set the seal on the decline of Spanish power and on the new hegemony of France.

135 The good deeds of Philip IV follow his soul heavenwards; Spanish kings were convinced that the one good result of struggles for earthly crowns was to secure for themselves and their subjects, for whom they were responsible, the blessing of a crown in Heaven.

REQVIESCAT ALABORIBVS SVIS, OPERA ENIM ILLIVS SEQVNTVR ILLVM. Apoc.

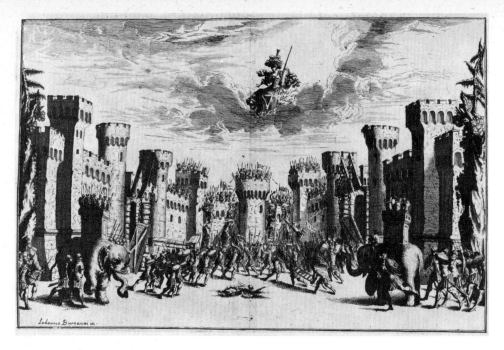

136 Design by Burnacini, the famous theatrical engineer and architect to the Viennese court, for a battle scene in the opera *Il Pomo d'Oro*. The society of the baroque imperial court liked to see their wars and quarrels glorified, tamed and reanimated in the guise of spectacle.

137, 138 Celebrations for the marriage of Leopold I; (*left*) an allegorical display showing the battle of the elements; (*right*) the equestrian ballet, with cavalry troops turned into a circus troupe. The performances of the Spanish Riding School which enraptured the American public in 1945 were a last reflection of this imperial artistry with horses.

139 Emperor Leopold I depicted on the column erected in thanksgiving for the end of the plague of 1679 in Vienna, designed by the theatrical artist Burnacini.

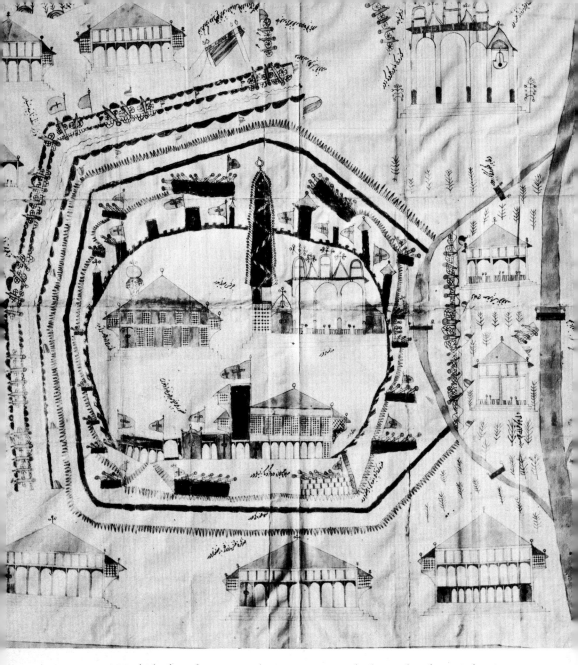

140 A Turkish plan of Vienna made in 1683, captured when Belgrade was taken in 1688.
Turkish espionage adroitly took advantage of peaceful Turkish missions which visited
Vienna before the war, as also of the French and Italian deserters who took service with the
Turks.

141 (*opposite*) Gate of Honour for Joseph I's entry into Vienna in 1690, designed by
Johann Bernhard Fischer von Erlach. Heaven and earth, the celestial state of God, Emperor
of Heaven, and all the Virtues are present at the high feasts of the emperor. In the
hands of imperial architects high baroque is in large measure an architecture of ceremony,
celebration, theatre. The triumphal columns were used by the architect again in his
design for the Karlskirche (plate 149).

142 *Sala terrena* of the Upper Belvedere, the palace of Prince Eugen, victor over the Turks. Their stone effigies and those of other 'rebels' here support the weight of the palace and with it the power of the Habsburg Empire, which owed its supremacy in the south-east to the exertions of Prince Eugen. Franz Ferdinand lived in the palace during the anxious years before the First World War, when that same power was disintegrating.

143 Permoser's *Apotheosis of Prince Eugen*, 1721. The penniless 'little *abbé*', whom Louis XIV refused to employ in his armies, rose in Vienna to be a great commander and the founder of the Habsburgs as a military power. He was friend and comrade-in-arms of the Duke of Marlborough, whose palace at Blenheim is the counterpart of the Belvedere.

144 Louis XIV as Emperor of the Romans in a festival play by Charles Perrault. The power-backed ideology here represented had a long life in France, from the Middle Ages to Napoleon (and after): the true emperor is in Paris, the true successor to 'Charlemagne' is the King of France.

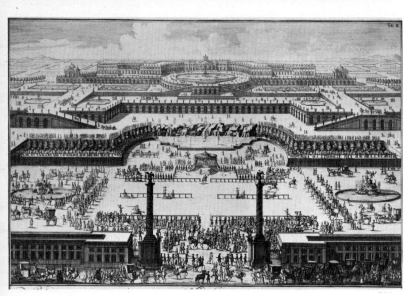

145 Illuminations for a festival at Versailles by Le Pautre. Even at night, the realm of the Sun King, Louis XIV, has to prove to the rest of Europe that it is 'Queen of the Night', the true centre of light ('enlightenment', *gloire* and political supremacy).

146 J. B. Fischer von Erlach's first design for Schönbrunn, before 1695. Schönbrunn was to be an Anti-Versailles and Super-Versailles (even before Versailles itself was finished). Vienna had not forgotten the scornful remarks about the 'poverty-stricken' Hofburg made by a prosperous Duke of Burgundy in the days of Frederick III.

147 Emperor Joseph I as victor over the Turks. Statuette by Matthias Steinle.

148 Grand portal of Kremsmünster, Upper Austria; Duke Tassilo, founder of the house
(in 777) is seen between two of its patrons, Charles the Great and Emperor Henry II.
Austrian Benedictine houses with their imperial salons and apartments inherited the
tradition of the Carolingian abbeys.

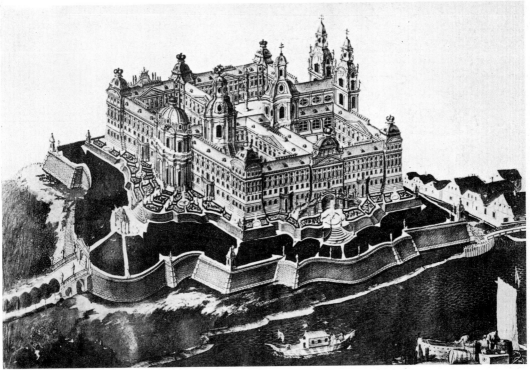

149 (*top*) Karlskirche, Vienna; see p. 237.
150 (*bottom*) Plan for the complete rebuilding of Klosterneuburg as the Austrian 'Escorial', impressive testimony to the importance of the Vienna-Madrid axis as a world-wide political force.

151 Scene from the opera *Costanza e Fortezza* presented at Prague in honour of the marriage of Charles VI in 1723. The rostrum mounted in 1621 by the victims of the Bloody Assize is now mounted by actors in an imperial spectacle.

In his own day Eugen was as much admired and fêted in the Paris of his great enemy as in the London of his great ally. He was complimented by Leibniz on his theological acumen (they were arguing whether the Jesuits in China should tolerate the Confucian religion). 'The prince can talk theology far better than I can talk war, since he was once a student and I was never a soldier.' In our own day his genius as a commander has been praised by Winston Churchill, descendant of Eugen's English comrade-in-arms, the Duke of Marlborough. In the Danube region, in the old Empire and in Austria he is honoured (above Maria Theresa) as the human embodiment of the fame and glory of the multi-national state and its benign presiding genius. His soldiers called him 'the little *abbé*' and he never felt at home in his palaces (Schlosshof, Ober-Siebenbrunn, Engelhartstetten, Promontor, Raczeve and Bellye), his two state residences in Vienna, the Winter Palace in the Himmelpfortgasse and the Belvedere (where he inhabited only the small lower building, separate from the main palace), or indeed in all the high official positions he held in Austria: he remained a remote visitor, 'a man who came from the country of the king of France' (Janko von Musulin).

Duke François Eugène of Savoy [plate 143], Prince of Piedmont, Margrave of Saluzzo, was descended on his father's side from the Carignani, a collateral branch of the reigning house of Savoy. This family had a mixed Germanic, Roman, Byzantine and even Armenian ancestry, but the French element far outweighed the rest. Just over a quarter of Eugen's paternal forebears had been related to the Capetians, the royal house of France. His more immediate antecedents on this side included Charles v, Kings Francis I and Louis XI of France, Lorenzo dei Medici and Charles the Bold of Burgundy. He was also connected with the family of St Thomas Aquinas and with the two great generals of medieval France, Bertrand du Guesclin and Olivier de Clisson. Eugen's mother was Olympia Mancini, a niece of Cardinal Mazarin. She was related to noble families in Rome and southern Italy and numbered a Borgia niece of Pope Alexander VI among her ancestresses. In Prince Eugen the European family and Mother Asia were combined. The European family was represented by the medieval imperial dynasties, the kings of France down to Francis I, the royal houses of England (Anglo-Saxon, Norman and Plantagenet), and other ruling dynasties past and present – Spanish, Portuguese, Scandinavian, Czech, Hungarian, Serbian, Bulgarian, Russian. The Asiatic element was by way of East European connections, which brought the princes and chieftains of a number of Mongolian tribes into the family tree.

Prince Eugen was born in Paris on 18 October 1663, the fifth child of the Count of Soissons, commandant of the Swiss Guards, and of Olympia Mancini, chief lady-in-waiting to the queen. The little '*abbé de Savoie*' (as Parisians called him in jest) was originally intended for the church. He was ill-favoured, had a slight hump and worst of all was poor. In 1680 his mother had to flee Paris under suspicion as a poisoner; two years later Eugen was also abandoned by his wealthy grandmother, Marie de Bourbon, because he had given up the idea of a clerical career. A friend, knowing he was eager for a commission in the army, obtained an audience for him with the Sun King. When they met, Eugen looked the king straight in the eye, an infringement of taboo, a broaching of the king's unapproachability which Louis could not tolerate. 'The request was modest, not so the petitioner. No one else ever presumed to stare me out so insolently, like a sparrow-hawk with his hackles up.' Louis' remark is typical of the man who meant to clip the wings of the self-seeking French aristocracy, to deprive them of their power and bind them to his throne. His sun brooked of no partners; the court must be filled with satellites, the government service with underlings.

The dukes of Savoy had been princes of the Holy Roman Empire. One of Eugen's brothers was already among the volunteers who flocked to the imperial banner in 1683 to defend Vienna against the arch-enemy of Christendom, the Turks. On 21 July of the same year Eugen secretly left Paris. On 8 August he was at Passau, where he offered Leopold his services. Eugen fought in the battle which delivered Vienna from the Turkish threat as a volunteer on the staff of Charles of Lorraine. It was his first taste of war. In December he was given command of the dragoon regiment previously led by his brother, who had died from battle wounds. At the age of twenty-two Prince Eugen became a major-general, at twenty-five he was field-marshal-lieutenant, two years later commander of the cavalry and at thirty field-marshal. In his seventeen campaigns fought in eight European 'theatres of war' (the baroque expression) he was nine times wounded. Eugen never spared himself. He fought the Turks in Hungary and the Balkans, the French and their allies in Italy, France and the Netherlands. In 1697 he was seconded to Augustus the Strong as his political adviser.[1] In the same year, in gratitude for the victory at Zenta, the emperor granted him a large estate between the Danube and the Drau. In 1700 Eugen commissioned Lukas von Hildebrandt, who had served under him in Italy as an officer with the engineers, to build him the Belvedere palace [plate 142]. In 1703, Prince Eugen became President of the War Council. He commanded the armies of three successive emperors, Leopold I (who died in 1705), Joseph I and Charles VI. At the battle of Turin in 1706 he defeated three French armies, entered Milan and was made governor-general of the Milanese.

One might say that on an earlier expedition to Italy (1700–01), Prince Eugen had resuscitated the obligations of vassalage owed by Italian principalities to the Empire through the financial contributions he exacted from Milan, Mantua, Parma, Piacenza, Modena, Tuscany and the rest. 'PRINCIPE EUGENIO LIBERATORE DI TORINO ASSEDIATA AN. MDCCVI CONDOTTIERE DI ESERCITI A NIUNO SECONDO ITALIA GLORIA!' So runs the inscription which still adorns Silvestro's marble statue of Prince Eugen adjacent to the town hall at Turin, a tribute to 'Prince Eugen, incomparable general and the glory of Italy'!

On 6 July 1708, Eugen and Marlborough defeated the French at Oudenaarde,

[1] In 1707 Peter the Great offered him the Polish crown, but Eugen preferred to remain in the emperor's service.

capturing Ghent and Bruges in the following winter. In his western campaigns of 1704–9, Eugen was opposed by some outstanding French generals (among them his kinsman Vendôme and Marshal Villars, who openly admired him). The unexpected death from smallpox of Emperor Joseph I in 1711 brought about the collapse of the Anglo-Austrian coalition.

Joseph's brother Charles, king-designate of Spain, lost no time in hastening to Vienna. In England it was feared that this new emperor (Charles VI) planned to become a world-ruler on the model of Charles V: he would have under his control Spain, the Netherlands, Italy and a Danube monarchy which was already penetrating deep into the Balkans. (Among his other exploits, Prince Eugen advanced as far as Sarajevo and in 1717 took Belgrade; he also had plans for marching on Constantinople, once the goal of Emperors Maximilian I and Charles V.) Marlborough fell from favour and his political opponents, now in power, were preparing to ally with Paris. It was at this threatening juncture that Prince Eugen was dispatched as a special envoy to London, where despite a jubilant reception he could do nothing to rescue the old coalition.

Serious disagreements over policy in Vienna earned Eugen the hostility of Spanish émigrés living in exile at the court of Charles VI, who urged a victorious progress back to Spain. Eugen nevertheless persuaded the emperor that it was necessary to make peace with France, and conducted the ensuing negotiations in person, Villars acting for the French. Their encounter was a courtly theatrical event on the world scale. The two leaders who had so often stood opposed on the field of battle, both of them masters in the art of war (the ceremony with which individual scenes were mounted can be seen from the extant battle-plan for Oudenaarde), now complimented one another with equal sincerity as masters of diplomacy and of *savoir vivre*. The peace of Rastatt was signed by Marshal Villars and Prince Eugen on 13 April 1714. From his Spanish inheritance the emperor received Lombardy, Naples, Belgium, a few fortified positions in south Germany and Mantua. The elector of Bavaria was reinstated in his territory, which had been occupied by the Austrians, and given an opportunity to exchange it for Belgium. Eugen had great hopes of this exchange (which came to nothing), since possession of Bavaria would have given the Danube monarchy leading importance in the Empire (and substantially altered the history of the Holy Roman Empire and the destinies of Europe in the nineteenth and twentieth centuries).

As a governor (he was variously governor-general of Lombardy, governor of Milan, of the Austrian Netherlands and Belgium and vicar-general of Italy) Eugen was regarded with great respect in the lands he administered. He said himself 'all my intentions are directed to one end only, to exercise my office in a way that wholly matches the public good . . . for in public affairs this is the road to faster progress . . . a sound government must see to it that every man receives his due.' His political economy never departed from the old domestic tradition, whether as regards the house of Habsburg, the emperor's 'houses' in Europe or the houses of the people.

'No man should be allowed to go hungry if there is no need for it.' This maxim, which he honoured on his own estates and as master of his own households, characterizes his practice of the arts of war and politics.

As a general he held it his duty to be economical in his use of men and made it his rule always to plan ahead, to foresee contingencies and never take a chance. Opting for peace was better than 'exposing oneself to an uncertain outcome', since nothing was 'more changeable than the fortunes of war'. Prince Eugen was as reluctant as any Habsburg to put his trust in the war-goddess Bellona or to Dame Fortune on her turning wheel. The extreme remedy of the great battle should be reserved for desperate situations, 'in extremis periculis extrema remedia'. Armed one must be, but more important still – as he never ceased to remind the last emperor under whom he served – was to look to one's finances. Without money, no armies, without armies, no defence for the emperor's hereditary dominions.

During the gloriously successful summers of his later life, in which he was surrounded by the brilliance of his palaces, his collections, his library, his gardens and his festivals, Prince Eugen saw threatening storm-clouds gathering over Austria. A presentiment of decline, a profound sense of coming disaster hovers over Vienna – though few perceive it – from the time of Prince Eugen and Emperor Charles VI to that of Joseph II. A totally unsentimental melancholy and the courage which looks heavy fate and death straight in the face are the true characteristics of high baroque. In the summer of 1734, prematurely old, Prince Eugen departed for the west and his last campaign. There was a young prince in the expedition whose allegiance to the imperial house Eugen wished to win. He asked this young man what made him happy (anyone able to answer this question reveals what he is). He replied, 'the same things which once made your highness happy, love and fame.' The young prince noted the conversation in the diary he kept of this campaign. He retained his admiration for Eugen, 'the secret emperor in Vienna'. When he himself was old he said, 'Who is there to set beside him?' The self-tormenting nature of his terrifying father (who signed his paintings in tormentis pinxi) early robbed the young prince of his capacity to love and be happy. It is an open secret that he was subject to despair and temptations to suicide. There remained fame, and that too tasted bitter at the last.

Exactly half a century separated the death of Prince Eugen from that of our young prince, Frederick the Great of Prussia. In the interval Frederick wounded the Danube monarchy past recovery. The death-dealing blows to the Holy Roman Empire and the imperial monarchy in Vienna were inflicted not by Napoleon but by the loss of Silesia to Frederick the Great which led to the defeat at Königgrätz in 1866.[1]

Eugen wanted to see the Empire opened up on the east and the old theatres of war in the west abandoned. His vision was probably of an Austria linked with 'those wide lands threaded by the Theiss, the Danube, the Drau and the Sava and washed by the

[1] Austria's defeat at Königgrätz and her enforced separation from the Empire was a direct consequence of the loss of Silesia, which in the Second World War still produced Germany's best troops.

Black Sea and the Aegean'. 'The lands wrested from the Turks should be settled with peasants from the heart of Europe, their heavily reduced populations being thus brought up to strength and the regions made self-sufficient through the introduction of modern methods of agriculture and manufacture.' Peace should come eventually in Europe through reconciliation with France, a goal which Prince Eugen, despite his 'private' grudge against Louis XIV, kept perpetually in view. If this proved impossible, an alliance between Austria, Prussia and Russia would at least keep the situation in Europe stable – in other words the 'League of the Three Emperors' to which men of the nineteenth century aspired.

'Gentlemen, you have but one *raison d'être*, to set a constant example, above all in the hour of greatest danger, but with so light a touch and serene a manner that none can take offence.' This demand Prince Eugen made of his officers is expressive of that Austrian 'understatement' which is better known from Hugo von Hofmannsthal's *Rosenkavalier*: 'lightness' is all, a lightness reached through being hard in secret on oneself but open and affable to others.

On 21 April 1736 Emperor Charles VI, always sparing of words, wrote in his diary: 'about eight-thirty news that Prince Eugen of Savoy, who has been in the employ of my house since '83, since '97 has achieved great exploits as commander in the field, in 1703 became president of the war council, since 1711 has been most useful to me in everything, has been found dead in his bed after a long illness. God be merciful to his soul. In his 73rd year.' Eugen's many enviers and enemies rejoiced that he was dead. Prince Liechtenstein, in a letter to the Prussian Crown Prince, had already predicted what his loss would mean in military terms. 'He was the greatest man of his century and when he dies he will probably not long be survived by an army which under his command won so many victories.'

Imperial baroque linked the people in town and country with the nobility and the clergy, secular and religious. Its influence reached out from urban palace and country residence to the peasant's furnishings in his single living-room, from the painted and stuccoed 'heaven' of the imperial salon in religious houses, from the 'sky-canopy' under which the emperor walked in procession, to the heaven of saints painted on the peasants' dwellings. This baroque made use of Spanish and Italian motifs, which it blended with features of the surrounding landscape; it can be found not only in the Habsburg hereditary dominions but also in much of the old imperial territory, not to mention Berlin, to the east far into Russia, and in the south-east in the Turkish Balkans. Imperial baroque is in the highest degree political, as is clear from its shaping of a world of feasts and ceremonies and its intense application to the representation of a reborn world-order on the grand scale. The culture of this baroque is Counter-Reformation, a manifesto of victory over Turks and 'heretics'; it is directed against the Sun King and his French rationality.

For the European public, the curtain on the great stage of this baroque, in which war and death would be figuratively enacted, went up for the first time in the Prague 'Theatrum' of 11 June 1621. The execution of the 'rebels' against the emperor and king of Bohemia took place on the open stage. In its original meaning a 'theatrum' was simply a raised rostrum. In the words of a contemporary account, 'the imperial judges were seated on the Althan near the theatrum which had been erected', and the three judges of the municipality accompanied the condemned to their execution '*auff die Bühne*', 'on the stage'. In 1652 the reigning emperor came in person to Prague. On his birthday, 13 July, a pillar to the Virgin was set up on the Altstadter Ring[1] as a victory monument (Prague had been plundered by the Swedes under Königsmarck as recently as 1648). This marks the beginning of the Counter-Reformation in Bohemia. In 1918 the Czechs took belated revenge and destroyed the monument.

The victory over the Turks made it possible for the arch-house and its aristocratic competitors to liberate the creative energies latent in the people. Despite its savagery, we cannot disguise from ourselves the ceremonial character of this 'war drama' in which Vienna, the city of the *Goldene Apfel*, and the Turkish army form an exciting and logical ensemble. Excitement and magnificence are already the keynote of Kara Mustafa's impressively martial and awe-inspiring approach to Vienna. He was 'Kara the Black' (from his dark complexion and melancholy expression) and he advanced on Vienna from Adrianople with an army so huge that it left behind for the victors' inspection pack-animals to the number of five thousand camels and ten thousand buffalo and oxen. Kara Mustafa (a great voluptuary, lord of three thousand concubines) travelled in a chariot smothered in silver down to the spokes of the wheels, a very Darius, Xerxes or Wallenstein. Wallenstein's own progresses, which had aroused the jealousy of the princes of the Catholic League, had also been spectacular set-pieces in the drama of war. Kara Mustafa was a Turkish Wallenstein, who aimed as grand vizier to win a caliphate for himself, with Vienna as its capital.

Next came the magnificent and terrifying spectacle of Vienna ringed with a sea of flames, the result of an order from Count Starhemberg, the city's defender, to set fire to the outer suburbs in the hope of depriving the Turks of cover and living quarters. Summer pavilions, summer cottages, churches, monasteries, inns and vineyards were all burned, leaving a scorched earth on which the aristocracy later built their mansions and gardens. In 1700, seventeen years after Vienna's liberation, Prince Eugen entertained six thousand guests to a masked ball in the grounds of the Belvedere, once the city's choicest vineyard. The palace itself was not yet built, so a temporary marquee was erected with ceilings and walls made from fifteen thousand ells of linen painted to simulate gardens.

During the siege Kara Mustafa kept his state in a tent pitched on a garden site in the ruined suburb of St Ulrich facing the castle. John Sobieski reported to his wife that Mustafa's tented town covered an area 'as large as Warsaw or Lemberg inside their walls'. The Turkish Wallenstein was content to leave technical matters to his excellent engineers and sappers, mostly Armenians or Italians, who had for their guidance sketches of the fortifications made as recently as the previous October

[1] Ferdinand II dubbed the Virgin his 'arch strategist'; the Virgin of el Pilar is still generalissimo of the Spanish army.

[plate 140]. He passed the time amusing himself with his women and bathing in the old Roman baths. Inside the invested city dysentery and hunger raged. At hours when the Turkish cannon were silent the womenfolk slipped over the walls to exchange fresh vegetables for bread, an offence Starhemberg made punishable by death on the gallows. The liberation only came after fifty-nine continuous days of bombardment.

The style of imperial baroque spread from Vienna and Austria into the states of Austria's Protestant allies – Sweden, Brandenburg, Holland and England – and became a European baroque. Crucial to it was the great synthesis which Johann Bernhard Fischer von Erlach (1656–1723) started to evolve about 1690 for the architecture of noble residences. Born a sculptor's son in Graz, Fischer von Erlach went to Italy at the age of fourteen. In Rome he gained admittance to the cultivated circle round 'the new Michaelangelo', Giovanni Lorenzo Bernini. A few years earlier Bernini had been invited with much ostentation to Paris, to rebuild the Louvre as a fitting symbol of the Sun King, but the French jibbed at his plans and the venture came to nothing. In 1689 (having also spent some time in Naples), Fischer was appointed court architect in Vienna, a post which carried the duty of giving daily instruction in architecture to the Crown Prince Joseph, who was also King of Hungary. In this way Fischer was drawn into the circle of 'Empire patriots' surrounding the heir to the throne, a circle which included men such as Graf Salm, Freiherr von Rummel (afterwards bishop of Vienna), Wagner von Wagenfels, the court historiographer, and Strattmann, the court chancellor. Fischer's general brief was to produce buildings whose art surpassed that of France and Italy. The idea of a 'Viennese Versailles' seems to have taken root shortly after the twelve-year-old Joseph's coronation as King of the Romans (1690); it may have originated with Leibniz, or even with Fischer himself. In 1690 Joseph already figures on a Gate of Honour as the true Sun King, Leopold-Jupiter, victor over the powers of darkness [plate 141]. Fischer's first great design for Schönbrunn [plate 146] was intended to put Versailles [plate 145], the wonder of the world, completely in the shade.

Few who look today at the great buildings of Old Europe reflect that these churches, cathedrals, castles and palaces are also symbols of the relentless struggles for power by which Europe was formed. In the high Middle Ages the French monarchy's gothic, spreading out from the Ile de France, captured a Europe whose limits were Scandinavia, Spain and Hungary. The Versailles of Louis XIV became the model, the unattainable ideal, for scores of European princes.

Versailles is 'the resting-place of Helios, the sun, who in this western garden of the Hesperides reposes from his labours'. *Quod sol in coelis id rex in terra*, 'as the sun is in the heavens, so the king is upon earth'. Versailles with its gold and silver was to vanquish and dissipate the hideous fear which lurked in the Spanish heart of Louis XIV, his fear of death, of the nobility, of Paris (during the last twenty-eight years of his life he paid only eight visits to the city and never slept there after 1666), of the masses. Louis burnt all the accounts relating to the building of Versailles: no one was to know what enormous sums it had cost.

The sun is displayed at Versailles in a thousand different ways, in pictures, symbols, cyphers, gold, silver, crystal and glass. Gold is the substance proper to the sun. There were plans for building an enormous temple of the sun, its main hall lined with mirrors, in the palace park. The king's bedchamber, like the apse in a christian church, lay toward the east as an architectural demonstration of the king's connection with the rising sun. The religious-political ceremonial which was set in motion each morning at half-past eight has no parallel outside the ancient imperial ritual of golden Peking, China's city of the sun. (Louis XIV greeted the eighteenth century with a banquet in the Chinese style.) In the liturgy of the court, the *lever* and *coucher* of the Sun King were the rising and setting of the 'light of the world'.

The saying, '*l'état, c'est moi*', is constantly ascribed to Louis XIV, but it is unlikely that he coined it himself; it does not occur even in his memoirs. Napoleon used it of himself, Bismarck said, '*Moi, je suis l'état*'. It is in any case uncharacteristic of the Sun King's political thinking (though not of the practice of his regime). Louis XIV saw himself as 'Sun': he was at all times and 'for all people' the visible centre of the divine world order as manifested upon earth. All his subjects should serve him: for them he served God.

Attention has often and rightly been drawn to the infantile traits in the religiosity which appeared in Louis as he grew older and more truculent, as also to the many repellent features of his character. But it must be acknowledged that this king, like no European before or since, styled his life in every particular as a work of high celebration. The first votary of his own cult, he executed his presentation of himself as the Sun King upon earth with such dignity and grandeur that even his harshest critics, when they met him in the flesh, were overwhelmed. We must have the courage to recognize the greatness of Versailles if we are to appreciate the greatness of the counter-design for Vienna.

Fischer von Erlach's design for Schönbrunn is a bold reconciliation of opposites such as Leibniz demanded when he spoke of space as an 'order of co-existences' and time as 'an order of successions' (in his correspondence with Clarke, opposing Newton, 1715–16). The height now occupied by the Gloriette (built to commemorate the battle of Kilin, 1756) was to be the throne of a 'Super-Versailles', the palace of the Roman Sun Emperor, whose four-horse chariot (the quadriga of Helios) should crown the central façade:

Swinging round in a powerful semicircle – a thoroughly royal motif – it binds together two wings, each on its own fit for a king's palace, and gathers the interminable breadth of the site into a huge circular lake. The view from one side is over imperial Vienna, on the other towards the Hungarian border: the man who was to inhabit this palace was also king of Hungary. The outside expanse is linked to the buildings by massive staircase structures: architecture which so completely dominates its terrain had probably not been seen in Europe since Palestrina built in Rome the Temple of Fortune, whose very ruins were Bramante's inspiration for the courts of the Vatican; not even the terraces of St Germain, the 'hanging gardens' so much admired by Wren, can compare with this (Hans Sedlmayr).

Fischer blends French, Italian and Roman motifs with his own inventions to project an imperial style which became exemplary for non-French Europe. 'The whole of Germany now began to look to Vienna, to which the great patrons sent their architects, including some of the most important of the younger masters; but whoever they might be – Pöppelmann, Welsch, Neumann – all were directly or indirectly influenced by ideas which had first come to Fischer.' From Austria the building wave spread to Bohemia and Silesia, Saxony and Poland, Franconia and the Rhine. It reached deep into Hungary, had outrunners in Savoy, swept over Berlin and washed as far as Stockholm.

This extension of imperial baroque was in part due to a younger architect, Johann Lukas von Hildebrandt, and his patrons. Prince Eugen provided him with building sites to the east and south-east, as well as in Vienna itself, while Schönborn, imperial vice-chancellor and afterwards bishop of Würzburg, through his family and political connections opened up the west for him. Hildebrandt built for Schönborn in Vienna and at Schönborn near Göllersdorf and was given the decisive voice in planning the residency at Würzburg. Hildebrandt also worked for many years for members of the Harrach family, in Vienna, at Bruck on the Leitha, at Aschach on the Danube, in Salzburg and in Linz. In 1700, having been introduced to imperial Vienna by Prince Eugen, Hildebrandt was appointed architect to the imperial court. Eugen had probably first come to know him during his campaigns in Piedmont, when he secured for him an appointment as field engineer with the imperial army. Born in Genoa, Hildebrandt received his training in military and civil architecture at Rome under Fontana and Cerutti, the papal officials who directed the works which changed the course of the Tiber. Fontana dedicated a treatise on architecture to King Joseph I and was proud to call himself imperial architect, Cerutti provided the Austrian army with plans for defence works in Hungary. The art of building for military and defensive purposes, which demanded thinking in terms of broad uncluttered spaces, was Hildebrandt's own point of departure as an architect.

One associates words such as 'fortress', 'wall', 'closed city' with constriction, anxiety and confinement. In Hildebrandt's baroque the 'drama of war' and manœuvre also fit into a space – the most unrestricted and uncluttered setting which could be achieved. The Belvedere palace Hildebrandt built for Prince Eugen (Blenheim, the mansion built by the English nation for the Duke of Marlborough is in a sense its counterpart) symbolizes through its sovereign mastery of the uncluttered terrain the liberation of the country from the Turks (the fortress *creates* uncluttered space!). But beside the fortress we now have the mansion which stands 'open' to the world, surrounded by its gardens and its landscape. The architectural weight of walls and roof are played down, giving one the illusion that the spatial volume of the body of the mansion (which can easily be overlooked) is a floating immateriality, lifted above its material limiting planes.

Conscious deployment of uncluttered space is equally a feature of baroque monastic rebuilding, as at the old Benedictine foundations of St Florian, Göttweig and Melk, where the space is sublimely caught and opened up through the combination of building, mountain, river and open country. The baroque revival of these monasteries is remarkable as an attempt at restoring the old Carolingian-Ottonian union between the Empire and the Kingdom of God (Leibniz comments on it approvingly in his *Braunschweiger Reichsannalen*). In that bygone era houses such as Reichenau and St Gall had given economic and military stability to the Empire and acted as lavish hosts to Carolingian rulers, whom they entertained with shows and banquets. They had been places of education for the aristocracy and workshops for the arts, combining a 'classical education' of an 'authoritarian humanist' type (Walter Rüegg) with learning and 'clerical culture'. The baroque houses of Austria aspired to this selfsame harmony (it is instructive that the historical schools of Melk and Kremsmünster took such a passionate interest in this period of their past [plate 148]). Church, cloister, 'imperial salon', library, art collections, 'cabinet of natural objects' formed an indivisible whole. The great staircases found in these houses are often an unfurled escutcheon proclaiming this last western communion between the separated spheres: at Göttweig, for example, the emperor, enthroned in the heavens as the Sun God, is surrounded by allegorical figures of the arts and sciences. These are both monasteries and imperial palaces, the cloister is a mansion. The different spheres – imperial and sacred, religious and political, scientific and artistic – intersect. Melk merges into its cliffs, Göttweig into its mountain – dazzling monstrances built into the rock of the victorious Empire (the Empire conceived as an imperial church!)

This *unio mystica et terrena* is especially obvious (and questionable) in the case of Klosterneuburg [plate 150]. Once the site of a Babenberg palace, Charles VI chose it as the place for an Austrian Escorial, a visible expression of his grief over the lost Spanish realm he had hoped to rule as Charles VII. His architect, Daniel Gran, approached his task somewhat differently, bringing to it an understanding of the Holy Roman Empire in its very Austrian continuation. In a letter to the senior members of the community he expounds his plan for the ceiling frescoes in the imperial salon' . . . the glory and majesty of the house of Austria, stemming from the Babenbergs, is heightened by the Habsburgs and prolonged in the Lotharingians. Here you have the best possible opportunity to allow 'Austrian piety' to play its part in your foundation.' In the original plan for Klosterneuburg this 'Austrian piety' – the religious-political piety and statecraft of imperial baroque – achieves a complete fusion between the emperor's precinct, the church and the cloister, and reintroduces the Carolingian-Ottonian eastwork and westwork, the twin romanesque poles of God's citadel and emperor's cathedral. The place of honour on the central pavilion is given to the gigantic stone imperial crown; the pavilion on the left is surmounted by the Austrian archducal hat, the right pavilion (never completed) was to receive the crown of Spain. Above the impressive staircase well soars the imperial eagle. The palaces of celestial and terrestrial emperor bear crowns of stone.

On the central fresco of Gran's National Library Charles VI is enthroned as cosmocrator, as ruler in heaven and upon earth, as Roman emperor, Hercules, lord of war and peace. About him weave in hymnic dance the choir of the virtues, the arts and sciences (as the 'school of Athens', in symbolic glorification of Vienna as the centre of 'world culture') and his historical exemplars. This is art drunk with victory. On the periphery of this sphere of light the 'vices' – Turks and Protestant preachers – are seen eddying in wild disorder down into the depths. Hovering near the imperial throne are the insignia of the Greek Empire (the goal of Maximilian I, Charles V, perhaps also of Prince Eugen). The Habsburg double eagle merges into the double eagle of Byzantium, into the Roman eagle, the eagle of the Old Empire, which here keeps watch over his church, as Dante saw him in Paradise.

The Karlskirche [plate 149] in Vienna was intended as the culmination of this imperial and cosmic style. Leibniz and Heraeus corresponded over the façade, Fischer von Erlach wrestled in his designs with the enormous demands made by this programmatic work. Its essence, he decided, should be summed up in a portico having the same function as the narthex of Hagia Sophia at Constantinople and of St Peter's at Rome. 'Vienna', says Heraeus, 'is called New Rome with a right equal to that once enjoyed by Constantinople, and the Karlskirche, like Hagia Sophia, is an imperial church.' Contemporaries such as Holler noticed the parallel and compared the two churches. Furthermore Holler discerned in the two colossal pillars erected in front of the church the columns of Trajan, 'with the assent of the gods' transported 'to our Vienna'. Casting about for an exemplar for the church's temple-like façade, he found one in the temple of Jupiter and Peace at Rome.

Heraeus, who drew up the symbolical programme for the church, intended it to embody Charles VI's political-religious programme down to the last detail. The two pillars already referred to contain references to Solomon, Constantinople, Rome, Charles the Great and Charles VI. As pillars of Charles V, they symbolize the Pillars of Hercules, the starting point of Spain's world empire. Emperor Charles VI makes this illustrious symbol his own, 'not only because he bears the same name, comes of the same dynasty, shares the same glory and brings back the Spanish crown' but also 'because in his eminent person he has conquered by his arms half the world surrounding this region (the Pillars of Hercules).' The symbolism of these pillars, decorated with crowns and imperial eagles, promoted Charles VI as the 'Spanish Hercules' and asserted his claim to the Spanish crown. In 1716 Leibniz suggested that the imagery on one of the pillars should relate to Charles the Great and on the other to the 'sainted' Charles of Flanders, 'the one as the emperor's forerunner in the Empire, the other as his predecessor in one part of his hereditary dominions'. The Empire, the Belgian Netherlands and Spain: the imperial programme of Charles VI is presented to the world as the Empire of Charles V. In the execution, however, the political aspect of the programme took second place to the religious: Heraeus reports in 1712 that for reasons of modesty the emperor would not allow himself to be shown receiving the *laudes*, the acts of ritual homage, and that they will be seen being offered instead to his baptismal saint, Charles Borromaeo.

Men had hailed Charles the Great as the new Solomon. In his preface to Fischer's

Historische Architektur, Heraeus gives a fulsome account of Charles VI as 'Solomon's surpasser'. The device Charles chose for himself, *constantia et fortitudo*, takes us back to the two 'colossal pillars' before the temple of Solomon at Jerusalem, Jachin and Boas ('it holds fast' and 'in it is strength'). Hagia Sophia was conceived as a 'New Temple of Solomon'. The Karlskirche, as a neo-Roman cosmic work of art, was intended to incorporate both St Peter's and the Templum Jovis et Pacis, just as its pillars 'were' the columns of Trajan and Marcus Aurelius.

This church of Emperor Charles VI was intended to represent the imperial edifices and orders of Old Europe, all its Holy Empires. When Charles VI died Europe observed with interest that his empire and realms appeared to be on the verge of total dissolution. The modern visitor to the Karlskirche may feel that Sedlmayr's comment on Klosterneuburg is just as applicable there: 'for all its richness, in contrast with the great works of the best period it smacks of cold calculation, hell and death'.

We may recall that Camus was repelled by the eclecticism of imperial and royal baroque as he experienced it in Prague and Vienna. Does not this baroque signify a presumption just as overweening and literally 'impossible' as that of Leibniz when he framed his thought with a synoptic view which took in the millennia of world history (this in a sense was Teilhard de Chardin's point of departure, but he thought in terms of millions)? In our modern world, rational, scientific, dominated by the coldly calculated political and economic interests of nation states, in a world where one position stands against another, would anyone still venture on a terrestrial-celestial symphony of this kind? The buildings and showpieces of this *Kaiserstil* and *Reichsstil* (like *Kaiser* and *Reich*, the terms are not simply interchangeable), are they or are they not the phantasmagoria, images, edifices and forms of madness, works of an imagination grown monstrously disproportioned?

The political, artistic and religious imagination whose energies had sustained the Old Europe was indeed entering on that great crisis which Goethe consciously experienced, the crisis which is still developing in our own day, when we face the 'crisis of the novel' and of our whole world of images. At the back of it, in the last analysis, lies the collapse of the old 'houses' which had stood firm for fifteen hundred years, the collapse of the old holy empires.

Fischer von Erlach was one who became aware of this painful truth. During the War of the Spanish Succession there was a building pause in Austria and the great architect had to seek commissions elsewhere. In the course of his travels his artistic convictions received a severe shock. The west rejected him, rejected imperial baroque. In Wittelsbach Bavaria the old political animosity had started to spill over into its architecture. The Prussian court under Frederick I, which Fischer visited in 1704 armed with a letter of introduction from Emperor Leopold I, refused to be converted. His visit to England probably fell in this same year, 1704, the year of Blenheim and a high point in the Austrian-English alliance. But now that he saw things through the eyes of the west, Fischer realized that for all their magic and sublimity his designs were unsuited to a cold northern climate. His flat roofs must be made sloping, his great apertures glazed in, his airy roof structures enclosed. His palaces thus become colder and more 'substantial'. Fischer turned his back on the great Utopia and sent his son, Joseph Emanuel, to school not in baroque Italy but in Utrecht, London and Paris. He wanted his son to be educated in the solid technical and mathematical disciplines and not, as he himself had been, as a universal artist.

'No performance because of the plague': so ran a notice posted outside a theatre in Vienna during the plague year 1679. Just as Silesian baroque emerged from the death throes of the Thirty Years' War, so did the Viennese world of imperial ceremonies and folk festivals revive under the threat of imminent death (from the Thirty Years' War, and later in 1679 from the plague, in 1683 from the Turks).

In February 1659 (ten years after the end of the Thirty Years' War) the most famous of the Viennese Jesuits' *Ludi Caesarei*, plays performed in the presence of the emperor, was played before Leopold I. *Pietas victrix sive Flavius Constantius Magnus de Maxentio Tyranno Victor* ('Piety Triumphant, or Flavius Constantine the Great, Victor over the Tyrant Maxentius') was the work of Nicolas Avancini, who taught rhetoric, philosophy and theology at the university, and relates the triumph of Leopold's illustrious 'ancestor' and pious exemplar over his internal and external foes. The victory of Constantine's army prefigures the present emperor's triumphs. Spectacular battle-scenes of this kind were great favourites with the public.

The text of *Pietas Victrix* includes stage directions for the lighting and acoustic effects (comets, lightning, 'infernal noises') and mechanical horrors (flying dragons, devils on serpentine chariots) used in performance. The influence of opera is both visible and audible. It was not uncommon for operas to have up to fifty scene changes. Figures flew through the air, boats moved on water, camels, elephants, bears, horse-men, cannons, even entire armies, made their appearance. Theatrical hunting and war scenes reflected those in the real 'theatre of war'. Opera came to Vienna from Italy, where it first appeared in the form of the sung play. The first operatic performance north of the Alps seems to have taken place in 1618 in Salzburg when *Il Perseo* was given in honour of Archduke Leopold of Austria; the opera was repeated there the following year, this time for Archduke Ferdinand, who was on his way to imperial coronation in Frankfurt. And it was for Ferdinand that the first operatic performance was given in Vienna, to celebrate his birthday in 1635.

Viennese music is found enjoying imperial patronage well before the line of emperor-composers starts with Ferdinand III. Maximilian I founded a *Hofkapelle*, whose members were required to 'warble in the Brabant fashion'. As time went on this Netherlandish style was superseded first by an Italian (1616–1715) and then by an Austrian vogue. Emperor Ferdinand III wrote a '*Drama musicum*' (1649), a play on the theme of earthly and heavenly love, and also composed masses, motets and hymns. The baroque emperors composed, played and conducted. Maria Theresa, who appeared in operas while she was a young archduchess, on one occasion was tempted to do so after she had come to the throne, but was dissuaded by the consideration that 'it would be contrary to decorum for a reigning queen to want to show herself *en spectacle'* (Khevenhüller). Imperial decorum did in fact require that the imperial-royal majesty and splendour be put on show, and for this the most appropriate vehicles were the operas and equestrian ballets given under imperial auspices. The grandest and most lavish of such spectacles were probably those mounted for the wedding of Leopold I and the Infanta Margareta. First there was an open-air pageant depicting the strife of the elements, a cosmic war [plate 137]. Duke Charles of Lorraine led the 'squadrons' of the air, Montecuccoli (who like Charles held a command in the imperial army) those of fire, Pfalzgraf von Sulzbach those of water. Earth – in green and silver, a pleasure garden with a rose-crowned Flora – was in the care of Prince Dietrichstein. Each element was accompanied by forty knights who led the way to the scene of action. A giant ship brought on the Argonauts and the Golden Fleece. A temple of eternity floated down from the clouds to disclose portraits of fifteen emperors from the house of Austria, the young empress in their midst. Then on came the sixteenth, Leopold himself, drawn on the chariot of glory and standing upright in a silver shell, to pay homage to his young wife. The equestrian ballet [plate 138] was given as a prelude to the opera. The piece chosen was the *Pomo d'Oro* [plate 136], whose punning title recalls the *Goldene Apfel* on the Stephansdom which the Turks so greatly coveted. The apple which figured in the opera was the Apple of Discord, which gave an excuse for bringing heaven and hell onto the stage.

The performance was written and talked about for years.

Half Olympus sat enthroned on a cloud, Neptune's sea horses stamped their way through the foaming main, churches split open at the impact of an earthquake. Dragons spitting fire flew down from the sky, the earth yawned to disgorge Charon the ferryman from the burning realm of Pluto and send him across the fiery flood.

Today the sea horses of Neptune stand in the park at Schönbrunn – fossilized mementoes of festive ebullience. One is struck, however, by the many representations of destruction and annihilation in the *Pomo d'Oro*, admittedly though they are fully in keeping with the dark side of the period and of baroque itself: burning churches, earthquakes, death and decay, the infernal powers, all take their place on the baroque stage alongside the triumphant will to live. Men were employed in their thousands on this production – which has all the stature of an act of state – and a hundred thousand guldens swallowed up. On three days a week the performances were thrown open to the public and the people made joint participants in this celebration of the Empire so newly arisen from the Thirty Years' War.

And so it continued. Under Joseph I the tradition of celebration was carried further until every important political and domestic happening was crowned with its musical festivity. Charles VI, himself a composer and a performer on the violin and harpsichord, increased the complement of the *Hofkapelle*. Viennese baroque opera, under the direction of Johann Joseph Fux, was now in its heyday, and Lady Mary Wortley Montagu, in a letter to Pope, has left for us a description of the opera *Angelica vincitrice di Alcina* performed in the open to celebrate the birth of the long-awaited heir to the throne in 1716, an event made doubly joyous by news of the defeat of the Turks at Peterwardein.

In 1723 the greatest musical event in Europe took place at Prague, the occasion being the coronation of Charles VI and his consort with the crown of Bohemia. Galli–Bibiena, 'master builder and perspective painter to the emperor', constructed a magnificent setting for the chosen opera, *Constanza e fortezza*, by Johann Joseph Fux [plate 151]. *Constanza e fortezza*, the emperor's motto, would find its stone embodiment in the Karlskirche; Fux here embodies it in music. Over a hundred singers and two hundred of the best instrumentalists in Europe were engaged for the event, which like the *Pomo d'Oro* was an act of state. The performance lasted from eight in the evening to one in the morning. The leading Prussian court musician, Johann Joachim Quantz, was so eager to attend that he enrolled himself in the *Hofkapelle* for the occasion. He reported to Potsdam, 'History has no more dazzling page of music than this festival.' The amphitheatre in the castle garden at Prague, which could hold about four thousand people, was crammed with an audience drawn from the nobility, the princes of the Empire, and members of high society and the musical world from Berlin, England, France and Vienna.

In 1741 Prague again witnessed a coronation, that of Charles Albert of Bavaria as king of Bohemia. On 30 May 1756 – Whitsunday, the high feast day of Christendom – began the eight-day long heavy bombardment of the city by Frederick the Great. Exploding churches and kingdoms, once a holiday spectacle, part of the emperor's games, after the death of Charles VI became everyday political realities. The conflicts in the Empire and the hereditary dominions made Maria Theresa and the counsellors she inherited from her father aware that an abyss was opening at their feet. *Finis Austriae*, the extinction of Old Europe – in 1918 and again in 1938 what had been prefigured in the festive entertainments of baroque became terrifying reality.

Baroque entertainments were expensive. Then as now (as the Republic of Austria, which tries to keep up the imperial musical tradition, knows to its cost), high fees were paid to Italian prima donnas: when Bordoni received 12,500 guldens for a couple of guest performances her rival Cuzzoni promptly demanded double. But the state coffers were empty. Charles VI had no money for his troops, which since Prince Eugen's day had gone to rack and ruin, and for a long while past he had had no money for necessary improvements in the administration. Hosts of beggars converged on Vienna, drawn there by the emperor's charity (beggars are especially common in Catholic countries because of their many religious houses and foundations). The puritans of the west were damming up both sympathy and poverty. In a rational, puritanical, well-regulated society there was no place for poverty: one put the poor into the army, the workhouse, the penitentiary, the factory. Leopold thought of beggars as his brothers – 'forgive me, brother', says the Spaniard to a beggar if he happens to have no change. So to the beggars he dispensed alms, and to the great lords and all who 'served' him rich presents. This was his imperial 'munificence', an attribute in which the monarch's obligation *'milte'* to 'reward' his comrades-in-arms with lavish gifts has become merged with specifically Spanish, baroque and Catholic traits.

The emperor never had any money and the credit of the state rested on the shoulders of Samuel Oppenheimer. The nobility enjoyed every kind of privilege. All the more lucrative taxes – customs, dues, tolls, etc. – had long since been farmed out to noblemen and officials. The emperors were convinced (and none more firmly than Charles vi), that it was wrong to 'deprive' such eminent people, even those who were clearly fit for nothing or still worse were shamelessly enriching themselves at the expense of the emperor and the state.

When Maria Theresa came to the throne the cabinets of other European states, competent in the handling of affairs and ready for war, were counting on the collapse of the Empire and of Habsburg rule. The state was almost bankrupt, in the fullest sense of the word: it had neither money, nor an army it could put into the field, and was saddled with an out-of-date 'civil service' composed largely of noblemen. This steep decline, following so closely on an epoch of the greatest brilliance, raises questions concerning the historical significance of the colossal 'extravagances' of the baroque emperors. How was it possible to indulge in celebrations which were enough to devour the resources of any state (even if the money came from the emperor's privy purse)? Why was corruption tolerated? What function was this celebration-culture of imperial baroque and all its attendant phenomena required to fulfil? Our present world is a product of the puritanical Protestant west (and in Catholic countries of its Jansenist counterpart); it is rational, bureaucratic, impersonal-objective. Ours is a technical civilization, from which Eros and Ludus are absent. Jan Huizinga was probably the first to chart fully the recession of the play element during the nineteenth century. It is of the essence of archaic, courtly, knightly, personal-subjective societies that play, feasting, celebration, war, cultus and art all hang together. 'There played the Franks', says the *Ludwigslied*, singing the victory of the Franks over the Normans in 881. Prince Eugen and his opponents in the European theatre of war were still 'playing out' – with great intelligence – the war-leadership ritual. 'Play is conflict and conflict is play.' The life of the Homeric heroes, the courtly life of the Middle Ages, the baroque way of life; all this was 'play', festival, celebration. Statecraft, the cabinet politics of the eighteenth century, was play raised to a fine art. Religious ritual is full of play. Baroque churches, paintings, statues, processions, theatrical performances, celebrations of the mass and other religious observances are play-festival-celebration all in one, play in honour of the God who plays, whom Plato and the Greeks had already discerned as *logos pais*.

Like all proper games, the game of courtly life is played in grim earnest. The Japanese knight who informed another of his father's death told him, 'your father has played death'. In this 'game of dying', Emperors Maximilian i, Charles v, Ferdinand i, Ferdinand ii, Leopold i and Charles vi proved themselves champions.

Admittedly, the industrial, engineering, technological and mechanical arts had their place in this celebration-world of courtly baroque (as in imperial China down to

1911), but their purpose was to give form to the festivities, to make life more artistic. Their application to the illiberal arts – connected with making money – was a secondary, less important matter. The high game of *ratio* (as in the games of late scholasticism and baroque theology and science) was put to wholly a-rational, pre-rational uses: man should live on the grand scale, artistically; man is created to re-present (still a favourite expression with Leibniz) the Godhead, beauty, the 'Great Order'; he is not created for the 'lowlier works', which make him unfree.

Presentation of life and of life as art – and of the 'Great Order' in Heaven and upon earth – is the reason for every 'putting on of state' and every representation staged by the festival-culture of imperial baroque. The festival-plays which bring before us Semiramis, Achilles, Trajan, Titus, Deborah, David, Spartacus, Sesostris, Romulus (names that figure in the emperors' theatrical programme between the years 1622 and 1740), that is to say, kings, heroes, saints and heroines from every period, all have the 'same' meaning, summed up in the play performed in Vienna on 4 November 1707 to honour the name-day of King Charles III of Spain, *La Conquista delle Spagne di Scipione Africano il Giovane*. In this play Scipio the Younger conquers Spain for the Romano-Latin world. The Empire is the true Rome. Present within the Empire is the whole of sacred antiquity, all that is good in human tradition, and it lives again in this lofty festival play.

Imperial baroque, both as the style of the Emperor and the style of the Empire, tries to overcome death by magnifying it and raising it to death in glory. 'Setting and not-departing is the peculiar power of the *Sun*/and through his power as creator/Man dies to rise again.' These are the words of an Austrian baroque poet, Abele von Lilienberg. The Spaniards who accompanied their king to Vienna, where he became Emperor Charles VI, brought with them their Spanish black, the colour of dignified death. In the eighteenth century the imperial city was thus once again subjected to Spanish influences, with fateful consequences. Spanish melancholy, and not the long overdue rationalism, became preponderant.

Outsiders (and with him this meant anyone outside his immediate family) saw Charles VI as 'the personification of an inaccessible and impersonal majesty'. The burden of responsibility started to weigh on him early, and in later years, after the death in infancy of his only male heir (1716), well-nigh crushed him.

At the age of eighteen Charles' father had sent him to Spain to win the crown of Charles V. He might have become a melancholic like Emperor Rudolf II had not his mother found him an excellent wife in Elizabeth Christine of Brunswick. Fourteen years old at the time, this doughty young woman allowed herself to be converted to Catholicism only when Protestant theologians persuaded her that 'divine Providence' had elected her for the Spanish crown. In his diary the king notes in his usual terse style 'Queen very beautiful, am thoroughly content'. 'Queen at night very loving'. In 1711, when the sudden death of his brother Emperor Joseph I forced him to return to Vienna, Charles left his young wife behind to govern Spain, which was now racked by civil war. Spain made her very unhappy, so much so that she longed to

S

take wings and fly away. She pins her hopes on the flying ship she hears has been invented in Lisbon and when it is available hopes to be able to visit her mother in Germany once a week. In 1713 the Queen was at long last released from Spain and entered Vienna as empress.

In Europe at large Emperor Charles VI (1711–40) was chiefly concerned to persuade the other powers to recognize his Pragmatic Sanction of 1713. The purpose of this fundamental law of the Danube monarchy was to foil the expectations of the many people who hoped that the disintegration of the Habsburg complex of dominions was imminent. The Pragmatic Sanction, a family treaty regulating the rights of succession, was concluded in 1703; having gone through the necessary formalities, in 1713 it became law by royal decree. The Habsburg possessions are declared indivisible and must descend by primogeniture, first to the direct male heirs of the reigning emperor (by 1713 Charles VI) and if they fail to his daughters. The provincial diets adopted the Pragmatic Sanction in 1712 and in 1722, the Hungarian diet following suit in 1723. The Pragmatic Sanction created the state of Austria, which Charles VI probably envisaged as the centre of a revived Holy Roman Empire within new borders. The emperor was particularly assiduous in wooing England, even to the extent of sacrificing his Ostend Trading Company which via Belgium was intended to represent the economic interests of the continental monarchy on the high seas. In 1718, thanks to the peace of Passarowitz secured by Prince Eugen, the Habsburg monarchy extended over a wider area than at any other time in its history: the Banat with Temesvar, parts of Wallachia, northern Serbia and Bosnia were all conceded by the Turks. But then came more wars in Spain and with France (not least over the Polish succession), and a last unfortunate war against Turkey (1737–9) during which Belgrade was lost. The growing weakness of the state could not be disguised.

King Frederick William I of Prussia was persuaded to recognize the Sanction (under the treaties of Wüsterhausen [1726] and Berlin [1728]) in return for some of the concessions the emperor so willingly offered. The father of Frederick the Great was not wholly lacking in patriotic feelings for the Empire. His son, who in any case hated his father, regarded such sentiment as a useless if not dangerous form of madness. The Pragmatic Sanction was eventually guaranteed by England, France, Russia, Spain and the Diet of Regensburg. Only Bavaria held aloof and was manifestly seen to be waiting for her chance. 'It was on this basis of international law that the hopes of Maria Theresa rested.'

Leibniz' great open and secret concern was lest the 'great order' of old Europe should prove an inadequate bridge over a chaos which the moulds of polity, art and theology might only temporarily contain. Prince Eugen's great anxiety was that the Habsburg state, because it was a work of art, might disintegrate. As preventive measures he recommended armed readiness, the recruitment of a disciplined army and an economic purge. But these were matters which Charles VI, for all his promises 'to look into them' as necessities of state, found highly uncongenial.

After a lifetime of almost uninterrupted good health, Charles VI was suddenly taken ill while on a hunting holiday at the Hungarian castle of Halbthurm. It is said that he was poisoned, either by intent or accident, by a dish of mushrooms, the famous '*plat de champignon*', which Voltaire maintained altered the history of Europe. The dying man was removed to the Favorita palace, just outside the gates of Vienna and there took leave of his family. His sense of imperial decorum did not desert him. He remarked that only two candles were burning for the extreme unction: as an emperor he should have had four . . . He consoled the weeping Charles of Lorraine: 'Do cheer up – though it is true that in me you are losing a faithful friend.' He died on 20 October 1740, between one and two in the morning. In the male line the house of Habsburg was extinct.

12

MARIA THERESA AND JOSEPH II

AN ENGLISH historian has remarked that Charles VI moved heaven and earth to secure his daughter's succession to the Habsburg hereditary possessions but did everything most calculated to make her unfit to rule them. She was not brought up as heir to the throne and was excluded from all affairs of state. One reason was that the emperor long thought he would be succeeded by a son or at least a grandson. But we should also appreciate that to an emperor of the Roman Empire, especially one brought up in the Spanish tradition, the thought of a woman as emperor and ruler of the Habsburg possessions must have seemed repugnant. Could a woman wear the imperial crown? Could a woman be *christus domini*, the Lord's Anointed, the vicar of Christ the King? Maria Theresa steadfastly refused imperial coronation, never more firmly than when she was at the height of her power. Emperorship was for males.

The woman who came so unprepared to the task of government inherited a situation of great confusion. During the last years of Charles VI the revenues of the state had fallen catastrophically. Prosperous provinces had been lost in unsuccessful wars. The army was underpaid and ill-commanded and seemed demoralized. She found her ministers, higher civil servants and a large part of the nobility in a mood of profound depression.

Maria Theresa (1740–80) was twenty-three when she came to the throne. Only a few hours after the death of Charles VI she was standing beneath the throne canopy to receive her ministers. In an informal speech she thanked them for their services to her father and confirmed them in office. On the following day, with her husband Francis Stephen, Grand Duke of Tuscany, at her side, she presided over the 'secret meeting', the Council of Ministers. The youngest of them was nearly seventy, the eldest, Count Starhemberg, whose brother had defended Vienna against the Turks over half a century before, was nearly eighty. These were survivors from the Leopoldine epoch. The secretary of state, Freiherr von Bartenstein, at least belonged to her father's generation. The general expectation, which he himself shared, was that he would be dismissed. He was a bourgeois upstart, the son of a philosophy teacher in Strassburg; still worse, he had been less than polite to Maria Theresa's husband, the Grand Duke of Tuscany. He was nevertheless confirmed in his office. 'Let him continue to do only what is good,' said Maria Theresa, 'and I will soon stop him from doing what is ill.' For the next fifteen years the prickly Bartenstein, precise and pedantic to a fault, was Maria Theresa's most influential adviser.

It may be wondered what Maria Theresa's troubles with her Habsburg possessions have to do with the Holy Roman Empire and with Europe at large.

From the beginning of the eighteenth century Austria, Prussia, Saxony and Hanover were developing as states whose centres of gravity lay outside the Empire. Austria's main interests were in south-eastern Europe, those of Brandenburg-Prussia in the north-east, Saxony's in Poland and Hanover's in England. Bavaria was waiting for a chance to resume, with French backing, the old 'office' of anti-emperor. Frederick the Great of Prussia was opposed to the idea of a Protestant emperor. At the diet in Regensburg, however, Prussian policies in the Empire and towards the Habsburg show Frederick increasingly in the role of an anti-emperor (which his father, Frederick William I, would never have contemplated playing).

The personal qualifications and qualities Maria Theresa brought to her inheritance included a fair knowledge of languages (Latin, because the public business of Hungary was conducted in that language, French, some Italian and a Viennese German not at all like the language of Lessing), a stout heart, indestructible vitality, which broke down only on the death of her husband, and a powerful urge towards self-assertion. At her side she had a husband to whom she was passionately devoted, Francis Stephen, Duke of Lorraine, who from the age of fourteen had been educated at the Viennese court. He was her 'Most Serene Duke, much beloved bridegroom', she was 'Your Dilection's most faithful bride Maria Theresa'. She wrote endearments to him in French and Italian: 'Aimez moi un peu', 'Adieu, Mausl; je vous embrasse de tout mon cœur', 'adio caro viso'. On 21 November 1740 she appointed him co-regent and in her early days even took his advice. He was a very able man and tried to set the state's finances in order by instituting a rigorous economy programme, so far as such a thing was possible at that period. For the rest of his life, however, he bowed to the sovereign will of his wife, whose passionate determination to be master was first awakened by her Hungarian coronation. Obsessed by it, she pushed first her husband and then her son into the background, creating a domestic drama which became what was virtually a European tragedy.

On 13 March 1741, shortly after the death of her third daughter, the Queen of Hungary and Bohemia and Archduchess of Austria (titles she assumed immediately on her father's death) gave birth to her first son, Joseph. 'I wish I were already in the sixth month of a new pregnancy,' she said when they laid the baby boy in her arms. The people of Vienna greeted the birth of the heir with jubilation and a painted contemporary horoscope predicts that the eagle of the 'Teutche Reich' will stay in the 'Haus von Österreich'.

Meanwhile, storm clouds had been gathering over Europe. In Bourbon Paris, Marshal Belle-Isle, who thought this was the moment to inflict a 'final' defeat on the house of Austria (the eternal dream of the military), was in the ascendant. From Madrid, the other Bourbon court, Elizabeth Farnese, the second wife of Philip V, was seeking an Italian dukedom for her second son, having already secured Naples and Sicily for his elder brother. In June 1741 the Spanish ambassador quitted Vienna. On 6 December 1740 Frederick of Prussia wrote in amiable terms to Maria Theresa and her husband. He then departed in secret to join his troops bound for Silesia, which he invaded without declaration of war on 16 December 1740. It was the signal for France, Bavaria and Spain to fall on the greatest – and to all appearance rudderless – prize in Europe, the hereditary possessions of Maria Theresa.

Frederick's veteran generals had implored him not to use his army to commit a breach of the peace, the aged Dessauer even going so far as to describe the king's plan as 'political profligacy'. (There were moments in the careers of Bismarck and Hitler when they were similarly opposed by conservative Prussians of noble antecedents.) Frederick's invasion of Silesia set off a chain reaction which led to both World Wars and ultimately to the dismemberment of Frederick's own territories, some of which passed under Russian or Polish rule.

'I am just off to Prussia,' writes Frederick to Voltaire, 'to receive homage without benefit of the flask of holy oil and those other useless and empty ceremonies intro-duced by ignorance.' He refused coronation at Königsberg, contenting himself with the homage due on accession. In terms of the old European world order one might say that the present metamorphosis of Königsberg, the capital city of the Prussian kings, into Kaliningrad is its third desacralization. Its first – a dissolution of the old sacral-political order – occurred when the Grand Master of the Teutonic Knights (a religious order of chivalry bound by its foundation and function to both emperor and pope) secularized his office and his Order's lands and became a secular ruler of Prussia. The second desacralization was that perpetrated by Frederick the Great. But this desacralized Prussia also harboured Kant, who in his works tried to build up a fabric which should compensate men deprived of God for the loss of the grand old order.

The emperors and kings of the old Europe looked on themselves as one great family; mutual support was a religious-political duty. Charles VI had taken young Frederick's part, and with some success. Frederick was now, through his marriage to a cousin of Maria Theresa's on her mother's side, actually part of the Habsburg family circle. But he rejected his wife, and she was left to live out her tormented and cheerless existence in isolation and unsupported.

Frederick epitomizes the greatness and limitations of the anti-feminine male. He had suffered deeply in his youth at the hands of his self-torturing father, who threatened to kill him and towards the end kept his son under lock and key.[1] These early experiences made Frederick long for one thing only, to be as much as possible and as soon as possible a man. It is possible, too, that his libidinous, wanton and highly intelligent mother (through Eleanor d'Olbreuse she was descended from the passionate great ladies of twelfth-century Aquitaine) aroused in him love-hate feelings which he suppressed.

[1] *Der Vater*, a novel by Jochen Klepper (himself a Prussian, who committed suicide under Hitler), gives an unforgettable portrait of Frederick the Great's father.

The intensely masculine Frederick (Janko von Musulin points out that no homosexual of any importance has ever come out of Austria) associated Maria Theresa with everything female, with shocking, shameful fecundity (she bore sixteen children), with 'accursed' gravid matter, with irrational forces of hatred. After his first victory over her on 10 April 1741 at Mollwitz (during which he lost his nerve and fled the battlefield) he chose as text for the thanksgiving service a passage from the First Epistle of St Paul to Timothy: 'Let the woman learn in silence with all subjection. But I suffer not a woman to teach, nor to usurp authority over the man, but to be in silence' (II, verses 11 and 12).

With a deadly sure instinct Frederick had hit upon the real justification for his existence as a lone male. St Paul had required women to be silent in church, and in consequence the church became a society of males. Frederick required women to be silent in Europe: Catherine of Russia, Madame de Pompadour, the woman in Vienna. Protestant males in Prussia and Germany detested Maria Theresa because they saw her as the genetrix of a male-murdering war (the guise in which Frederick's propaganda was clever enough to present her). She was branded as the woman who begrudged the hero what he had so bravely won, in other words, Silesia. Conversely, Frederick made an equally monstrous impression on Maria Theresa (at one time he was thought of as a possible husband for her). She referred to him as that 'vicious beast', 'barbaric neighbour', *ennemi sans foi et sans loi*. In a letter to her son she once described him as 'a stage king, or rather a stage despot', that is to say she regarded Frederick's dissembling, in which he was a past master, as an evil disintegration of his personality: the outward appearance was deceptive, the inner reality deceitful. Frederick struck her two fatal blows: he forced her to give up Silesia, and by fraud he involved her in the infamous partition of Poland.

People have always found it difficult to understand why Maria Theresa went to such lengths to keep Silesia, which after all was only one province out of many, and still rebuke her for it. It must be realized that like Frederick III and Charles V she was animated (in the strictest sense of the word) by the belief that to surrender a single right or territory would amount to sacrilege, bringing in its train the far greater sacrilege of the total disintegration of all the lands entrusted to her rule. She was also convinced that time was not on her side, a conviction shared by her son, Joseph II, who was always conscious of the threat of imminent destruction hanging over the monarchy, always conscious that he had 'no time'.

One may regard Maria Theresa's religious-political feelings of responsibility towards Silesia and the souls of her Silesian subjects as 'eccentric', 'mythic', typically Habsburg. The history of Europe down to 1945 shows that her political instinct was right. The loss of the rich Silesian territories jolted the old Holy Roman Empire out of the ellipse it had formerly described between the male-female, Catholic-Protestant, poles. The old Empire had been 'unattached', 'broad', flexible, organic, multicoloured; these qualities perished in the fall. The new Germany which Prussia carried off as booty from the patrimony of the Holy Roman Empire became domineering, aggressive, bureaucratic and militaristic. Silesia made a significant addition to the unproductive possessions of the king of Prussia: it was rich not only in resources but in men. It was Silesia that made possible Prussia's policy of conquest within the Empire which in time swallowed up one territory after another (bringing her to the Rhine and leading in 1866 to the annexation of the kingdom of Hanover). Again, the road Frederick took with his first invasion of Silesia in 1740 led straight to Königgrätz and the forcible expulsion of Austria from the Empire (1866), which was followed by Austrian losses in the Balkans. Thereafter Hungarian magnates dictated the policies of the Danube monarchy. But the clash with Russia in the Balkans was yet to come.

On 10 April 1741 Frederick of Prussia defeated the unprepared and poorly equipped Austrians at Mollwitz. During the next few months meetings between France, Spain and Bavaria (held in secret at Nymphenburg) and between France and Prussia show that the powers were already arranging the share-out of the Austrian inheritance.

On 19 June 1741 Maria Theresa set out for Pressburg and her coronation as queen of Hungary [plate 153]. She addressed the Estates in Latin, promising to rule the Hungarians like a mother, and after coronation in St Martin's church set out, still attired in the mantle of St Stephen and his sacred crown (which to many Hungarians is still the symbol of legitimate rule over Hungary), to ride her magnificently caparisoned black horse up the coronation mound. *Vivat domina et rex noster!* As 'king' of Hungary Maria Theresa brandished the sword of St Stephen to the four quarters of the heavens: was she not 'a daughter of Ghengis Khan', whose ancient peoples of the steppe had by this same gesture signified their claim to rule in all four quarters of the wind?

News of the alliance concluded between France and Prussia reached Pressburg only at the beginning of July. Its impact is reported by Robinson, the English ambassador. 'The ministers fell back in their chairs as white as corpses, one heart only remaining undaunted, that of the queen.' Maria Theresa's courage is borne out by one of her own remarks during those anxious days. 'I am only a poor queen, but I have the heart of a king.' Robinson, afterwards Lord Grantham, strongly advised the queen to give up Silesia and reach an understanding with Frederick while she had the chance. On 27 July she came unexpectedly into the room where the ambassador was giving her husband news of the Nymphenburg treaty. Robinson walked over to the window and pointed to the Danube as it rushed past in full spate far below: 'the flood of your Majesty's tribulations will increase from hour to hour, just as that flood is mounting down below'. Her Austrian advisers also favoured surrender. The situation was made still more unpleasant by the attacks on the queen emanating from the Hungarian opposition; some of the most obnoxious libels were burned by the hangman under the gallows. Against this mounting mood of depression, at the end of the summer Maria Theresa made a hurried departure for Vienna to take part in the procession of 10 September to commemorate the deliverance of the city from the

Turks in 1683. As she approached she found troops preparing to defend Vienna against an anticipated Bavarian attack and returned the same day to Pressburg. On 11 September she appeared dressed in mourning and wearing St Stephen's crown before both houses of the Hungarian diet, and as it were incited the Hungarians to 'insurrection'; that is, she asked them to mobilize, a decision which could only be taken by the diet. The force of her presence overcame the distrust of centuries (the distrust the Hungarians felt for 'Vienna' and the Habsburgs – which was reciprocated by the Austrian who remarked about this time that he would sooner see Maria Theresa trust herself to the Devil than to the Hungarians), and for Maria Theresa the Hungarians agreed to mobilize.

On 15 September the elector of Bavaria made a ceremonious entry into Linz, accompanied by French troops which had crossed the Rhine a month earlier and now sported blue and white cockades, the colours of Bavaria, as a sign of their secondment to Bavaria for the conquest of Austria. The Viennese, some of whom had Bavarian sympathies, awaited the attack with bated breath. The wars between Frederick and Maria Theresa – the two Silesian wars (1740–42 and 1744–5), the war of the Austrian succession (1740–48) and the Seven Years' War (1756–63) – can here be touched on only briefly. Frederick's disturbance of the equilibrium in the Empire reduced France's eastern neighbours, as also Bavaria, to the position of French satellites. The goal striven for by Richelieu and Mazarin was at last within reach and in 1742 Charles Albert of Bavaria, the protégé of France, was elected emperor (1742–5). To Maria Theresa he remained the 'Elector of Bavaria', and she never referred to him by any other name.

Bavarian and French troops captured Prague and Bohemia. To gain a breathing-space, Maria Theresa concluded with Frederick the Peace of Breslau (11 June 1742) which allowed him to keep Silesia. The Austrians retook Prague and Bohemia and drove Emperor Charles VII from Bavaria, Munich falling on 13 February 1742.

In the following year Maria Theresa set out from Vienna for her coronation in Prague, where three sumptuous Turkish pavilions were in readiness for her outside the equestrian gateway. There were fears in the city of a repetition of the bloody assize which followed the battle at the White Mountain, but Maria Theresa had more than her share of the *clementia austriaca*, which she describes as 'that Austrian clemency towards unworthy subjects implanted in me'. The coronation took place on 12 May and of the Wenzel crown she writes: 'it is heavier than the crown of Pressburg and looks like a fool's cap. She used the sword of St Wenzel to dub her first knights.

Maria Theresa stayed in Prague for over a month. She gave careful instructions to the commissioners appointed to deal with those who had deserted to the enemy, telling them to distinguish between the 'completely disaffected', the 'novelty-seekers' and the 'frivolous'. No one was condemned to death and within a few years nearly all those subject to penalty had received a full pardon.

The fall of Walpole in 1742 brought England into the war on the side of Austria and against the two Bourbon states, France and Spain. The plan was for the Austrians to join the English in crossing the Rhine in an effort to win back the duchy of Lorraine (Maria Theresa's only sister was married to Charles of Lorraine) and so recover old imperial territories from France.

The Lorrainers were lighting joyful bonfires on the heights of the Vosges to greet their young prince and Austrian troops in Alsace were already within sight of Strassburg when the situation was altered by a fresh breach of the peace by Frederick II, his third to date. On 22 May 1744 he had entered into a 'Union' with the emperor (Charles VII), the Elector Palatine and the Landgrave of Hesse-Cassel, whose stated object was to 'rescue German liberty and protect it against the tyranny of the house of Austria'. Such slogans had been the common coin of French propaganda in the seventeenth century. Now 'imperialist' propaganda was pressed into service against the troops of Maria Theresa, at the very moment when they were poised to win back for the Empire the territories on the far side of the Rhine it had lost a century before. Ever since their loss a promise to recover these *avulsa imperii*, the lands stolen from the Empire, had figured in the solemn engagements every emperor swore to on his election.

Frederick did what he could to persuade the sultan into a war of aggression against Austria and to foment a Protestant uprising in Hungary. He himself invaded Bohemia, spreading such havoc that the inhabitants had to take to the woods to escape the plundering Prussians. Prague, that ill-used city, surrendered on 16 September 1744, but ten weeks later, after fierce street fighting, in which the Austrians were joined by Praguers embittered by Prussian looting, the Prussians were expelled.

The sudden death of Emperor Charles VII at Munich on 20 January 1745 made possible the conclusion of the separate peace of Füssen between Austria and his son, Max Joseph. The Wittelsbachs got back Bavaria, which Maria Theresa had wanted to keep in compensation for Silesia, and consented to the election of her husband, Francis Stephen of Lorraine, as emperor. The election duly took place at Frankfurt on 13 September, but not before the ambassadors of Prussia and the Palatinate had left the city in protest.

Maria Theresa came to Frankfurt for the coronation, the only occasion in all the forty years of her reign when she crossed the borders of her own possessions. She refused, however, her husband's pleas that she should be crowned empress beside him. Emperor she could not be; queen of Bohemia and Hungary she was, and with no one by her side.

Goethe includes an account of this coronation in his autobiographical *Dichtung und Wahrheit*, basing it on 'stories told by older people who were present'. The road Maria Theresa took to Frankfurt is a fair indication of what 'the Empire' meant at that period and where it was at home: in its towns, at the seats of its bishops and at the courts of petty princes. In the eighteenth century the south-west of Germany was known in common parlance as '*das Reich*'. One halting place was Nuremberg, the city associated with the Hohenstaufen, with Charles IV and with Maximilian I, from which Maria Theresa wrote, 'I would have been very happy to talk to all the patricians' wives if we had not had to travel for thirteen hours and then spend three hours giving audience, with no opportunity to change.'

It was on 4 October that Francis rode to the cathedral of Frankfurt for his coronation, wearing the mantle of the duchy of Lorraine, a territory he no longer possessed, and the crown of Jerusalem, a kingdom defunct five centuries before. After the ceremony he walked in solemn procession to the Römer. He was now decked out in the coronation robes of Frederick II of Hohenstaufen, plus the insignia of the Holy Roman Empire and the imperial crown. Goethe describes an episode which took place as the procession passed Maria Theresa, who watched it from the balcony of the Frauenstein. Remarking that her looks were 'fair above the average', he continues:

As her husband in his odd attire passed by on his way from the cathedral, exhibiting himself so to speak as the ghost of Charles the Great, he jestingly raised both hands to draw her attention to the orb and sceptre and the quaint gloves he had on; whereupon she burst into uncontrollable laughter, to the great pleasure and edification of the watching crowd which was thus privileged to behold the wholesome and unaffected harmony prevailing between the foremost married couple in Christendom. But when the empress, in salutation to her husband, flourished her handkerchief and shouted her own *'vivat'*, the enthusiasm and rapture of the crowd knew no bounds and it seemed the shouts of joy might never end.

In his poetry and philosophy Goethe 'wraps up' the thousand-year-old Empire (in the double sense of the term, as understood by Hegel, the Swabian who on his mother's side was Austrian). It is worth pausing for a moment to decode some of the cyphers in his remarkable account of the coronation and its attendant episodes. Goethe characterizes the coronation, and even the ship-board reunion between Maria Theresa and her husband (she had come from Aschaffenburg, he from Heidelberg) as *märchen*, benign recollections of folk memories. Francis saw himself as the ghost of Charles the Great: the emperors from Otto I to Charles V had seen themselves as Charles the Great's successors, the people as his reincarnation. At Frankfurt in 1745, in the eyes of people whose understanding of the world was imprinted by Protestantism and modernity, the sacral imitation had become a postlude. The liturgy, the high pomp, the solemn union of heaven and earth, were reduced to an agreeably human game and masquerade. The 'sole' memento of that high union was the successful marriage between Francis and Maria Theresa. The *laudes*, the hymns the old Empire offered in salutation to its redeemer-king (Sumerian salutations preserved in the royal psalms of David and used at all the solemn coronations of the Middle Ages) rang out at this coronation as popular 'enthusiasm'.

At the high feast of Christmas in this same year Maria Theresa concluded with Frederick the peace of Dresden, under which she renounced Silesia and Frederick recognized her husband's election as emperor. The peace of Aachen (1748), made necessary by England's negotiations with France, restored Belgium to Maria Theresa's possession but entailed Habsburg losses in Italy to the Spanish Bourbon.

The succeeding period was occupied with internal judicial and administrative reforms (including the introduction of a system of fixed taxation) whose object was to curtail the excessive privileges enjoyed by the nobility throughout the Habsburg possessions. Count Haugwitz, the minister responsible (son of a Saxon general and himself formerly *Landespräsident* in Silesia), took Prussia as his model. The trend was towards centralization; the separate chanceries for Bohemia and Austria were abolished, which meant the end of Bohemian independence. At the same time, in the interests of external preparedness, Prince Kaunitz set in train the great *renversement des alliances* (ratified in legal form by treaties concluded at Versailles in May and August 1756) by which the house of Austria became the ally of its arch enemy, the house of Bourbon; opposed to them were Prussia and her new ally, England. The English ambassador found it humiliating that Maria Theresa should throw herself 'into the arms of France'. She denied it – 'I am not throwing myself into his arms, I am placing myself at his side' – and pointed out that England had already concluded a treaty of alliance with Frederick. Like his predecessor, who had told her she would have to abandon Silesia, the English ambassador treated her like a child in political matters, and she found this irritating.

War over Silesia and the Empire was again imminent, only this time the Empire was ranged on the side of Austria. An attack by Frederick launched the Seven Years' War (1756–63), during which the English fought the French on the high seas and made world conquests, in America and India. Despite serious defeats at Kolin (1757) and Kunersdorf (1759), Frederick held his own against Austria, France, Russia and Sweden. Kunersdorf might have been a total disaster had the Russian generals not failed to pursue their advantage (Frederick found it very strange that they did not). The Brandenburg 'miracle' – deliverance in the nick of time from seemingly impossible situations – was already at work. For Frederick this particular miracle was soon followed by another, Russia's withdrawal from the war on the death of Tsarina Elizabeth and her successor's willingness to become Prussia's ally (1762). The Tsar in question, Peter III, an infantile pervert of cruel habits, was deposed by Catherine II, who repudiated the alliance. But Frederick's Prussia had been saved and occasional defeats did nothing to halt the conquering progress. The miraculous deliverance of 1762 was a precedent Dr Goebbels clung to in 1945. It seems, indeed, that from time to time he cheered the 'Führer' with the thought that the Brandenburg 'miracle' had been inherited by the Third Reich and that miraculous deliverance from the chancery bunker might hourly be expected – which was what Goebbels wanted to make himself and the German people believe.

France and Sweden having withdrawn from the war, in February 1763 an exhausted Austria concluded with Frederick the peace of Hubertusburg, under which Prussia kept Silesia. Prussia had become one of the 'great powers' of Europe. Henceforth, for as long as the Empire existed, the tension between Austria and Prussia would overshadow all other relations inside Germany and in the Empire (and continue to do so down to 1866).

Playing on the psychology of German Protestant masculinity, Frederick in his propaganda spoke derisively of the 'petticoat conspiracy' against him of Maria

Theresa, Elizabeth of Russia and Mme de Pompadour.[1] The impression Prussian ultra-masculinity left on a romantic young woman of ultra-feminine sensibility emerges from a sketch entitled *The Prussians* which Joseph's young wife, Isabella of Parma, left among her papers at her early death. Partisan and in many ways unfair to her subject, she clearly regarded the Prussian regime as a unique affront to feminine – and human – dignity, as the following extracts show:

The fundamental law of the Prussian state is despotism, tyranny of the most absolute kind, supported by an out-and-out military form of government. The ruler has unrestricted control over the destiny of his subjects. . . . The army is lord and master, for the past three generations every Prussian has been a soldier. . . . The King of Prussia has a wide array of talents. Circumstances have made a soldier of him. He keeps rigidly to his decisions and sees that they are carried out to the letter. His generals are robots whom he controls, even his most important ministers are nothing but inferior clerks; both are denied any knowledge of their master's true intentions. . . . He is the foremost field commander of his century, particularly when it comes to attacking in strength. His advance never falters. No one loves him, rather he is much hated, and his officers are afraid of him. Fear of the king and his all-seeing eye is a more effective spur than ambition and patriotism. . . . When he wants to charm, no one could be nicer. Nature, having endowed him with everything necessary for greatness, gave him in addition a cold, barbaric, unsympathetic heart. . . . The prisons of the country are full to bursting. His family, like his country, is ruled by the crack of the whip. . . . He is very jealous of his good name. If one of his generals makes a reputation of his own he at once falls from grace. . . . He has a high opinion of his own worth, other men he disdains. He never asks advice, even the slightest suggestion of dissent costs a man his favour. He scoffs at the religions and respects none of the boundaries erected by providence or the old lawgivers for the protection of human society. He knows nothing of injunctions, whether human or divine. . . . Immediately his own interests are affected, anything is justified. The consequences of such an attitude soon make themselves felt. One notices a decline in morals throughout his dominions and the general prevalence of doubt. . . . His chief goal was to raise Prussia to the rank of a great European power and to obtain for her in Germany the place once held by Austria.

Isabella fell into a decline after giving birth to Joseph's only child to survive infancy (a daughter) and eventually died. Joseph watched night and day at her bedside. 'I have lost everything,' he wrote to his brother (the future Emperor Leopold II) after the funeral. His mother when her daughter-in-law lay dying said, 'I love her so much that I am bound to lose her. Her death will be a sacrifice demanded by Heaven.' The remark is indicative of what lay deep down in mother and son, two protagonists in the drama within the house of Austria who were as close to one another on one level as they were remote on another. Both were rooted in the old sacrificial order which with baroque had taken on a new lease of life: an

---

[1] Maria Theresa was alleged to have written a fawning letter to Mme de Pompadour at the time of the *renversement des alliances*. In all probability the letter was a fake, inspired by Frederick himself. In 1915 Thomas Mann, then in his ultra-Prussian and chauvinistic period, quoted it against Maria Theresa as evidence that 'the author of the chastity commission, the pious and faithful wife' was a hypocrite.

order which assumed that men were created in order to sacrifice themselves fully, unaffectedly, with resolution and without embitterment. This was still the order under which Mozart lived, wresting from it that inner serenity which makes for happiness. Joseph II often felt it weighing on him like a monstrous burden, a burden he was fated to carry like a curse.

On the evening of his coronation as King of the Romans at Frankfurt on 3 April 1764 he wrote a letter to his mother, who had stayed in Vienna:

> If, dearest mother, you will continue to regard me merely as your son and your subject, I shall be at the summit of happiness. I beg you not to spare yourself in commanding me, restraining me, chiding me, just as in the past, for I need your guidance, and the little good in me is due solely and exclusively to your care and concern; this honour must be allowed to be yours.

The son had not spared himself. For his part, however, he would have liked the 'painful comedy' in Frankfurt over and done with as quickly as possible. Frederick the Great, the 'Enlightener' whom Joseph first admired and afterwards detested, would have said the same. It was Maria Theresa – and not her husband the emperor – who insisted on the election of Joseph as King of the Romans during his father's lifetime (so that he could eventually succeed without further formality).

Goethe wrote at the request of his father (a Frankfurt patrician) an eye-witness account of the happenings of 'the great days' of election and coronation and later incorporated it into *Dichtung und Wahrheit*. The three ecclesiastical electoral princes, the archbishops of Mainz, Trier and Cologne, came riding to the election in person, their mantles trimmed with ermine. They were followed by the proxies of the lay electors, dressed in the old Spanish style. When the election was completed the cry went up 'long live Joseph II, King of the Romans'. Joseph himself was captivated by the shouts of joy 'which refused to die down' and vowed, 'I will do everything in my power not to disappoint the people's pleasure if I really become their elected emperor.' A touching example of traditional fealty to the Empire was set by the old and ailing Landgrave of Hesse-Darmstadt who prostrated himself before Emperor Francis and kissed his feet, acknowledging him as his lord. One might say the gesture was one of *proskynesis*, 'as in the time of Justinian', but what had then been central at this last coronation under the Holy Roman Empire was but an episode.

Young Goethe observed the coronation procession very closely:

> The emperor was quite at home in his robes and one saw both emperor and father writ large on his frank and dignified countenance. The young king by contrast trailed along wearing his engulfing garments and the insignia of Charles the Great as though they were a disguise, and as he caught sight of his father could not refrain from an occasional smile. The crown, for all its padding, stood out from his head like an overhanging roof. The dalmatic and stole, although skilfully taken in and adjusted to his figure, did not sit well on him. Sceptre and orb were cause for admiration, but it was agreed that the whole outfit would have looked better on a well set up figure, more suited to carrying it off.

Charles the Great and the Ottonian emperors had appeared to their people as high priests, priest-kings; the Hohenstaufen had aspired to do the same. But now the priestly vestment had become a costume and men judged the young King of the Romans on his performance as an actor.

It is noteworthy that only the three ecclesiastical electors appeared in person. 'The empty places of the secular electors at the coronation banquet were an indication to the King of the Romans that the great men of the Empire had no desire to accentuate the pomp of the festivities by their presence.'

Joseph was a lonely figure, never more so than when for reasons of state Maria Theresa and Kaunitz forced him into a second marriage with a Wittelsbach princess, Josepha of Bavaria. He found her repulsive, describing her after their first meeting as 'small and stout, totally without the bloom of youth, having a spotty pock-marked face and horrible teeth'. Even Maria Theresa recoiled when she first met this unfortunate young woman.

In his loneliness Joseph plunged himself into work on behalf of the state he saw threatened with collapse. The Bavarian marriage was intended to pave the way for the great project of exchanging Upper and Lower Bavaria for the Austrian Netherlands. But it was this very plan that led to the last struggle between Frederick the Great's Prussia and the Habsburg monarchy for supremacy in the Empire. From a Habsburg Bavaria it might have been possible to start rebuilding the Holy Roman Empire in the Catholic regions adjoining the Habsburg possessions. There was no future for a Holy Roman Empire which contained Prussia, a state organized on strictly military lines, whose estimate of the other states and political groupings of the Holy Roman Empire was determined by the size of their armies and the extent to which they could be used as political agents working against Vienna. The tragedy of Joseph II was that he allowed himself to be forced into adopting the weapons, battle-grounds and political methods of his opponent and paid no further heed to the fragile, loose-knit, untaut fabric which was the Empire. He became just as determined to impose his 'will' in the Empire as in his Habsburg possessions.

Maria Theresa observed this development in her son with mounting dismay, but the sudden death of Francis in 1765 had broken her heart. She had her long tresses shorn, distributed her clothes to her ladies-in-waiting and her jewellery to her daughters. During the fifteen years that remained to her she never appeared in anything but widow's weeds. 'Even the sun looks black to me,' she wrote at Schönbrunn that autumn. A scrap of paper found in her prayer-book contained a note, written three years after the emperor's death, of the years, months, weeks, days and hours their married life had lasted: the total came to over a quarter of a million hours of happiness! This must appear a truly archaic bounty of bliss, quite immeasurable when compared with the fleeting days, hours, moments of happiness experienced by those with a 'modern' sensibility to life. Goethe confessed that in the whole of his life he experienced only a few days of unalloyed happiness.

At the age of twenty-four Joseph was now co-ruler with his mother in Austria:

'Not before it was time', as Kaunitz remarked on Joseph's death, twenty-five years later. The Habsburg possessions were seething with discontent from Belgium to Hungary. When it was not openly rejected, the monarchy attracted only scorn and ridicule; isolated, it seemed on the point of extinction. 'It was always my will-power alone,' wrote Joseph shortly before his death in 1790 in his farewell letter to his great ally, Catherine II of Russia. Once the most hated man in Europe, in the nineteenth century and after Joseph became the symbolic figure of the upright ruler, the emperor who was servant of his people, protector of the poor, the widow and the orphan, the liberator of peasants and Protestants.

Emperor Joseph II was born on 13 March 1741 and received the names Joseph Benedictus Augustus Johannes Antonius Michael Adam. Benedictus was after his godfather, Pope Benedict XIV, the enlightened and pro-reform correspondent of Voltaire, and the other names were those of nearer and remoter relations of the young archduke; but it is interesting that as types Joseph's baptismal names are representative of mankind as seen by the christian west: thus we have Adam, the first father, Joseph, foster-father of Jesus, Augustus, in the Middle Ages regarded as the divinely elected founder of the Holy Empire, John, the Beloved Disciple, Anthony of Padua, the great saint of the Counter-Reformation, Benedict, patriarch of old Europe's monastic houses in their thousands, and Michael the archangel, celestial guardian of the Holy Empire.

Maria Theresa had wanted the tiny prince to be called Charles, in memory of his grandfather Charles VI and of Charles V and of Charles the Great before him. Joseph was substituted at the last minute on the suggestion of her mother Elizabeth, the ex-Protestant Welf princess, who begged Maria Theresa to call her baby after the foster-father of the Lord out of gratitude for an easy delivery.

The Empress loves the emperor (her son Joseph) to distraction and nothing pleases her more than to see him loaded with praise and approbation; yet she likes to command and direct him, to know everything he does or intends. When they are together there is perpetual wrangling, each constantly contradicting the other.... All this, and their difference of opinion on nearly every issue, is public property, since both speak of it openly, so that you will find officials and people generally declaring allegiance to one party or the other, that of the emperor or the empress, and swearing that they are or will be persecuted on that account. This not only makes a very bad impression in the country and on the foreign ambassadors, but also is extremely damaging in affairs of state and disheartening all round.

These impressions are recorded by Leopold, Joseph's younger brother by six years and in due course his successor. He is an unsparing critic of the state of affairs in Austria and of the imperial family, his mother not excepted. Of Joseph (who figures as '*imperatore*' in Leopold's private Italian shorthand) he has this to say:

The emperor is very talented, capable and energetic, he has a quick understanding, a good memory and a command of languages, so that he can talk well and on paper is even better. He is a hard, forceful and ambitious man, whose every word and deed is calculated to attract praise and enhance his reputation in the world. He does not tolerate contradiction, his principles are arbitrary, violent and vehemently-held, and he is imbued with the harshest and most extreme form of despotism. Anything he has not thought of himself he dismisses with contempt; he will have about him only men who are without talent, who obey him and him only like automata and leave him with all the glory for whatever is achieved.

As we have seen, Isabella of Parma, Joseph's first wife, spoke in almost identical terms of Frederick II of Prussia:

He believes that his talent gives him the advantage over everyone else and allows him to lord it over them, he has contempt for everyone, he makes unbelievable, despotic and extremely stupid speeches about the measures he intends to take against officials or whole nations, Hungary, the Netherlands and the rest, how he will take away their privileges and so on, and when all this becomes public he is naturally hated, feared and criticised . . . he loves no one and thinks only of himself. . . .

With quiet spite and much circumstantial detail, Leopold accuses Joseph of ingratiating himself with the lesser folk and of mixing with them in totally unsuitable fashion:

He believes what they say at once and without question. . . . He makes frighteningly harsh and despotic speeches about abolishing privileges, threatens strong measures, says he will declare the state bankrupt and denies he is bound by any undertaking he subscribes to while he is co-ruler with the empress. All this talk has the effect of making him generally odious and leaves no one to like or appreciate him. He alarms everyone by his autocratic ways and no one trusts him; knowing this only disposes him to be all the more cussed and to greater bewailing of his lot, complaints about the country and so forth. He has no love for anyone, anyone at all.

Suddenly in the middle of this destructive criticism Leopold has a good word to say for his brother: 'towards us he is honourably most attentive, offering us his confidence, friendship and trust'. Trust was what Joseph was looking for when he courted 'his' peoples. Trust is a key word with Maria Theresa, recurring again and again in her letters. Trust was the one bond which could restrain people and ruler, the European family of peoples, from the plunge into chaos. Greatly troubled, Maria Theresa warned her daughter Marie Antoinette of the revolution she foresaw in France. She had never been to Paris, but she realized that the young royal couple reigning there were not the type to win popular trust or to inspire confidence in the Estates, the nobility and the bourgeoisie. In addition, every moment of her days and nights was filled with fears that Joseph was gambling recklessly away, to the detriment of the internal order, the most important credit the ruling house possessed, the trust of the people. Coerced by Joseph and Kaunitz, Maria Theresa reluctantly consented to the most unfortunate political act in her career, the (first) partition of Poland. Russia under Catherine II was advancing into Europe. Turkey seemed ripe for partition, but Maria Theresa made difficulties. Catherine then allied herself with Frederick II of Prussia with the object of partitioning Poland. Afraid that Austria would 'come off short', Joseph and Kaunitz joined in. Maria Theresa wept as she signed the deed of partition on 21 August 1772. 'I do not understand this policy. I do not understand why two godfathers should get together with their superior force to oppress an innocent nation.' She was sure the deed 'would shatter the foundations on which the security of those unaffected by it depend.'

'Loyalty and faith have been lost for all time.' Maria Theresa's perceptive comment illumines the history of Europe from her day to the present. The successive partitions of the Polish state signified the 'liquidation' of a thousand-year-old member of the European family of nations. 'Are we to die for Danzig?' people asked in France in 1939. Hitler's invasion of Poland and the German-Soviet pact which compounded Poland's (fourth) partition were the first shots which ushered in the Second World War. The earlier partitions of Poland ushered in the era of the French Revolution and the end of the Holy Roman Empire. They provided the precedent for future 'new orders' in Europe, from Napoleon's to Hitler's. Europe had become a passive object to be parcelled out by the victor of the moment among his satellites and collaborators. The partitions brought Russia well forward into the west. They brought Prussia in 'her' Poland not only territory but also a population the Prussians feared and held in both hatred and contempt, a group many would have preferred to see annihilated. This hatred of Poland would play a continuing and fateful role: in 1870, 1900, in 1933 and in 1939.

Joseph II did not share his mother's anguished vision of the remote and terrifying future. He visited Galicia, Austria's main acquisition, and on his return to Vienna set himself with great verve to the task of civilizing those destitute regions. It must be admitted that culturally and technically Austrian Poland became the most highly developed of all the Polish territories and the nucleus of the Polish revival.

What, we may ask, did Joseph II really wish to accomplish? The equestrian statue of Imperator Josephus in the Josephsplatz in Vienna [plate 158] – in its total architectural effect one of the finest squares in Europe – has a Roman-Imperial look, reminiscent of Trajan or Marcus Aurelius. (Marcus Aurelius was born in Vienna.) One might say that late Roman 'enlightenment' found its reincarnation in the dirigism of Emperor Joseph and his 'Josephine', Jansenist civil servants. Government called for the serious-minded, hard-headed direction of the people from above. Government was conducted by the first servant of the state, in other words the emperor, who was his own chief civil servant, and by officials schooled to deny themselves in the service of the state. The grim earnest of the Josephine civil servant left its unmistakable stamp even on Franz Grillparzer, the poet who celebrated the imperial mission of the house of Austria. Grillparzer turned his back on happiness: all he wanted was to work.

In 1783 the municipality of Buda offered to erect a memorial to Joseph in what was by now the capital of Hungary. Joseph declined, in terms characteristic of the man:

When all errors have been eradicated and true love of the fatherland and the public good again has its rightful place, when methods of instruction have been perfected and men's minds illumined thereby . . . when trade and traffic have come to such a flowering that we have no further need of foreign goods, then, and only then, shall I merit a memorial column:

now I do not, since the only effect of the transfer of the department of taxes and administration to Buda has been that the inhabitants of that city sell their wine at better prices and collect higher rents for their houses.

The eradication of error has loomed large in the programme of revolutionaries. It was the goal of the English puritans in 1640 and equally of the Jacobins, above all Robespierre. Emperor Joseph II wanted to make revolution from above, because he feared that the 'backward' Habsburg lands would otherwise be left still further behind in the future.

'One needs much courage and an even greater measure of patriotism to be an innovator in our present century,' wrote the twenty-four-year-old Joseph in a memorandum expounding his programme to his mother. 'Great things will have to be accomplished at a single stroke.' Joseph wanted to lead the 'subjects' of the Habsburg possessions towards an 'imperial patriotism': he meant them to come together as free men in a common 'fatherland'.

Free men, not least the princes of the arch-house, needed programmes and guide-lines for their education. These Joseph II and his brother Leopold II (who in principle also aimed at revolution from above, though he thought to achieve it by different, more flexible means), set out to provide. 'The theorists and programme planners of the American and French revolutions in their formulation of the great doctrine of the period concerning the innate equality and value of all human beings produced nothing more radical than can be found in the directives for the education of Habsburg princes.'

The magnitude, both in success and failure, of what Joseph and Leopold accomplished as reformers can only be fully measured when it is realized that the years which saw the movement for American independence (in which Joseph and more especially Leopold took a deep interest) and the approach of the French Revolution were also years during which Vienna was attempting a radical reconstruction of the state: hence the measures providing for the reform of the schools and universities and peasant emancipation, the patents of toleration for Protestants and Jews, the abolition of the censorship, and the various legal and penal reforms.

The Josephine revolution from above failed – in great things, rather than small – because there was no concomitant alteration in the structure of society. That this was one reconstruction Joseph had no wish to see is made plain in his treatment of Bohemia.

'Our father, father of the peasants, see how we are beaten, our father we can no longer bear it, our daily bread is taken from us!' So runs a revolutionary 'Our Father' which was the 'prayer' of Czech peasants who in 1775 were in revolt against their landlords: some freedoms they claimed, had already been granted in writing by Emperor Joseph, but the proprietors' agents refused to publish them. One of the ringleaders, Matthias Svoika, bore a startling resemblance to Joseph II and could have been taken for his brother. The peasants marched on Prague, burning noblemen's houses as they went. They were mowed down by troops who had Joseph on their side. One of his mother's most cherished schemes was thus brought crashing to the ground. Whereas she had envisaged the transformation of robot-like serfs into a free peasantry of tenant farmers with a stake in the soil, Joseph favoured keeping the large estates intact. He had no faith in the petty nobility, still less in the 'people', and regarded the great landed proprietor as the crown's surest support. The Bohemian serfs therefore remained serfs and the landlords went on exploiting the peasants. In 1781, now sole ruler, Joseph thought the abolition of serfdom would 'put everything to rights', but by then it was too late; the Bohemian (and Hungarian) higher nobility were too firmly in the saddle.

The serious consequences of Joseph's failure to initiate agrarian reforms in his eastern possessions are all too evident today: Poland, Czecho-Slovakia, Hungary, Rumania and the rest have become communist countries not only because they were overrun and occupied by the Red Army but also because in all of them land reform was either non-existent or inadequate. During the nineteenth century the self-assertive Hungarian magnates were Vienna's harshest opponents. This feudal aristocracy led the monarchy into the First World War and in the nineteenth century prevented the reconstruction of the Danube monarchy as a league of free peoples. The Hungarian magnates ruled their Slovak, Rumanian, Croatian, German and Jewish 'subjects' just as they did their peasants. The misery of the serfs in Hungary and still more in Siebenbürgen was brought home to Joseph when he made a tour of the country in 1773, to inspect schools, hospitals, prisons, rural and urban housing, factories, etc. He found they were treated like cattle or worse. 'That is shocking,' he remarked, as he listened to the peasants' complaints and saw the flogging stool on which they suffered their humiliation, women and children included. The leaders of a Siebenbürgen peasant revolt which broke out towards the end of 1784 appealed to Emperor Joseph for his support; one of their demands was that the noblemen should vacate their offices and so make way for imperial civil servants. Emperor Joseph did not, as hostile Hungarian propaganda alleged, conspire with the rebels. Activity of that kind was left to his successor Leopold II, who in fact supported a form of imperialist Jacobinism in Hungary, with the idea of keeping the nobility in check. Joseph was not completely inactive, he saw to it that the defeated rebels were humanely treated and put a stop to the punitive raids by bands of volunteer noblemen.

Earlier that same year, Hungarians dressed in mourning were to be seen standing outside the castle at Pressburg, as a closed coach rolled past on its way to Vienna. One Hungarian magnate reports, 'I have heard from trustworthy Germans in Pressburg that there was a sudden downpour, tears sent from Heaven to accompany the sorrowful cortege. Who would still dare to say that the God of the Hungarians is dead?' In the twelfth century German knights and imperial bishops had brought the God of the Germans to the east lands at the point of the sword. For centuries, the Slavs and other peoples of the east had resisted him as the God of their oppressors. The Hungarian magnates believed that the God of the Hungarians had given them dominion over the inferior peoples under the sway of the Hungarian crown. This divinely appointed rule was more than symbolized by the crown of St Stephen: the crown was itself their empire and now, on this April day in 1784, it was being removed to Vienna.

On 18 February 1790, as a gesture of reconciliation towards rebellious Hungary, the dying emperor ordered the crown to be sent back. 'The Almighty,' he remarked, with stoic resignation, 'is destroying my life's work even during my lifetime.' We have not so far touched on this emperor's attitude to the 'Almighty' or on his relations with the church and the pope. In his determination to rule the church Joseph reminds us forcibly of the emperors and kings of the Middle Ages, starting with Charles the Great. In his conviction that it was his duty to reform and educate the church and clergy he was well in line with a much older tradition, and many of his so-called innovations, pilloried by hostile propaganda as 'Josephine' domination and terroriza-tion of the church, were in fact the fruit of projects started under Maria Theresa, whose ecclesiastical advisers based themselves on Lombard precedents.

We have seen that Joseph looked forward to the day when 'all errors are eradi-cated'. As a new Charles the Great, a new Otto, a new Maximilian I, he tried to reform the church so thoroughly that all 'pagan ceremonies' all 'superstitions' were rooted out. The radicalism of Joseph's church legislation has still not been surpassed, either by later revolutionaries or by the Communists (who in the successor states could base themselves upon it). Joseph dissolved the contemplative orders (Carthusians, Carmelites, Capuchins), stigmatizing them as clubs of 'non-doers'. Hundreds of monasteries and churches were secularized and converted to secular uses. 'The monarchy is too poor and backward to allow itself the luxury of maintaining non-doers. What the state needs are active, educated priests who will teach the virtues of philanthropy, not barefoot beggars who go about in rags.' Joseph's threat to divert the great wealth of the church into secular channels for the good of the state and society remained only a threat, but a powerful one.

There were two sides to the emperor's reforming work for the church (in which he was assisted by like-minded 'enlightened' Catholic clerics). On the one hand was a radical and revolutionary 'purification', so drastic that it attacked valuable institu-tions at their most vital points and all but destroyed them. On the other was the education and further training provided for the clergy in seminaries and universities, reforms which were in large part responsible for what can be described as the modern Catholicism of the twentieth century. In regions where the Josephine reforms did not penetrate (Poland for example), Catholicism is still so backward that it funks coming to grips with our technological and industrial civilization and has retreated into a ghetto.

Joseph's claim to the traditional rights of the old emperors and kings *vis-à-vis* Rome (medieval kings of Hungary, for example, claimed the right to censor papal bulls before they were published in the country), inevitably brought him into conflict with the pope. Here, too, recent tradition was also fully on his side. Maria Theresa had taken Rome's earnest protests over her government of the church as a personal insult, and when her son Leopold became governor of Tuscany she instructed him to act towards the pope as 'a good son, yielding to the Holy Father in all matters concerning religion and dogma' but also to 'be a sovereign and refuse to tolerate even the slightest interference from the Roman curia in matters of government'. Joseph was as determined as any medieval king or emperor to keep the pope from meddling in his affairs. He held that the first duty of his bishops and clergy was to serve their emperor and king as good citizens.

In 1782 men were treated to the impressive spectacle of a 'Canossa in reverse', the journey of Pius VI, the sixty-five-year-old pope, to Vienna to plead in person with the emperor for the rights of the church as Rome understood them [plate 156]. A few days before his arrival Eybel, professor of canon law at Vienna, published a pamphlet *What is the Pope?* which he had written at the emperor's request. In it he declares that the rights enjoyed by the Vicar of Christ are not unique to the Pope but extend to all bishops as successors of the apostles; the Pope merely represents the wholeness of the church. (These propositions and topics still figured on the agenda of the Second Vatican Council, 1964.) Eybel, standing both on the old and on the more recent (Jansenist) tradition, further asserts that the head of state derives his power directly from God and that he has the right and duty to guide and supervise the operations of the church. We may recall that on the eve of the Thirty Years' War Melchior Goldast performed a similar service for the Holy Roman Empire with his collection of traditions and sources. The pope obtained very little from his meetings with the emperor but was grateful for what he got. Joseph had his way over all the questions he regarded as crucial to his authority; the pope promised, for example, to ensure that the Hungarian bishops implemented the emperor's decrees. Joseph's offer to raise one of the pope's nephews to the ranks of a prince of the Empire was favourably received.

Pope Pius VI's journey to Vienna had a sequel the following year. On Christmas morning 1783 the Holy Father was expecting to receive the king of Sweden in audience and had prepared an address suitable for a Protestant ruler. He rose from his throne and to his astonishment found before him Emperor Joseph. As Joseph reported to Kaunitz: 'there I was in Rome, and my arrival was like a bombshell'. During his stay Joseph conducted himself as an ostentatiously pious Catholic, zealously visiting the churches. His companion on these excursions was King Gustavus III of Sweden, who had by this time arrived, and was obliged to join Joseph in his genuflections, whether he liked it or not. The emperor was determined to prove to Rome that he was neither antichrist nor a barbarian – not even a new Luther. The populace gave him a rousing reception.

Joseph willingly lent himself to such comedies on his visits to other parts of Europe, for example France and Russia. They helped to keep his loneliness and besetting anxieties at bay. His contacts with Frederick the Great, Catherine II and above all the Paris of the Enlightenment, only heightened his anxieties. He was aware that Europe was on the move and must have asked himself what chance there was for his monarchy in face of Russia and Prussia, and of peoples in a rising state of ferment. Fourteen years before the outbreak of the French Revolution Joseph had already foreseen it from Vienna and warned his sister Marie Antoinette: 'the revolution, if you fail to avert it, will be an atrocious one.'

'There is revolution in my organism,' wrote Joseph in his mortal illness to his brother Leopold. The Netherlands and Hungary were in uproar. His attempt to head off the revolution from below by forestalling it with a revolution from above appeared to have failed. Hungarian noblemen chased out the emperor's land surveyors and made bonfires of the imperial decrees, chanting the 'Marseillaise' and *Ça ira* (in Latin) as they burned. The counter-revolution camouflaged itself by speaking the language of the revolution. The Hungarian rising of 1956, like the Hungarian risings of the nineteenth century, was supported as much by profoundly reactionary elements as by those which were evolutionary and genuinely concerned with freedom and progress.

Emperor Joseph II died at the very moment when the French Revolution was flaring up into a European conflagration which could not fail to affect the Holy Roman Empire. Emperor Joseph had no great feeling for the Empire and his church policy had further estranged him from its Catholic Estates. The last decades of the Holy Roman Empire's history are overshadowed by the antagonism of Austria and Prussia and in the west by the renewed threat from a France whose ensign was no longer the lilies of Bourbon but the cockade of the Revolution.

Comte de Bulkeley, who in 1772 was the French king's ambassador to the Perpetual Diet in Regensburg, described '*le corps germanique*' as perhaps the most complicated structure ever to have existed. The task of the French ambassador, like that of all his predecessors since the Thirty Years' War, was to keep an eye on German affairs and alert the diet against encroachments on its authority by the imperial court. France was still the Guardian of German liberty: as de Bulkeley observes with self-conscious pride, 'Germans of goodwill recognize that the credit for having founded the German constitution belongs in essence to Cardinal Richelieu.'

The imperial constitution had ten basic components: the Golden Bull, still regarded as the fundamental law, the *Concordata nationis Germaniae*, the *Ewigen Landfrieden*, the *Reichsmatrikel* of Worms, the *Reichesexekutionsordnung*, the promises made by emperors on election (*Wahlkapitulationem*), the treaties of Westphalia, the imperial peace treaties made in the seventeenth and eighteenth centuries and the *Reichsabschiede* (decisions made by the imperial diet before its temporary suspension).

The Empire was not a state but a system of dispensing justice [plate 159]. Leibniz is very clear on this point. Samuel Pufendorff, the great seventeenth-century Protestant jurist, had already pointed to its judicial function as the prime task of the Empire, exceeding in importance any accumulation of power. There were three superior tribunals from which justice could be obtained, the *Reichskammergericht*, the *Reichshofrat* (since the treaty of Westphalia these two had been on an equal footing and it was left to the plaintiff to decide where he would bring his suit), and the imperial diet, which acted as the final court of appeal and of last instance. 'There are only three places,' says Pütter, 'where the unity of the Empire is still on view: Vienna, which is the seat of the imperial court, of the *Reichshofrat* and of the *Reichsvizekanzler*; Regensburg, which is the seat of the Imperial Diet, and Wetzlar, which is the seat of the *Reichskammergericht*.'

The *Reichskammergericht* was composed of Catholics and Protestants in equal numbers. The *Reichshofrat* had six Protestant and eighteen Catholic members, all appointed by the emperor. It was the supreme court for members of the German aristocracy, for hearing feudal suits, and for dealing with matters arising from the administration and constitution of the Empire. It was the organ of the emperor as supreme judge in the Empire.

Joseph II pressed successfully for a speedier handling of the many actions which for years had been hanging fire. As a young barrister pleading in the *Reichskammergericht*, Goethe was familiar with the finical procedures of these courts; it is no wonder that his Mephisto jeers at the encrusted legal system which had turned a benefit into a hindrance. The three high courts continued, nevertheless, to make a positive contribution right down to the end and because of their impartiality enjoyed a high degree of confidence. Their greatest success was in preventing smaller territories and lordships directly dependent on the Empire from being swallowed up by the larger states. These petty lordships, counties, principalities, imperial towns, knightships, 'which criss-crossed the entire Empire like a net', through their variety kept in being the culturally productive world of the old Empire.

This cultural world was fruitful still; it was the nursery of the free creative spirits – Lessing and Wieland, Schiller and Goethe, Hölderlin, Hegel and Schelling – whose coming brought the great springtime of the intellect in the late eighteenth and early nineteenth centuries. Wieland, a mocker and a son of the Enlightenment, (whose irony and force we have only now begun again to appreciate), in his old age bestowed high praise on the old imperial constitution which he thought far more conducive to human culture and freedom than French democracy. The Empire was no dying corpse, 'it provided the framework for the greatest and most unhampered cultural flowering ever to have grown from German soil'.

The two great academical constitutional lawyers of the day, Johann Jakob Moser and Stephan Pütter (both of them Protestants) were entirely in favour of the imperial constitution. Even as late as 1801, Karl Ernst Adolf von Hoff, a young observer who was very critical of the degenerate constitution of his own day, remarked that if the old constitution had survived 'in the form presented to us by our lecturers in constitutional law, we should still be the happiest people on earth'. The Germans were only 'happy' in the bosom of the old Empire – under an order, that is, of infinite complexity and mutability, perpetually bubbling with dissensions and disputes. The new state (of the nineteenth-twentieth centuries) overstrained the Germans, demanded too much of them, and corrupted their political imagination from the start.

The imperial diet was an unmanageable and cumbersome institution. The great

152 Allegory of Austria's acquisition of territories by marriage and by conquest. The picture appeared in 1744, a time when Europe was confidently expecting the collapse of Habsburg power in Vienna.

153 (*left*) Maria Theresa in her Hungarian coronation robes.

154 Allegorical meeting of Maria Theresa and Frederick the Great marking the Peace of Hubertusburg, 1763. The two great enemies never in fact met.

THERESIENS LEZTER TAG.

155 Maria Theresa's last hours. She died sitting upright on her couch.

156 The meeting between Joseph II and Pope Pius VI at Marienbach outside Vienna. The pope failed to persuade Joseph to give up his ecclesiastical policy.

157 Allegory of Joseph II's Toleration Patent, 1781. Issued eight years before the outbreak of the French Revolution, the Patent provided one of the legal bases for the construction of the modern state.

158 (right) Emperor Joseph II by Zauner. The statue makes obvious reference to the celebrated equestrian statue of Marcus Aurelius and honours Joseph as a great new philosopher-emperor.

160 Coronation procession of Leopold II on the Römerberg at Frankfurt in 1791. Right to the end the ceremonial of the Empire was preserved and Leopold's coronation followed the detailed procedure laid down in Charles IV's Golden Bull.

161 (*right*) Domestic scene at the Vienna court, *c.* 1800. Empress Marie Thérèse is teaching her children their evening prayers, with her husband, Emperor Francis II, her mother, Queen Maria Caroline of Naples, and her sister, Marie Christine, looking on.

159 (*left*) Seat of Justice with the imperial arms at Rottweil, late eighteenth century. The judicial responsibilities towards the countries and peoples of the Empire retained by the supreme judges of the Imperial Courts were the last links which held the Empire together before its final dissolution.

162 (*top*) Emperor Francis II and Napoleon after the battle of Austerlitz. Francis had to make his illegal abdication so that Napoleon could try to revive the Empire of Charlemagne.
163 (*bottom*) King Rudolf I and his sons represented in a historical pageant for the silver wedding of Emperor Francis Joseph, 1879. In Austria the imperial past was preserved only in meaningless theatrical gestures.

crush and confusion astonished Lady Mary Wortley Montagu when she visited Regensburg with her husband in 1716. The last diet in the old style had been dissolved in 1654. Up till that time the diet met for only short sessions and concluded its proceedings by issuing a decree (the *Reichsabschied*) binding on all the Estates of the Empire. From 1663 the Perpetual Diet sat permanently at Regensburg as a standing conference of the Estates. In this assembly Prussia aspired to the position of an anti-emperor (a word which goes back to Kaunitz and the younger Trauttmansdorff). Mirabeau once remarked that Prussia was not a state at all, but an army. In this last phase Prussia in general acted as the spokesman of the larger principalities, the emperor as the ally of the smaller, some of them minute. The real achievement of the imperial diet was a 'passive' one: 'the German imperial diet guaranteed the political survival down to 1803 of even the tiniest principalities of the Empire.'

From Regensburg, the intelligence centre of the Empire, went forth an unbroken stream of false reports and propaganda announcements by this or that party. Joseph did himself a great disservice when in 1782 he cancelled all stipends in the Empire still paid by the emperor and so cut off the only reliable source of news.

All the constitutional offices of the diet were in the hands of Catholics. It was presided over by the *Principalkommissar* and its business was managed by the deputy of the elector of Mainz, known for this purpose as the *Reichsdirektoriale*. The final practice of voting by the two *corpora*, (these were the two most important parties in the diet and can be broadly characterized as Lutheran and Catholic) became established only in 1721. While the Lutheran *corpus* emerges as a closed body composed of dynastic members (Saxony, Brandenburg-Prussia, etc.), the *corpus catholicorum* appears far more varied, consisting of many types of Estates and regarding itself as 'the Empire'. In the Catholic *corpus* ecclesiastical princes were very much in the majority. The diet had three 'colleges': the Electoral college, which down to 1779 had nine voting members (three ecclesiastics, Cologne, Mainz and Trier, and six laymen, Bohemia, Brandenburg, Saxony, Bavaria, the Palatinate and Hanover); the *Fürstenrat* (council of princes), which numbered a hundred votes wielded by about twenty deputies and was controlled by Austria; and the *Städtekollegium*, which was only finally written into the constitution at the peace of Westphalia, a time when the political importance of the imperial towns was already declining. This college was only called into consultation when the two others had already cast their vote. The imperial towns, and this includes even the Protestant towns, remained in the emperor's pocket down to the very end.

'Why must Germany have an emperor?' asks one flysheet, to which the Reichsfreiherr von Soden replied in 1787, 'in order to preserve in the smaller states the cultural life peculiar to themselves'. The Empire was still divided into ten circles, of which the ideal type was the Swabian Circle. Its circle diet (*Kreistag*), held each May, was attended by the ambassadors of the emperor, Prussia, France, Russia, Great Britain and Denmark, all accredited to the *Kreisdirektor*, the Duke of Württemberg. The Franconian and Upper Rhenish Circle (which until the eighteenth century included Savoy) also continued to be of some importance. Worms and Mainz ran their circles together in a personal union. In the Westphalian and Lower Saxon circles the consequences of the Reformation were particularly apparent.

The predominant elements in the Empire were the church and the nobility. The boundaries of Catholic dioceses were written into the imperial constitution. Catholic bishops, and a few abbots, ranked as Estates of the Empire. Of the seven pre-Reformation archbishoprics only four survived, Mainz, Cologne, Trier and Salzburg (the others were Magdeburg, Hamburg, and Besançon). In the last century of its history, the imperial church was just as aristocratic as it had been in the days of Otto the Great.

The German nobility was far from homogeneous. There was a clear-cut distinction between the imperial nobility (imperial princes, imperial counts, imperial knights) and the provincial nobility. The great preserves of the imperial nobility were the cathedral chapters, on which a specified number of seats were reserved for those of noble descent. Because of increasing competition from the new nobility, during the eighteenth century the number of generations over which the noble descent had to be proved rose from about four or five to eight. The provincial nobility were politically totally insignificant, which made them all the more anxious to assert themselves. This assertiveness was one reason for the nobility's declining prestige, which was particularly marked in southern Germany.

The first real threat to the equilibrium of the Empire arose from the problem of the Bavarian succession. The possible claimants (two of them Hohenzollerns) all lacked legitimate heirs and France (with the Polish example freshly in mind) feared that the strife between Austria and Prussia over Bavaria might in the end lead to the partition of Germany. Catherine of Russia was at pains to set herself up as the guarantor of the imperial constitution, hoping by this means to win recognition as a member of the European family of great powers.[1] She looked on the Empire as a kind of select club and felt it a slur not to belong (A. Tratschewsky). Frederick pinned his faith on Russia as Prussia's last hope; 'la Russie seule nous reste', he wrote on 13 March 1778. The political and diplomatic struggle for the Empire was not simply a struggle between 'Berlin' and 'Vienna', since in both camps there was disagreement as to the best course. In October 1777 Frederick's brother Henry suggested that Austria and Prussia partition Germany between them. A year later we find Maria Theresa and Kaunitz seriously considering the exclusion of Joseph from the succession in Austria; Joseph himself toyed with the idea of renouncing Austria and taking up residence as emperor in Frankfurt.

During the war over the Bavarian succession (1778–9) between Frederick and Joseph the Empire was officially neutral. Kaunitz having tried in vain to persuade the Empire, that is to say the Diet, to act as arbiter in the conflict, the only recourse was to seek Franco-Russian mediation. The peace of Teschen concluded between Berlin and Vienna on 13 May 1779 was guaranteed by France and Russia and ratified by the

[1] Compare the present position of Russia in the DDR and that of the western powers in the Federal Republic.

Empire. In return for agreeing to the cession of a small area on the Inn to Austria (it contains Braunau, Hitler's birthplace), Frederick secured the guarantees he needed for the union of Ansbach and Bayreuth with Prussia, which in turn ensured Prussian predominance in the Empire.

The peace of Teschen is also important for another reason. Russia, which from the time of Peter the Great had close links with German ruling houses, now became extremely active in the Empire. The Russian ambassador filled the role in the Empire which the emperor had lost – that of a disinterested arbiter – and was held in greater esteem than the French, whose task was to promote France's own imperial policy. Russian influence penetrated into the smallest German principality and no court was better informed of opinions in Germany than St Petersburg. The Russians found Weimar particularly reliable in this respect since its duke for a time was attracted by the idea of combining with other princes to form a kind of 'third force' between Frederick the Great and Vienna. Goethe, who was one of his ministers, is scathing in his comments on Frederick the Great, whom he compares, for example, to the Ashanti chieftain Opokku, a man so laughably uncultured and deluded with grandeur that the defeat of an enemy confirms his opinion of himself as the world's only giant.

The last battle in and over the Empire was a battle over the imperial Church. The election of Archduke Max Franz (the youngest son of Maria Theresa) as coadjutor of the archbishopric of Cologne and Münster gave Frederick opportunity for painting the future of the Empire in the most alarming colours: he warned that a Habsburg secundo-geniture, embracing all the Rhenish bishoprics (after secularization) from Liège to Strassburg, was being plotted (Frederick spoke with authority – his ancestors had acted similarly in Prussia) and pointed as a further danger to the sees in the south-east which had already been earmarked for the princes of Tuscany: Grand Duke Leopold, Joseph's brother, had ten sons.

The prince-bishops of the Empire were further disturbed by Joseph's plans for reforming the church in Austria. In order to gain control, Joseph needed to revise the diocesan boundaries, since the imperial sees of Passau, Salzburg (not then part of Austria), Constance, Augsburg, Freising and Chur still held ecclesiastical jurisdiction over suffragan sees and churches in Austrian and Habsburg territory. Joseph's argument that the new arrangement would provide more direct pastoral care cut no ice with the prince-bishops of the Empire, who regarded themselves first and foremost as imperial princes and saw only that their rights were being attacked. Joseph's plan for the reorganization of the Austrian church as it eventually emerged provided for dioceses whose boundaries coincided with those of the civil government and for a church subordinated to the state. It is astonishingly close to the 'Civil Constitution of the Clergy' drawn up in the early days of the French Revolution.

The confiscation of ecclesiastical estates under Joseph II caused great indignation in the Empire and created a stir throughout Europe. In January 1788 King Peter III of Portugal ordered public prayers to be offered for an emperor so blinded by the devil.

Clerical propaganda described the emperor as 'antichrist', as in the days of Henry IV, Henry V, Frederick I, Frederick II and Ludwig of Bavaria.

In Austria itself Joseph was opposed by Kaunitz, who wanted the reform to be confined to Austria. Kaunitz found his former pupil more and more dislikeable. As he would write to Trauttmansdorff on 21 December 1789, 'You know as well as I do how much this unhappy man [the emperor] deserves the opprobious title "perpetual wrecker of the Empire".'

Was he indeed the wrecker of the Empire? Joseph's reforms eventually drove the ecclesiastical princes of the Empire into the Protestant League of princes which Frederick had founded in 1785 in the hope of strengthening Prussian influence. The old confessional parties among the Estates transformed themselves into an Austrian and a Prussian party. It should be noted that the *Corpus Catholicorum* in the Empire was not the same as an emperor's party, which despite Lutheran princes' assertions to the contrary as such scarcely existed. In reality there was a sharp cleavage between the Catholic Estates and the emperor, so much so that the Catholic opposition often found itself obliged to side with the *Corpus Evangelicorum*. 'In my view,' wrote Kaunitz in February 1787, 'for a long time past the religious difference in Germany has been merely a matter of political pretext and catchword, so that if the imperial court and the more powerful princes acknowledged the Confession of Augsburg today, the Protestants would declare for Catholicism tomorrow.'

There was a danger about 1785 that the Empire would be forced to take sides and be drawn as the appendage of a Prussian or an Austrian party into the cabinet politics of the great powers. This was ground on which the Empire, because its structure made it deficient in 'power', i.e. armies, could not compete. Goethe, as Weimar's 'minister for war', cut down the duke's army during the war of the Bavarian succession to avoid becoming involved. His drama *Die Vögel* is directed equally against the black eagle of Prussia and the double-headed eagle of Austria.

In the early 1780s there was in fact some resurgence of Empire patriotism, which found sympathizers in Protestant princes such as Carl August of Weimar, Franz of Anhalt and Carl Friedrich of Baden, but this trend was halted by the tug-of-war which developed in 1787 over the election of Karl Theodor von Dalberg, who had had a hand in the education of Carl August, as coadjutor of Mainz. He was the candidate of both Austria and Prussia, having good relations with both courts, but in the event owed his election to Prussia's purchase of the chapter's votes. It was at this period, when the shock of Joseph's ecclesiastical measures was still great, that Prussia really became influential in Germany. Frederick was dead, and the Prussian minister Hertzberg courted south German support by spreading rumours that Frederick at the end had been ready to embrace Catholicism and that his successor Frederick William II, or perhaps one of his sons, was ready to turn Catholic for the sake of becoming emperor.

'It was Dalberg's tragedy that the third party, the party of the Empire, did not exist just when he so urgently needed to use it.' Vienna and Berlin both distrusted him and left him in the lurch. He disappointed Austria by joining the League of Princes, despite his promise not to do so. Undaunted by his rebuffs, Dalberg set about reconciling the League of Princes with the emperor, and in the autumn of 1787 presented Vienna with a plan for the judicial reform of the Empire. Joseph might dismiss Dalberg as a fool and a dreamer, but his proposals contained in embryo what has since been realized in the European tribunals of the Common Market countries, in the High Authorities and in the Council of Europe. Needless to say the plan met with an unsympathetic hearing in Vienna and Carl August had an equally cool reception in Berlin; neither court had any further interest in reforming the Empire. 'After the summer of 1788 imperial reform did not so much as enter anyone's thoughts, whether in Berlin or Vienna' (Aretin).

In 1789, on the eve of the Great Revolution in France, Austria's situation appeared to the emperor as desperate, no less desperate than Prussia's had appeared to Frederick the Great when he contemplated what might happen after his death. The Netherlands – a Catholic province – were in an uproar as a result of Joseph's high-handed actions and his attempts to impose ecclesiastical reform. The risings against Austria in Liège, Belgium, Galicia and Hungary all had Prussian backing. In the Empire, however, the revolt in the Netherlands was no special cause for excitement. What did make a strong impact was the revolution at Liège of 18–19 August 1789 and the bishop's flight to Trier.

Prussia, whose support of the revolutionary movements in Hungary, Bohemia and Belgium had hitherto been clandestine, now sent troops to support the rebels, under pretext of acting 'as the imperial executive' to put down the revolution. But Max Franz, the Elector of Cologne, saw no reason why he should not do to King Frederick William II and his minister Hertzberg what Frederick the Great had once so readily done to Joseph, and branded Prussia as a lawbreaker. Within six months of the storming of the Bastille Prussia was exposed before the now thoroughly alarmed Empire as the supporter of revolutionary movements and obliged to retreat from Liège. 'As a factor in power politics the Empire was admittedly negligible, militarily speaking it had no significance. Yet in virtue of its tradition and its rootedness in justice, it still had the power to frustrate designs whose success depended on a violation of the law.'

Max Franz now set about making plans for a reform of the Empire and for a new league of princes. By 1790 his prestige was such that a flysheet published at Regensburg could propose his election as Roman Emperor. After Joseph's death some attempt was made to detach the imperial crown from the Habsburgs. The house of Zweibrücken might provide a candidate and Frederick William II had brief thoughts of becoming one himself. Saxony and Prussia favoured a long interregnum, until Austria had been dealt a knock-out blow.

'We have been a great power, but are so no longer. One must resign oneself to the fact.' 'War is such a detestable trade, contrary to all humanity and happiness!' 'An indifferent peace is better than a victorious war.' With these and similar aphorisms the ageing Maria Theresa had sought to deter Joseph from his wars with Frederick.

'I want to look death in the face,' she said to her son. For her, death was 'like going from one room into another'. She had the curtains left undrawn, although the rain poured down without ceasing. 'I am not having good weather for my journey.' On 29 November 1780, at about nine in the evening she hoisted herself from her couch. Joseph rushed to her side. A few minutes later she was dead.

'Your country has killed me, the loss of Namur is my death agony, the loss of Brussels my end.' Thus Joseph on his death-bed in 1790 to the Prince de Ligne. And indeed the deterioration in the Netherlands and in Joseph's state of health went hand in hand. He was not afraid of death and like his mother wanted to look it in the face. This 'latter day Carolingian' had already sent a letter to the Hungarian court chancery revoking all the edicts issued in Hungary during his reign with certain significant exceptions: the patent of toleration, the law abolishing serfdom and the law relating to the organization of the clergy.

After receiving extreme unction, the dying emperor remarked to Rosenberg, his chief lord-in-waiting: 'I do not believe the poet is right who says that the passage from the throne to the tomb is so terrible. I have no regrets at having to leave the throne. The one and only thing that troubles me is that despite all my efforts I have made so few men happy.' On 17 February the dying emperor had news that his beloved young niece Elizabeth of Württemberg, wife of Archduke Franz, the nephew he would dearly have liked to bring up as his successor, had died in great agony having given birth to a still-born child. He asked Rosenberg where Elizabeth was to be buried and was told 'in the *Hofkapelle*'. 'That will not do,' replied Joseph, 'that is where I shall be and I would not like to disturb the little one's rest.' On 19 February he had himself dressed in the white uniform of a marshal, even down to the boots. He dictated his last letters reclining in a chair and died about five in the morning.

The Prince de Ligne, 'Prince of French Europe' (as he is called by Dumont Wilden, his biographer), grieved that no one mourned the emperor and foresaw that before long the Monarchy would understand what it had lost. When that time came, would not travellers exclaim in astonishment over the hospitals, schools, prisons, orphanages he had built, artisans acknowledge that he was their protector, peasants that he too had laboured and heretics that in him they had their best defender?

13

THE UNFINISHED SYMPHONY

'PRINCES should reflect that they cannot humiliate others without humiliating themselves.' 'The most important thing is that princes should convince themselves that all men are equal. They can do what they are called on to do only through serving the people.' These and similar maxims figure in the instructions Leopold II wrote down for the education of his twelve children. To his favourite sister Marie Christine, governess of the Netherlands, he once wrote:

I believe that the sovereign, even a hereditary sovereign, is merely the delegate and appointee of the people for whom he exists, that to them he should dedicate all his thought and toil . . . I believe that executive power belongs to the sovereign, but legislative power to the people and their representatives, and that at each change of sovereign the people can introduce new conditions.

Leopold II, the last emperor of the Holy Roman Empire who was still emperor when he died, occupied the office for a bare eighteen months (30 September 1790 – 19 March 1792). At his baptism on 5 May 1747 he received the names Peter Leopold Johannes Antonius Joachim Pius Gotthard. The first name, Peter, is significant; it was given to him at the request of his godmother, Tsarina Elizabeth, to perpetuate the memory of her father, Peter the Great. Pietro Leopoldo, as Leopold was officially known when he was Grand Duke of Tuscany (which he ruled initially for his father Francis Stephen), showed himself at least as daring an experimenter in government as his Russian patron and namesake. In an engraving by Goetz, the court painter, we see the cradled infant as a 'porphyrogenetos' (that is to say one 'born in the purple', like the children born to reigning emperors in Constantinople). The purple-born is shown with crown and golden fleece, his cradle bears as ornament the crowns of his house and the archducal hat, and has half-moons for rockers; the string is pulled by an imperial eagle, who has the sword of the Empire and the keys of St Peter. Using the symbolic language of late baroque, the artist has assembled every one of the claims advanced by wearers of the imperial crown or their imperial propagandists, from Charles the Great downward. In the row of statues, starting with Louis the Pious, which adorns the façade of the town hall of the former coronation city of Aachen, that of Leopold is the last.

Leopold, who had been moulded in his youth by the spirit of the French and

Italian Enlightenment (Montesquieu, Muratori, the Encyclopedists), was mentally very alert, having a particular interest in the natural sciences (he was an enthusiastic experimental chemist). He seems to have had a real flair for sensing the undercurrents and underlying tendencies of his age. While regent of Tuscany he kept himself informed about developments in the movement for American Independence and added copies of American documents, for example the Pennsylvania Constitution of 28 September 1776, which he had acquired either from Benjamin Franklin or his own agent Mazzei, to the dossier for his projected Tuscan constitution.

Leopold turned a critical eye on the state of affairs in the Danube monarchy quite early in his career; his *Riflessioni sopra lo stato della Monarchia* describes the situation as he found it on a journey to Vienna in 1778. Appreciation of the tasks and potentialities inherited by the Danube monarchy as successor to the Holy Roman Empire has been shown by Winston Churchill and a host of other political commentators from the Anglo-Saxon world: they see in it a form of commonwealth whose open, multinational structure can be compared with that of the United Kingdom of Great Britain (Lord Acton, for example, makes a direct reference to Great Britain in his defence of the multi-national monarchy centred on Vienna). After two catastrophic world wars, even political opponents and enemies of the Danube monarchy have admitted that in this Little Europe of the Danube region there was once a real chance of creating a true league of nations. An umbrella organization of this kind which took the smaller and smallest nations under its wing would also have helped to stabilize the European balance of power, overweighted by a heavily armed new Germany and the hugeness of Russia. These potentialities were still present in the mind of Crown Prince Rudolf and Archduke Francis Ferdinand, who were painfully aware that opportunities were being wasted – not least because of the rigidity of the monarchy's foreign policy.

Leopold, whose plans for internal reform were in essence far more radical and audacious, in short more revolutionary, than those of his brother, realized that to implement them he needed external and internal peace (something which Joseph had tragically failed to see), and time in which to work them out. What he contemplated was nothing less than the transformation of archaic-aristocratic political structures based on personal kinship ties and ecclesiastical hierarchies, lordships and class relationships, into a technological and industrial 'open society'. Leopold had recognized something which to the discredit of Europe and the freer half of the world many of our statesmen and politicians still fail to grasp: that an 'active' foreign policy is incompatible with the internal action necessary to adapt society to the demands of the twentieth century.

Leopold had perceived the vital connection between disarmament and internal reform while he was Grand Duke of Tuscany. On 1 November 1777 he instructed his adviser Gianni to draw up a plan for replacing the Tuscan armed forces by a civilian militia (he also disbanded the Tuscan fleet); Maria Theresa had recommended Joseph to make cuts in the army as early as August 1765. Leopold's plan for a civilian militia was in keeping with his aim to develop Tuscany as a model state in which the citizens were encouraged to take an active part in local government. He realized that the great struggles of the future would be struggles over the structure of society and men's place in it.

Leopold's reforms in Tuscany have to be seen in relation to the state of affairs in the Danube monarchy which so constantly occupied his attention. He noted the discontent of all classes of the population and in particular the unpopularity of a government which acted so despotically in its expenditure of men. The administration was in a state of utter confusion; disorder, anarchy and corruption were rife. Poor education was chiefly to blame. Leopold was convinced of the monarch's duty to educate his subjects as citizens willing and able to take responsibility. He particularly deplored the poor education given to women and girls, which inculcated only a taste for luxury and sentimentality.

Leopold realized the importance of experiment in politics. In the old Europe politics had been a 'game', an adventure embarked on by great lords, bound up with hunting, war and feasting. With Leopold politics, and for him this meant first and foremost internal politics, became a carefully thought-out scientific experiment. He believed in trying out reforms in one or two places before extending them, if necessary in a form modified in the light of experience, to the whole area covered by his rule.

Leopold . . . deliberately applied the methods he had found to work in the laboratory to solving the problems of human co-existence, the political and economic problems; and in so doing he found himself in tune with the times, for at almost no period before or since has there been a greater conviction that political problems are susceptible to 'scientific solutions' (Adam von Wandruszka).

This 'enlightened' conviction was shared, however, only by small circles of his high officials and a few secular and ecclesiastical princes. There is no saying what good effects might have followed for Europe if Leopold had been able to reform the Habsburg lands in the light of his Tuscan experience.

All Emperor Leopold II had time to do when he succeeded Joseph in Vienna was to carry out some emergency 'first aid' in an effort to calm peoples already seething with unrest. He restored the Hungarian constitution, reinstated the 'Bohemian-Austrian chancery' and the chanceries for Siebenbürgen and Illyria and set up a chancery for Galicia. He intended the kingdoms and provinces to have the widest possible degree of autonomy. The emperor came to an understanding with Prussia (Convention of Pillnitz), made peace with the Turks – and died.

Austria's wars with revolutionary France and with Napoleon, which lasted from 1792 to 1815, carry us beyond the end of the Holy Roman Empire. Napoleon, backed by German princes to whom he made promises (which he honoured) of crowns, lands and rich booty, systematically destroyed the old Empire. By the grace of Napoleon, Bavaria and Württemberg became kingdoms. The knell of the old Empire was already sounded when the imperial princes in the west formed themselves into the

Confederation of the Rhine under Napoleon's protectorate. The imperial church, for a thousand years the prop and stay of the Holy Roman Empire, was broken up for good. Sweeping changes in 1803 completed the secularization of ecclesiastical foundations begun at the Reformation and also accomplished the 'mediatization' of the towns directly dependent on the Empire (which with only six exceptions now passed under the control of secular princes). The secularized lands on the right bank of the Rhine went by prearrangement (secret negotiations had started as early as 1795) to princes with lands on the left bank which under the peace of Lunéville (1801) were surrendered to France. In some of the secularized territories all the church lands and revenues became the property of the new ruler. In others, while the new ruler was free to dispose of property not used for strictly ecclesiastical purposes, he was made responsible for meeting the costs of providing divine service and instruction and for the upkeep of establishments used by the public at large.

In permitting this liquidation of the imperial church the 'new Charlemagne' dealt the Holy Roman Empire its death blow. Charles the Great had created the imperial church and laid the foundations of the Holy Roman Empire. The 'second Charlemagne' dissolved the imperial church and assumed the style of an emperor. The emperor in Vienna was justifiably afraid that the new emperor in Paris intended to claim for himself the supreme imperial office, that of Roman Emperor of the Holy Roman Empire.

In France, obsequious churchmen 'happy to have discovered someone to restore the church's liberty, never tired of comparing Napoleon with Charles the Great' (Karl Fürst Schwarzenberg). Charles the Great, it was said, had been the first French Emperor. Ever since the twelfth century French propaganda had sought to devalue the Roman emperor by calling him 'German'. Now the true Charles-emperor had appeared. Napoleon proceeded to set up electorates on the old model and to create an imperial nobility whose dukes he invested with provinces. At his coronation he used insignia allegedly or actually descended from Charles the Great. The pope had to be present to administer to the self-crowned emperor the rite of unction as a sign of consecration. For a millennium men had debated what it was that had happened at Rome on Christmas Day 800: this was Napoleon's solution. Napoleon next revoked his predecessor's donation to the pope and invaded the Papal State. Finally he made it known that emperors of the French were crowned in Paris and in Rome.

Napoleon married himself into the old family of nations by taking to wife Marie Louise, daughter of Emperor Francis II. It was a nuptial union intended to conciliate the old Europe with the new and to confer on Napoleon himself the highest possible legitimacy. His son became 'King of Rome' and imperial eagles adorned his cradle, as also the escutcheons and banners of the new imperial realm.

Paris, true city of light, had long been a kind of anti-Rome (had not the university of Paris once claimed to judge popes?); it was now to be the true Aachen and the true Rome. Napoleon wanted to have the pope beside him in Paris, just as Charles the Great had probably wanted to keep his pope in Aachen. In Paris, too, palaces of the *reguli*, the sub-kings, should arise around the gleaming new palaces of the emperor.

The new Augustus-Charles-Alexander had thoughts of proclaiming himself Emperor of the West and was so acclaimed by his army when he reached the North Sea. As an exile on St Helena he had time to reflect on the conquering progress of his career. It had started in Egypt, where from the Pyramids 'forty centuries looked down' on him; he judged that the imperial office itself was between four and five thousand years old. In Egypt, so he now averred, he and his army might well have gone over to Islam (this possibility also occurred to men around Hitler and Himmler): as a new Alexander he could have founded a world empire in the east. To medieval men Alexander the Great was the patriarchal emperor, prototype of Christ the Celestial Emperor (Alexander is shown in medieval cathedrals ascending heavenwards in a kind of aerial balloon). The French bishops in their pastoral letters commended the veneration of the new Charles to the faithful: he was the chosen of the Lord of Hosts. The new imperial catechism and the imperial legislation for schools make much of the harmony between imperial throne and altar. Earlier on, however, Napoleon had shown no reluctance in assuming the role of those most christian kings of the Middle Ages who brought all possible pressure to bear to make the popes amenable. Philip the Fair had threatened Boniface VIII through his French national council. Napoleon cowed his pope, held in captivity in Savoy, through a French national council which German and Italian bishops were also commanded to attend.

The Napoleon of the Hundred Days proclaimed his new constitution on a festival he called the 'Field of May', the name given to the great Carolingian assemblies. This fustian flourish highlights the peculiarly theatrical and artificial quality of all attempts at Empire once the Holy Roman Empire was no more. In their own way they are demonstrations, acts of propaganda. The last attempt at a similarly contrived link-up with the past was Hitler's translation of the 'relics' of the Duke of Reichstatt during the Second World War.

We have it on the authority of Alfred Loisy, a distinguished French historian of religion and a critic of Christianity, that the ancient Carolingian liturgical prayers beseeching God for an imperial victory were offered for Napoleon III shortly before his capture and defeat by the Prussians in 1870. Loisy was among a choir of school-children which greeted the weary and ailing man on his way to the front. The King of Prussia, Bismarck and the Crown Prince all found the proclamation of the Prussian King as emperor in Louis XIV's Galérie des Glaces at Versailles an almost unbearable farce. The new emperor spoke not a word to Bismarck all day, and during the banquet even refused to look at a design for an imperial coat of arms. Shown a portrait of himself painted by a patriotic artist with the insignia of the old emperors he commented, 'It makes me look like a priest of Baal'.

William I of Prussia was not crowned at Versailles in 1871. Bismarck held that 'the true crown' lay in Vienna. The Hohenzollerns asked to have it, but the Viennese government refused. Thanks to the initiative of the Crown Prince, the first diet of the Second Reich was opened with the emperor seated on an ancient imperial throne from Goslar, on which Henry IV, Philip of Swabia, Otto IV and Frederick I had once sat enthroned. In 1809 the throne had been sold for a song to a Goslar tinsmith who intended to melt it down. By a lucky chance it escaped this fate and was ultimately recognized by Klaproth, the discoverer of uranium, as a 'rare and ancient object' and purchased for three thousand marks by a brother of William I who was a collector of antiquities. But the Hohenzollerns still needed a crown for their new Empire. William I and his son Frederick agreed on a style which resembled the octagonal crown of Otto the Great, and a wooden model of it was on view in the Hohenzollern museum at Monbijou on the Spree until shortly before the end of the Second World War, when it was burnt in the fire which destroyed the whole building.

The Crown Prince (in the line of Prussian rulers Frederick III) succeeded his father when he himself was mortally ill. He wished to be known as Frederick IV, that is to say as the successor of Emperor Frederick III, father of Maximilian I. Bismarck telegraphed an immediate veto: he was utterly opposed to any move which proclaimed, or even implied, that the German empire he had fabricated was the successor to the Holy Roman Empire.

Historical play-acting, especially when he could appear in the guise of an old German emperor, appealed greatly to Emperor William II ('Kaiser Wilhelm'). He staged festivals of chivalry at the Marienburg, decked himself out with the Virgin's cross of the Teutonic Knights, carried about with him the crooked stick used by Frederick the Great and was even deferential to the emperor in Vienna. During his exile at Doorn he worked on a monograph dealing with the evolution of the imperial baldachin. He had a reconstruction of Constantine's labarum made for his palace chapel, with the intention, so it is said, of having it borne before him at the end of that world war in which, as the new Constantine, he would have triumphed over the heathen surrounding him on east and west.

We are reminded of the motives imputed to Otto I at the battle at the Lech in 955, motives which no doubt also inspired his imperial bishops and faithful followers: the king makes peace and attests his saving power as king through victory in battle. Faith and security – both are created by the sword. The victorious king pacifies the German peoples and brings the Empire into being, therefore to him belongs the imperial crown.

'What an uplifting sight: the German peoples invincibly shoulder to shoulder and ready for bloody battles against the enemies of the fatherland. A people filled with such a united will to victory and dedicated to the continuing influence of German culture and the German way of life, may feel justifiably conscious of the support of him who is the Almighty Lord of battles and of the destinies of mankind.' Thus Kaiser Wilhelm on 10 September 1914, yet the decisive blow had already been struck the day before, on the Marne.

A month earlier, in Berlin, the Kaiser had issued his call to arms in which he invoked the thousand-year-old German trust in the sword, applying it to the new situation. 'Since the Empire was founded forty-three years ago, it has been the burning preoccupation of myself and my predecessors to preserve world peace and to promote in peace our vigorous development. But our enemies begrudge us our success. Hitherto, conscious of our responsibility and might, we have tolerated all the open and secret acts of hostility against us in east and west and beyond the seas, but now they want to humiliate us.' Kaiser Wilhelm's feeling that his Empire was under attack was as acute as that of any medieval imperial theologian when he contemplated the challenge offered to his Empire from Byzantium in the east and from the kinglets of the west.

Two weeks later the emperor bade farewell to the first regiment of infantry guards, who were leaving Berlin to go into action. He drew his sword from the scabbard and brandished it over his head: 'It is our ancient glory to appeal to the German people and its sword. And the entire German people has grasped the sword, down to the last man. So I too draw the sword, that with God's help has been left for so many decades in its scabbard.'

Millions of Germans fought in the Great War, enlisted in their 'tribes' under their 'princes', 'as in the Middle Ages.'

Two world wars and the technological and industrial revolution have accelerated a development which began with Napoleon's liquidation of the Holy Roman Empire. Deliberately uprooted, the colourful diversity of life in Europe has gradually withered away. The great drive to make countries, political institutions and men uniform and conformist, the drive so successfully promoted by Richelieu, Mazarin, Louis XIV and the great revolution, in the nineteenth century also made its impact on the German central core of Old Europe. Englishmen and continental Europeans assisted alike in the forward march of this process through which Europe developed its technical, economic and military potential and made for itself new and freely-expanding labour markets, spheres of influence and battle-grounds. Much has been lost to Europe as a result: personality becomes rarer, almost non-existent. Take a look at a hundred faces from the Holy Roman Empire, for example the men and women who frequented Goethe's 'Buchenwald' near Weimar, and then at the ten thousand faces ground into conformity in the Buchenwald concentration camp – the 'same' Buchenwald – and a regression is all too obvious. In the course of a single century millions of subjects, 'citizens' who pay their taxes to a state and become its cannon fodder, have lost their old identities.

The Holy Roman Empire had contained within it many fatherlands and mother-lands, all the greater and lesser principalities and lordships which it sheltered under its roof. Goethe remained a Frankfurter all his life. Schiller a Swabian in exile. Beethoven's 'fatherland' was Bonn, and Max Franz, the last Elector of Cologne 'his' elector. The youngest son of Maria Theresa, Max Franz, may here serve as a model for all the various types of German princes who still soldiered on, even during the Empire's last decades. For some of his predecessors in 'the holy city of Cologne' the

Empire had provided nothing more than a personal claim to dignity, importance and pomp. In 1706, Elector Joseph Clemens had claimed as arch-chancellor of the Holy Roman Empire for Italy (*Archicancellarius Imperii per Italiam* once figured among the titles of the archbishop of Cologne) the right to wear a cardinal's robes and to exercise all the right of a member of the sacred college, apart from electing the Pope. This, so he said, was 'his privilege', which he intended to restore. The aim of Elector Max Franz was to reform Cologne and to serve the Empire. He belonged to the younger generation of German princes which did such fruitful work as reformers and enlighteners during the very last years of the Empire's history: they built schools and universities, founded laboratories for medical and scientific research, encouraged industry, agriculture and the craft trades.

'I have no nephews or family whom I ought to help, no mistresses or bastards to make a nest egg for.' Elector Max Franz walked about Bonn quite unattended, dressed in a shabby grey overcoat. He cut down the personnel of the court and had an easy, unforced relationship with the townspeople. Georg Forster, who was a defender of the French Revolution, mentions that in 1790 he saw the elector helping a poor woman with a heavy basket – proof, he says, of the man's genuine humanity. The elector of Cologne possessed to the full that 'affability' which had struck people in the first Rudolf of Habsburg, in Maximilian I and in other members of the arch-house.

'It shall be my lifelong endeavour,' says Max Franz in a private letter, 'to protect the weak and oppressed; and I shall be guided solely by the justice of their cause, not by my personal advantage.' He made fundamental reforms in elementary education and in the training of school teachers; in 1786 he founded the university of Bonn. His political faith emerges from the following declaration: 'I will endeavour to uphold the constitution of our German Empire, on which the well-being of so many individuals depends, ignoring any expectations of advantage men may offer me, and I shall always speak in the language of truth, the language of justice, leaving to others the language of politics.' Max Franz was an imperial patriot with a very clear perception of how things now stood. Greatly though he grieved for his sister, Marie Antoinette, he refused to contemplate an armed attack on the French Revolution and declared against any intervention.

Max Franz had no use for the French *émigrés* who were so busy organizing the counter-revolution on German soil, and to the day of his death inveighed against them as immoral, war-mongering, '*émigré*-vermin'; he found it particularly odious that – thanks largely to their ecclesiastical connections – they should use Germany as a platform (they still do) from which to denounce the French Revolution and the dawning of the new era as anti-christian and the 'satanic advance' of democracy. Max Franz refused to allow them into his lands. He held that the fugitive aristocracy were guilty whichever way one looked at it: 'they had either brought on the revolution by their unrestrained, self-seeking, scheming conduct, or else, through their cowardly behaviour, which ran counter to their duty, they had allowed the revolution to gain the upper hand by escaping abroad to posture and swagger as enemies of their fatherland, whereas they should have stayed to expend their property and blood for the sake of preserving a sound order.'

Max Franz deliberately set out to mediate between Vienna and the princes of the Empire. During the early days of the war he continued to work on his plans for reforming the courts of the three ecclesiastical electors and warned against any involvement of the Empire in a war with the French Revolution; if war there must be, he thought the emperor should be given quasi-dictatorial powers for the duration. He left Bonn for the last time on 3 October 1794, only a few days before the French entered the town. Afterwards he remarked to the Austrian ambassador with bitter irony that things had gone so far that there was doubtless nothing left for him but to put on the red cap and become a Jacobin. His greatest remaining wish was to make a tour of America. In April 1800 he transferred his residence to Vienna, where he died on 27 July 1801, at the age of forty-four, and was buried in the Capuchin vault.

Ernst Moritz Arndt, who was no friend to the clerical order or to the Ancien Régime, or for that matter to Austria, travelled through the lands of the electorate during the French occupation and set down his impressions. 'The rule of Max, that humane and liberal prince of the house of Austria, seems to have set a new tide of life flowing among the people. He was generous in his patronage of all the peaceful arts, tended the young growth of the university, followed the example of his great brother by reinstating the human intellect in its sacred rights, sought to put fresh life into manufacturing enterprises, and by discarding all pomp – a necessity only to the weak – stood forward as the first citizen of his state. The electorate of Cologne was thus one of the happiest of lands, until war broke out and ravaged the lovely countries of the Rhine.'

Like so many of his imperial forebears, Max Franz was very musical. He played stringed instruments, in later life taking especial pleasure in the viola, and had his voice trained. In Vienna he joined in the music of his brother's household and helped Joseph to decide which new operas were worthy of presentation. Max Franz welcomed the new German movement represented by Gluck, Haydn, Mozart. His connection with Mozart began in 1775, when the composer wrote the opera *Il re pastore*, first performed at Salzburg on 23 April of that year in honour of the eighteen-year-old prince.

Beethoven was born and brought up in Bonn, the capital of the electorate of Cologne. His father, the tenor Johann van Beethoven, was a member of the electoral chapel. When Beethoven went to Vienna to study under Haydn, Max Franz continued his stipend of four hundred guldens and paid him another five hundred as a subsistence allowance. Beethoven's name figures in the projected 'establishment' for the new electorate being founded at Münster (Cologne having vanished in 1803). He is mentioned as remaining without stipend at Vienna, 'pending his recall'. Beethoven intended to dedicate his first symphony to 'his' elector, but Max Franz died before the work was finished. It was as an unfinished symphony that the Empire descended to its successor states.

'Five thousand years measure the flight path of the imperial eagle, as he makes his way from the temple towers of Eridu towards the setting sun, towards the evening mists veiling the future of the atomic age.' Thus Prince Karl Schwarzenberg, a contemporary Czech historian whose forebears belonged to the Estates of the Holy Roman Empire. In his *Adler und Drache* he brings before us the complementary images which testify to this continuity: the eternal emperor, the patriarchal king Gayomart, and Adam, the first lord of creation, as seen on the orb of Rudolf II in Prague; the sun-bearing emperor, the Sumerian God-king enthroned on his roll seal, facing Otto IV on a Golden Bull; the conquering emperor, Alexander the Great, as he appears on the Sidon sarcophagus, standing beside Charles V as painted by Titian; the emperor who restores an ancient and sacred legal order after doing battle with 'pagan' godless enemies, Darius the Great triumphing over false kings and Leopold the Great (as the Court Chronicle describes Leopold I) triumphing over the Grand Turk; the peace-creating emperor, Augustus, and his clan standing before the Altar of Peace, Francis I of Austria returning home from the war of liberation; hunting emperors, King Bahram in pursuit of the wild boar and Francis Joseph I in pursuit of the deer; the fertility emperor, Pharaoh Scorpion hoeing, Emperor Joseph II ploughing; the feasting emperor, Assurbanipal at a banquet on a relief from Nineveh, Charles IV at his coronation banquet from a manuscript of the Golden Bull; the emperor of Eternal Rome, Augustus enthroned with the goddess Roma on the *gemma augustea* (now in Vienna), Frederick I enthroned in the city of Rome (from a Golden Bull); the emperor who renews the sacred imperial past and the rightful order, Marcus Aurelius in his equestrian statue at Rome, his 'brother' Joseph II in his equestrian monument at Vienna.

The Empire moves from country to country, one imperial capital taking over from another, the imperial relics, the Empire 'incarnate', being transmitted from one generation to the next:

The great kings of antiquity carry the images of the gods with them, Napoleon receives at Aachen the reliquary of Charles the Great, even the museums of our great modern cities are still fragmented replicas of the old hoards of relics. A special thread of continuity binds together the imperial cities, and the present inhabitants of an erstwhile capital may continue to regard it as high and holy. A thread thus runs from Eridu to Babylon, from Babylon to Istachr, Beleukia, and Alexandria; Alexandria itself is heir to Memphis and Thebes; Alexandria's new sovereign brings its treasures to Rome, from Rome one thread leads to Constantinople, but another runs to Aachen and thence to Vienna.

When Joseph came to Rome the populace made him welcome with the greeting *'siete a casa'*: Rome was where the emperor belonged. Goethe noted on his Italian journey that a sizeable number of Romans would have preferred Joseph's government to that of the papal regime. The Romans' liturgical salutation to the emperor – *conservet Deus* – first rang out eleven centuries before Haydn composed his 'God save our Emperor' for Francis II, the last Roman emperor: that same Emperor Francis II who as Emperor Francis I of Austria deliberately chose to place the imperial double-headed eagle on the crest of the Danube monarchy. Until 1860 the Roman Church continued to offer its prayers for the Emperor Francis (and in due course Francis Joseph) in the old form: the decree of the Congregation of Rites instituting the new forms introduced under the concordat of 1860 cites the canonized emperor, Henry II, as Francis Joseph's predecessor. Prayers for the emperor were offered after 1815 even in the Protestant state churches of Brunswick and Mecklenburg, and at Zara the ancient *laudes* could still be heard in our own day; they were sung for the last time for Emperor Charles, at Easter 1918.

The imperial insignia were not allowed to fall into French hands. Francis, the last Roman Emperor, rescued them from Aachen and Nuremberg and had them taken first to Regensburg, then to Vienna, then to Budapest, and lastly to Temesvar, the capital of the Banat which lay between Siebenbürgen and Belgrade: one might almost say that the 'Empire' had taken refuge with the 'Turks'. In 1801 the imperial insignia – the '*rich*' – were brought to the Empire's last resting-place, the treasury of the Hofburg at Vienna.

With the passing centuries the crown treasure gradually took on the character of relics. We know that the holy lance was very early regarded as a relic in the narrowly ecclesiastical sense. In the oldest inventories the holy lance, together with the fragments of the true cross, takes precedence over the imperial crown. The 'imperial cross', the name given to the reliquary containing these fragments, is more powerful and impressive than the crown itself; it is indeed the most monumental piece of goldsmith's work displayed among the insignia. The feast in honour of the holy lance was introduced into the Roman Church by Innocent VI at the request of Charles IV; later a feast of the nails of Christ's cross was instituted, celebrated on the second Friday after Easter.

These relics of the Holy Roman Empire are relics of a world order founded on the sacred households of the God-Emperor in heaven and upon earth which endured for five thousand years. Today people look at them as one looks at a spectacle and at works of art – yet once they were what men believed in and the condensed manifestation of the Empire's saving power. There they are: the imperial crown, a sacred octagon combining the earthly and the heavenly Jerusalem, surmounted by the bow which demands that the kings of the earth pay due service to the King who is Emperor in heaven as upon earth; the imperial sword, always borne point uppermost, whose inscription – *Christus vincit* – *Christus regnat* – *Christus imperat* – echoes the ancient victory song addressed to the victorious *Christus imperator* in the *laudes* following the imperial coronation and is a prayer for further victories; the Hohenstaufen orb, which ascribes to the Emperor, by placing the globe in his hand, the attributes of Jupiter: in antiquity the orb was surmounted by Nike the victory goddess, in the Holy Roman Empire by the cross. Emperor Otto I had once worn the star-strewn mantle and the tunic fringed with tintinnabula, part of the vestment of the high priest. Embroidered into the coronation robe made for King Roger II in 1133–4, which is now in the treasury at Vienna, is an Arabic song in praise of Palermo: 'here where days and nights may pass in delights, changeless and unending, one is filled with feelings of respect and devotion and a stimulating sense of sharing in happiness, in the continuance of well-being and in the sustenance provided by whatever activity is needful'. What is this but a reminder of the earthly paradise created by the prince of peace?

The Empire created peace, that was its mission. It was the mission ascribed to Otto the Great by his contemporaries and comrades-in-arms. To create peace the Emperor must be and must become the prince of peace; first and last, that was his function. *Il re pastore*, shepherd king, prince of peace, was the title of the opera with which Mozart saluted the Archduke Maximilian, the young man many hoped would become emperor and renew the Empire. Latterly the prince of peace has been gradually withdrawing from the field, into the realm of music and literature. Hölderlin's prince of peace in his marvellous hymn *Die Friedensfeier* (only discovered in London after World War II) is a mythic figure, with traces of Napoleon and Christ. When Hugo von Hofmannsthal, together with Max Reinhardt, founded the Salzburg drama festival in Mozart's city after World War I as a means of reconciling the peoples, he was invoking that mythic prince of peace who hovers as the spirit of reconciliation behind his works and who once, as a child, as the child-king in the 'tower', conjured up the oldest visions of humanity. The divine child is the playing child, the *logos pais* seen by the early Greeks at play with the terrestrial ball.

Peace in the Empire, peace because of the Empire: this Great Peace was the goal emperors and kings, imperial princes, bishops and abbots, ecclesiastical and secular Estates strove for as they met in the imperial diet and fought their literally interminable campaigns. The theme of peace among men and peace between God and man is the point at which the great thinkers whose intellectual and psychic roots were implanted in the Empire intersect: Meister Eckhart, Nicholas of Cusa, Leibniz, Goethe. In them and because of them the old powers recede, the Empire to become an inward empire of mankind, the Holy Roman Church to become an invisible church of the Holy Spirit. We see this many-sided process starting with Joachim of Flora and still at work in Kant and Hölderlin; it has yet to come to an end.

The Empire is no longer in a position to assert itself on the old battlefields of this world. Those who bore rule in it always disappointed expectations by demanding peace instead of giving it. Hence it is that today – after our catastrophic wars – we find ourselves with boundaries which almost match those of the old Empire of a thousand years ago: the Elbe and Saale boundaries of Germany in the age of Otto the Great were not very far removed from the existing frontier between the German Bundesrepublik and the Deutsche Demokratische Republik, which politically speaking belongs to a different hemisphere.

The year 1833 saw the last meeting of the three heads of the Holy Alliance, the alliance which some people (visionary Germans living in Russia, for example Madame de Krüdener) hoped would manifest the old Holy Roman Empire in a new trinity: a peace league of three christian churches, a true league of nations. This conference between the Tsar, the Emperor of Austria and the King of Prussia took place at the castle of Münchengrätz in northern Bohemia, in whose chapel the remains of Wallenstein were finally interred, a century and a half after his death. Shortly before the conclusion of the Peace of Westphalia, at Wallenstein's own castle in Friedland, the last Swedish commander had asked for a table to be brought in: 'Peace is always stronger than war'.

In present-day Vienna, only a few paces away from the treasure chamber in the Hofburg which contains the relics of the Holy Roman Empire, there is a perpetual coming and going of international congresses and conferences, not least important among them the meetings of the Atomic Energy Commission of the United Nations. The flags of the nations old and new which co-inhabit this one world are displayed in brotherly contiguity on the Hofburg façade. The halls are filled with discussions and disputes, seemingly 'interminable', as in the days of the imperial diets and their successor, the Perpetual Diet at Regensburg. Nearby are the relics of the Holy Roman Empire, issuing to all men their warning against settling these conflicts in forms which lead to self-destruction.

BIBLIOGRAPHY

The bibliography lists first books characterized as 'general'; these titles are not repeated in the bibliographies for each chapter which follow. The 'general' section is divided into three: the works listed in section A by and large cover the whole period, those in section B cover the whole or a substantial part of the period dealt with in chapters 2–6, those in section C do the same for the period dealt with in chapters 7–13. Additional titles in English which the English-speaking reader may find useful are marked with an asterisk. For an even fuller bibliography the reader is referred to the German edition of the book (*Das Heilige Römische Reich*, Berne–Munich–Vienna, 1967).

ABBREVIATIONS

MIÖG *Mitteilungen des österreichischen Instituts für Geschichtsforschung*, Vienna
HZ   *Historische Zeitschrift*, Munich
DA   *Deutsche Aussenpolitik*, East Berlin
ZRG   *Zeitschrift für Religions- und Geistesgeschichte*, Brühl-Cologne

GENERAL: A

O. Brunner. *Land und Herrschaft*, 3rd ed., Brunn–Vienna, 1943

*J. Bryce. *The Holy Roman Empire*, first published 1864, last revised ed. 1906

H. U. Engel. *Die Strasse nach Europa. Reichskleinodien und Kaiserkrönungen*, Hamburg, 1962

*R. Dybowski, O. Halecki, J. H. Penson, W. F. Reddaway, eds. *A Cambridge History of Poland*, Cambridge, 1941–50

H. Fillitz. *Die Insignien und Kleinodien des Heiligen Römisches Reiches*, Vienna–Munich, 1954

F. Gaupp. *Deutsche Fälschung der abendländischen Reichsidee*, Berne, 1946

F. Heer. *The intellectual history of Europe*, translated by J. Steinberg, London and New York, 1966

W. Honneke. *Formwandel und Probleme des Abendlandes*, Biberach, 1951

J. Huizinga. *Homo ludens. A study of the play-element in culture*, translated by R. F. C. Hull, London, 1949 (first published 1938); New York, 1955

R.L.John. *Reich und Kirche im Spiegel französischen Denkens. Das Rombild von Cäsar bis Napoleon*, Vienna, 1955

W.König. *Idee und Geschichte des Welttheaters in Europa. Sine dramaturgische und szenische Gestaltung von Aeschylos bis Paul Claudel*, Vienna, 1951

A.Mirgeler. *Geschichte Europas*, Freiburg, 1953

H.Nicolson. *Monarchy*, London, 1962; issued as *Kings, Courts and Monarchy*, New York, 1962

P.Rassow. *Die geschichtliche Einheit des Abendlandes*, Cologne–Graz, 1960

R.R.Rohden. *Die Idee des Reiches in der europäischen Geschichte*, Oldenburg, 1943

E.Rosenstock-Huessy. *Die europäischen Revolutionen und der Charakter der Nationen*, Stuttgart, 1951

P.E.Schramm. *Sphaira, Globus und Reichsapfel*, Stuttgart, 1958

P.E.Schramm and F.Mütherich. *Denkmale der deutschen Könige und Kaiser*, Munich, 1962

K.Schwarzenberg. *Adler und Drache. Der Weltherrschaftsgedanke*, Vienna–Munich, 1958

V.Valentin. *Weltgeschichte*, Cologne–Berlin, 1939

L.Bittner. 'Der Titel Heiliges Römisches Reich deutscher Nation', *MIÖG*, 34, 1913

A.Diehl. 'Heiliges Römisches Reich deutscher Nation', *HZ*, 156, 1937

GENERAL: B

*G.Barraclough. *Medieval Germany 911–1250*. Essays by German historians, translated with an introduction, 2 vols., Oxford, 1938

*Ditto. *The origins of modern Germany*, Oxford, 2nd ed., 1947

K.Bösl. *Die Reichsministerialität der Salier und Staufer*, Stuttgart, 1950–1

C.Dawson. *The making of Europe*, London, 1932

G.Falco. *The Holy Roman Republic*. Translation by K. V. Kent, 1964, of the 2nd ed., Milan–Naples, 1954

H.Fichtenau. *Grundzüge der Geschichte des Mittelalters*, Vienna, 1947

R.Folz. *L'idée d'empire en Occident du 5e au 14e siècle*, Paris 1953 (with bibliography)

L.Génicot. *The contours of the Middle Ages*, translated by L. and R. Wood, London and New York, 1967

M.Goldast. *Monarchia S.Romani Imperii*, 1611–14, reprinted, Graz, 1960

Rhabanus Maurus Haache. *Rom und die Cäsaren. Geschichte des Cäsaropapismus*, Düsseldorf, 1947

K.Hampe. *Deutsche Kaisergeschichte in der Zeit der Salier und Staufer*, 8th ed. revised by F.Baethgen, Leipzig, 1943

J.Hashagen. *Europa im Mittelalter*, Munich, 1951

F.Heer. *Die Tragödie des Heiligen Reiches*, Stuttgart, 1952 (full bibliographies of the older literature)

Ditto. *The Medieval world*, translated by J.Sondheimer, London, 1961; New York, 1962

W.Holtzmann. *Das mittelalterliche Imperium und die werdenden Nationen*, Cologne–Opladen, 1953

K.G.Hugelmann. *Stämme, Nation und Nationalstaat im deutschen Mittelalter*, Würzburg, 1955

H.U.Instinsky. *Bischofsstuhl und Kaiserthron*, Munich, 1955

H.Kampf. *Das Reich im Mittelalter*, Stuttgart, 1950

E.H.Kantorowicz. *The king's two bodies. A study in medieval political theology*, Princeton, 1957

R.Latouche. *The birth of western economy. Economic aspects of the dark ages*, translated by E.M.Wilkinson, New York, 1960; London, 1961

R.Maschke. *Der Kampf zwischen Kaisertum und Papsttum*, Constance, 1955

L.Santifaller. *Zur Geschichte des ottonisch-salischen Reichskirchensystems*, Vienna, 1954

F.Schneider. *Die neueren Anschauungen der deutschen Historiker über die Kaiserpolitik des Mittelalters*, 6th ed., Weimar, 1943

P.E.Schramm. *Kaiser, Rom und Renovatio*, Leipzig–Berlin, 1929

G.Schreiber. *Gemeinschaften des Mittelalters*, Münster, 1948

H.Steger. *David Rex et Propheta. König David als vorbildliche Verkörperung des Herrschers und Dichters in Mittelalter*, Nuremberg, 1961

W.Ullmann. *Medieval papalism*, London and New York, 1949

Ditto. *The growth of papal government in the Middle Ages. A study in the ideological relations of clerical lay power*, London and New York, 1955

W.Wegener. *Böhmen, Mähren und das Reich im Hochmittelalter (919–1253)*, Cologne–Graz, 1959

Deutsche Königspfalzen. Beiträge zu ihrer historischen und archäologischen Erforschung. Veröffentlichungen des Max-Planck-Instituts für Geschichte, 11/1, Göttingen, 1963

D.Gerhard. 'Neusiedlung und institutionelles Erbe – zum Problem von Turner's "frontier", *Ein Leben aus freier Mitte, Beiträge zur Geschichtsforschung (Festschrift Ulrich Noack)*, Göttingen, 1961

K.L.Lampe. 'Die europäische Bedeutung des deutschen Ordens', *Blätter für deutsche Landesgeschichte*, 88, 1951

W.Schlesinger. 'Die geschichtliche Stellung der mittelalterlichen deutschen Ostbewegung', *HZ*, 183, 1957

BYZANTIUM:

A.Michel. *Die Kaisermacht in der Ostkirche (843–1204)*, Darmstadt, 1959

O.Treitinger. *Die oströmische Kaiser- und Reichsidee nach ihrer Gestaltung im höfischen Zeremoniell. Vom oströmischen Staats- und Reichsgedanken*, 2nd ed., Darmstadt, 1956

GENERAL: C

F.Baethgen. *Europa im Spätmittelalter*, Berlin, 1951

Bodan Chudoba. *Spain and the Empire, 1518–1643*, Chicago–London, 1952

*J.H.Elliott. *Imperial Spain, 1469–1716*, London, 1963; New York, 1964

P.Frischauer. *Die Habsburger. Geschichte einer Familie*, Vienna–Berlin, 1961

O. Geschliesser. *Der Reichshofrat, Bedeutung und Verfassung, Schicksal und Besetzung einer obersten Reichsbehörde von 1559 bis 1806*, Vienna, 1942

L.Gross. *Die Geschichte der deutschen Reichshofkanzlei von 1559*, Vienna, 1933

R.A.Kann. *Werden und Zerfall des Habsburgerreiches*, Graz–Vienna, 1962

J.van Klaveren. *Europäische Wirtschaftsgeschichte Spaniens im 16./17.Jahrhundert*, Stuttgart, 1960

Götz Freiherr von Pölnitz. *Die Fugger*, Frankfurt, 1960

M.Dugast Rouille, etc. *Les grands mariages des Habsbourgs*, Paris, 1955

E.Schaeffer. *Habsburger schreiben Briefe. Privatbriefe aus fünf Jahrhunderten*, Leipzig, 1935

M.Uhlirz. *Handbuch der Geschichte Österreichs*, 4 vols., 1927–44

A.Wandruszka. *The house of Habsburg*, translated by C. and H. Epstein, London and New York, 1964 (2nd German edition, Stuttgart, 1956)

CHAPTER 2: THE EMPIRE OF CHARLES THE GREAT

C.A.Bouman. *Sacring and Crowning. The development of the Latin ritual for the anointing of kings before the 11th century*, Groningen, 1957

*D.Bullough. *The age of Charlemagne*, London and New York, 1965

J.Calmette. *Charlemagne, sa vie et son oeuvre*, Paris, 1945

W.Ensslin. *Gottkaiser und Kaiser von Gottes Gnaden*, Munich, 1943

H.Fichtenau. *The Carolingian Empire*, translated (in shortened form) by P.Munz, 1957

P.Mennicken, etc. 'Der Aachener Dom', articles in the special number *Aachen zum Jahre 1951* of the Rheinischen Vereins für Denkmalpflege und Heimatschutz

W.Metz. *Das karolingische Reichsgut*, Berlin, 1960

Th.Schieffer. *Winfrid-Bonifatius und die christliche Grundlegung Europas*, Freiburg, 1954

H.Schnitzler. *Der Dom zu Aachen*, Düsseldorf, 1950

P.E.Schramm. *Die Anerkennung Karls des Grossen als Kaiser. Ein Kapitel aus der Geschichte der mittelalterlichen Staatssymbolik*, Munich, 1952

P.Classen. 'Die Verträge von Verdun und Coulaines 843 als politische Grundlagen des westfränkischen Reiches', *HZ*, 196, 1963

H.Fichtenau. 'Byzanz und die Pfalz zu Aachen', *MIÖG*, 59, 1951

F.Heer. 'Die Renaissance-Ideologie im frühen Mittelalter', *MIÖG*, 57, 1949

W.Rüegg. 'Der autoritative Humanismus der Karolingerzeit', *Agora* 12, 5 Jg. 1959, p. 12

P.E.Schramm. 'Karl der Grosse. Denkart und Grundauffassungen – Die von ihm bewirkte Correctio', *HZ*, 198, 1964

CHAPTER 3: THE OTTONIAN EMPIRE

G.A.Bezzola. *Das ottonische Kaisertum in der französischen Geschichtsschreibung des 10. und beginnenden 11. Jahrhunderts*, Graz–Cologne, 1956

A.Brackmann. *Kaiser Otto III. und die staatliche Umgestaltung Polens und Ungarns*, Berlin, 1939 (Abh.d.Preuss. Adademie der Wiss.)

M.Buending. *Das Imperium Christianum und die deutschen Ostkriege vom 10. bis zum 12. Jahrhundert*, Berlin, 1940

J.Deer. *Die Entstehung des ungarischen Königtums*, Budapest, 1942

J.Deer. *Heidnisches und Christliches in der altungarischen Monarchie*, Szeged, 1934

H.Grundmann. *Betrachtungen zur Kaiserkrönung Ottos I*, Munich, 1962

R.Holtzmann. *Geschichte der sächsischen Kaiserzeit (900–1024)*, Munich, 1941

M.Lintzel. *Die Kaiserpolitik Ottos des Grossen*, Munich, 1943

J.Bernhart. 'Bischof Udalrich von Augsburg', *Augusta*, 955–1955, Munich, 1955

C.Erdmann. 'Das ottonische Reich als Imperium Romanum', *DA*, 6, 1943

Festschriften 962–1962: 'Renovatio Imperii': Atti della Giornata Internazionale di Studio per il Millenario (Ravenna, 4.–5. Nov. 1961), Faenza 1963; Festschrift zur Jahrtausendfeier der Kaiserkrönung Ottos des Grossen, *MIÖG*, Ergänzungsband XX, 3 vols.

L.Hauptmann. 'Universalismus und Nationalismus im Kaisertum der Ottonen' (Festschrift Hugelmann, p. 189)

F.Heer. 'Deutsche und europäische Perspektiven der Lechfeldschlacht', *Tausend Jahre Abendland*, Augsburg-Basel, 1956

★K.Leyser. 'The battle at the Lech, 955', *History*, 50, 1965

H.Löwe. 'Kaisertum und Abendland in ottonischer und frühsalischer Zeit', *HZ*, 196, 1963

CHAPTER 4: THE EMPIRE OF THE SALIANS

W.Plöchl. *Geschichte des Kirchenrechts*, Vol. II, Vienna–Munich, 1962

R.Sprandel. *Ivo von Chartres und seine Stellung in der Kirchengeschichte*, Stuttgart, 1962

W.von den Steinen. *Canossa, Heinrich IV. und die Kirche*, Munich, 1957

CHAPTER 5: SACRUM IMPERIUM: THE EMPIRE AND IMPERIAL IDEOLOGY
UNDER THE HOHENSTAUFEN

P.A.van den Baar. *Die kirchliche Lehre der translatio imperii Romani bis zur Mitte des 13. Jahrhunderts*, Rome, 1956

W.Goez. *Translatio imperii*, Tübingen, 1958 (see esp. pp. 104 and 157)

H.Grundmann. *Neue Forschungen über Joachim von Fiore*, Marburg, 1950 (see esp. p. 25)

E.Hellmann. *Die Reichsidee in deutschen Dichtungen der Salier und frühen Stauferzeit*, Berlin, 1963

W.Kaegi. *Chronica Mundi*, Einsiedeln, 1954

F.Kempf. *Papsttum und Kaisertum bei Innocenz III. Die geistigen und rechtlichen Grundlagen seiner Thronstreitpolitik*, Rome, 1954

E.Klingelhoefer. *Die Reichsgesetze von 1220, 1231/2 und 1235. Ihr Werden und ihre Wirkung im deutschen Staat Friedrichs II.*, Weimar, 1955

P. E. Schramm. *Kaiser Friedrichs II. Herrschaftszeichen*, Göttingen, 1955

A. de Stéfano. *L'idea imperiale di Federico II*, new ed., Bologna, 1952

H. Thillmann. *Papst Innocenz III*, Bonn, 1954

O. Brunner. 'Abendländisches Geschichtsdenken', *Neue Wege der Sozialgeschichte*, Göttingen, 1956, pp. 168, 184

Th. Mayer. 'Papsttum und Kaisertum im hohen Mittelalter', *HZ*, 187, 1959

A. Stickler. 'Imperator Vicarius Papas', *MIÖG*, 62, 1954

W. Ullmann. 'Cardinal Roland and Besançon', *Sacerdozio e Regno da Gregorio VII a Bonifacio VIII*, Rome, 1954

A. Walz. 'Papstkaiser Innocenz III., Stimmen zur Deutung', *Sacerdozio e Regno . . .*, Rome, 1954

E. Wolf. 'Heilsgeschichte im Geschichtsbewusstsein und im geschichtlichen Ablauf des europäischen Mittelalters', *Christentum und Geschichte*, Düsseldorf, 1955

CHAPTER 6: HABSBURG, LUXEMBURG, WITTELSBACH: THE EMPIRE FROM 1273–1438

O. Berthold. *Kaiser, Volk und Avignon. Ausgew. Quellen zur anti-kurialen Bewegung in Deutschland in der ersten Hälfte des 14. Jahrhunderts*, Berlin, 1960

A. Blaschka (ed.). *Kaiser Karls IV Jugendleben und St. Wenzelslegende* (with German translation), Weimar, 1956

F. Bock. *Reichsidee und Nationalstaaten. Vom Untergang des alten Reiches bis zur Kündigung des deutsch-englischen Bündnisses im Jahre 1341*, Munich, 1943

W. M. Bowsky. *Henry VII in Italy. The conflict of Empire and city-state 1310–1313*, Lincoln, Nebraska, 1960

*Meister Eckhart. *Selected treatises and sermons*, translated by J. M. Clark and J. V. Skinner, London and New York, 1958

A. Gerlich. *Studien zur Landfriedenspolitik König Rudolfs von Habsburg*, Mainz, 1963

F. Heer. *Meister Eckhart*, Frankfurt, 1956 (with bibliography)

Bede Jarrett. *The Emperor Charles IV*, London, 1935

R. L. John. *Dante*, Vienna, 1946 (see esp. pp. 30, 83, 187)

K. Mommsen. *Eidgenossen, Kaiser und Reich. Studien zur Stellung der Eidgenossenschaft innerhalb des heiligen römischen Reiches*, Basel–Stuttgart, 1958

J. Pfitzner. *Kaiser Karl IV*, Potsdam, 1938

G. Rabuse. *Der kosmische Aufbau der Jenseitsreiche Dantes*, Graz–Cologne, 1958

L. Weisz. *Die alten Eidgenossen*, Zürich, 1940

F. Heer. 'Zur Kontinuität des Reichsgedankens im Spätmittelalter', *MIÖG*, 58 1950

G. Stadtmüller. 'Die ungarische Grossmacht des Mittelalters. Ungarn als antemurale christianitatis', *Hist. Jahrbuch*, 70, 1950

H. Steinacker. 'Die Habsburger und der Ursprung der Eidgenossenschaft, *MIÖG*, 61 1953

CHAPTER 7: THE RISE OF THE HOUSE OF HABSBURG (1438–1519)

*C.M.Ady. *Pius II*, London, 1913

H.Ankwicz-Kleehoven. *Der Wiener Humanist Johann Cuspinian: Gelehrter und Diplomat zur Zeit Kaiser Maximilians I*, Graz, 1959

O.Benesch–E.M.Auer. *Die Historia Frederici et Maximiliani*, Berlin, 1957

R.Buchner. *Maximilian I., Kaiser an der Zeitenwende*, Göttingen, 1959

J.Calmette. *Les grands Ducs de Bourgogne*, Paris, 1949

H.Fichtenau. *Der junge Maximilian (1459–1482)*, Vienna, 1959

H.Forestier and H.Drouot. *Bourgogne, Morvan*, Paris, 1959

L.Hommel. *Marie de Bourgogne ou Le grand héritage*, Brussels–Paris, 1951

I.Irmscher (ed.). *Renaissance und Humanismus in Mittel- und Osteuropa* (collection of sources), 2 vols, Berlin, 1962

M.Lanckorenska. *Die christlich-humanistische Symbolsprache und deren Bedeutung in zwei Gebetbüchern des frühen 16. Jahrhunderts, Gebetbuch Kaiser Maximilians und Breviarium Grimani*, Baden-Baden, 1958

*R.J.Mitchell. *The laurels and the tiara* (study of Pius II), London, 1962; New York, 1963

H.T.Musper (ed.). *Kaiser Maximilians I. 'Weisskunig' in Lichtdruck-Faksimile*, 2 vols., Stuttgart, 1956

W.Oberhammer. *Die Bronzestatuen am Grabmal Maximilians I*, Innsbruck, 1955

Ch.Oursel. *L'art de Bourgogne*, Paris, 1953

A.Schmidt (ed. and transl.). *Aeneas Silvius' 'Germania'* and J.Wimpfeling's *Responsa et replicae ad Eneam Silvium*, Cologne–Graz, 1962

F.Schmidt. *Eine neue Fassung der maximilianischen Selbstbiographie*, Vienna, 1950

A.Schulz. 'Der Weisskunig', *Jahrbuch der Kunsthistor. Sammlungen des AH. Kaiserhauses*, VI, 1887

Lewis W. Spitz. *Conrad Celtis. The German arch-humanist*, Cambridge, Mass., 1957

J.Strelka. *Der burgundische Renaissancehof Margarethes von Österreich und seine literar-historische Bedeutung*, Vienna, 1957

H.Ullmann. *Kaiser Maximilian I*, 2 vols., Stuttgart, 1884–91

R.Vaughan. *Philip the Bold. The Formation of the Burgundian State*, London and Cambridge, Massachusetts, 1962

Glenn Elwod Waas. *The legendary character of Kaiser Maximilian*, New York, 1941

K.Wehmer. *Mit Gemälde und Schrift. Kaiser Maximilian I. und der Buchdruck*, Stuttgart, 1962

B.Widmer. *Enea Silvio Piccolomini – Papst Pius II*, Basel–Stuttgart, 1960

A.Coreth. 'Dynastisch-politische Ideen Kaiser Maximilians I.', *Mitteil. des österr. Staatsarchivs 3*, 1950

H.Federhofer. 'Die Niederländer an den Habsburgerhöfen in Österreich', *Mitteil. der Komm.f.Musikforschung, Nr. 6, Akad.d.Wiss.*, Vienna, 1956

R.John. 'Die wirkliche Herkunft des A.E.I.O.U.', *Österr. Akademische Blätter, 9–10*, 1963

A.Lhotsky. 'Die Bibliothek Kaiser Friedrichs III', *MIÖG*, 58, 1950

A.Lhotsky. 'AEIOU. Die "Devise" Kaiser Friedrichs III. und sein Notizbuch', *MIÖG*, 60, 1952

H.Wiesflecker. 'Maximilian I. und die habsburgisch-spanischen Heirats- und Bündnisverträge von 1495–96', *MIÖG*, 67, 1959

CHAPTER 8: THE EMPIRE ON WHICH THE SUN NEVER SET

H.Bernkamm. *Das Jahrhundert der Reformation. Gestalten und Kräfte*, Göttingen, 1961 (particularly valuable for the essay on Luther and summaries of recent work on other great figures of the Reformation)

G.de Boom. *Charles-Quint, prince des Pays-Bas*, Brussels, 1943

K.Brandi. *Kaiser Karl V*, 2 vols., Munich, 1937, 1941; 6th ed., Munich, 1961
English translation by C.V.Wedgwood, *The Emperor Charles V*, London, 1939

K.J.Burckhardt. *Gedanken über Karl V.*, Munich, 1954

R.Carbis. *Historia de la leyenda negra hispano-americana*, Buenos Aires, 1943

F.Chabod. *Lo Stato di Milano nell' Impero di Carlos V*, Rome, 1934

F.de Cossio. *Carlos V*, Madrid, 1941

H.von Einem. *Karl V und Tizian*, Cologne, 1960

*G.R.Elton. *Reformation Europe 1517–1559*, London–Glasgow, 1963; New York, 1964

E.Fabian (ed.). *Urkunden und Akten der Reformationsprozesse am Reichskammergericht...*, vol. I, 1530–4, Tübingen, 1962

J.Gregor. *Das spanische Welttheater*, Munich, 1943

J.Hantsch. *Die Kaiseridee Karls V.*, Graz–Vienna, 1958

J.Heckel. *Im Irrgarten der Zwei-Reiche-Lehre. Zwei Abhandlungen zum Reichs- und Kirchenbegriff Martin Luthers*, Munich, 1957

F.Heer. *Die dritte Kraft – der europäische Humanismus zwischen den Fronten des konfessionellen Zeitalters*, Frankfurt, 1959

J.Jacquot (ed.). *Les Fêtes de la Renaissance, II: Fêtes et cérémonies au temps de Charles-Quint*, Paris, 1960

J.Lortz. *Die Reformation in Deutschland*, 2 vols., Freiburg, 1941 (see esp. pp. 47, 199, 243)

M.Mittler. *Mission und Politik. Untersuchungen über das Kolonial-Imperium Karls V.*, Zürich, 1951

M.Monica. *La gran controversia del siglo XVI acerca del dominio español sobre America*, Madrid, 1952

B.Monsegu. *El Occidente y la Hispanidad*, Madrid, 1949

Götz Freiherr von Pölnitz, *Anton Fugger I., 1453–1535*, Tübingen, 1958

A.von Randa. *Das Weltreich-Wagnis und Auftrag Europas im sechzehnten und siebzehnten Jahrhundert*, Olten–Freiburg, 1962

P.Rassow. *Karl V. Der letzte Kaiser des Mittelalters*, Göttingen, 1957

K.Repgen. *Papst, Kaiser und Reich, 1521–1644*, Tübingen, 1962

M.Salomies. *Die Pläne Kaiser Karls V. für eine Reichsreform mit Hilfe eines allgemeinen Bundes*, Helsinki, 1953 (note bibliography)

R.Schmidt. *Deutsche Reichsstädte*, Munich, 1957

G.Schwarzenfeld. *Karl V., Ahnherr Europas*, Hamburg, 1954

J.Soder. *Die Idee der Völkergemeinschaft. F. de Vitoria und die philosophischen Grundlagen des Völkerrechts*, Frankfurt, 1955

J.Strelka. *Der burgundische Renaissancehof Margarethes von Österreich*, Vienna, 1957

S.Troescher. *Deo et Caesari fidelis perpetue. Kaiserbilder und Reichssymbole in der westlichen Reichsromania*, Brussels, 1943

A.Truyel y Serra. *Die Grundsätze des Staats- und Völkerrechts bei Francisco de Vitoria*, Zürich, 1947; 2nd ed., 1957

Royall Tyler. *The Emperor Charles the Fifth*, London, 1956 (note list of sources and bibliography, p. 321)

E.Wolf. *Idee und Wirklichkeit des Reiches im deutschen Rechtsdenken des 16. und 17. Jahrhunderts*, Stuttgart, 1943

R.Bernheimer. 'Theatrum mundi', *The Art Bulletin*, vol. xxxviii, no. 4, December 1956

J.Lecler. 'Les origines et le sens de la formule: Cuius regio, ejus religio' (*Recherches de science Religieuses*, 38, 1951

A.Truyel y Serra. 'Die spanische Kolonialethik im Goldenen Zeitalter', *Saeculum*, III, 1952

CHAPTER 9: THE MADRID–VIENNA AXIS

Qu.Aldea. *Iglesia y Estado en la España del siglo XVII*, Comillas Santander, 1962

K.Bibl. *Maximilian II. Der rätselhafte Kaiser*, Hellerau, 1929

G.R.Hocke. *Die Welt als Labyrinth*, Hamburg, 1957

José Antonio Marvall. *La philosophie politique espagnole au XVIIe siècle dans ses rapports avec l'esprit de la Contreréforme*, Paris, 1955 (French translation of the first Spanish edition, Madrid, 1944)

G.Mecenseffy. *Geschichte des Protestantismus in Österreich*, Vienna, 1956

O.Schürer. *Prag*, 5th ed., Prague, 1943

A.E.Stahl. *Die spanischen Habsburger im spanischen Drama*, Vienna, 1953

H.Sturmberger. *Kaiser Ferdinand II. und das Problem des Absolutismus*, Munich–Vienna, 1957

K.Vossler. *Spanien und Europa*, Munich, 1952, p. 148

A.Angyal. 'Das rudolphinische Prag', in J. Irmscher, *Renaissance und Humanismus in Mittel- und Osteuropa*, II (see above, Chapter 7)

A.Anyal. 'Das Problem des slawischen Barocks', *Wissenschaftl. Zeitschrift der Ernst Moritz Arndt-Universität Greifswald*, VI, 1956–7

G.Mecenseffy. 'Habsburger im 17. Jahrhundert. Die Beziehungen der Höfe von Wien und Madrid während des dreissigjährigen Krieges', *Archiv für öst. Gesch*, 121, 1957

V.L.Tapié. 'Baroque slave et l'Europe centrale', *Accademia nazionale dei Lincei*, CCCCIX, 1962, Rome

CHAPTER 10: FROM THE GREAT WAR TO THE GREAT PEACE

D.Albrecht. *Richelieu, Gustav Adolf und das Reich*, Munich–Vienna, 1959

F.Dickmann. *Der Westfälische Friede*, Münster, 1959

Carl C.Eckhardt. *The papacy and world-affairs as reflected in the secularisation of politics*, Chicago, 1937

K.Repgen. *Die Römische Kurie und der Westfälische Friede*, vol. I, *Papst, Kaiser und Reich 1521–1644*, Tübingen, 1962 (see F.Dickmann, *HZ*, 197, 1963, p. 161)

D.Meinert. *Von Wahl und Krönung der deutschen Kaiser zu Frankfurt am Main. Mit dem Krönungsdiarium des Kaiser Matthias aus dem Jahre 1612*, Frankfurt, 1956

H.-Ch.Messow. *Die Hansestädte und die Habsburgische Ostpolitik im Dreissigjährigen Kriege (1627–8)*, Berlin, 1935

P.Rassow. *Forschungen zur Reichsidee im 16. und 17. Jahrhundert*, Cologne–Opladen, 1955

A.Wandruszka. *Reichspatriotismus und Reichspolitik zur Zeit des Prager Friedens von 1635*, Cologne, 1955

*F.Watson. *Wallenstein, Soldier under Saturn*, London, 1938

E.Wolf. *Idee und Wirklichkeit des Reichs im deutschen Rechtsdenken des 16. und 17. Jahrhunderts*, Stuttgart, 1942

R.Dietrich. 'Landeskirchenrecht und Gewissensfreiheit in den Verhandlungen des westfälischen Friedenskongresses', *HZ*, 196, 1963

P.Negri. 'Urbano VIII et l'Italia (1623–1644)', *Nuova Rivista Storica*, 6, 1922

CHAPTER 11: THE EMPIRE IN THE BAROQUE AGE (1657–1740)

I.Bog. *Der Reichsmerkantilismus. Studien zur Wirtschaftspolitik des Heiligen Römischen Reiches im 17. und 18. Jahrhundert*, Stuttgart, 1959

M.Braubach. *Prinz Eugen von Savoyen*, 4 vols., Vienna, 1963–5

B.Grimschitz. *Johann Lucas von Hildebrandt*, Vienna–Munich, 1959

F.Hadamovsky. *Barocktheater am Wiener Kaiserhof, mit einem Spielplan (1625–1740)*, Vienna, 1955

H.Hantsch. *Prinze Eugen als Staatsmann und Mäzen*, Graz, 1963

*N.Henderson. *Prince Eugen of Savoy*, London, 1964

F.Heer. *Leibniz*, Frankfurt, 1958

J.C.Horn. Introduction to *G.W.Leibniz, Grundwahrheiten der Philosophie-Monadologie*, Frankfurt, 1962 (parallel French and German texts)

R.F.Kreutel. *Im Reiche des Goldenen Apfels. Des türkischen Weltenbummlers Evliva Celebi denkwürdige Reise . . . anno 1665* (German translation of Celebi's narrative), Graz, 1957

A.T.Leitich. *Vienna Gloriosa, Weltstadt des Barocks*, Vienna, 1947

*R.W.Meyer, transl. J.P.Stern. *Leibniz and the seventeenth century revolution*, Cambridge, 1952

R.Krug von Nidda. *Eugen von Savoyen*, Vienna–Zürich, 1963

Th.Schüssel. *Kultur des Barock in Österreich*, Graz, 1960

R.Topka. *Der Hofstaat Kaiser Karls VI*, Vienna, 1954

Th.Zacharias. *Joseph Emanuel Fischer von Erlach*, Vienna, 1960

H.Zwingmann. *Der Kaiser in Reich und Christenheit im Jahrhundert nach dem Westfälischen Frieden*, 1913

R.Bernheimer, 'Theatrum Mundi', *The Art Bulletin*, vol. XXXVIII, no. 4, December 1956

A.Coreth. 'Pietas Austriaca, Wesen und Bedeutung habsburgischer Frömmigkeit in der Barockzeit', *Mitt. des. österr. Staatsarchivs*, 7, 1954

P.Gasser. 'Das spanische Königtum Karls VI. in Wien', *Mitt. des österr. Staatsarchivs*, 6, 1953

F.Hartung. 'L'état c'est moi', *HZ*, 169, 1949

J.van Klaveren. 'Fiskalismus-Merkantilismus-Korruption', *Vjschr.f.Soz. und Wirtschaftsgesch*, vol. 47, 1960

G.Otruba. 'Prinz Eugen und Marlborough: Die Geschichte einer Freundschaft', in O.Hietsch (ed.), *Österreich in der angelsächsischen Welt*, Vienna–Stuttgart, 1961

O.Redlich. 'Die Tagebücher Kaiser Karls VI', *Srbik-Festschrift*, 1938

Th.Schieder. 'Prinz Eugen und Friedrich der Grosse im gegenseitigen Bilde', *HZ*, 156, 1937

H.Sedlmayr. 'Die politische Bedeutung des deutschen Barock', *Epochen und Werke*, II, Vienna, 1960

H.Zelzer. 'Österreichisches Barock und der angelsächsische Raum', *Österreich und die angelsächsische Welt*, 1962 (see G.Otruba, above)

CHAPTER 12: MARIA THERESA AND JOSEPH II

Klemens Graf zu Brandis. *Die Habsburger und die Stephanskrone*, Vienna–Zürich, 1937

F.Fejtö. *Un Habsbourg révolutionnaire, Joseph II*, Paris, 1952

*G.P.Gooch. *Maria Theresa and other studies*, London and New York, 1951

M.C.Goodwin. *The papal conflict with Josephinism*, New York, 1938

H.H.Hoffmann. *Adelige Herrschaft und souveräner Staat*, Munich, 1962

A.Hubert. *Die Politik Kaiser Josephs II., beurteilt als Protagonisten von seinem Bruder Leopold von Toskana*, 1877

L.Jedlicka (ed.). *Maria Theresia in ihren Briefen und Staatsschriften*, 1955

H.Kretschmayr. *Maria Theresia*, 2nd ed., Leipzig, 1938

J.Miskolczy. *Ungarn in der Habsburger Monarchie*, Vienna, 1959

P.Reinhold. *Maria Theresia*, Wiesbaden, 1957

H.Rothfels. *Ostraum, Preussentum und Reichsgedanke*, Leipzig, 1935

D. Silaghi. *Jakobiner in der Habsburger Monarchie*, Vienna, 1961

A. Wandruszka. *Leopold II.*, 2 vols., Vienna, 1963–5

F. Engel-Janosy. 'Joseph II. Tod im Urteil seiner Zeitgenossen', *MIÖG*, 44, 1930

F. Hartung. 'Der aufgeklärte Absolutismus', *HZ*, 180, 1955

O. Hintze. 'Der österreichische und der preussische Beamtenstaat im 17. und 18. Jahrhundert', *HZ*, 86, 1901

A. von Martin. 'Die Problematik des Josephinismus', *Archiv für Kulturgesch.*, 33, 1951

A. Wandruszka. 'Le istruzioni di Franceso di Lorena per il figlio Leopoldo', *Archivo storico italiano*, 1957

CHAPTER 13: THE UNFINISHED SYMPHONY

W. Andreas. *Carl August von Weimar. Ein Leben mit Goethe, 1757–83*, Heidelberg, 1953

Prince J. E. Arenberg. *Les Princes du St. Empire et l'époque napoléonienne*, Bruxelles, 1951

K. O. von Aretin. *Die Konfessionen als politische Kräfte am Ausgang des alten Reiches. Ein Beitrag zur Problematik der Reichsauflösung* (Festgabe Joseph Lortz, Baden-Baden, 1958)

S. S. Biro. *The German Policy of revolutionary France, 1792–97*, Harvard, 1957

M. Braubach. *Die vier letzten Kurfürsten von Köln. Ein Bild rheinischer Kultur im 18. Jahrhundert*, Bonn, 1931.

M. Braubach. *Kurköln. Gestalten und Ereignisse aus zwei Jahrhunderten rheinischer Geschichte*, Münster, 1949

E. Bussi. *Il diritto pubblico del Sacro Romano Imperio alla fine del 18° secolo*, Padua–Milan, 1957–9

F. Meinecke. *Weltbürgertum und Nationalstaat*, Munich–Berlin, 1936

W. Mommsen. *Die politischen Anschauungen Goethes*, 1948

H. Rössler. *Napoleons Griff nach der Karlskrone. Das Ende des alten Reichs*, Munich, 1957

F. G. Schultheiss. *Die geistlichen Staaten beim Ausgang des alten Reiches*, 1895

H. v. Srbik. *Das österreichische Kaisertum und das Ende des Heiligen Römischen Reiches 1804–06*, Berlin, 1927

K. Stoye. *Die politischen und religiösen Anschauungen des Freiherrn Friedrich Karl von Moser (1723–1798) und sein Versuch einer Regeneration des Reiches. Ein Beitrag zur Geschichte des Reichspatriotismus im 18. Jahrhundert*, Graz, 1959

E. Walder. *Das Ende des alten Reiches. Quellen zur neueren Geschichte*, Hist. Seminar der Universität Bern, 1948

K. O. von Aretin. 'Höhepunkt und Krise des Deutschen Fürstenbundes. Die Wahl Dahlbergs zum Coadjutor von Mainz (1787)', *HZ*, 196, 1963

A. H. Benna. 'Das Kaisertum Österreich und die römische Liturgie', *Mitteil. des öst. Staatsarchivs 9*, 1956

H. Hausherr. 'Goethes Anteil am politischen Geschehen seiner Zeit', *Jahrbuch der Goethe-Gesellschaft*, 11, 1949

H. Hausherr. 'Der Minister Goethe und die äussere Politik Carl Augusts', *HZ*, 169, 1949

H.Holldack. 'Die Neutralitätspolitik Leopolds von Toskana', *Hist. Vierteljahrsschrift*, 30, 1936

W.Mommsen. 'Zur Bedeutung des Reichsgedankens', *HZ*, 174, 1952

J.Rinieri, S.J. 'La secolarizzazione degli stati ecclesiastici della Germania', *La Civiltà Cattolica*, 57, 1906

Ditto. 'Le cause della secolarizzazione dei beni ecclesiastici della Germania', *op.cit.*, 56, 1905

A.Scharnagl. 'Zur Geschichte des Reichsdeputationshauptschlusses vom Jahre 1803', *Hist. Jahrbuch*, 70, 1950

Frh.von Schewinger. 'Der Reichsgedanke in Süddeutschland, Franz von Roggenbach', *Hist. Jahrbuch*, 62–69, 1949

H.v.Srbik. 'Goethe und das Reich', *Jahrbuch der Goethe-Gesellschaft*, 4, 1939

W.von den Steinen. 'Mittelalter und Goethezeit', *HZ*, 183, 1957

INDEX

INDEX

William, Count of Holland, anti-king, 87

William, Archbishop of Mainz, 26, 37

Wittelsbachs, 11, 117

Worms, 138, 265, 268; Concordat of (1122), 62–3, 39; treaty at (1521–2), 176

Wyclif, 54, 119–20

Zuñiga, Baltasar, 193–4, 202

Zwingli, Swiss theologian, 54, 152